A HISTORY OF HUNTING
IN HAMPSHIRE

By Dighton

H.R.H. THE PRINCE OF WALES, AFTERWARDS GEORGE IV.

[*Reproduced by gracious permission of H.M. The King*]

A
HISTORY OF HUNTING
IN HAMPSHIRE

BY

BRIGADIER-GENERAL J. F. R. HOPE, C.B.E., D.S.O.

WINCHESTER :
WARREN AND SON LTD.
THE WYKEHAM PRESS
1950

MADE AND PRINTED IN GREAT BRITAIN
BY
WARREN AND SON LIMITED
THE WYKEHAM PRESS, WINCHESTER.

ACKNOWLEDGMENTS

THE author wishes to acknowledge the great debt he owes to the following noblemen, ladies and gentlemen who have helped him in a great many ways by the loan of diaries, the giving of much information, and the answering of very many questions with wonderful patience. Without their ready assistance the book could never have been written :—The Hon. F. A. Baring, Colonel F. G. Barker, C.B.E., Miss Barker, M.F.H., Major Jack Blake, Major-General S. S. Butler, C.B., C.M.G., D.S.O., Captain Sir George J. R. Cooper, Bart., Captain A. F. Coryton, Major P.P. Curtis, M.C., A. W. H. Dalgety, Esq., Lieut.-Colonel The Lord Dorchester, O.B.E., Captain Lionel Edwards, G. P. E. Evans, Esq., Mrs. George Jonas, Sir Owen F. Morshead, K.C.V.O., D.S.O., M.C., J. C. Porter, Esq., Sir N. E. O. Rycroft, Bart., W. J. Yorke-Scarlett, Esq., John Simpson, Esq., B. Warner, Esq., and Mrs. Paul Woodhouse, who very kindly supplied much useful information from the files of the *Hampshire Chronicle* of which she is the Editor.

He has also to thank H.M. The King and the following noblemen, ladies and gentlemen for permission to publish, the loaning of pictures, diaries, books and other help :—The Rt. Hon. the Earl of St. Aldwyn, Lady Apsley, H. Aris, Esq., Mrs. J. C. Atkins, R. Beddington, Esq., Isaac Bell, Esq., Lieut.-Colonel J. A. Butchart, D.S.O., and Mrs. Butchart, Miss Butler, C. L. Chute, Esq., M.C., Lady Cope, Brig. E. W. Chadwick, M.C., Ralph S. Dutton, Esq., F.S.A., James Eggar, Esq., Kenneth Glover, Esq., Lieut.-Colonel L. T. Goff, The Rt. Hon. The Earl of Hardwicke, M.F.H., Lieut.-Colonel C. E. St. J. Harris-St. John, D.S.O., Major Edward Harris-St. John, M.C., A. Henry Higginson, Esq., Major J. C. Humphrey, Major F. H. T. Jervoise, T.D., F.S.A., Brigadier M. W. Selby-Lowndes, D.S.O., Mrs. Mackenzie, Gwen Lady Melchett, Lieut.-Colonel Sir George Ll. T.-G.-Meyrick, Bart., M.F.H., Lieut.-Colonel J. H. Nicholson, M.C., Brigadier-General E. W. M. Powell, C.B., C.M.G., D.S.O., O. T. Price, Esq., Mrs. Pritchard, Captain C. M. R. Schwerdt, C.V.O., C.B.E., R.N., Colonel J. B. Scott, The Rt. Hon. The Earl Spencer, T.D., Lieut.-Colonel J. H. Walford, D.S.O., M.F.H., Lieut.-Colonel His Grace The Duke of Wellington, Mrs. Witherby.

My grateful thanks are due to Miss C. Mills for the accurate and attractive drawing of the Hunt buttons reproduced on the paper jacket and facing page 16.

DEDICATION

To the Sportsmen of Hampshire
past, present and future

CONTENTS

LIST OF ILLUSTRATIONS

FOREWORD

EVERYONE who has hunted in Hampshire will welcome General Hope's book. There are many also in Hampshire and elsewhere who, although perhaps themselves, not participating in hunting will find, I think, much to interest them in the many historical facts and people mentioned in this book.

From the earliest day Hampshire has been noted in the annals of the chase in all its forms. Although we do not possess the stretches of grass of the Midlands, we have a country so diversified that the working of a pack of hounds can be seen in all its variety by those who love houndwork.

This book provides a fund of historical facts and the names of many bygone and present followers of the chase. It will remind many of us of past days and recall friends met in the hunting field now, perhaps, half forgotten.

General Hope has performed a monumental task in amassing all the names, facts and dates of the various Hampshire packs, their masters and followers. This book, apart from its historical interest, provides a most useful source of reference. The author has not spared himself, and as I know, has travelled many miles to tap various sources of information. He has been most persevering in extracting facts and tales from all and sundry connected with hunting.

GEORGE MEYRICK.

November, 1950.

PREFACE

AN attempt has been made to collect and save from oblivion some of the history of Hampshire sport. When the book was started some danger existed that hunting, the most ancient pursuit of mankind, might be interfered with by legislators who were ignorant of country life. Happily their efforts proved abortive.

Hampshire may not be a hunter's paradise, but it provides every type of country within its boundaries, much of it, too, of great beauty—forest, heath, rolling downland, woodland, marsh and strongly-fenced vales. In recent times it has suffered in common with all countries from that curse of hunting, barbed wire. Downs and pastures have been ploughed, villas, bungalows and chicken farms have spread their ugliness over much pleasant country, and, lastly, the electrification of some railways have all added difficulties to hunting.

In spite of all difficulties and the financial losses of two world wars hunting still flourishes and no established pack of foxhounds has failed to recover itself, though some did not hunt during the war years.

The county has produced some very renowned huntsmen —Thomas Smith and Thomas Assheton Smith were both Hampshire men : some of the writers of the greatest of hunting classics were Hampshire men.—Colonel John Cook, Mr. Thomas Smith, Mr. F. P. Delmé-Radcliffe : some well known sports-men and authorities on all matters concerning hounds and hunting, though not Hampshire men, have hunted Hampshire packs—Mr. John Warde, Mr. J. T. Villebois, Mr. George Evans. The county can claim, too, the first and only Royal Master of Foxhounds, H.R.H. The Prince of Wales, afterwards George IV. Kings and queens have hunted in the Hampshire forests for a thousand years and more. Though not Hampshire born Winchester College, can claim two of the greatest poets of the chase—George Turberville and William Somerville. The boar, wolf, stag, buck, hare and fox have all played their part in training hardy, active, quick-witted men. It is worthy of note that the greatest huntsmen usually excelled in other ways and were men of marked ability. The 1st Duke of Wellington, one of the greatest Englishmen of all time, was devoted to foxhunting and always preferred to have foxhunters on his staff. The sky blue and black of the Salisbury Hunt frequently was seen behind the lines with his hounds in the quieter times of the Peninsular War. No one was a better supporter of foxhunting in Hampshire in his later days.

Long may it flourish and breed hardy men and good will in the county. In the words of the 16th century writer : " Wherefore I say that hunters shall go into Paradise when they die, and live in this world more joyfully than any other men."

J. F. R. H.

Preston Grange, 1950.

CORRIGENDA

Page 52. *For* Mr. Kingcote *read* Mr. Kingscote.
For Capt. M. P. Haworth *read* Capt. M. E. Haworth.
For R. Pearse *read* R. C. T. Pearse.

Page 71. *For* R. Pearse *read* R. C. T. Pearse.

Page 105. *For* Lord Hedley *read* Lord Headley.

Page 184. *For* huting *read* hunting.

Page 258. *For* William Colyer *read* William Collyer.

Page 272. *For* Jack Baily *read* Jack Bailey.

ADDITIONAL CORRIGENDA

Page 53. In the list of masters, *against* 1923-24 *delete* Capt. R. Orred, tenant of Farleigh House, Basingstoke.

Against 1924-25, *below* Lieut.-Col. C. G. Mangles, *add* Capt. R. Orred, tenant of Farleigh House, Basingstoke.

Page 86, line 21. *For* Lieut.-Col. C. G. Mangles and Captain R. Orred, 1923-24, *read*
Lieut.-Col. C. G. Mangles, M.C., 1923-24.
Lieut.-Col. C. G. Mangles, M.C., and Capt. R. Orred, 1924-25.
line 35. *For* Lieut.-Col. C. G. Mangles and Capt. J. B. Scott, 1924-25, *read* Lieut.-Col. C. G. Mangles, M.C., and Capt. J. B. Scott, 1925-26.

Page 87, line 7. *For* 1926-27 *read* 1926-29.
below line 7, *insert* Mr. G. P. E. Evans, 1929-32.
line 15. *For* 1927-32, *read* 1932-33.
Transfer line 15, Mr. G. P. E. Evans . . . *to end of line* 19, . . . own packs, *to page* 89 *and insert below line* 12.

Page 89, line 15. *For* Mr. G. Evans and Mr. B. Hamilton, 1934-35, *read* Mr. G. P. E. Evans, 1934-35.

Page 92, line 10. *For* Lucknow *read* Mhow.

Page 94, line 16. *For* show-umping *read* show-jumping.

Page 120, footnote 4, line 3. *For* 1918 *read* 1908.

Page 121, line 14. *For* 1848-49 *read* 1948-49.

Page 123, line 18. *For* After the war *read* Before the war.

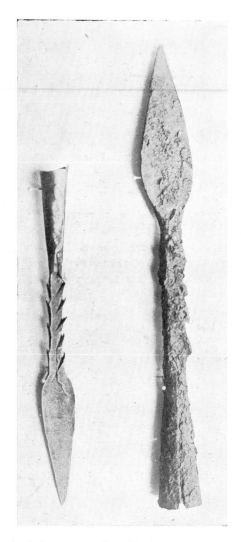

The photograph of these two mediaeval barbed spearheads is reproduced by the kind permission of Major A. G. Wade, M.C., F.S.A. The one on the left is from Suffolk and that on the right from Bentley.

CHAPTER I.

HUNTING IN HAMPSHIRE IN EARLY DAYS.

Few records of early hunting in Hampshire exist. In Saxon days it was a duty of able-bodied men to hunt. The food obtained was of great value and the training in hunting the wild boar, the wolf and, to a rather less extent, the stag, demanded courage and physical fitness combined with quick and resolute action. All kings and nobles were hunters, and perhaps as early as the days of King Canute[1] Forest Laws were made to protect beasts of the chase in Royal forests. These were amplified and made more severe by William the Conqueror and his unpopular son William Rufus, the former substituting mutilation for fines, and enjoining the penalty of death in certain cases. Hampshire has many place names recalling Saxon days if few records. Woolmer Forest was Wulfmæres Gemære and doubtless the wolf was hunted there by the kings. It is interesting to note the discovery of a wolf spear found by Major A. G. Wade, F.S.A., at Boars Hill on the boundary of the late Lord Baden Powell's estate of Pax Hill, Bentley. Wolf-hanger also is a well-known H.H. fox covert by Bramdean Common. The etymology of " Wolvesey " is presumably Wolves Eyot or Island, and denoted the place, either where the killer of a wolf was rewarded and whither he brought the wolf's head to prove his deed, or the place where the tribute of wolves' heads levied by King Edgar from the Welch was paid (c. 970). Wolvesey traditionally was the Royal palace of the Saxon kings before it became only the Bishop's Palace. William the Conqueror built his palace between the Square and the High Street of Winchester, the only relic of which is one pillar of an entrance gate behind the Butter Cross, and the Church of St. Lawrence is on the site of the Chapel Royal. Henry I made the Castle his palace, doubtless owing to the fact that he had usurped the throne and wanted security from his elder brother Robert Duke of Normandy.

The name Boars Hill is suggestive of the chase, and not far away in Surrey, the Manor of Bacsete (now Bagshot) was held in grand sergeantry for the service of hunting the boar. Boars

---

[1] The " Charta de Foresta " of Canute is stated by Manwood to have been issued from Winchester in 1016. Its authenticity is doubtful, but it is reasonable to suppose that some regulations for the control of the Royal Forests did exist before the Norman Conquest.

were still hunted at Windsor in 1617 in James I's reign and existed in England as late as 1680. The famous Alfred was thoroughly trained as a hunter at 12 years of age. Bishop Asser, in his Life of Alfred written in 879, calls him " a most expert and active hunter and excelled in all the branches of that most noble art, to which he applied (himself) with incessant labour and amazing success." His two sons were instructed in Latin and Saxon and also in hunting and horsemanship. Alfred's saying is a sound one for all time : " If thou hast a sorrow, tell it to thy saddlebow, and ride thee singing, forth." His grandson Æthelstan followed in his footsteps as a great hunter and soldier. From a defeated King of Wales he levied " Hawks and sharp-scented dogs, fit for hunting wild beasts." Harold, the last Saxon King, is portrayed with hawks and hounds in the Bayeux tapestry.

William the Conqueror considerably extended the New Forest.[2] There is no evidence, however, that he destroyed any churches and there is evidence from the Doomsday survey that he avoided afforesting cultivated land. He retained the Manor of Lyndhurst in his own hands, holding it, at first, under Amesbury Abbey. The murderess Elfrida had given it to Amesbury Abbey ; she also had founded the Abbey of Wherwell, near Andover, further to expiate her crime. Her stepson King Edward the Martyr, whom she caused to be murdered in 979 at Corfe Castle, Dorset, was also a hunting king, and when he met his end, he was seeking rest and refreshment from his stepmother after hunting in the Royal forest nearby.

William Rufus met his end hunting in the New Forest, as did his brother Richard and his nephew Richard. William was justly hated by both Norman and Saxon. In the words of the Chronicle : " In his days all righte fell and all wrong in the sight of God, rose." His senseless cruelty, and lack of principle or religion, had made him hated by all parties, Norman and Saxon, Church and people. His death was hoped for by many, both in England and in Normandy. Neither the exact place, nor the name of his slayer, are known for certain. Many legends arose afterwards about his death and Walter Tyrrell's flight. The Chronicle simply relates that he was shot at the chase by one of his friends. His bones, with those of King

---

[2] William I found about 75,000 acres of land practically uninhabited ; he added from 20 to 25,000 acres of sparsely inhabited land, moving about 500 families. To this he again added about 10,000 acres of village commons, woodlands, or waste along the River Avon and near the coast. The Forest was then about 30 miles from North to South.

Canute and others, now lie in one of the mortuary chests on the choir screens at Winchester Cathedral, completed by Bishop Fox in 1525. Even in the Cathedral the remains of William Rufus have not remained in peace. He is supposed to have been buried under the tower which fell down in 1107. Henry de Blois undoubtedly collected the remains of many of the most illustrious princes and placed them in the Holy Hole in the 12th century. Bishop Fox again translated them in the 16th century. The inscription translated runs : In this chest, and in that opposite to it are the remains of Canute and of Rufus, of Emma, queen, and of Wina and Alwin, bishops. Another inscription runs, on the opposite side : In this chest A.D. 1661 were promiscuously laid together the bones of the princes and prelates, which had been scattered about by sacrilegious barbarism A.D. 1642. On 7th July, 1797, Mr. Henry Howard of Corby Castle and Mr. Hastings surgeon to the North Gloucester Militia inspected the bones in the chests. In the third and fourth chests no skull was found, but they were full of thigh and leg bones, one set of which, in the third chest, is much smaller and weaker than the rest. This, with the supernumerary skull in the second chest, might possibly have belonged to Queen Emma. The fifth chest held five skulls, two of old men ; they might be the skulls of the Bishops Wina and Alwin.

No doubt after the Cromwellian desecration it was utterly impossible to identify the remains. Probably, however, scientists could have arranged them with considerably greater accuracy than was attempted.

It is significant that no inquiry concerning William Rufus' death was ever made. The Forest Laws were undoubtedly rigidly applied in the New Forest, Alice Holt, and Woolmer Forest, and probably in early days in Pamber, Chute and Bere Forests. Briefly, these laws were altered as follows :—

In 1184 Henry II substituted fines for death and mutilation by the Assize of Woodstock.

In 1215 Magna Carta repealed many of the most oppressive laws.

In 1217 and 1228 new charters set forth that no one should lose life or limb for first offences and disafforested all lands afforested since William Rufus' time.

12th Century.

The Royal Manor of Odiham was visited by Henry I in
1116. Whatever Royal residence existed there was repaired in
1130. It is also stated by Holinshed that Henry I was a keen
boar hunter which he truly describes as a " very dangerous
exercise." The Royal park at Odiham existed from a very
early date. Hugh the " Parker " is mentioned in 1130. From
Odiham the King could have hunted in Alice Holt, Woolmer
or Pamber Forest, but no records exist.

In King Stephen's time the Manor of Brockenhurst was
held by grand sergeantry by the finding of litter for the King's
bed and hay for the King's horses, should he come to hunt
there. Stephen was unlikely to have called on this service
often during his troubled reign. Henry II confirmed this
grant. Henry II granted the Manor of Little Weldon in
Rockingham Forest to his Chamberlain, Osbourne Lovel. This
manor, called also Hunters Manor, was held in grand sergeantry
by the service of being master (magister) or custodian (custos)
of the Royal Buckhounds : both terms are used in charters.
Kings then hunted from Rockingham Castle in Northamptonshire all the forest around, a tract of 24 miles long by 12 miles
wide. The Lovels held the appointment till 1316. Then
Thomas de Borhunte, a name also spelt Boarhunt and very
suggestive of his calling, held in right of his wife Margaret
Lovel till 1340, when he was succeeded by her second husband
William Danvers. On his death, in 1361, the manor and office
passed to Mary de Borhunte, daughter of Sir John de Roches
and widow of Sir John de Borhunte, and so to her second
husband, the famous Gascon Knight, Sir Bernard Brocas. This
loyal and gallant knight fought for his English overlord and
king in France, Scotland, Gascony, Brittany and Spain. Among
his many offices he had served as Chamberlain to the Queen,
King's Warden and Ambassador, Constable of Aquitaine,
Controller of Bordeaux, Captain of Calais, as well as master of
the Buckhounds. He fought at Crècy, Poitiers and Najara.
His tomb in Westminster Abbey was well deserved. He died
full of honour in 1395 and his family held the office of hereditary
master of the Buckhounds until 1663, when Thomas Brocas
sold the manor and the office to Sir Lewis Watson, afterwards
Lord Rockingham. Henry II did more to foster sport as he
founded the Royal Mews at Winchester by buying a piece of
land called La Park outside the Castle gate and now called
Oram's Arbour. At first five falcons were kept there. In

1183, 1185 and 1197 sums were spent on the King's houses at Freemantle. This hunting lodge near Kingsclere was used for the hunting in Chute Forest and Freemantle Park, but the expenditure on the two earlier dates probably also signify the adding of amenities for the reception of his famous mistress, the Fair Rosamond. Robert of Gloucester's *Chronicle*, at any rate, says :—

> " Boures had the Rosamond about in Engelond,
>   Which the King for her sake made ich understond,
>   Waltham Bishops,—in Castle of Wynch,
>   Atte park of Freemantle, atte Martelstow,
>   Atte Woodstocke, and other places."

Henry's redoubtable son Richard I leaves no hunting stories in Hampshire; he did, however, visit Freemantle on one occasion in April 1194 on his way to be recrowned at Winchester on April 17th. Richard I[3] had little time for hunting in England, but he was a great hunter as well as soldier.

In John's reign, for some reason a considerable number of facts relating to hunting in the County have been preserved, and his name is preserved in two hills near two of his hunting lodges.

13th Century.

King John built a castle at Odiham of which the ruined keep still remains. It was built on 20 acres of meadowland belonging to Robert " the Parker." King John visited this castle on twenty-four occasions during his reign, presumably to retire to, with a sense of security, after the hunting day was over. In 1215 it was from Odiham he set forth to Runnymede to sign the " Magna Carta " which was published throughout the kingdom and sworn to by every hundred moot and town moot, and remains the foundation of the liberty of an Englishman. To Odiham he returned after this fateful act. The great charter was badly wanted; the gallows creaked with the victims of his Forest Laws. At Beaulieu it is said that Caius Appulyarde, the local executioner, gave the thumbs of their fathers to their children to play with. King John founded Beaulieu Abbey in 1205, traditionally owing to a very bad dream in which he was scourged by the Cistercian Monks, whom he had ordered his bodyguard to ride down at Lincoln, when assembled with their

---

[3] Manwood relates a hunt of Richard I's in 1194 in Sherwood Forest which took him to Barnesdale in Yorkshire, a good 40 miles. The hart was not killed and was protected by special Royal Proclamation : " No person should kill, hurt or chase the said hart, that he might safely return into the Forest again."

abbots by his order in 1204.   Though the order was not
obeyed, the King felt the smart of the blows next morning.
Some effect must have been achieved on the tough conscience
of the King as he gave no less than 1,050 marks and £300 besides
other valuable donations in kind towards the building.   It was
completed by Henry III.   To Freemantle King John repaired
no less than thirty-seven times.   Local tradition says that the
peculiar animal forming the wind vane on Kingsclere Church
was set up by the local inhabitants to show their gratitude to
the particularly virulent type of harvest bug, alleged to have
driven the King and his minions away.   His thirty-seven visits
seem to show that this joy may have been prematurely expressed.
King John's Hill, near Kingsclere, commemorates this evil and
idle king's predilection for the neighbourhood.   In 1204 King
John gave Mathew de Wallop the custody of the gates and gaol
at Winchester " for the service of keeping at his cost our birds
put into the castle to be mewed, finding one servant to mew
them and keep throughout the mewing time and he shall find
three hounds for each season."   This Mathew, an ancestor of
Lord Portsmouth's family, received two carncates[4] of land at
Preston Candover, and 100 shillings of land at Bramdean for
his services.   A modern house called " Fawkners " commemorates this holding, but the position of the two carncates
cannot now be recognised with any certainty.

   At Wardleham, now Worldham, near Alton, King John
built a lodge for convenience in hunting Alice Holt and Woolmer
Forests.   It was probably of wood and of a temporary nature,
but his name is still remembered by King John's Hill nearby.

   The Forest of West Bere was also visited by this king, who
stayed with William de Briwere at Ashley Manor.   The Forest
of Bere was divided by the River Itchen into East and West
Walks.   This William de Briwere seems to have been a very
privileged person as, in the minority of Henry III on July 3rd,
1219, the bailiffs of the New Forest were ordered to let his dogs
chase bucks in the forest up till Michaelmas.   Again, on
August 9th, permission was given him to chase anything in the
forest, provided neither bow nor greyhound were used.   The
permission to chase the hart or red deer in a Royal forest is an
almost unheard of privilege.   On August 18th, 1221, an order
was given to John of Monmouth (presumably Lord Warden)
or his bailiffs of the New Forest, to give for that season liberty

---

   [4] A carncate or hide equals 100 to 120 acres, according to the soil: a year's work for
a plough team of oxen.

of chase to the dogs of William Briwere. The next year, on July 8th, his dogs were allowed to chase bucks. On July 30th, in 1223, he was again allowed to use his buckhounds in the New Forest; these are specified as "*canes damericos currentes,*" the use of bow or greyhound. "*leporarius*" was not allowed him. The Bishop of Salisbury was allowed to receive five bucks from the Forest in 1223 and eight bucks in 1226, and four bucks from the Forest of Clarendon in 1224. The King's uncle, William, Earl of Salisbury, was not allowed to starve, receiving ten harts and 20 bucks from the New Forest in 1221, also five harts from William Briwere's Bailiwick. In 1222 the Earl again had three harts from the New Forest and in 1224 this Earl was allowed to take in the Forest six harts and twelve bucks, presumably in this case, he himself or his own men hunted them. In 1227 Ela, Countess of Salisbury, was allowed one buck for the marriage feast of her daughter Mary; the Earl was then dead. In 1227 we find the King's Huntsman, Master Grey, with his staghounds "*cervericiis*" and two of Hubert de Burgh's huntsmen, John le Fot and John le Berner, with their stag and buckhounds, were allowed to take 30 harts and 30 bucks. These huntsmen were allowed one bow apiece, but Hubert de Burgh was Justiciar of England and Henry still a minor till 1232.

Henry III was more cultured than his father John, but weak, obstinate and a believer in absolute power. He was forced, however, to confirm the great Charter and the Carta de Foresta which mitigated the appalling harshness of the Forest Laws under Rufus and John. An example of this may be given in a local instance quoted by Woodward. On September 2nd, 1227, an order was given allowing William Sazmuket, then in prison at Winchester on suspicion of having killed a fawn in the New Forest, to be let out on safe bail until the justices of the forest should hold their court. Newly assarted (*i.e.*, grubbed) lands were allowed to be cultivated in Pamber and Chute Forests and at Freemantle. A considerable grant from the Royal Manor at Odiham was made to Patric de Cadurcis, now called Weston Patrick. He was given the right to enclose and fence his new lands. Few records of hunting in Chute Forest exist. It stretched from Hurstbourne Tarrant into Wiltshire, Doles Wood and Doiley Wood and Manor mark the site of one walk of this forest, the East walk of which was called Finkley. Henry III sent his huntsman Roger de Stopham to take deer in Michael de Columbers' bailiwick of Diggersley (now Doiley) and Finkley and ordered Michael to aid him until the King should come into those parts. In the same year Michael had to find timber for a new kitchen and buttery, a dispensary, a drawbridge and joists for two turrets and a chamber over the gate, all for Winchester Castle, where, incidentally, Henry III of Winchester was born. In 1235 Avice de Columbers was ordered to allow the constable of the Castle beams for the King's dispensary and " saucery " there.

In 1267 a plea was heard at Winchester by William de Kenet, Lord of Colemore, claiming the right to be quit of expedition or lawing. This barbarous custom was to strike off three claws of the forefeet of all dogs that could not pass through a certain standard, *i.e.*, they were large enough to poach deer. The so-called " Rufus stirrup " in the Verderers Hall at Lynd-hurst is shown as the local standard, but the stirrup is probably of late Tudor 16th century origin.

Henry II granted land at Eyeworth to Roger Bateson " *in capite*" for the service of finding litter for the King's bed and hay for his horse when he came to hunt there. At Eling and Redbridge in the New Forest also, the heirs of Cobbe and Richard de Baudet held by finding 50 and 100 arrows respec-tively. In the Woolmer Forest area the Manor of Acangre, now Oakhanger, was held on a hunting tenure, the Lord having to keep a pack of white hounds when the King came to hunt there. The St. John's, the Earls of Pembroke and the Lords de la Warr succeeded each other as Lords of this manor. The pack of white hounds was not a difficulty, the " rache " being generally white (see explanation of terms of venery at end of chapter). During this reign the family of Daundeley, who had held Chilton Candover Manor since the Conquest, became Royal huntsmen. They had taken to calling themselves de Candover at this time and two entries of interest appear ; in 1269 the King ordered the men of Basingstoke to pay Richard de Candover £10 to purchase himself therewith two horses, and again in 1271 they had to provide William de Candover mainten-ance for himself and two horses, three servants and 25 of the King's dogs " moving about wages," for 54 days at a cost of £4. 16s. 0d. The country would have been ideal for hawking and conveniently close to Winchester, but it would be interesting to know what exactly the 25 dogs hunted on the downs. Some relics exist of the family—a stone coffin to Johan de Candover in the buried church by the site of the old manor house, a child's stone coffin, King's Down and a copse called Ruxers (Rexhurst), also the unique yew avenue which led directly to the manor house might have existed in their day. A good instance of the Forest Laws being still very much operative was given early in Edward I reign. The Steward of the New Forest, Walter de Kanc, was indicted for very serious offences against the Forest Laws. He had caused false entries to be enrolled as to the disposal of the King's deer, naming, in 1271, one John le Espaniell, yeoman to the Queen, as taking 20 does for the behoof of the Queen, when this yeoman was in foreign parts with the Queen. The Verderers were duly amerced (fined) for a bad presentation. The Verderers and foresters said that Walter despoiled the forest of 500 beasts and upwards during his stewardship and sent the venison where he wished. He was fined " £5,000—namely, for each beast £10." This, however, was by no means the end. " For other beasts which he caused to be taken without number and without warrant, and for the waste made by him of his bailiwick as well of venison as of vert—because it is not possible to estimate it—at the will of the King and Queen." Apart from the enormous fine, being " at the will of the King " meant that his life and the lives of his family and the whole of his property were at the King's mercy ; really at the mercy of the convicting court. His life was closed and he could only hope for a quick release. He had doubtless taken liberties thinking King Henry was old. Several of his underlings were involved, too, but he was rightly held responsible, and was soon shown that Edward I was not a man to be trifled with. In 1280 the Abbot of Beaulieu was indicted at Winchester " for receiving Brother Richard, his convert and Richard de Rames his servant, indicted for trespass of venison with snares and other engines in a close made fine with the King for 40 marks, came and brought the Queen's writ by which the Queen pardoned the Abbot and convert for the trespass aforesaid—and gave the 40 marks for the work of the Church." The wily ecclesiastic knew who to go to in his troubles when fairly caught and the Queen did a cheap benefaction at the same time.

Edward I was a great soldier and a great hunter. In 1285 he caused a new hunting lodge to be built in Bramshott Manor to hunt conveniently the Forests of Alice Holt and Woolmer. The upper chamber was seventy-two feet long by twenty-two feet wide and it is interesting to find two chimneys provided as well as two garde-robes and six windows of glass. A small chapel was provided, and a large hall entirely built of wood was also built for the general company with a kitchen nearby.

The mason's wages came to £11 and the materials £6. 13s. 0d. Six thousand three hundred wooden shingles were used for roofing. Edward visited his new lodge for a week in 1285 and four times between 1290 and 1302. His Queen was not forgotten and had a small garden there for her own use. In his youth as Prince, Edward had beaten the famous outlaw Adam de Gurdon in single combat near the Pass of Alton[5] not far from Bentley. He gallantly spared his life and took him to see his mother who was staying at Farnham Castle nearby. De Gurdon was pardoned and became a loyal subject, receiving the post of Ranger of Alice Holt and Woolmer Forests, which post he held till 1304 when his son-in-law John de Venus succeeded him. Adam de Gurdon lived at Temple where the Earl of Selborne now lives, but the house does not show signs of its mediaeval origin. De Gurdon should be remembered as the giver of the " La Pleystow " or play place to Selborne Village in 1271, which is the open space near the church there and still retains its ancient name (now Plestor) and provides a playing ground for children. Edward I also used the Royal lodge at Lyndhurst and his Queen often used it too, when Edward was engaged in war. No less than twenty oaks were felled to make laths for the Queen's Manor House at Lyndhurst. A king's chapel is also mentioned in 1285. By Edward I's time the New Forest had been reduced to some twenty miles from North to South, and thirteen miles from East to West. The acreage was 92,000 of which 27,000 were in private hands.

Edward II apparently used yet another lodge at Kingsley as he had a chapel built there. It seems curious that three lodges should have been built so close together as Worldham, Bramshott and Kingsley, even if chiefly built of wood. Edward I's lodge, however, was certainly in Bramshott as various Royal documents were addressed from " Brembeshete " and a formal legal enquiry about the King's rights was held at " Brembleshute," two of the sixty-two variations of spelling indulged in by our ancestors for this manor. Edward I granted Freemantle to Reginald FitzPeter for life and the lodge fell into ruin. The King does not seem to have objected to this. The Crown regained possession in 1386. Large sums had been expended in repair of the park palings in Henry III's reign and gifts of venison were sent frequently from Freemantle Park to

<hr/>

[5] " The Pass of Aultone " may also have been near Chawton Park. In deeds of Edward II it is described as where the high ground falls into the plain. The name still exists in " Pease Way Close " and a Pace Way nearby. *Chawton Manor and its owners.*

various people in Henry III's reign and also in the reign of Edward I and II, once even as far as to Carlisle. It remained in Royal hands till 1640, when it was bought by Lord Cottington of Hamworth. In Cromwellian times this ancient Royal park was granted to the arch-regicide President Bradshaw, when Lord Cottington's estates were requisitioned. The name " Cottington Hill " is often used for King John's Hill.

Local people of importance were frequently made " Parkers " as Sir William Sandys of the Vyne and Sir William Kingswell of Sydmonton. Its site is marked by the names Freemantle Park Farm, Freemantle Park Down, and Park Coppice. A trough in the down grass is shown as the site of the Royal fish ponds.

14th Century.

The Wars of the Plantagenets necessitated the buying and breeding of " great horses." Studs were established at various places, among others at Odiham in 1312. Grooms received 2*d.* a day and each four colts received one bushel of oats and two bushels of bran, *i.e.*, at 40lbs. to the bushel of oats, 10lbs. a day, the normal army ration of late years.

No mention of the stud is made after 1360-61, when some of the best mares, with others from the Windsor and Guildford studs, were sold and the profits given to William of Wykeham to pay for repairs at Windsor Castle. It was thought, as usual, after some successful campaign, that it was unnecessary to keep up the war horses.

The park at Odiham was assigned to Queen Margaret in 1299 and to Queen Isabella in 1327. It was still well stocked with deer in 1630 after its grant to Lord Zouche in 1617-18. After that no more is heard of it and presumably it was disparked in Cromwellian times.

Edward II, though not a great soldier, was a very keen huntsman. He employed, too, a first-rate professional huntsman in William Twici. He was a light-hearted king and his private expenses record the following :—" Item paid at the Lodge of Wolmer when the King was stag-hunting there, to Morris Ken, of the kitchen, because he rode before the King and often fell from his horse, at which the King laughed exceedingly. A gift, by command, of twenty shillings." It is possible that Ken might have been willing to fall off again for so ample a reward. In the New Forest one Peter Spelman held a carncate of land by the service of finding for Edward II an esquire clad in coat of mail, for forty days in the year, and whenever the King came to the village (Brockenhurst) to hunt, litter for his bed and hay for his horse. The King could obviously live hard when required, though not a lover of the hard life.

On July 27th, 1313, the King's Buckhounds, under the mastership of John Lovel, King's Yeoman, visited Pamber Forest and other forests in Hampshire, Wiltshire and Berkshire. His hounds were kenneled at Hunters Manor in Rockingham Forest. For this trip he took with him twenty-four buckhounds, sixteen greyhounds and one bercelet. He was ordered to take in Hampshire :—twelve bucks and four harts in the Forest of Wolvermore (Woolmer) ; six bucks in Freemantle ; six bucks and eight harts in the Forest of Pamber on the same occasion.

Fifty-eight bucks, thirty-four harts and forty hinds were ordered to be taken by the masters of hart hounds and harriers in the Forests of Nottingham, Derby, Huntingdon, North-ampton and Essex. Stags would be fat and in their prime in July. The season was May 3rd to September 4th.

On November 10th of the same year John Lovel was sent to take eight hinds and ten bucks again from Pamber. At this date the redoubtable William Twici (called also " Twety," " Twyti," " Twity ") was " Huntsman to the King of England " and probably carried the horn. His " art of venerie," written in French, though Twici, was a native of Twyford in Berkshire, is our first written hunting authority. His pay as huntsman was 9d. per diem and his son " Little Will " received 3½d. The master or keeper of the buckhounds received 12d. a day. William Twici died in 1328 and was buried at Reading Abbey, not far from his birthplace.

The King's hounds travelled vast distances in these days. In October he was hunting in Wiltshire, in December Lovel was in Dorset and Somerset. The mastership was no sinecure. Great quantities of venison were salted down for the use of the court, and also for the fleet. These long journeys must have kept men, horses and hounds very fit. It was not till Henry VIII's reign that a hound van is heard of when five shillings was spent to buy ten ells of canvas " to cover the cart with the King's hounds."

In 37 Edward III, 1363, Sir Bernard Brocas obtained free warren of Beaurepayr, Bradle(y), Stevynyton (Steventon), Farnham, Hannynton, all Hampshire manors, and most of them long held by his descendants.

Richard II must have used the New Forest for hunting as he built a "hall" within the lodge in 1388, now the "Verderers' Hall," which existed practically unchanged till badly mauled in a so-called restoration in 1851. The prisoners' dock, hewn out of solid oak by axe and adze, and the "bar" between court and body of the hall are of very early date. The panelling, now forming a wainscote on the walls, was originally in the Henry VIII rooms over the hall, destroyed in 1851. The Royal Arms have interest as they are of Charles II, during whose reign the Earl of Oxford held the last Great Justice seat in Eyre for the Royal forests south of the Trent in 1669-70. The tables, too, are fine, probably of Tudor date. The "Rufus" stirrup is also probably of that date. This is mentioned in chapter V, page 101. The despoilers of this beautiful hall brought the walls down to eight feet and built a barn roof abutting the King's house. They inserted mullioned windows of brick and plaster in place of the original stone. In 1904 the hall and the fine old house adjoining were altered with some attention to tradition and some knowledge of architecture and at long last the King's house attained a bathroom.

The Wars of the Roses most certainly interrupted the pursuit of all beasts of the chase, and no records have survived.

15th Century.

The second Sir Bernard Brocas and hereditary master of the Royal Buckhounds took part in a bold attempt on the life of Henry IV at Windsor in 1400. He was duly convicted of treason and executed at Tyburn. He was not, however, drawn and quartered. His last words were noble : " Blessed be God that I was born, for I shall die this night in the service of the noble King Richard." Henry IV, though far from secure on his throne, promptly reversed the attainder and forfeiture of his estates, and allowed his son William to succeed to the family estates and also the mastership of the Royal Buckhounds. William, who was M.P. and High Sheriff for Hants, by marrying Joanna Sandys as his second wife, received the Vyne in dower. The family for the next two generations, another William and his son John, seem to have hunted for the White or the Red Rose impartially and not to have mixed politics with their duties.

16th Century.

Henry VII was no hunting man, but his son Henry VIII had a passion for the chase and rode extremely hard until his obesity drove him to the degraded sport of shooting the deer driven by dogs in enclosed parks. Hampton Court was the last "forest" to be created by Royal Decree. The old hereditary Royal pack must have become somewhat useless in these days and Henry started a privy pack, with George Boleyn Viscount Rochfort as its first master in 1528. From this pack descended the Royal Buckhounds, which existed until 1901. George Boleyn, like many of Henry's friends, came to the block in 1536. His crime was simply that Henry was tired of his sister Queen Anne and the family. On the day of Queen Anne's execution Henry had waited impatiently to throw off hounds until he saw the flag notifying her execution run up to the mast. Little is known of his hunting in Hampshire except that he did so. In 1531 the King had visited the Vyne where lived his Chamberlain, Sir William Sandys, First Lord Sandys of the Vyne, and the following items occur in his payments :—

	s	d
"To the keeper of Baroper (Beaurepaire) - -	6	8
To the keeper of Mr. Pawlet's and Lord Sandys' parks (Hackwood and Morgaston) - -	13	4
To the servant of the Lord Chamberlain for bringing a stag to the Vyne which the King had stricken before in Wolmer Forest - - -	10	0 "

Lord Sandys held many other appointments of importance— Treasurer of Calais, Captain of Guisnes, and also he was keeper of Farnham Castle. He retired from political life after the divorce of Queen Katharine of Arragon, but still looked after the King's deer. In 1535 he sent his brother to Queen's Park (now Great Park Farm, Mortimer). He found hounds and hunters and their servants there, who attacked him and "hurt him sore." He reports young Trapnell as having killed twenty of the King's deer on the borders of Windsor Forest. "Two years ago he slew a great hart and carried him away in a cart." Lord Sandys retired to a lodge in the Forest of Woolmer and was granted material for its repair from the Manor of Worldham which had fallen into Royal hands after the attainder and execution in 1513 of Edmund de la Pole, Earl of Suffolk. A fine soldier and an honest man, Lord Sandys died in 1540 and was buried in the Holy Ghost Chapel at Basingstoke.

During the Tudors hunting became degraded. Queen Elizabeth preferred shooting deer in a park where they were driven into netted passages whilst the Queen and her courtiers were seated in pavilions and shot the deer with arblasts. When younger, however, it is related that King Henry's " man minded offset, rose to chase the deer at five." In Lord Berkeley's Park she once shot twenty-seven deer without his knowledge and in his absence. She gained money by granting the right to empark and then announced her intention of coming to stay. These sporting progresses were by no means always appreciated by her subjects, but heads were insecure and they had to submit, and try to appear pleased In September of 1600, soon after the disgrace of her old lover Essex, Queen Elizabeth and her court amused themselves with hunting and hawking at Hanworth and in the New Forest. Richard Whyte relates : " Her Majesty is very well, and exceedingly disposed to hunting for every second day she is on horseback and continues the sport long." Hackwood House, now the seat of Lord Camrose, was originally a hunting lodge of the Paulets in Queen Elizabeth's time. It was greatly enlarged after the Restoration and the destruction of Basing House by Cromwell. The first enlargement was completed in 1687 and in the next enlargement, between 1759 and 1765, the Fifth Duke of Bolton greatly altered the house. The old banqueting hall, open to the roof, had a floor inserted and lost its original character, but is still a very handsome room. In 1794 Thomas, First Lord Bolton, built a new north front 24 feet from the original one and connected it to the wings by corridors. Finally, between 1807 and 1830 the south front was altered by Wyatt to correspond with the north front.

Abbotstone House was another princely hunting lodge of the Paulets (it had a hundred rooms), rebuilt by the First Duke of Bolton, Lord Chamberlain, about 1700 and there he entertained Queen Anne. Povey in 1719 states that " he caused two vast large hawkes to be fixed on the top of the banquetting houses just before the entrance into the house." The house decayed and was pulled down at the end of the century and the Grinling Gibbons' carving was taken to Hackwood. Elizabeth started her progress into Hampshire on September 5th, 1601, the same day as the Duc de Biron headed an embassy to her from the French King, the ducal train consisting of some four hundred nobles and gentlemen. She stayed no less than thirteen days with the Marquis of Winchester at Basing.[6] Thither went the Duc de Biron, and waited with his escort for the Royal appearance. The Queen came out accompanied by the High

---

[6] What Thomas Tooke, Clerk of the Kitchen at Basing House, thought of the visit, he expresses in a letter : " . . . where all things for so great entertainment, but elbow room and good will, were wanting." On Sunday the Frenchmen supped at Basing and on Monday and Tuesday they dined, *when we were of them delivered.*"

Sheriff, and with her attendants. At first she passed the ambassador without noticing him, but when he had dutifully followed her for about 20 yards, cap in hand, and bowing low to his horse's mane, she stopped, took off her mask and received him most graciously. He was quartered at the Vyne during her stay at Basing, furniture with plate and hangings being sent from the Tower and fine furniture came also from Hampton Court, besides seven score of beds and other furniture provided by the Hampshire Squires. The Queen visited the Duke at the Vyne in return and it is recorded that they hunted and feasted together in princely fashion. Returning to London in October, holding Biron by the hand, she pointed with ghoulish delight to the heads that decorated the Tower saying, " It is thus, they punished traitors in England." Sad to relate, the Duc de Biron, soon after his return to France, lost his own head. Elizabeth said that " she had done that in Hampshire that none of her ancestors ever did, neither any prince in Christendom could do, that was, she had in her progress in her subjects' houses entertained a Royal ambassador and had royally entertained him." She once stopped at Liphook on her way to Cowdray and it is recorded that she shot a red deer in the Royal Forest of Woolmer. Possibly she stayed at the Anchor Inn at Liphook as later on her successor Queen Anne did, but more likely she would continue her journey to Cowdray House.

17th Century.

Hunting had a friend in James I, somewhat ungainly and uncouth as he was. He utterly repudiated park hunting, but was guilty of hunting trapped hares on his journeys. To teach the English again the art of the chase he had a famous Frenchman sent to him well versed in all ancient laws of the chase and the art of venerie as practiced by the French kings. He pardoned the hereditary master of the Royal Buckhounds, Sir Pexal Brocas, but this decadent member of a distinguished family deserved no pardon. Unfortunately no details are known of his Hampshire visits to Sir Benjamin Tichborne,[7] but it is certain that he would insist on being provided with sport after deer or hare. King James stayed also at Bramshill in 1620 with the builder of that beautiful house, Edward Lord Zouche of Harringworth. A very unfortunate accident happened the next year in Bramshill Park when George Abbott, Archbishop of Canterbury, shot a

---

[7] Sir Benjamin earned James I's friendship by galloping to Winchester to proclaim him King as High Sheriff without waiting for orders. He and his four sons were all knighted.

A HISTORY OF HUNTING IN HAMPSHIRE

by

Brig.-Gen.

J. F. R. Hope

1950

HAMPSHIRE HUNT

GARTH HUNT

NEW FOREST HUNT

Dress

TEDWORTH HUNT

VINE HUNT

HURSLEY HUNT

Silver

HAMBLEDON HUNT

NEW FOREST
BUCKHOUNDS

keeper Peter Hawkins, instead of a stag whilst on a visit there. The Archbishop gave a pension of £20 a year to the widow and fasted every month on a Tuesday, the day of the sad accident.

Prince Henry and Prince Charles were both good horsemen, trained by the famous William Cavendish, Duke of Newcastle, at Welbeck who also instructed Charles II, James II and Prince Rupert. The Duke was the greatest authority on the art of horsemanship of his age.

Prince Henry's death was a national calamity with far-reaching consequences and he never lived to see Bramshill completed which, tradition says, would have been his home. The Prince of Wales' feathers still adorn the house which now belongs to Lord Brocket.[8]

Few records of the Stuarts in Hampshire exist as huntsmen, but it is recorded that in 1637 King Charles I and all that hunted with him in the New Forest were " roundly wet." It is also recorded that " scarce a room in his house (the King's house at Lyndhurst), has held out the rain." In the next year timber was provided for " making bridges and causeways to secure His Majesty's riding over the bogges and moores there." One, known as the King's Passage, near Matley, may have been made at this time. Between 1634 and 1672 both Charles I and Charles II greatly improved and rebuilt the King's house and most of their work exists to-day. Stabling for forty horses was added. A census of deer (1670) taken in the reign of Charles II shows in the New Forest :—

103 Red Male.   1,409 Fallow Male.
254 Red Rascal.[9]   184 Fallow Rascal.

The dimensions of the Hampshire forests may be of interest. The New Forest in Charles II's time (1681), 92,365 acres ; it is now 30 acres more. Alice Holt about 2,000 acres. Woolmer Forest, 6,000 acres. Forest of Bere, 1,500 acres. The Forest of Bere seems to have been peculiarly unprofitable to the Crown. Though the Crown was " to be supplied with deer without stint," the Crown usually got none. The warden, however, also had a right to be supplied without stint ; it is not recorded that the warden got none. Winchester College had a purlieu[10]

---

[8] The house was rebuilt in 1605 incorporating portions of the ancient home of the Foxleys. In 1637 it belonged to the 2nd Earl of Antrim and in 1640 to Robert Henley. From 1700 till very recently it belonged to the Cope family. It is again for sale, 1950.

[9] Rascal means deer not fit for venison.

[10] A " purlieu " was a " clear place," a term used of forest land disafforested and bounded by immovable marks.

there and the right to be supplied with " two bucks, one for the purlieu and one as composition deer." This forest was enclosed in 1812.

A story of some interest is given in *The Diaries of Dummer* edited by A. M. W. Stirling, 1934 relating to hunting in Hampshire. It is said that the famous, or infamous, Judge Jeffreys had hunted a stag with " the Knight of Chawton." He was on his way to Winchester Assizes, probably in 1685 when Dame Alice Lisle was condemned to be burnt alive. A conversation is alleged to have taken place as follows :—

Knight : " The distance is a dozen miles ; but come with me, and we will make free with *my old friend* Stephen Terry of Dummer Manor, like myself a staunch friend of Church and State, and I can ensure a welcome for the Lord Chief Justice."

Jeffreys (taking out an ivory tablet) : " Forsooth, he is a well affected Hampshire gentleman, and as such I will wait upon him, and perhaps in his loyalty he will rehorse me to Winchester."

The Lord Chief Justice was well entertained and pressed to stay the night, but made on to Winchester that night.

The story is not mentioned in *Chawton Manor and its Owner.*

There are several points of difficulty in the story.

Stephen Terry bought Dummer Manor from his cousin Frances Soper. He was a " cursiter " in the Chancery Office. He could not have been born before 1666 and would have been only 19 years of age in 1685. Richard (Martin) Knight died as an undergraduate at Cambridge in 1687. He would have been 16 years of age in 1685. An additional difficulty is that Chawton was let to Lord Wiltshire, and three Paulets were born there in 1684, 1685 and 1686. The two young squires could hardly have been very *old friends.*

Chawton Manor possessed two parks, one of considerable extent, 1,000 acres, valued at 4*d.* the acre, and one of 100 acres valued at 18*d.* the acre in 1350. The Great Park is still called Chawton Park and has been a great home of sport till the Second World War when it has become like so many woodlands, a mutilated and tangled ruin.

In 1337 at the death of Hugh de St. John no acreage is mentioned, but " another park " is mentioned " of which the pasture is worth yearly beyond the sustentation of the deer (ferarum) 5s., and the pannage, when it happens, 6s. 8d."

This seems the only mention of Chawton Park as a deer park, but doubtless the deer would still exist in Stuart times. The great bank and ditch boundary of the park on one side is very plain still.

Queen Anne did not hunt in Hampshire forests and her interest in the deer was ill rewarded by an attack of rheumatism. Whilst on a journey to Portsmouth, the Queen came out of the road at Liphook and, reposing herself on a bank, still called Queen's Bank, about half a mile to the East of Woolmer Pond, saw her keepers drive the whole herd of five hundred red deer before her. The Queen spent the night at the Anchor Inn at Liphook. The herd was reduced to fifty by the Duke of Cumberland's time when the Royal huntsman and six yeoman prickers in scarlet and gold, rounded them up and took them to Windsor. The forest was disafforested in 1857.

The last king to stay in the New Forest was George III, who used the King's House in 1789. He was attended by the " Bowmen and Archers " in all his rides. He also stayed a second time with Sir George Rose at Cuffnells at Lyndhurst.

Madame D'Arblay relates that the people smashed down palings and hedges and even windows when allowed to see the King at dinner, but " were perfectly civil and well behaved." Charles Davis came with the Royal Buckhounds in Lord Eroll's and Lord Rosslyn's masterships in 1836, 1848 and 1852, about two thousand people attending the meets. These were the last occasions when the Royal hunting liveries were seen in the Forest.

In 1851 the Deer Removal Act was passed and the fine herd of indigenous red deer, after the Royal pack had secured what they required, was handed over to indiscriminate slaughter. A few, however, survived by crossing the River Avon on to private property, and, when the zeal of destruction abated, returned to their old haunts in the Royal forest. A few still exist. The fallow deer which are now hunted are not of English origin but were introduced by the Romans.

The Forest of Pamber seems never to have attracted much Royal interest. The St. John and Paulet families held the bailiwick of this forest from 1298 when Walter de Eversley granted it to John de St. John. The most interesting custom in connection with this forest was that of the Tything Man Lord. He was elected yearly on July 20th and held his court in an orchard seated in an elbow chair. He sat with his hat on, all others stood uncovered. The steward swore the jury and charged them in the usual manner. Then a large bundle of sticks were brought, about two feet six inches long, on which were entered their customs and usual presentments. They refused to recognise Mr. Powlett Wright as lord who was the representative of the St. Johns and the Paulets. In 1793 the case was tried at Winchester and Mr. Richard Benyon, the then lineal representative, was established as lord. Despite this verdict a court of the Tything Man Lord was held as late as 1817. King James I had granted the right to hold courts leet, view of franc pledge, and swainmote to Messrs. Waller and Purcell, during a short interlude in the long Paulet-St. John holding of the forest rights, which they quickly repurchased. The Tything Man Lord claimed the right to hunt to Windsor Forest. The continuance of such a claim, whether exercised or not, is against all custom. A forest also could have no lord of the manor. The kings gave away plots of land from this forest on many occasions. The parks formed wholly or partially by these gifts show the former great extent of the forest.

Sherbourne Park and Morgaston; St. John family before 1245.

*Hackwood Park; Breboeuf family, 1223 and 1280.

Bramley Park; St. John family, 1245.

*" Hangre," now Stratfieldsaye; de Saye family, 1261.

Cufould Park; de Cowdray family, 1268.

" Prewet," now Park Prewet; St. John family, 1302.

*Heckfield Park; enclosed in 1328. Robert de Manefeu, son of John, a verderer of Pamber Forest, had licence for some 90 acres.

*Bramshill (2,500 acres) and Hazeley Park were formed out of Pamber Forest partly, but chiefly from the disafforested land of Eversley.

The Bishop of Winchester had his chaces at *Farnham, Waltham and Wield and the Park of East Meon.

The Prior of St. Swithun's had his park at Wooton or *Manydown which was much larger in those days. It was licensed in 1332. Hugh de Despenser visited it with twelve horses to hunt with Prior Richard of Enford in 1324 before its licence. The Church appeared to be risking trouble but Despenser was a Royal favourite. In 1361 and in 1364 the King's huntsmen were there in force. In 1430 one Robert Peverill was amerced (fined) for poaching "*cum canibus suis intravit in parcum domini et ibidem occidit unam feram nomine 'pricket.'*"[11]

The park at King's Somborne was acquired by John of Gaunt by marriage with Blanche, daughter and heiress of Henry, Earl of Lancaster. When his son Henry Bolingbroke became King it became Crown property and remained so till Charles I disposed of it. It was a very early park as in 1200 William de Ou received licence to enclose, and also received the righ to chase hare, fox, cat and wolf. Deer disappeared when palings were broken in Sir Thomas Wyatt's rebellion in 1554, but 215 deer are mentioned thirty-seven years later. None are mentioned by the Parliamentary Commissioners in 1651, when it was disparked.

[11] A pricket is a buck in his second year.

* The author has not attempted to give all parks in the County enclosed by Royal Licence, but only those which happened to include parts of the Royal Forest of Pamber and King's Somborne is mentioned as one which became a Royal park by marriage. Those marked with an asterisk still exist as parks.

EXPLANATION OF TERMS IN VENERIE.

Bercelet. A shooting dog, used to help the archer, both to range and find the quarry and also to hold it or retrieve it. A type of mastiff was used. It was in common use for buck hunting. Derivation : French " Bercer," to hunt especially with the bow.

Berner, bernier. Anciently, the man who paid his dues to his lord in brenage or bran bread for his hounds. Afterwards the feeder or kennelman.

Cervericus (see *Rache*). A hart hound.

Damericus or *deimericus* (see *Rache*). A buck hound.

Fewmets, fumes, fewments. Droppings of deer.

Greyhound (French *levrier* or Latin *leporarus*). A swift hound hunting by sight. Often white in colour, but the master of game preferred " red fallow." A constant companion of his master in war, the chase, or at home. Speed was essential and ability to seize and hold stag, wolf or boar. " Good, kindly and clean." Fierce only with wild beasts. Probably the Irish wolf hound would be near to the type.

Limer or *lymer.* This was a hound specially selected when young for its nose. Used on a leash or liam to track game or in tufting a warrantable stag. He appears to have resembled a bloodhound in contemporary pictures. He lived with his master and slept in his room.

Rache, brache, canis curreus. This was a hound which hunted by scent in a pack. The Book of St. Albans speaks of " a kenell of rachys " but "a mute of houndes." In colour, often white or white with black markings, sometimes mottled. A.S. raec, a hound. Generally coupled together and led by a berner till wanted. Presumably the " cervericus," a hart hound, would be stronger and larger than the " deimericus " or buck hound, again the buck hound was probably larger than the " vulpericus " or foxhound, and the " canis heirettis " or harrier.

HEREDITARY MASTERS OF THE ROYAL BUCKHOUNDS.

1. Osborne Lovel (Henry II).
2. William Lovel.
3. Hamon le Venour, 1216 (Henry II).
4. William Lovel.
5. John Lovel, *ob.* 1316.
6. Thomas le Borhunte, *ob.* 1340, *jure* Margaret Lovel.
7. William Danvers, *ob.* 1361, *jure* Margaret Lovel.
8. Sir Bernard Brocas, 1363, *ob.* 1395, *jure* Mary de Borhunte.
9. Sir Bernard Brocas (2), executed 1400.
10. William Brocas (1), *ob.* 1456.
11. William Brocas (2), *ob.* 1484.
12. John Brocas, *ob.* 1492.
13. William Brocas (3), *ob.* 1506.
14. John Brocas, 1508–1512.
15. George Warham and Ralph Pexall, 1512–1514, *jure* Anne and Edith Brocas.
16. Ralph Pexall, 1514–1540, *jure* Edith Brocas.
17. Sir Richard Pexall, *ob.* 1571.

EXPLANATORY PEDIGREE.

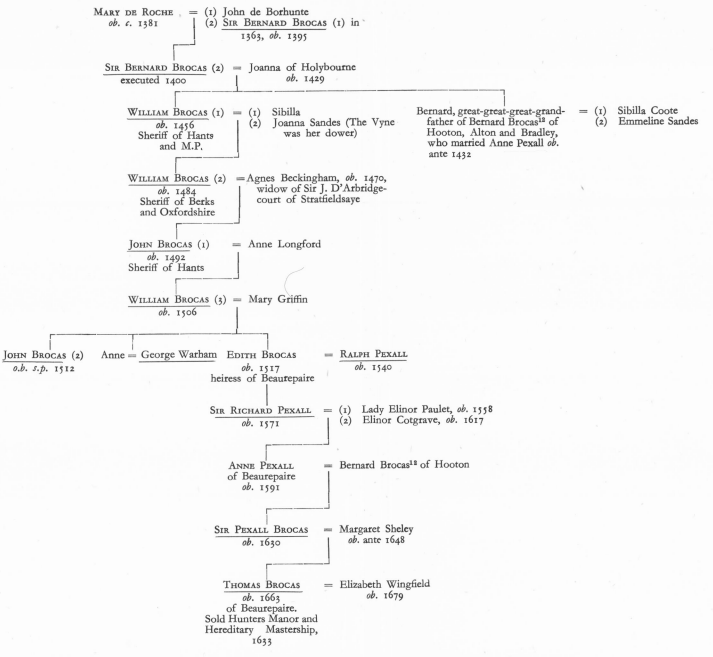

MARY DE ROCHE = (1) John de Borhunte
ob. c. 1381   (2) SIR BERNARD BROCAS (1) in
                   1363, *ob.* 1395

SIR BERNARD BROCAS (2) = Joanna of Holybourne
executed 1400   *ob.* 1429

WILLIAM BROCAS (1) = (1) Sibilla   Bernard, great-great-great-grand-   = (1) Sibilla Coote
ob. 1456   (2) Joanna Sandes (The Vyne   father of Bernard Brocas[12] of   (2) Emmeline Sandes
Sheriff of Hants   was her dower)   Hooton, Alton and Bradley,
and M.P.   who married Anne Pexall *ob.*
                                                        ante 1432

WILLIAM BROCAS (2) = Agnes Beckingham, *ob.* 1470,
ob. 1484   widow of Sir J. D'Arbridge-
Sheriff of Berks   court of Stratfieldsaye
and Oxfordshire

JOHN BROCAS (1) = Anne Longford
ob. 1492
Sheriff of Hants

WILLIAM BROCAS (3) = Mary Griffin
ob. 1506

JOHN BROCAS (2)   Anne = George Warham   EDITH BROCAS   = RALPH PEXALL
o.b. s.p. 1512   *ob.* 1517   *ob.* 1540
                                          heiress of Beaurepaire

SIR RICHARD PEXALL = (1) Lady Elinor Paulet, *ob.* 1558
ob. 1571   (2) Elinor Cotgrave, *ob.* 1617

ANNE PEXALL   = Bernard Brocas[12] of Hooton
of Beaurepaire
ob. 1591

SIR PEXALL BROCAS = Margaret Sheley
ob. 1630   *ob. ante* 1648

THOMAS BROCAS = Elizabeth Wingfield
ob. 1663   *ob.* 1679
of Beaurepaire.
Sold Hunters Manor and
Hereditary Mastership,
1633

[12] Her cousin and so restored the old name of Brocas to the Royal Buckhounds and
to Beaurepaire.

The last so-called Bernard Brocas died in 1861, but the last true Brocas of Beaurepaire died in 1777 ; in the female line Roche Court continued in the family.

Names of masters of the Royal Buckhounds are underlined.

18. Sir John Savage, till 1584, married widow of Sir Richard Pexall.
19. Sir Pexall Brocas, *ob*. 1630.
20. Thomas Brocas sold Hunters Manor to Sir Lewis Watson afterwards Lord Rockingham 1633.

N.B.—The manor of Little Weldon, or Hunters Manor, was near Rockingham, in Northamptonshire, and so, well placed for the hunting of Rockingham Forest. Rockingham Castle, as a Royal hunting seat, was afterwards succeeded by Windsor Castle. Rockingham Forest was some 30 miles long by 12 miles wide until fairly recent time.

NOTES ON THE BROCAS FAMILY.

The first ancestor of the Gascon Knight Sir Bernard Brocas who came to this County was Arnald, killed at Bannockburn in 1314. The second, Sir John, was appointed Vallettus to the King and then, in 1314, "*custos equorum regis*," a position of great responsibility. The price of "Great horses" in 1330 is of interest. £120 was paid for one, a grey with a black head. £70 was paid for another, and for a third, a bright bay with white hind fetlocks, £50 was paid. To obtain the comparison with modern days, the multiple would be not less than 40.

Sir John received a tunic of blue and a cape of white Brussels cloth. He had at least six Royal studs under his charge and was a warrior and diplomat as well as a "Master of Horse." He held a command at the seige of Calais, was ambassador to Alfonso XI of Castile and negotiated concerning the marriage of Edward III's daughter to Pedro the Cruel. The Brocas family were first connected with Hampshire in 1337 when he obtained the lands of one Boew, an outlaw, at Basingstoke.

On the failure of a male heir in 1512 on the death of John Brocas, Henry VIII specifically excluded male kinsmen in favour of Edith and Anne Brocas. In this he followed the grant of August 15th, 1316, to Thomas Borhunte, "Venour le Roy des deymers." Henry VI had limited the succession more sensibly to heirs male. The influence of Cardinal Wolsey is probable, Ralph Pexall, husband of Edith, being in his retinus. Henry VIII seems to have ignored the old Royal Buckhounds, and the masters had the greatest difficulty in extracting their modest stipend. Sir Richard Pexall's claim was allowed by letters patent in Queen Mary's reign.

Sir Pexall Brocas claimed a position in James I's Coronation ceremony, but his claim was refused. This is not to be wondered at as his life was not a reputable one. That he was pardoned in 1603 for "all riots and unlawful assemblies before March 20th last past," did not prevent his being sentenced, in 1612, to do "open penance at Paul's Cross where he stood in a white sheet and held a rod in his hand," for "secret and notorious adulteries with divers women." He is then supposed to have gone to the Lord Mayor with thirty men in scarlet and demanded a dinner for his penance.

Charles II also refused Lord Rockingham's claim to attend the Coronation so the old hereditary office had lost its importance and never recovered it.

CHAPTER II.

18th CENTURY HUNTING.

In the 18th century hunting the fox gradually became more popular than hunting the hare. In Hampshire it will be seen that various gentlemen used to bring their hounds and hunt where they were likely to have sport. There were no boundaries laid down, though in a few established Hunts, such as the Charlton Hunt, custom had given some sort of claim to what is now called " a country." The fox was ceasing to be vermin and became, as the century progressed, the chief " beast of chase," supplanting both the stag and the hare. The fact that H.R.H. George Prince of Wales, afterwards George IV, changed his staghounds to foxhounds in 1793 marked definitely the change of fashion. Hampshire can claim one of the earliest regular packs of foxhounds; and the fox was hunted with hounds in the 17th century in the New Forest as will be shown.

There is good evidence[1] that Henry, the 3rd Lord Arundell of Wardour, kept a pack of hounds at Breamore in Hampshire from about 1690 till his death in 1694, and that this pack was handed down and kept by the 4th and 5th Lords, then apparently by the latter's son-in-law James Touchet, 6th Earl of Castle-haven. Finally, in 1782, this pack was disposed of by Henry, the 8th Lord Arundell of Wardour, and bought by the famous Hugo Meynell of Quorndon Hall and so they became incorporated in the Quorn Hounds. Mr. Meynell had started his

---

[1] " Nimrod," in his article on the Chace in the Quarterly Review reprinted in *The Chase, the Turf and the Road*, published in 1837, mentions a letter he had received from James Everard, 10th Lord Arundell of Wardour, dated February 1833. "A pack of foxhounds were kept by my ancestor Lord Arundel between the years 1690 and 1710 and I have memoranda to prove that they occasionally hunted from Wardover Castle in Wiltshire and at Brimmer in Hants (Wardour and Breamore), now Sir Edward Halse's (Hulse), but then the occasional residence of Lord Arundel. (At that time his main residence.) These hounds were kept by my family until about the year 1745, when the Sixth Lord Arundel died (he died 30-6-1746) when they were kept by his nephew the Earl of Castlehaven, until the death of the last Earl of that name, about the year 1782. The pack were then sold to the celebrated Hugo Meynell, Esq., of Quorndon Hall, Leicestershire, and hence it is possible they may have in fact contributed to the establishment of that gentleman's fox-hunting fame." Lord Arundell had two nephews, James and John the 7th and 8th Earls of Castlehaven. James died in 1769 and John in 1777. Perhaps both kept the hounds; it is not possible now to say. It would appear that they may have been returned to the 8th Lord Arundell for disposal in 1782.

career as M.F.H. at the age of 18 in 1753. The facts leading up to the formation of this pack were briefly as follows : Thomas, the 2nd Lord Arundell of Wardour, had raised a regiment of horse at his own expense for King Charles I. He was badly wounded at the Battle of Lansdown and died at Oxford on May 19th, 1643. As he was dying he must have heard of the surrender of his castle to the rebels. His wife, Blanche, a daughter of the Earl of Worcester, had held out from April 29th to May 8th. She was forced to surrender on honourable terms which were not kept. Henry, the eldest son, afterwards 3rd Lord Arundell, hearing of this, came and besieged his father's castle and by springing a mine recaptured the castle from Edmund Ludlow the rebel commander. He did not get much benefit from his loyalty in Charles II's reign as from 1678 to 1683 he was imprisoned in the Tower of London on information given by that lying impostor Titus Oates. In 1685, however, he was made a Privy Councillor and in 1686 Lord Privy Seal. After James II's abdication he retired from public affairs. As Wardour Castle was dismantled and ruinous he lived at Breamore and hunted in both Hampshire and Wiltshire. The 8th Lord Arundell of Wardour built the modern mansion in the years 1768-76 from the designs of Payne the architect. Wardour Castle was never restored, but it is not known where the hounds were kenneled during the period of the pack's existence, 1690–1782 ; probably at Breamore or at Wardour as required.

The following packs of foxhounds were started in Hampshire during the 18th century and have maintained a nearly continuous existence as foxhounds ever since, though in the case of the N.F.H. there was a gap from 1798 to 1800 and in the case of the Vine Hunt from 1942 to 1948 they ceased to have a separate establishment for the time being owing to the Second World War and the sale of their kennels.

1745. Mr. William Evelyn's Hounds started hunting in Hampshire in the " H.H." country.

1781. Mr. Vincent Hawkins Gilbert started his pack in the New Forest. They became the New Forest Hunt in 1784.

1795. Mr. William John Chute started his foxhounds at the Vyne. The pack became " The Vine Hunt."

In the 17th century it would appear that the fox was hunted by private packs in the New Forest, but it seems that he was still regarded as vermin as the following extracts from the churchwarden's accounts at Eling would show :—

		s	d
1675.	Pd. to my Lord Sandis'[2] huntsman for 2 foxheads -	2	o
1682.	Gave to Sir John Coventry's huntsman for 6 fox-heads - - - -	6	o
1683.	To Sir John Coventry's huntsman for 2 foxheads -	2	o
1683.	To Sir John Mill's[3] huntsman for 1 Foxhead -	1	o
1685.	„ „ „ 6 „ -	6	o
1686.	„ „ „ 5 „ -	5	o
1688.	Pd. Henry New for 3 foxheads which Sir William Gooreing killed when he lay at Lyndhurst which foxes were killed about Langley and Ipley -	3	o
1691.	Mr. Cromwell's[4] huntsman for 1 foxhead -	1	o
1724.	Pd. Lord Duke's[5] man for 9 foxheads - -	9	o
1724.	To Sir Richard Mill's[3] man for 5 foxheads - -	5	o
1724.	To the Lord Duke's man for 2 foxheads -	2	o

An early 18th century pack of foxhounds was kept by Mr. Charles Wither, 1684–1731. This gentleman succeeded to Oakley Hall in 1697 and married in 1707 Frances Wavell of an old Yorkshire family. He was High Sheriff of Hampshire in 1708 and M.P. for Christchurch 1726–31. His most important work was Commissioner of Woods and Forests, which office he undertook in 1720. It kept him busy. According to his journals : " I am up every morning at four and abroad till ten at night." He wrote regularly when away to his daughter Anne, who did not go to Court gaieties like her sisters, but stayed at home and did much for her father. He lived, officially, at Cranburn Little Lodge, near Windsor. In one letter he says " I beg you will tell me all about the fox hunting." In October 1731 there was a great stir for his return to Oakley : " I would have Dick the postillion come hither with the four horses on Wednesday ; pray let him set out early in the morning on

[2] William 5th Lord Sandys who sold the Vyne about 1649 and retired to Mottisfont Abbey. He died without issue in 1688. His father, Colonel Henry 4th Lord Sandys, was mortally wounded at Bramdene fight, March 29th, 1644, fighting for King Charles I and died April 6th. The loyalty of this family caused the sale of the Vyne which they had held since 1386.

[3] Sir John Mill and Sir Richard Mill were subsequent owners of Mottisfont Abbey. Their family arms are on the Bargate of Southampton. A descendant was the first M.F.H. in the Hursley country. Sir John Mill's father, also Sir John, married Margaret the eventual heiress of the Sandys family, a daughter of Colonel Henry Sandys.

[4] Mr. Richard Cromwell of Hursley, the unassuming son of Oliver Cromwell, nick-named " Tumble Down Dick," married Dorothy Major, the heiress of Hursley. He died at the Lodge there on July 12th, 1712, in his 86th year, ruined by his grasping daughters.

[5] Charles 2nd Duke of Richmond and Lanox, K.G., K.B., succeeded in 1723 and died 1750.

CHARLES WITHER (THE YOUNGER) OF HALL PLACE, M.F.H.
c. 1708-31.

PAULET ST. JOHN'S HOUNDS AT DOGMERSFIELD PARK, c. 1750.

Mounted figures probably Paulet (afterwards Sir Paulet), Ellis, and Goodyer St. John. Boy driving probably Sir Henry Paulet St. John, 2nd Baronet, b. 1737. Lady probably Mary, second wife and mother of the boy.

The sky of the lower picture is really part of the lake shown in upper picture. Originally one picture with yet another portion, landscape only, painted for Rev. Ellis St. John of West Court, Finchampstead, and it remained there until that property was sold by Lieut.-Colonel C. Harris St. John, D.S.O. Now the property of his son Major Edward D. Harris St. John, M.C., by whose kindness it is reproduced.

Wednesday, that he may be here betimes for the horses to have some rest. Let Webb go to James the waggoner and tell him to provide to bring my goods and the maids by his wagon on Saturday. Tell Ned I would have the hounds kept fresh for me, for I think I have not been so well these twenty years as I am now, and shall hunt shortly." He came home but, despite his cheerful letter, he died in the November following.

In an earlier letter he speaks of " Henny "—Henrietta Maria, his elder daughter (who married Mr. E. Bramston)—saying she " hunts tomorrow in her new habit, which is garter blue gogram, laced with gold lace." This would probably have been with the Royal Hounds, but it is not definitely stated. She was going to a ball at Windsor that night. An interesting picture exists of Charles Wither in a tight-fitting hunting frock with belt open at the neck for a black stock and he wears a hunting cap. He carries a whip in his gauntleted left hand. A French horn is on the table (see Plate III facing page 26).

Mr. Wither was fourth of his family to own Hall Place, as Oakley Hall was then called; his family were a younger branch of the Withers of Manydown which estate they held on lease from the priors of St. Swithun's Monastery and the Dean and Chapter of Winchester Cathedral from 1389 to 1863 when the Manydown leaseholds were bought, only to be again sold with Tangier Park and all the property remaining in 1871 to Mr., afterwards Sir Edward, Bates. Oakley Hall has also left the family.

A letter dated 21st October, 1731, quoted by Mr. A. F. Leach in his *History of Winchester College*, page 375, written by Miss Osborn from Chilbolton to her brother Robert Byng, M.P. for Plymouth, gives a picture of the life of " Commoners " at Winchester College in the early 18th century.

" You that are in the midst of the Beau Monde and think of nothing but Foreign Dukes, etc., will not be entertained with what I can relate from hence, which only consists of the pleasure of the Field, where last Monday we were particularly well pleased. For by invitation we had Dr. Burton, the Master of Winchester School, and his ten young noblemen's sons that live with him, for which he has £200 a year for each and is as a private governour to them and they also have the advantage of a publick school at the same time, which surely must be a fine way of educating them.

" These with four other young gentlemen of the School met us in the field a-hunting. They and their attendance and ours made in all forty people, and after very good sport all came home to dine here. Indeed, I have not seen a finer sight than those boys and their master together."

Some of these pupils of Dr. Burton were of interest :—

Lord Deerhurst, born in 1721, died unmarried in 1744. His brother, Hon. George W. Coventry, born 1722, succeeded as 6th Earl 1751 and died 1801. He married the famous Maria Gunning, eldest of the three beauties. Hon. John B. Coventry who took the name of Bulkeley and died 1801. Lord Ossulston, born 1716, became 3rd Earl of Tankerville 1753 and a Lieutenant-General at 27, died 1767. Lord Brooke, born 1719, succeeded as 8th Baron, 1727, becoming Earl Brooke in 1746, and Earl of Warwick in 1759; he died 1773. " Master Wallop " John, eldest son of 1st Earl of Portsmouth (then Viscount Lymington), born 1718, died 1797. Lord Drumlanrig, eldest son of 3rd Duke of Queensberry, killed by accident 1755. Sir Robert Burdett, succeeded as a Baronet at his birth in 1716, died 1797. His grandson, Sir Francis, married Sophia Coutts, the great heiress. He married Elizabeth, daughter of Sir Charles Sedley, the well-known wit.

The most likely pack of hounds with which this party hunted would be Mr. Paulet St. John's hounds an illustration of which appears facing page 27, and which are next mentioned. He probably moved his hounds from Dogmersfield to Farley Chamberlayne and *vice versa*. Chilbolton would be about ten miles from Farley Chamberlayne and twelve miles from another possible pack, the Quarley Hunt, a picture of which is shown in the National Gallery of British Sports and Pastimes at Derby House, founded by the late Mr. Walter Hutchinson of Stanbridge Earls, Romsey. The picture is called " Full Cry " and shows the master and four hunt servants in livery and was painted probably about this time by James Seymour, 1702–52. The Prince of Wales received four-and-a-half couple of hounds from the Quarley Pack in 1791.

The five horsemen shown in the picture are in green coats, with red collar and cuffs, four of them—undoubtedly hunt servants—wear spare stirrup leathers round their bodies, over the shoulder. It is not known who was master of this pack in James Seymour's day. Later in the century, however, they were hunted by joint-masters, Lieut.-General Charles FitzRoy, 1st Lord Southampton, who was born in 1737 and became a

Baron in 1780 ; his joint-master was Colonel Beaver of Penton who had served in the 27th Regiment (Royal Inniskilling Fusiliers) and in the Hampshire Fencibles. Lord Southampton lived at Whittlebury, near Doles, in the Andover district which was burnt down in the 3rd Lord's time with much of its contents. Quarley would be conveniently placed between the two masters. Colonel Beaver is mentioned by Mr. Stephen Terry as helping the Devon hunting visitors in the 1780's. Mr. William Poyntz calls these hounds the Quarley Hunt in 1791, but Mr. FitzRoy's in 1792. The pack were sold in 1794. The pack depicted is far beyond the style of an ordinary country squire. Traditions of the kennels and hunt servants' cottages exist in the locality, but the actual subject of the picture remains somewhat of a mystery. James Seymour was the leading sporting artist of his day and the picture is full of interest.

The next mention of foxhunting known to the author appears to be the inscription on Farley monument, near Winchester. The monument is erected to the memory of a horse, the property of Mr. (afterwards Sir) Paulet St. John, 1704-80. His local connections were many, being M.P. for Winchester 1734-41 and 1751-55, M.P. for Hants 1741-47, Mayor of Winchester 1771 and High Sheriff for the County 1728. He was created a Baronet in 1772. It is recorded that his horse, " in the month of September 1733, leaped into a chalk pit, *a-foxhunting*, 25 feet deep, with his master on his back and in October 1734 he won the Hunters' Plate on Worthy Down and was rode by his owner, and entered in the name of ' Beware Chalk Pit.' " Mr. St. John was the son of Ellis Mews of Winchester who assumed the name of St. John when his wife, Frances, succeeded to the St. John estates of Farley Chamberlayne. He himself married three heiresses and was the ancestor of the St. John Mildmays, lately of Dogmersfield. The only other evidence of Sir Paulet's hounds was a large hook in an oak tree near the house at Dogmersfield, on which tradition said the carcases for his hounds were hung.[6]

In addition to these, the following packs of foxhounds were brought into the county or were kept in the county for hunting the fox during the 18th century.

The 4th, 5th and 6th Earls of Craven[7] brought in their packs to Dummer, near Basingstoke, and hunted the Andover-

---

[6] From information given by Isabel, Lady St. John Mildmay, 1948.

[7] The 4th Lord, Fulwar, succeeded in 1739 and died in 1764, his cousin William, 5th Lord, carried on till 1769, and his nephew William, 6th Lord, till 1791.

Kingsclere district.   Lord Stawell of Marelands, Bentley, and
Hinton Ampner House, Alresford, kept hounds, Mr. William
Poyntz of Midgham, Berkshire, brought his hounds to Overton
for some years.   Mr. Russell of Greywell and Hoddington,
Basingstoke, Mr. Thomas Land of Park House, Hambledon,
Colonel Thomas de Burgh of Belmont (later Warnford Park),
all kept packs which hunted fox.   The Dukes of Richmond and
Bolton brought their hounds by permission to the New Forest.
Mr. Barber of Fremington, near Barnstaple, Devon, used to
come to the Star Inn, Andover.   Mr. Richard Smith of Crux
Easton also kept a popular pack of foxhounds at the latter end
of the century.

Some account of these gentlemen is given, but very little is
known of their actual hunting achievements.

An amusing tale is told of William, the 3rd successive
Lord Craven to bring his hounds to Dummer.   The tale well
illustrates the lack of boundaries and casual manner of hunting
where foxes were likely to be found.   Lord Craven, as recorded
by Mr. Stephen Terry the Diarist, had missed his fox in Highclere Park.   He asked a labourer if he had seen him.   The man
was a wag and also preferred Squire Smith's hounds of Crux
Easton, answered, " Oh aye, I seen 'im, and he stopped and
had a bit of a chat wi' me ! "   " Indeed," said Lord Craven,
" and what did he say to you ? "   " Why, he axed me if I could
tell 'un whether ut were me Lord's hounds or the Squire's as
was after 'un, so I told 'un ut was most likely me Lord's, abin
the Squire was out yesterday. 'Ah,' said he, 'I thought so, that's
just how 'tis ; that's the reason why I can stop and have a chat
with you, abin you see, when the Squire's after me I have no
time to spare.' "   However, Lord Craven killed his fox and had
the best of the labourer whom he met again, saying, " Your
friend the fox stayed chatting with you too long and paid the
penalty of all idlers."

Many gentlemen kept a pack of harriers and hunted their
own property and that of friends and neighbours.   As foxhunting became popular, they went farther afield, but there were
fewer packs of foxhounds and so their country was very large.
Foxes being still not preserved with any strictness, masters of
hounds moved their packs to a district where sport was likely,
or to places where friends wanted them to hunt.   In the 19th
century it will be seen how in the H.H. country the Hambledon
and the Hursley Hounds started, also later Sir John Cope's large

country was divided into the Garth and the South Berks. This process necessitated accurate boundaries which were not always obtained without recrimination.

In the 18th century a hasty breakfast was often taken in the kitchen, and an old yeoman who had hunted with three Lord Cravens was most indignant at the late hours kept by the last lord. " We," he said indignantly, " took care to be at the covert-side before dawn ; we killed our fox early and had a good long afternoon for drinking." Actually hounds and horses were slower, the scent lay better before the sun was up and they found the drag of the fox returning from his night's hunting for food and hunted up to his lair. This became unnecessary when foxes were more plentiful and inconvenient when large fields turned out, many coming from a distance. In the 17th century foxes were found by two or three couple of hounds only used as " tufters," as in stag hunting, and the pack was in couples until slipped on the " View Holloa " being given by the huntsman.

Meetings after hunting were most convivial and were social occasions which greatly assisted the sport and kept good fellowship.

An extract from a poem or doggerel called the " Fox Chace," relating a hunt of George Villiers, 2nd Duke of Buckingham, in the Bilsdale country is given as it so well shows the earlier method, a relic of stag hunting.

Verse 3.

Then in Wreckledale scrags
We threw off our dogs,
In a place where his lying was likely ;
But the like ne'er was seen
Since a huntsman I have been ;
Never hounds found a fox more quickly.

Verse 4.

There was Dido and Spanker,
And Younker was there,
And Ruler that ne'er looks behind him ;
There was Rose and Bonny Lass,
Who were always in the chace,
These were part of our hounds that did find him.

Verse 5.

Mr. Tybballs, cries, Away,
Heark away ! Heark away !
With that our foot huntsman did hear him.
Tom Mossman cries, Codsounds,
Uncouple all your hounds,
Or else we shall never come near him.

The poem was published in the latter end of the 17th century by William Ouley, a very likely date would be 1686 or 1687, after the Duke's disgrace and retirement from the Court and all its intrigues. Three couple of hounds are mentioned by name as finding the fox. On the "Hark away" being cried the foot huntsman uncouples the rest of the pack. The Duke's French servant, Leppin, sounded the horn at the death, being doubtless an expert at blowing the "Mort" for a stag, as described in the following verse :—

Verse 17.

> Then Leppin took a horn
> As good as e'er was blown;
> Tom Mossman bid him wind his Death, then
> The country people all
> Came flocking to his fall;
> This was honour enough for a Frenchman.

A foot huntsman is also mentioned with the Charlton Hunt founded about 1679 by the Duke of Monmouth with Mr. Roper as his first huntsman. The Charlton Hunt, later named the Goodwood Hunt, ceased in 1813. Squire Roper retired to the continent after the Battle of Sedgemoor and returned after the Battle of the Boyne, when he was employed again with this hunt; he died out hunting in 1715. No doubt this method of hunting would be used also by the packs visiting the New Forest in the 17th and early 18th century, and probably by the 3rd Lord Arundell of Wardour.

Mr. W. Poyntz.

A regular hunting visitor to North Hants for a good many years was Mr. William Poyntz of Midgham, near Newbury. His portrait appears opposite. A man of good family, whose father, Stephen, had bought the property of Midgham. His father had become a man of some importance, whose appointments were very varied, ranging from tutor to Lord Townsend's children to Ambassador Extraordinary and Minister Plenipotentiary at the Congress of Cambray, 1727, Governor to William, Duke of Cumberland, 1730, and a Privy Councillor in 1735. It is probable that this rise to fame was largely due to his marriage with Anne Maria Mordaunt, sister to Charles, Earl of Peterborough, and Maid-of-Honour to Queen Caroline. The son William was born in 1734 and the Queen, his uncle (the Earl of Peterborough) and the Duke of Cumberland were sponsors. At his father's death in 1750 Mr. Poyntz found country life pleasanter than the pursuit of fame at court.

By Gainsborough.

WILLIAM POYNTZ OF MIDGHAM, M.F.H. and manager of the Prince of Wales' Hounds.

WILLIAM HARRISON.

Huntsman to Lord Stawell of Marelands, Bentley, and Hinton Ampner House, c. 1780–96.

When master of his own affairs, his mother dying in 1771, he lived a peaceful, comfortable and somewhat eccentric life at home and visiting friends. Hunting the fox and dancing were his hobbies. His hunting establishment was a simple one. John Topper, his huntsman, was assisted by his valet, John Child, and sometimes by a boy to help in taking on the horses. A good many horses were kept at grass in the park and all could be bought with no warranty and half-an-hour for trial. His hunters were only corned the night before hunting and on the morning of hunting. He travelled with four horses and postillions and latterly he was equipped with his gun and two terriers, in case a pheasant or a hare could be added to the bag ; hunting in the saddle had then become too strenuous for him. Mr. Poyntz's picture by Gainsborough shows him leaning against a tree, gun in hand, with a favourite spaniel. The peaked cap in his hand is unusual ; it somewhat resembles that of Mr. Charles Wither (see portrait facing page 26).

Wherever he stayed he would ask for a little dance and the maids were duly summoned. Mr. Poyntz would choose the youngest and prettiest. Despite his passion for the dance he did not like draughts or " great inroads of wind " as he termed them, and whilst staying at Hurstbourne Park he arranged a comfortable chat with the housekeeper and a youthful charmer in the housekeeper's room. When seated in red coat and frilled shirt warmly and happily, before a cosy fire, he was found out by Lady Portsmouth and retrieved from his den. His ready wit, however, mollified his hostess's displeasure.

Little is known of his actual hunting. He used the Red Lion, Overton, for his kennels and himself used an inn opposite called after him, the Poyntz Arms, but now demolished. There he entertained neighbouring squires and would also have small dances. Freefolk Wood he hunted usually on Mondays and Wednesdays, picking up on Wednesdays perhaps a tired fox and some of his stray hounds. His staff cheerfully left hounds all over the countryside to get home at their discretion, while John Topper made a useful public house cast. Mr. Poyntz gave up his Hampshire country to the Prince Regent in 1791 probably—he certainly did so by 1793—and helped the Prince with the management of his hounds. His friendship with the Prince did not leave him quite unscathed and probably hastened his hunting on wheels. His country was afterwards part of Mr. T. A. Smith's country around Andover and the Overton-Whitchurch country, afterwards Mr. Chute's. He

D

married Isabella Courtenay and his eldest son, William Stephen (1778–1840), married the heiress of the unhappy Montagues, who, after her home Cowdray had been burnt, and her brother drowned in 1793, saw her own two sons drowned when boating at Bognor in 1815, thus fulfilling the monkish curse of the destruction of the family by fire and water said to Sir Anthony Browne, K.G., at Battle Abbey in 1738. Mr. Poyntz died in 1809 at the London home of his sister, Countess Spencer, to whom he left his estates. His most unpleasant eccentricity was the sale of his hounds at Tattersall's for £5 for the 50-odd couples. One hound only was wanted by the buyer and the rest were resold for their skins.

Lord Stawell.

Henry 2nd Lord Stawell was born in 1757, the son of the Right Hon. Henry Bilson Legge (1708–64), fourth son of the 1st Earl of Dartmouth. He owned several houses, at Maple-durham ; Marelands, Bentley, near his kennels at Great Lodge, Alice Holt ; and also Hinton Ampner House, near Alresford. He inherited his title from his mother Mary, created Baroness Stawell of Somerton, daughter of Edward, Lord Stawell. He hunted the country Farnham, Odiham, Basingstoke, and some times he hunted around Andover. His huntsman Will Harrison (whose portrait appears facing page 33) is remembered for some peculiar characteristics of stature and speech. He was a very short man and his heels barely reached below the saddle flaps. When spurring his horse along he was heard to exclaim one day " I might as well stick my spurs into oblivion "—his spurs only goading the saddle flaps. He was fond of grand words. On being asked by his master what was the best way to get water at some kennels he was building he answered, " My Lord, I have duly considered the matter and, in my opinion, the best plan would be *to erect* a well." On one occasion he ran a fox into the grounds of Waverley Abbey from the Holt. The gardener remonstrated with him for riding over the lawns saying " Even my master and mistress don't ever ride there." " Don't they," said Harrison with a sniff, " and I never saw better riding in my life ! But, I will tell you what, my man, we shall lose our fox owing to your nasty stinking violets." Another hunt servant to Lord Stawell, George Sharp, went to be hunts-man to the Prince of Wales, though much against his will at the time.

Not much is remembered of Lord Stawell's hunting, but on one occasion his hounds ran a fox to ground in Hurstbourne Park having found in Farnham Holt. This gives a point of some 24 miles, a truly wonderful hunt; more particulars would be of great interest. From his kennels near Basingstoke he hunted the country around, usually staying with his friend the Duke of Bolton. Once when hunting at Hackwood he found a vixen and a litter of six cubs in Spring Wood. The vixen got away, but all the litter were killed in two hours. He gave up his hounds in 1796 displeasing his Hampshire supporters, who had acceded to all demands made for their retention.

As many tales of ghostly visitations both at Hinton House and at Marelands have been recounted and also published and the name of Lord Stawell has been mentioned with that of his steward, Isaac Mackrel, as the probable causes of the many and curious disturbances, it is fair to this nobleman's memory to state that the rumours concerned his grandfather who died suddenly of apoplexy at Hinton on April 2nd, 1755, and the steward was killed in the following year by the fall of a stack of bavins. Both these men were of very evil repute.

The worst manifestations occurred between 1767 and 1771 during the tenancy of Mr. W. H. Ricketts and his wife. Despite a week's visit by her brother, the famous Admiral John Jervis, Earl St. Vincent, the efforts of Captain Luttrell of Kilmeston, and offers of money rewards, the mystery remained. Lord St. Vincent insisted on his sister removing from the house and asylum was given her by the Bishop of Winchester at Wolvesey Palace. The old house at Hinton was pulled down in 1787 as tenants could not be induced to stay there and the owners did not wish to live there. A new house of Georgian type on a different site was built and has been twice greatly altered since then, but only because of the varied tastes of succeeding owners. Bones in a box were found when the old house was pulled down; these were buried without expert examinattion.

The Georgian house forms the background of the picture of the H.H. Meet at Hinton House by Mr. T. Smith in December 1819, when in the occupation of Mr. R. J. Heysham, a prominent member elected in 1813. Lord Stawell was a member of the old club under Mr. Ridge's presidency. He died in 1820 when the barony expired. His only daughter Mary, by marrying John, Lord Sherborne, carried the family estates to the Hon. J. T. Dutton, their second son, the grandfather of the present owner.

Mr. J. Russell.

Lord Stawell's country between Basingstoke and the Golden Pot and around Herriard and Preston Oakhills was next hunted by Mr. Joseph Russell of Greywell. Mr. Russell was a first-rate sportsman and has been described as a fine looking old man with white hair. He had been a solicitor in Essex and had married Lady Betty Birmingham. This lady was the daughter of Lord Athenry created Earl of Louth. When he died in 1799 the earldom became extinct. She was a very agreeable, affable lady and good looking. Her costume in the field was striking as she wore a scarlet body to her habit, with, according to Mr. Stephen Terry, H.H. Buttons,[8] over a dark riding skirt.

Mr. Russell kept his hounds at North Warnborough, but he himself lived at Greywell till 1802 when he moved to Hoddington. Lord Stawell's old huntsman, William Harrison hunted his hounds at first and then John Major, a first-rate huntsman when sober.

Mr. Joseph Russell can claim the honour of being the first M.F.H. to instruct the famous Tom Smith who was brought up at Shalden, the home of his father. William Harrison taught him the names of the hounds and often discussed hunting with the boy. He would say, " Well, Master Smith, and what became of our fox to-day?" He often got not only a prompt but a very shrewd answer.

Mr. Russell used to say that he committed no sins during the hunting season as he hunted six days a week and went to church twice on Sundays and so had no time to do anything wrong. An account of a very remarkable hunt, written by Mr. Russell himself, appears in Appendix " A."

Little of his sport has come down to us, but a fine run took place on November 1st, 1803, from Dogmersfield to Liphook, a point of some 13 or 14 miles, reported in the *Sporting Magazine*. Mr. Russell does not appear to have been a member of the H.H. His retirement was caused by an altercation with Mr. J. T. Villebois, a tenant of Preston House, where he kept a pack of harriers. One day Mr. Villebois changed on to a fox and ran from Preston Copse, killing above Amery Wood, near Alton. Mr. Villebois and Mr. Smith of Shalden Lodge were alone with hounds and a picture showing Mr. Villebois

---

[8] This may be the first example of the Lady's Button. She appears at any rate to be the first local lady follower.

just taking the brush celebrated the occasion. Mr. Russell heard of this run and remonstrated with Mr. Villebois when they next met. He ended by saying : " You had better hunt the country yourself." To this Mr. Villebois replied : " If you really mean that, I will." This he did the very next season, 1804, until his death, to the great satisfaction of the country and entirely at his own expense as will be shown in the next chapter.

Mr. T. Land, 1790.

In the latter end of the 18th century two gentlemen hunted fox in parts of what became afterwards the Hambledon country. The first, Mr. Thomas Land of Park House, Hambledon, was a bit of a character. He believed in hunting at daybreak and, in fact, he would bivouac at night by the covert he intended to draw if it was at any considerable distance. Often he threw off at his kennel, situated near large woodlands, and found the drag of a fox attracted by the smell of horse flesh. He hunted deer in the Forest of Bere in the summer and started cub-hunting in September with the same hounds. After two or three days they were quite steady and would take no notice of deer. Mr. T. Smith attributed this to the fact that Mr. Land did not use young hounds for the deer. The head keeper of the forest was very angry at his hunting there as he had no permission whatever to do so. Mr. Geary, the keeper, had hounds for the purpose, but his son hunted with Mr. Land, and so did Lord Scarborough, Colonel of the York Militia, then at Portsmouth, and many of the neighbouring gentry. He used to poach fairly regularly on the Duke of Richmond's Charlton Hunt and the Duke sent a messenger to ask him to forbear and to keep within a certain line. The messenger was well regaled but no arrangement was made and the messenger returned a little the worse for liquor. He gave the following laconic answer from Mr. Land " That he had hunted the country before his Grace was born and he hoped to do so after he was dead and damned." This story is given by Colonel John Cook, a contemporary (though a younger man) and a Hampshire man. "Aesop " says that Mr. Land ran a fox from Highden Wood to Petworth and Lord Egremont objected and sent a servant to tell him to whip off. He puts somewhat similar words into the mouth of Will James, Mr. Land's huntsman : " Tell your master I hunted before he was born and hope to do so after he is dead and buried." This is undoubtedly an inaccurate memory of the tale.

The 3rd Duke of Richmond moved the Charlton Hunt Kennels to Goodwood and had the hounds from 1757 until his death in 1806. The pack was presented by the 4th Duke to H.R.H. The Prince Regent in 1813. Tom Grant, the old huntsman, spoke of the future role of the hounds as " to hunt calves or donkeys " (*i.e.*, the carted deer).

Yet a third version of this story is given in Nimrod's *Hunting Reminiscences*, Chapter X, p. 197. He refers to a celebrated yeoman, " Mr. Laund," hunting part of the Hambledon country and calls him a capital sportsman of the old school. He relates that on one occasion the Duke of Richmond met Mr. Laund at the same covert, both intending to draw and each laying claim to it. The Duke became angry, when Mr. Laund thus addressed him : " It's no use my Lord to put yourself in a passion. I've just thow'd 'em in, and if there's a fox in the covert they'll find him, and between us both we shall kill him ! But, if your Grace puts yourself in such a passion, as I hunted the covert before you was born, I shall hunt it after you are dead." In this version the Duke of Richmond is probably correctly given instead of Lord Egremont. The story of the meeting and words used (in all three cases more or less the same) does not appear likely or so natural as that given by Colonel Cook. These three stories are given to show some of the difficulties of an hunting historian.

Mr. Land died in 1791 and was buried at Hambledon, so he was wrong in his calculation. The Duke was born 1734-35, and lived until 1806.

Colonel T. de Burgh (before 1793).

Another gentleman who had a small pack of foxhounds was Colonel Thomas de Burgh who became Lord Clanricarde. This gentleman lived at Belmont (later Warnford Park). A facetious person once chalked on the gates :

" Oh what a blundering Irish Dog
Who calls this a mount when 'tis but a bog."

It was, however, afterwards most thoroughly drained by Mr. E. R. Tunno.

The gallant Colonel was said to have given up his hounds to join the Duke of York's expedition to the Netherlands. This was not actually a fact. He did, however, raise the 88th Regiment (the Connaught Rangers) in September 1793. The regiment proceeded to Holland, but the Colonel was promoted Major-General and sent as G.O.C. to Elba, where he remained in 1796-97. It is presumed, therefore, that he was more efficient than some of the colonels appointed to the new regiments raised for these unlucky operations, one of whom, at least, had never held the King's commission previously. Whilst at Elba, General de Burgh and also General O'Hara at Gibraltar both earned the sweeping disapproval of Nelson in 1797 when refusing to spare him 1,000 or 1,500 men for raids. " Soldiers," he reported, " have not the same boldness in undertaking a political measure that we have ; we look to the benefit of our country and risk our own fame every day to save her ; a soldier obeys his orders and no more." (*Fortescue IV*, II, p. 797.)

Colonel de Burgh gave his small pack of foxhounds to the Prince of Wales. This probably occurred in 1793 when the Colonel raised the 88th Regiment and the Prince of Wales started fox hunting on February 11th of that year. When General de Burgh returned from his period of service he kept a pack of harriers. He has, however, been wrongly claimed as a master of the Hambledon Foxhounds.

Mr. T. L. Sclater-Matthew, 1780's ?

Mr. Thomas Limbrey Sclater-Mathew of Tangier Park was born in 1742. In 1772 his uncle John Limbrey made over Tangier Park to him, and he lived there till his death in 1809. He hunted the greater portion of the Vine country and Sherborne Wood was his favourite meet. Probably Mr. Sclater-Mathew got together his pack soon after he came to live at Tangier and probably continued to hunt for some twenty years. The Rev. J. E. Austen-Leigh states that he gave up hunting some years before he died. Nothing is known of the sport shown. His huntsman, John Adams, has left a name behind him, not, however, in his professional capacity, but as a toper. After his master gave up hunting Adams practised as a farrier and cow doctor whenever he was sober enough to exercise his calling, and when very drunk on one occasion at Oakley Hall he is said to have cut off a cow tail and sent it up to the Hall on a plate, saying that it would do for Squire Bramston's dinner. Remains of kennels exist at Tangier. Mr. Sclater Mathew's father Richard had married Magdalen daughter of John Limbrey of Hoddington House and Tangier Park. Mr. Limbrey was born in 1703 and succeeded in 1738. He, too, may have hunted a pack of hounds, but no evidence exists.

CHAPTER III.

THE PRINCE OF WALES AT KEMPSHOTT.

In 1788 the Prince of Wales, afterwards George IV, leased Kempshott Park from its new owner, Mr. J. C. Crook of Stratton. Some ten years before this date the owner at that time, Mr. Philip Dehany of Farleigh Wallop, had pulled down the old manor house and built a Georgian mansion, the main elevation of which and a plan of the principal rooms are given facing pages 48 and 49. These and plans of the other floors and basement have only very recently been found at Windsor Castle and are published by gracious permission of the King.

This home again was much altered by Mr. Edward W. Blunt in 1832 in the Italian style. The illustration facing page 40 bears no relation to Kempshott, though it was stated to do so on the caption. The print is from a plate etched in 1788 from a pen and water-colour picture by George Rowlandson made in 1787. Its correct title is " The Return," forming one of a series of six fox hunting scenes purporting to show George IV when Prince of Wales. The set was in Lord Carnarvon's collection and three of this set were shown at Burlington House in " Masters of British Water-Colour " in 1949, this picture being one of the chosen three. It had previously been exhibited in Amsterdam 1936, Country Life Exhibition 1937 and at the Louvre in 1938. Despite this publicity nothing was known of its true history and the actual print from which this reproduction was made was loaned to the author by Sir Nelson E. O. Rycroft whose grandfather Sir Nelson lived at Kempshott and who sold the estate after the death of his father in 1925.

So far as is known the Prince of Wales did not own a pack at the time when the picture was made. He would not be flattered at the artist's pointed reference to his increasing stoutness, if the figure having his spurs removed be indeed that of the Prince. On the other hand, the presence of ladies in the hunting field was most unusual at this time, and no such bevy of beauty would be likely to attend the hounds of any private person. The huntsman certainly bears no resemblance to the dapper George Sharpe whose portrait is given facing page 41.

It has been traditionally supposed that the gracious lady looking over the balustrade was Mrs. FitzHerbert. This

From a Drawing by Rowlandson

"The Return"

possibly H.R.H. The Prince of Wales (afterwards George IV) returning to Kempshott after hunting.

GEORGE SHARPE ON "MONCK."

Huntsman to the Prince of Wales and afterwards to H.M. King George IV, 1791 - 1822. (Reproduced by the courtesy of Kenneth Glover, Esq., F.R.I.B.A., to whom the copyright belongs.)

beautiful and witty lady was frequently at Kempshott. Her maiden name was Mary Anne Smythe of the Hampshire family of Smythe then of Brambridge Park. She had married in 1775 Mr. Edward Weld of Lulworth Castle, Dorset, brother of the founder of Stonyhurst College, and on his death in 1778 she married Thomas FitzHerbert of Swinnerton whom she also survived, to marry to her sorrow, George, Prince of Wales, on December 15th, 1781. The marriage was not recognised by the Royal Marriage Act, but the Prince's affection for her, while it lasted, was one of the nobler features of his character. It is said, on good authority, that her miniature was hung round his neck when he died.

The *Hampshire Chronicle* records a stag hunt on January 30th, 1790, from Hackwood Park. The deer crossed the River Loddon between Basingstoke and Basing and then, swinging left-handed over the Sherborne Fields, passed *via* Shothanger, Worting, Kempshott, Farleigh, Highwood to Preston Oakhills. Here, His Royal Highness was thrown out of the hunt; hounds, however, ran on through Herriard Common, Lasham, to Shalden where the deer was taken in the kitchen of a cottage. There had been many casualties among the followers and only four were present when the deer was taken. It is of considerable interest to know that the Prince then wore " a uniform of the Hampshire Hunt." He is said to have conversed with his usual affability with every gentleman present. This may account for his losing the hunt. It cannot now be certain what staghounds are referred to, but it is possible that the Royal Buckhounds may have been brought to Hackwood through the Prince's agency.

No other hunt is mentioned in 1790, but in July of that year the Prince attended Winchester Races with a greater number of the nobility than ever before remembered, among whom were the Dukes of Bedford, Bolton and Queensbury; Marquis of Clanricarde, Earl of Portchester, Earl of Portsmouth, Earl Stawell Lord Viscount Palmerston, Lord John and Lord William Russell, Lord Bishop of Winchester, Dean of Canterbury, Lord Rosehill, Lord Southwell, Lord Cavan, Lord Montcalt, two members for the City and County, Sir Harry St. John Mildmay, Sir Thomas Miller, Sir J. Lade, Sir Harry Tichborne, Sir Harry Featherstone, Sir Charles Mill, and " a great concourse of the first families in the kingdom, in the most superb and splendid equipages, formed a scene so highly descriptive of the richness of this island, that it struck several foreigners of distinction who were present with silent astonishment."

The Prince started as a master of staghounds in January 1791. Luckily, the author is able, by the courtesy of Sir Owen F. Morshead, K.C.V.O., D.S.O., M.C., Librarian to H.M. The King, to give many details of this hunt and of the foxhounds, from the diary of William Poyntz of Midgham whom the Prince appointed as his manager. The diary, bound in vellum and enclosed in a green morocco case, is still in the Royal Library. A slip is pasted inside :—

" In case of my death, I desire this book may be delivered with my most humble duty to His Royal Highness George Prince of Wales.

Midgham.   (Signed)   WILLIAM POYNTZ.
       Christmas Day, 1796."

The book appears to be exactly as he left it ; some slips of paper with the names of horses which he had meant to fill in, the original bits of blotting paper used last in 1793, were still in place. Mr. Poyntz did not enter accounts of the hunting in 1794 and 1795.

Thirty-nine couple of staghounds were in kennel made up as follows :—

        5 couple from the Duke of York.[1]
        8½   ,,   ,,   Lord Egremont.
        3   ,,   ,,   Lord Craven.
        1½   ,,   ,,   Lord FitzWilliam.
        15   ,,   ,,   Lord Stawell.
        4½   ,,   ,,   the Quarley Hunt.
        ½   ,,   each from the Duke of Bedford, Lord
                     Donegall and Mr. Panton.

Thirty-four hunters were in the stables ; their prices ranged from 45 guineas to 200 guineas. Some were sold, some exchanged and some given away, but about thirty hunters were always in the stable. Mr. Ridge, the master of the H.H., was the lucky recipient of a horse called Herodotus. The Duke of

---

[1] H.R.H. The Duke of York kept a pack of foxhounds at Weybridge. This pack received an invitation to hunt in the Vine country on one occasion, and Lord Stawell went out from Hackwood to see them. His opinion of them was far from complimentary : " Sir, they are worse than you can possibly imagine ; they can neither draw, nor run, nor hunt ; they all stink, and want brimstone ; there is only one dog amongst them that looks in the least like a foxhound ; and the only thing worth going out for was to hear old Squire Harwood grumbling and cursing the huntsman for a fool."

York, Lord Melbourne and Mr. Dutton also received presents of horses.

The servants were :

Head Groom	-	John Gascoygne (or Gascoyne).
Huntsman	-	George Sharp.[2]
Whipper-in	-	George Dean.
,,	-	John Farrell.

The hunt liveries were green plush with gold facings.

Neither the Prince nor his manager came out at first but George Sharpe had a trial day on January 1st, 1791. An old New Forest stag ran to Dummer and back and was taken by the Kitchen Wall. This unenterprising old stag was let out of the paddock and killed on January 4th, having " by chance broke his thigh." A hind was also uncarted on January 1st and was killed by Hatch Warren. On January 5th Mr. Poyntz came out with one other local person, Mr. Timberley. They had " a good chace when the hounds behaved remarkably well." This was far more like a hunt and hounds covered quite a nice country through Farleigh Park, Axford, Preston Candover, by Chilton Wood, across the valley to Wield and Heath Green, through the Grove to " Maidstead." At a farmyard in Medstead the stag was taken. Spellings of places and people are erratic and are usually corrected. The only mischance to mar a pleasant gallop over much open country was the loss of one of Lord Egremont's bitches " Jealousy " who ran under George Sharpe's horse and was killed. On January 7th the Prince himself came out and a field of eleven, including Lord John Russell, Sir Henry St. John Mildmay, Mr. Coulson Wallop and Mr. Terry. Quite a good hunt rewarded the Prince and his small field. The stag was turned out by the turnpike gate on the Basingstoke road and ran *via* Hatch Warren, Farleigh paddocks, Inn Wood and Upper Kempshott Wood : here hounds changed on to a fox for nearly an hour, running to Hackwood Park. A " halloa " eventually put them right and they ran through St. John's Wood, crossing the Western Road to Manydown, through Malshanger, and the stag was finally taken at Ashe Park *an hour after dark*. The *Hampshire Chronicle*, however, relates that the gentlemen of the Hampshire Hunt joined in this run, and that His Royal Highness dined with them at the Wheatsheaf, Popham

---

[2] George Sharpe died on January 28th, 1830, aged 74 and was buried at Dummer. Mr. Poyntz always omits the final " e " of his name. Both spellings are used for the family in the Dummer registers, but the final " e " is given to George and rather predominates.

Lane, after " *the morning's sport*." Whether this is an inaccuracy of the reporter, or whether the Prince and the gentlemen of the H.H. abandoned the hunt for their dinner is not now apparent. We hope that it was the former. On the next day, Saturday, His Royal Highness hunted with Mr. Ridge and the H.H. and afterwards entertained them to dinner at Kempshott.

News of good sport must have been spread as on January 10th twenty-three were in the field, including Mr. Ridge, M.F.H., and Mr. Portal of Laverstoke and his brother Mr. John Portal of Freefolk were among them. The stag took them from Weston Down by Micheldever and Thorney Down to Avington. Here the stag was coursed by a sheep dog and fell on his head jumping a fence " which nearly killed him." This sounds an unusual accident for a stag unless very blown. As time went on many Hampshire sportsmen, whose names will appear in various chapters of this book, came out with H.R.H.'s pack : Mr. Powlett-Powlett, Sir Henry Tichborne, Mr. Delme, Mr. George Ricketts, Mr. Rodney, Rev. R. Lowth and the Rev. C. Powlett, the two H.H. poets and others. An invariable supporter was Mr. Edwards, sometimes accompanied by his wife, a good horseman and keen sportsman, but unfortunately he overspent his income considerably and ended in very reduced circumstances. Among distinguished visitors, presumably stay-ing at Kempshott, were : H.R.H. The Prince of Wurtemburg, Lords Barrymore, Granard, Paget, Rowden and Sackville ; Lord Charles Somerset and frequently Lord John Russell, sometimes accompanied by his wife. An occasional name of a French emigré occurs but never such a crowd as Mr. Terry describes in his diary.

Mr. Poyntz does not, however, always give the names of those out and he was often not out himself when he says " informed by George Sharp " in the account of the hunt. Mr. Terry gives 1792 as the year of the great hunt for the French emigrés. Ten post horses from Demezy's at Hartford Bridge were sent for to supplement the royal stables. Prince William turned out on a pony, but soon disappeared into a deep ditch. A crooked running hind was selected to help the foreigners. She was uncarted in the Park before some 500 horsemen. The foreigners were soon all over the countryside. Three times, at a check, the Frenchmen, with their long curly horns worn over their shoulders, put hounds onto a hare and George Sharpe was nearly driven mad. Some fifty out of the huge field reached the end of the hunt. Mr. Terry states that

Rowlandson drew a clever drawing of this hunt dated 1792.
The Frenchmen did not like early hours as is shown in Mr.
Powlett's song, page 96 :

> " See from France yon petit maître,
> Thus exclaims the puny creature.
> ' Comment sortir avant l'aurore
> Sans déjeuner ?   'Tis a great bore ! ' "

Mr. Terry on another occasion horrified the Frenchmen by
clutching Prince William by the knee and so preventing him
falling off at a jump at the corner of Gander Down.   The
Prince was on a Hartford Bridge hack, presumably a poor
performer.   The jump was off the turnpike road near North
Waltham.   When the Prince thanked young Terry the foreigners
cheered, but at first they were horrified at his boldness in touching a prince of the Blood.

On Friday, May 6th, 1791, the Prince of Wales gave *an
elegant dinner* at Popham Lane to all the Hampshire farmers
over whose grounds he had hunted during that season.

On the 6th of January, 1792, Mr. Poyntz mentions several
distinguished-sounding names among the field—Marchioness
and Mademoiselle de Coigny, Prince Tarente, Comte Belsance,
Lord and Lady John Russell and Master Russell, among others.
The hunt was from Popham Beacon, through Black Wood to
Laverstoke, back to West Stratton, where the stag was taken at
Godings Farm.   The account finishes with the following
pungent note :   " The hounds were kept waiting by the ladies
one hour and three-quarters during an easterly wind.   Wonderful
effect it had upon Prince Tarente."

Mr. Poyntz himself undoubtedly preferred the fair sex in a
nice warm room with a bright fire and out of a draught.   Some
of the comments in his diary are rather amusing.   On
February 16th, 1791, a gentleman named Mr. Kippington " had
a damned fall " ;   Comte Belsance on January 3rd, 1792,
" suffered a fall but not wounded."   The keen Mrs. Edwards on
February 9th, 1792, " fell but not hurt."   A foreign lord of a
name quite indecipherable is said to have " started " ;   others,
but not he, are announced as " came in."   On February 9th,
1792, Mr. Poyntz notes himself as " particularly smart, new
scarlet uniform, new breeches, boots and cap."   Luckily he had
no falls to damage his finery.

On February 11th, 1792, Mr. Ridge brought his hounds with Joe Hall and Phil Gosling from Kilmeston to Kempshott at the Prince's invitation.   It was probably on this occasion, when Mrs. FitzHerbert was hostess but did not hunt, that Lady Jersey and Lady Cunningham, with Mesdames Hodges and Sturt, attended and joined the field.   Charles James Fox had also meant to hunt and was booted and spurred, but gout prevented him riding or even walking, and he remained indoors.   The presence of these somewhat renowned ladies caused much local excitement and comment.   Hounds found a good fox in Woodmancote Holt at 3 p.m. and ran till dark when he was lost.

On Saturday, November 14th, 1792, a stag turned out at Kempshott gave an excellent run of five hours and was taken at the upper end of Hyde Street in Winchester.   His Royal Highness took a post-chaise from the George Inn back to Kempshott.

When the Prince went out hunting, two, three and even four horses were noted as being out for his use.   This, presumably, was to keep pace with his rapidly increasing weight.   In 1791 the Prince hunted nine times with his staghounds and in 1792 eight times.   In 1792 the Prince sent his hounds to the New Forest and George Sharpe informed Mr. Poyntz that he killed nine stags and took two alive in eleven days' hunting.   The sport with the staghounds seems to have been good ; many long runs were recorded.   Sometimes hounds were run out of scent and laid out at night to recover the line next day and try and capture the stag.   Stags occasionally, and hinds more often, died as the result of a really severe hunt.   Sometimes, if no one was up with hounds, the deer might be killed or seriously mauled by hounds.

There is no doubt fit men and fit horses were required, but Mr. Stephen Terry remarks on the poor condition of the Royal hunters.   Young Terry on a fit pony was often able to help in stopping hounds to allow the Prince to catch up.   The royal hunters probably had too much to eat and too little exercise.   Rumour said that the head groom was promoted owing to the beauty of his sisters who formed an inferior seraglio to the establishment.   The Prince also kept some beagles at Kempshott   The only occasion they are mentioned is on a visit when frost and snow prevented hunting the stag in February 1792.   Apparently they showed very little sport.

In February 1793 the Prince changed his pack from stag-hounds to foxhounds. The hounds had all been foxhounds and there would have been little difficulty in changing their quarry : they would seldom encounter wild deer in their country. He hunted Mr. Poyntz's old country, around Overton, Andover and Whitchurch, and some of the H.H. country. He had 33 couple of hounds in kennel and 32 hunters were in his stables, probably 37, as five more names appear on a slip of paper whose names Mr. Poyntz wished to check. The hunting days were Monday, Wednesday and Friday.

George Sharpe took hounds out on February 13th and found in Brick Kiln Copse, ran for one and a half hours and killed. On February 13th Sharpe found a brace of foxes in Burley. Nine couple ran one to ground after a three-quarters of an hour hunt, while 16 couple ran the other to ground in Doiley Wood after a five and a half hour hunt. According to the Rev. J. E. Austen Leigh the first hunt was at Southington Scrubbs after a bagged fox and he tells a story of a gentleman telling Sharpe that he must " take care to kill him whatever you do ; never mind about sport to-day ; your business is to give your hounds blood. If I was you, I would not give him more than five minutes law." Sharpe is supposed to have answered briefly : " You make yourself easy, and keep quiet ; I am not going to give him more than one." This story does not agree with the diary[3] but Mr. Poyntz did not come out himself until February 15th, when ten local gentlemen also appeared, including Mr. Powlett-Powlett, Mr. Austen[4] and Mr. Graeme. A fox was found in Freefolk Wood and was " very handsomely killed " in a farmyard in Southington village after a hard burst without any checks.

On February 18th a hard run took place from Cranborne Wood ending in the fox being extracted from a rabbit hole in Nutley. This fox had given a good run through Freefolk, Laverstoke, Litchfield, Waltham Frimleys, Popham and Woodmancote Holt. The Harwoods of Dean, father and son, and Mr. Scott[5] were out on this day.

The Prince came out after this promising start on February 23rd. Hounds found in Dean's Heath and killed in the oven of a brew house in North Waltham village. Their

[3] It appears a secret trial arranged by the huntsman. Mr. Poyntz would not know of a " bagman."

[4] Presumably the Rev. George Austen of Steventon Rectory, father of the famous Jane.

[5] Presumably Mr. James Scott who bought Rotherfield Park in 1808.

next fox from Cranbourne beat hounds near the Stratton turnpike gate.

Sport continued to be quite good throughout the season. Fields were never large, which is a great help in a cold scenting country ; the biggest field was thirty-four. On March 30th, 1793, Mr. W. J. Chute of the Vyne and his brother Thomas came to see the new pack of foxhounds. They had a good hunt but did not see a kill as the fox got to ground and no terrier was out. The near neighbours like the Harwoods of Dean, Newton and Coulson Wallop of Hurstbourne, Austens of Steventon, Mr. Edwards of Worting, seem to be regular supporters. Mr. Thomas Smith of Tedworth, Mr. Tankerville Chamberlayne of Cranbury and even Messrs. Edward and Henry Morant from Brockenhurst are sometimes in the field. The Prince himself is only recorded as taking the field on two occasions in 1793. His hard living and his enemy the gout were making hunting too arduous a pursuit for his weakened frame. His heavy drinking at Kempshott had a bad effect on the neighbouring squires, but it had the worst possible effect on the Prince himself, who had to have a powerful village woman called Nanny Stevens to nurse him. This sturdy dame even helped him out of his bath, while his lazy valet looked on without offering the slightest assistance. The gradual physical decline went on till the Prince's legs could hardly support his ponderous body. About 1820 the following strange device[6] was adopted to enable the Prince to mount a horse. An inclined plane was made for his wheeled chair which led up to a mounting platform. A kind of crane with pulleys then gently uplifted the Prince from his chair and placed him in the saddle. The Prince must originally have been endowed by nature with very good physique, proved by the two following tales. It is related that the Prince in the early 1790's took less sleep than almost any man in the kingdom. On his journeys down to Kempshott from Carlton House, he generally travelled by night merely wrapping himself up in a large pelisse, and on arrival taking his gun and going out shooting without other rest. It is also related of him that on a journey to Newmarket he ordered the postilions inside the carriage and he and Charles James Fox rode the horses.

[6] An entry exists in Queen Victoria's diary which shows that this contrivance was seldom, if ever, used : " Dec. 17, 1838. Lord M. (Melbourne) said he believed George IV never rode after he was King ; Lord M. remembers him riding with him, but says he was very nervous ; he used to hunt when quite young which Lord M., of course, can't remember, and had two places in Hampshire for hunting." As late as 1828, when Don Miguel of Portugal was visiting the King, a meet of the Royal Buckhounds was arranged at Salt Hill. The King went as far as ordering a new pair of breeches, but no further. H.R.H. liked to think he could still hunt.

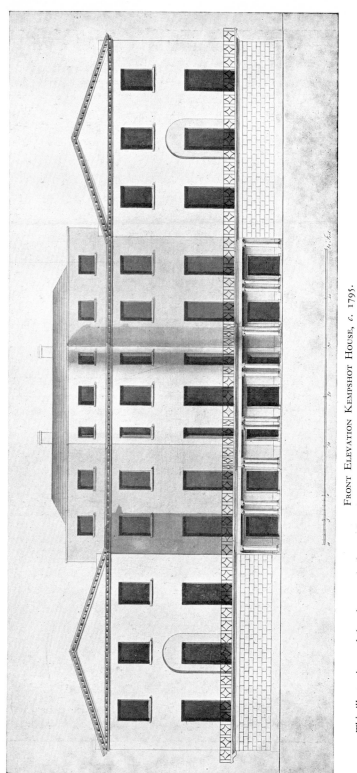

FRONT ELEVATION KEMPSHOT HOUSE, c. 1795.

This illustration and the plan overleaf were found, amongst others, in the Royal Archives at Windsor in 1949 and are reproduced by the gracious permission of H.M. The King.

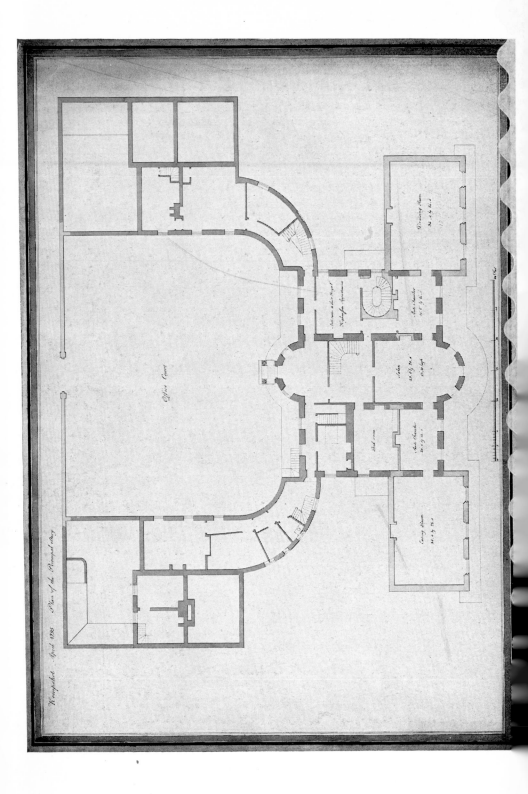

The Prince was not above playing tricks on his neighbours and some of them were in very questionable taste. His nearest neighbour was Mr. Thomas Terry of Dummer, father of Stephen the diarist. Mr. Terry was asked to dine, and an invitation was a command. Mr. Terry got into his smartest clothes, including a new pair of canary-coloured knee breeches with beautiful silk stockings to match. The dinner pursued its lengthy course and at last Mr. Terry started to walk home. He walked the quickest way down the footpath past the glebe but was not in a condition to easily negotiate the stiles which then existed on the path. During dinner the Prince had had the stiles well tarred. The state of Mr. Terry's garments next morning was, of course, horrible and his feelings for his host were anything but grateful.

One of the last incidents of the Prince's life at Kempshott was his honeymoon with Princess Caroline of Brunswick, his most unfortunate wife. He introduced her to all his boon companions and the time can hardly have been a happy one. Lady Jersey is supposed to have promoted the match as the Princess was so unattractive that she hoped she might keep her power over the volatile prince or even increase it. The Queen also favoured this liaison, so as to break the Prince's devotion to Mrs. FitzHerbert. The Prince did abruptly break off his relations with Mrs. FitzHerbert in 1794, having fallen a victim to Lady Jersey's mature charm. Not till 1799 did he again live with Mrs. FitzHerbert. His marriage to Princess Caroline of Brunswick was a tragic failure from their first interview. This took place at the Duke of Cumberland rooms in St. James's Palace. The Prince embraced her, turned round and walked away, saying to Lord Malmesbury, the only witness of the scene, " Harris, I am not well, pray get me a glass of brandy." Water was suggested, but indignantly repudiated. In 1796 they separated for ever.

In October, 1795, the Prince took a lease of Northington Grange, near Alresford, then the property of Mr. Henry Drummond (jun.) whose father, the great banker, had recently transformed the old Inigo Jones' manor house of the Henleys into a Palladian mass. The Prince paid £5,000 for the stock and fixtures and no less than £500 for the beer alone. Mr. Drummond had buried his servants' quarters well underground, but apparently did not grudge them a very handsome allowance of beer. Whilst at the Grange he made friends with the great

E

Admiral Rodney, his neighbour at Old Alresford House, and
Mr. Charles Graeme of Dean House, Kilmeston. It would
appear that it was not found possible for His Royal Highness
to hunt his pack at the Grange owing to the objections of the
Hampshire Hunt and covert owners.[7]   Perhaps for this reason
the Prince of Wales took Crichel House, the property of Charles
Sturt, Esq., M.P.   This house stands in a fine park about eight
miles from Blandford, Dorset, and the estate provides very good
sport of all kinds.   H.R.H. paid a rent of £1,300 a year for the
house and sporting, and a further rent of £300 a year for Dean
Farm nearby. He also bought Mr. Sturt's hounds and so
acquired a country to hunt in.   Few records exist of his hunting
in Dorset, but the following reliable evidence exists. Firstly,
when Mr. James John Farquharson of Langton House
(M.F.H., 1806–1858) was speaking at the ceremony in 1858
when he resigned his long period of control and was receiving
his presentation portrait, he said : " The first person he had
hunted with had been George IV, then Prince of Wales, when
he lived at Critchel and bought Mr. Sturt's hounds."

There is also an entry in the diary of the Hon. Robert
Digby, now in possession of Lord Digby, bearing the date
8th November, 1797, which runs as follows : " The gentlemen
all went out to see the Prince of Wales' foxhounds throw off at
Sydling Wood where they killed a fox." Sydling Wood is
still a good covert in the Cattistock country.

There are other references to H.R.H.'s stay at Crichel in
Dorset. One mentioned by Lord Ribblesdale in his book *The
Queen's Hounds* relates the Prince Regent returning from hunting
with the Rev. William Butler. They were discussing the
drinking capacities of some of the neighbouring boon companions. The Prince asked if the Rev. William thought a
certain gentleman "was a three bottle man?" The Rev. William
thought the story untrue, adding " he would be as drunk as a
Prince." H.R.H. did not relish this comparison at the time, but
bore no malice. At a levée some years later he was heard to
mutter : " The Reverend William Butler ; I shall not forget the
Reverend William Butler." Nor did he forget, as shortly afterwards he presented him to a nice Crown living.

Recently bills have come to light at Windsor showing that
H.R.H. was still in occupation of Crichel during 1799 and 1800.

---

[7] The *Hampshire Chronicle* of January 9th, 1796, records a remonstrance having been
sent to H.R.H. on this matter.

In the *Hampshire Chronicle* of June 24th, 1799, the following notice is found : " The Prince of Wales is about to change his country residence to Northington Grange[8] near this city, to which place his books and other valuables have lately been removed. His Royal Highness is reported to continue very unwell."

In June 1799 the Prince of Wales was present at Winchester Races for the whole week, but he lodged with Sir H. P. St. John Mildmay, Bart. During his stay he inspected the new organ at Winchester Cathedral built by Avery, and listened with keen appreciation to several recitals played by Mr. Chard. In July 1800 His Royal Highness again attended Winchester Races and had the pleasure of seeing his horse " Knowsley " win the King's Plate. His Royal Highness attended the Race Ball at St. John's Rooms on Tuesday evening, 8th July, but again lodged with Sir H. P. St. John Mildmay. In this year the Prince definitely bought the Pavilion, Brighton from the executor of the late Mr. Weltje where he had many alterations and additions carried out. Brighton then became his only country residence, and he had there a beautiful pack of harriers. It seems improbable, therefore, that the Prince of Wales ever occupied Northington Grange for a second tenancy.

Though hardly able to ride a horse at all without great discomfort, H.R.H. took great interest in the Royal Buckhounds. In 1813, when the Duke of Richmond left England to assume the governorship of Canada, he presented his famous Goodwood Pack (the former Charlton Hunt going back to the Duke of Monmouth's and Mr. Roper's days) to the Prince. George Sharpe hunted this pack, assisted by Charles Davis, his son-in-law, who afterwards became so great a celebrity with the Royal Pack and hunted them for so long. His interest continued after he became king in 1820, and the old lumbering pack of staghounds with its yeomen prickers in attendance, disappeared to give place to a fast pack of English foxhounds with all their drive and high courage. The hunt lost something of its picturesqueness, but the royal liveries were still very attractive and the pack a very handsome one. So great a revolution in the royal establishment had not taken place since King Henry VIII founded his Private Pack.

[8] The Grange is about 6½ miles from Winchester. The Prince certainly had possession of it in 1799, since in a letter to Lady Elgin, dated 2nd August, 1799, he says : " You had best write a line to Hicks at the Grainge, Hampshire, to let him know what night you intend to be there." On 2nd October, 1800, the Prince again writes to Lady Elgin : " That place (' Grange ') is no longer mine." He probably had a short tenancy, but was prevented from personally living there.

CHAPTER IV.

THE H.H.

MASTERS OF THE H.H.

[1745–49   Mr. W. Evelyn, St. Clere, Ightham, Kent; and Harmsworth, Alresford, Hants.]

1749–95   Mr. T. Ridge, Kilmeston Manor, Alresford.

1795–1802 Mr. W. Powlett Powlett, Little Somborne, Winchester.

1802–03   Committee: Mr. J. T. Villebois (Chief Manager), Admiral Calmady and Mr. Kingcote.

1803–37   Mr. J. T. Villebois, tenant of Harmsworth, Alresford.

1837–42   Major C. R. Barrett, Cheriton, Alresford.

1842–45   Mr. A. Onslow, Upton House, Alresford.

1845–47   Capt. M. P. Haworth, New House, Ropley.

1847–50   Lord Gifford.

1850–52   Committee: Messrs. E. Knight, Chawton House (Manager); J. W. Scott, Rotherfield Park; F. J. E. Jervoise, Herriard Park.

1852–55   Mr. R. Pearse, South Warnborough Lodge.

1855–56   Mr. E. Knight, Chawton House.

1856–62   Mr. E. Tredcroft, Alresford.

1862–84   Mr. H. Deacon, Ropley Cottage.

1884–88   Mr. A. H. Wood, Froyle Place; and Arlebury, Alresford.

1888–89   Committee; Messrs. F. Coryton, Liss Place, Petersfield; M. Knight, Chawton House, Alton; F. M. E. Jervoise, Herriard Park, Basingstoke.

1889–95   Mr. F. Coryton, Liss Place, Petersfield.
           Mr. F. M. E. Jervoise, Herriard Park, Basingstoke.

1895–99   Mr. F. Coryton, Liss Place, Petersfield.
           Lieut.-Col. R. Knox, The Holt, Bentley.

1899–1909 Mr. F. Coryton, Manor House, Greatham.
           Mr. A. T. E. Jervoise, Herriard Grange, Basingstoke.

1909–15   Mr. G. P. E. Evans, Hunt Lodge, Ropley.

1915–19   War Committee.
           Mr. F. Coryton (Chairman), Manor House, Greatham.

1919–21   Mr. A. P. Robinson, Hunt Lodge, Ropley.

1921–23   Major A. C. Bovill, M.C., Hunt Lodge, Ropley.
1923–24   Lieut.-Col. C. G. Mangles, M.C., Hunt Lodge, Ropley.
          Capt. R. Orred, tenant of Farleigh House, Basingstoke.
1924–25   Lieut.-Col. C. G. Mangles, Hunt Lodge, Ropley.
1925–26   Lieut.-Col. C. G. Mangles, Hunt Lodge, Ropley.
          Capt. J. B. Scott, Rotherfield Park, Alton.
1926–29   Capt. J. B. Scott, Rotherfield Park, Alton.
          Mr. G. P. E. Evans, Hunt Lodge, Ropley.
1929–32   Mr. G. P. E. Evans, Hunt Lodge, Ropley.
1932–33   Mr. G. P. E. Evans, Hunt Lodge, Ropley.
          Mr. M. Hastings, tenant of Burkham House, Alton.
1933–34   Mr. G. P. E. Evans, Hunt Lodge, Ropley.
          Mr. M. Hastings.
          Mr. B. Hamilton.
1934–35   Mr. G. P. E. Evans, Hunt Lodge, Ropley.
1935–37   Mr. G. P. E. Evans and Mrs. Evans, Hunt Lodge, Ropley.
1937–39   Mr. G. P. E. Evans, Hunt Lodge, Ropley.
          Lieut.-Col. M. R. F. Courage, D.S.O., Preston House, Basingstoke.
1939–44   Lieut.-Col. M. R. F. Courage, D.S.O., Preston House, Basingstoke.
1944   Mr. H. A. Andreae, Moundsmere Manor, Basingstoke.

During the later years of the 18th century and during the earlier years of the 19th century, the age of the casual hunt was passing. Fox hunting became increasingly popular, fresh hunts sprang up and boundaries had to be arranged and more rigidly adhered to. No authority existed to arrange such boundaries and troubles arose with certain autocratic squires. In Hampshire, luckily, no serious troubles arose ; in most cases the arrangements were made quite amicably. The nearest approach to trouble occurred when that fine sportsman Mr. Garth started hunting the Hampshire portion of Sir John Cope's great country. Excellent authority exists for saying that in this instance the Whebleites (Berkshire) greatly resented the starting of the Garth hounds. An irascible Irishman from the Berkshire side wished to settle the matter in a duel with a Garth champion. It is said that the peace-making efforts of the Reading magistrates were of no avail and it took the intervention of the Iron Duke himself to prevent a meeting. Whether or not these be the facts, the records which existed until recent years have apparently been lost or destroyed and so the author leaves the names of the parties unrecorded.

Many of these packs were subscription packs and so meets had to be advertised and adhered to. Incidents, such as the Iron Duke roaming the country to find Mr. Chute's hounds, became impossible.

The following packs of foxhounds were started in Hampshire during the 19th century :—

> 1800.—The Hambledon Hunt Club. Mr. T. Butler, first master.
> 1810.—Mr. Ellis St. John's foxhounds, afterwards Sir John Cope's foxhounds, now the South Berks and the Garth.
> 1826.—Mr. Thomas Assheton Smith's foxhounds, afterwards the Tedworth Hunt.
> 1837.—Rev. Sir John Barker-Mill's foxhounds, which in 1840 became the Hursley Subscription Hounds, now the Hursley Hunt. Military packs of draghounds, the Aldershot, the Longmoor (M.I.) and the Bordon Draghounds (R.A.), have been allowed to hunt fox in parts of the H.H. country.

It may be noted that certain of the 19th century Hampshire masters have left names which will always live as acknowledged authorities on sporting matters as well as great sportsmen— Mr. J. T. Villebois, Colonel John Cook[1], Mr. Thomas Assheton Smith, Mr. Thomas Smith[2], Mr. John Warde, Mr. George P. E. Evans, Sir George L. Tapps-Gervis-Meyrick, Bart.

In addition to these gentlemen, Mr. F. P. Delmé Radcliffe, then resident at Shawford House, near Winchester, Honorary Secretary of the Hambledon Hunt, 1831, and afterwards M.F.H., the Hertfordshire Hounds, 1835 - 1839, was author of *The Noble Science of Fox Hunting,* 1839.

W. Evelyn, 1745-59.

It has always been stated that Mr. William Evelyn of St. Clere, Ightham, Kent, and Harmsworth, near Alresford, Hampshire, was the 1st Master of the " H.H." He certainly hunted in the H.H. country with his own hounds. He is said to have been " a very polished and popular gentleman." Very little is known of his hunting except that he rode a grey stallion, the sire of many good hunters. He probably hunted part of

---

[1] Author of *Observations on Foxhunting,* 1826.

[2] Author of *Extracts from the Diary of a Huntsman,* 1838 ; *The Life of a Fox,* dated from Hill House, Hambledon, June 10th, 1848.

the season in Kent and part in Hampshire. His father, born 1686, was the first of St. Clere; he had married an heiress, Frances Glanville, and he had assumed that name himself. On her death, however, he resumed his own name and married Bridget Raymond of Langley, Kent, Mr. Evelyn's mother. He was succeeded in his Kentish property by his daughter Frances who married Colonel Alexander Howe, who took the name and arms of Evelyn in 1797, presumably on his father-in-law's death. He had a son William who died unmarried in his father's lifetime, and whom Jane Austen describes as a " Yahoo," who had thought all his life more of horses than of anything else. Jane Austen was not a lover of field sports though her family was a very sporting one. She, however, much enjoyed a drive with Mr. Evelyn in Bath with his " very bewitching Phaeton and four." Mr. Evelyn presumably ceased to hunt from Harmsworth in 1749, but it was not sold till 1778. He continued to hunt apparently in Kent, as an entry in Mr. Wither Bramston's[3] account book of February 26th, 1780, records: " To Mr. Evelyn's huntsman for a couple of hounds, £1. 11s. 6d." The only other mention of Mr. Evelyn in local records is in a letter of 1775 from the Rev. George Austen of Steventon Rectory (father of Jane the famous authoress), in which, he says, that Mr. Evelyn was organising a ploughing match between his own Kentish ploughman to compete against the Hampshire champion ploughman for a rump of beef.

It would appear, therefore, that Mr. Evelyn, a member of an ancient and distinguished family who have held Wotton since 1579, and was distantly connected with the famous diarist, hunted much of the country with his private hounds, but is most unlikely to have founded the Hampshire Hunt.

Mr. T. Ridge, 1749-95.

The real founder of the Hampshire Hunt was the next master, Mr. Thomas Ridge of Kilmeston Manor.[4] His hounds were kenneled at the Manor House, Kilmeston. He was the father of no less than twenty-one children of whom nineteen grew up to man and womanhood. The Manor House was

---

[3] Mr. Wither Bramston, born 1753, married Mary Chute, daughter of Thomas Lobb Chute of the Vyne, succeeded to Hall Place or Oakley Hall in 1790 as heir to his mother Henrietta Maria Wither, heiress of Charles Wither the younger; she had married Edmund Bramston who died 1763. Mr. Wither Bramston rebuilt Oakley Hall in 1795 and Dean Church in 1818. He died in 1832. He was presumably keeping up his grandfather's pack to some extent (see pp. 26, 27).

[4] The Rev. J. E. Austen-Leigh (sexagenarian) writing in 1865 of his reminiscences rightly refers to Mr. Ridge as " the venerable founder of the H.H."

enlarged to hold this considerable family and still stands much as he left it, though the entrance has been changed.

Mr. Ridge is mentioned twice by Cobbett in his *Rural Rides*: On November 18th, 1822, riding from Alresford to Hambledon, he passed through "*Kilmston*." "Here is a house, that was formerly the residence of the landlord of the place, but is now occupied by one of the farmers. This is a fine country for fox hunting, and Kilmston belonged to a Mr. Ridge who was a famous fox hunter, and who is accused of having spent his fortune in that way. But what do people mean? He has a right to spend his income, as his fathers had done before him. It was the Pitt system,[5] and not the fox hunting; that took away the principal." Again on November 11th, 1823, riding from Easton to Petersfield, he goes *via* Bramdean and says: "A little on our right, as we came along, we left the village of '*Kimston*' where Squire Graeme[6] once lived, as was before related. Here, too, lived a 'Squire Ridge,[7] a famous fox hunter, at a great mansion, now used as a farm house; and it is curious enough, that this 'Squire's son-in-law, one Gunner,[8] an attorney at Bishop's Waltham, is steward to the man[9] who now owns the estate."

The first mention of the present title "The H.H." occurs in an advertisement in the *Hampshire Chronicle* on March 8th, 1784, as follows :—

"THE NOBLE DIVERSION.
The members of the H.H. Society are requested to meet at Mr. Vernon's at Popham Lane on Thursday next, the 11th instant.

J. DYSON ⎫
T. BOWMAN ⎭ *Stewards*."

In another notice of March 29th, 1784, the members are styled "the Gentlemen of the Hampshire Hunt."

Towards the end of his time Mr. Ridge took a small subscription. No doubt the education of his family was making a

---

[5] It was not the "Pitt System" but the Squire's nineteen adult children who caused the sale of the property.

[6] Mr. Charles Graeme, member of the old and new clubs, Father of the Hunt, Honorary Secretary for many years till his death in 1833, when his son succeeded him. A friend of the Prince of Wales, and a great sportsman. He lived at Rotherfield, New House, Ropley, Dean House, Kilmeston, and died at Alresford.

[7] Mr. Thomas Ridge, M.F.H., was the son of George Ridge, who bought Kilmeston Manor in 1739. The manor was sold in 1810 to Edmund Smith.

[8] A descendant of Mr. Gunner, Miss Gunner of Bishop's Waltham provided Mr. Schwerdt with the photograph of Mr. Thomas Ridge.

[9] "The man" was Mr. Walter Long of Preshaw who bought the property from Edward Smith in 1812.

large inroad into his income. Members of the old Hunt Club met for monthly dinners served at 3.30 p.m. at the White Hart, Winchester, the Swan at Alresford, and the Wheatsheaf, Popham Lane. At the latter house, Mr. Vernon's, the Club kept an excellent cellar of port wine, but this was seized by the creditors most unfortunately when the proprietor became bankrupt in 1795.

The only possession of the Hunt Club now remaining is a handsome double snuffbox for " Irish " and " Rappee," presented in March 1812 by Gorges Lowther. It has a galloping fox and " Tally-ho " embossed on the lid. Mr. Gorges Lowther of Ovington was elected a member in 1811. He commanded the Fawley Troop of Yeomanry Cavalry.

Meets were early in the morning, as in the words of one of the Hunt songs :—

> But ere the sun has reached the skies
> Fresh as the morn we gaily rise,
> Then free from care, from pain, from sorrow,
> Haste to Thorny Down to-morrow.

The Hunt songs, given at the end of the chapter, were written by the Rev. Charles Powlett of Itchen Abbas, 1728–1809, the eldest illegitimate son of Charles, 3rd Duke of Bolton, and Mrs. Lavinia Bestwick (the original " Polly Peachum " of " Beggar's Opera " fame), whom the Duke subsequently married in 1751.

Special drinking glasses were used with " the boot and spur " on them. These were used before the Prince of Wales' feathers became the H.H. crest.

Hunt dinners have taken place, generally annually, up to 1939, when the last one was held at Burkham House, the residence of the chairman, General Sir George Jeffreys, K.C.B., K.C.V.O., C.M.G. War and austerity have prevented them being held of late years, but it is hoped that they will start again shortly.

Hunt Uniform.

In Mr. Ridge's time the members of the Hunt wore blue coats in the field. One of the Hunt songs keeps this tradition in memory :—

> Checked by sheep cots in the valley,
> Men of weight gain time to rally,
> Mopping his front and double chin,
> Each heavy blue comes puffing in.

The blue coat was succeeded by red by a rule passed on January 18th, 1799. The alteration was proposed by Mr. Charles Graeme and passed unanimously. Judging, however, from existing coloured engravings, several members wore blue well into the next century. The old blue uniform with white Kerseymere waistcoat with gilt buttons, black knee breeches and silk stockings with buckled shoes is retained as the Hunt evening dress.

The Hunt button was originally silver with a large blue enamel " H.H." on it. This proves that the Hunt was the Hampshire Hunt, though often referred to as the Kilmeston Hunt from the master's residence.

The silver button was changed to a large brass one with H.H. on it during Mr. Ridge's mastership in 1785. Another change took place at the very end of the old club ; the exact date cannot be found, either in the Hunt archives or at Windsor Castle.

On April 25th, 1795, it is first mentioned that the members of the Hunt wore the Prince of Wales' feathers surmounting the monogram H.H. The grant was made perhaps verbally to Mr. Ridge by H.R.H. The Prince Regent who lived at Kemp-shott House from 1788 to 1795 ; he kept hounds there, first to hunt the carted deer, and then, in February 1793, the fox. In 1795 the Prince rented Mr. Henry Drummond's house, the Grange, near Alresford. The Prince seems to have wished to again reside at the Grange in 1799 but, though he obtained possession of the place, he was apparently prevented from actually again living in Hampshire. Having hunted his hounds in part of the H.H. country by permission, the grant of the right to wear his own crest was probably a courteous acknowledgment of this privilege. Each successive Prince of Wales has given his gracious consent to this honour and each Prince of Wales has been duly elected an honorary member of the Hunt Club. From the Grange also the Prince is said to have hunted with the H.H. It is sad to relate that, of the forty-three members of the old Club whose names are known, only one descendant still owns an estate in the H.H. country—Sir Anthony H. J. Doughty Tichborne, Bart. Another member, Mr. J. C. Jervoise, described as of Herriard, was actually of Idsworth, Horndean, a distant cousin of the Jervoises of Herriard.

Mr. W. Powlett Powlett, 1795 - 1802.

On Mr. Ridge's resignation on April 25th, 1795, the Club was immediately re-formed at a meeting held at Winchester on April 25th. It was resolved that there should be twenty-five members besides the President; that it should be called the Hampshire Hunt; that it should meet on October 12th and every first Friday in every month to April, inclusive; hounds to be kept at Bishops Sutton from the second week in October till the first week in March; Mr. W. Powlett Powlett, of Little Somborne and afterwards of Lainston House, was elected perpetual President with control of huntsman and other servants. Two stewards were taken in rotation for the monthly meetings, beginning with the oldest members of the old Club. Dinner to be on the table at 5 p.m. Bill to be called for at 9 p.m. precisely. A wise rule, too, was passed that any bet or match made at the Club could be called off by paying two guineas to the stewards of the meeting next morning. The money was applied to the purchase of the cup, annually run for at the H.H. Races on Worthy Down or Tichborne Down. Mr. Powlett's huntsman's name was Green; nothing is known of his capacity. A good run is recorded on November 12th, 1798, when a fox from Beauworth was hunted to a garden at Twyford. There he was lost in a bed of artichokes for an hour. Finally, this stout fox jumped the garden wall, swam the Itchen, and was killed at Compton. The *Hampshire Chronicle* relates that " from the length of the chase, the hounds and horses seemed much fatigued, and the gentlemen were highly satisfied with their day's sport."

Mr. Powlett Powlett was very lame and went about on crutches wearing a long laced-up boot on his withered leg. He is said to have worn a grey coat with a blue spencer over it and a peculiar hat made specially by Camis at Alresford, very much turned up at the brim to let the rain off. He could not mount without assistance. When master he regularly drew Freefold Wood where a good breed of fox existed, which always ran to Sherborne Wood. Mr. Powlett Powlett resigned in 1802. At Mr. Powlett Powlett's resignation the Club resolved " that the hounds and country were the property of the present members of the Hunt; that they are to receive them from Mr. Powlett, who has offered the Hunt the kennels at Sutton, which they have agreed to purchase off him at a valuation."

A Committee, 1802-03.

A Committee consisting of Mr. John Truman Villebois, tenant of Preston House, Admiral Calmady of Woodcote, Mr. Kingscote, tenant of Hinton House and afterwards New Place, Alresford, took over the management. Mr. Villebois was chief manager.

J. T. Villebois, 1803-37.

Mr. John Truman Villebois, known to the countryside as "Squire Villeboy," was the eldest son of Mr. William Villebois, a member of a French family that had settled in Ireland. On his mother's side he was great-grandson of Sir Benjamin Truman, brewer, of the famous firm of Truman, Hanbury and Burton. He was born at Feltham, Middlesex, in 1772, educated at Harrow and Oxford, and soon after coming of age he settled in Hampshire. He was tenant of Preston House from 1796 to 1808 and he kept a pack of harriers there in a yard by the kitchen garden, still called the "kennel yard."

Both "Aesop" and "Nimrod" give a story of Mr. Villebois and Mr. Russell which is partly true, but had nothing to do with Mr. Villebois taking the mastership of the H.H. It is said that Mr. Villebois' harriers found a hare in Preston Copse and changed on to a fox which they ran ten miles and killed by Amery Wood, near Alton. Mr. Russell, having succeeded Lord Stawell, considered this his country. It is probable that he was annoyed and expressed his annoyance when he met Mr. Villebois. The dialogue is reported to have ended as follows :—

Mr. Russell : " You had better hunt the country yourself."

To this Mr. Villebois replied : " If you really mean that, I will."

Such a hunt did take place and Mr. Villebois had the kill painted with himself holding up the dead fox. This picture hung in his dining room till his death.

The only effect of Mr. Russell's retirement, however, was to give back to the H.H. that part of the north of their country round Farnham, Odiham, Alton and Basingstoke, formerly hunted by Lord Stawell and Mr. Russell, which compensated for the loss of the south of their country taken over by the Hambledon Hunt. Mr. Ridge's country, stretching from Farnham to Romsey, had included this northern portion.

In the hunt mentioned Mr. Villebois' only companion at the kill was Mr. Thomas Smith of Shalden Manor, who was father to the famous Tom Smith of Hambledon.

Mr. Villebois had become a member of the Club in 1796. His brother Henry, a keen foxhunter and first-rate whip, became a member of the H.H. in 1801 and also of the Benson Driving Club in the same year : he died in 1847. His son, another Henry, was Master of the V.W.H. from 1850–54. The third brother, Frederick Read Orme, was for a time in a Cavalry regiment and in 1833 he succeeded Mr. Thomas Smith in the mastership of the Craven : he died in 1851, leaving his hounds and horses and £1,500 to the Craven Hunt. He was buried in Burghclere New Church. Mr. Villebois seems to have acquired from his ancestry something of Huguenot austerity combined with business efficiency. His servants, hounds and horses were all excellent and in every possible way he was an ideal master of foxhounds. The hounds were moved to Harmsworth in the year 1803,[10] and were bought by Mr. Villebois in 1804. The money was invested in three per cent. consols by the Trustees, Lord Rodney, Hon. William Gage and Charles R. Barrett. By 1837, when the Squire died, this money had become £3,550. 16s. 4d. One of his old servants said of him that he was " a right good master ; when he said a thing was to be done we knew it must be done and no mistake ; and it is a very good thing for a servant to know that of his master."

Squire Terry, in some doggerel verse, gives another side to his character :—

> I think as I run my season once more,
> How kind and how good Villebois was to the poor ;
> If any were sick, it was he found them out,
> And he asked more than once, " What's the parson about ? . . ."

He had the strongest sense of duty and communicated it to all about him. Possessed of ample means, he required no subscription and not even an earth was stopped at the Hunt expense. The same discipline was observed in house and kennels as was observed in the field. The Rev. J. E. Austen-Leigh recounts : " It was sufficient for Villebois to rein in his horse and exclaim with his sonorous and somewhat stern voice,

[10] Probably remains of Mr. Evelyn's kennels still existed, but Mr. Villebois undoubtedly built new kennels there.

' Gentlemen, I fancy hounds have checked ! ' in order to make every man remember that he was wrong." He was always carefully dressed, which is shown in the only portrait that has survived to the author's knowledge, reproduced in Mr. C. F. G. R. Schwerdt's *The Hampshire Hunt*, and by the courtesy of Mrs. Schwerdt and Captain C. M. R. Schwerdt, c.v.o., c.b.e., R.N., also in this volume.

His hospitality, however, was great and his farmers' dinners to all who farmed over fifty acres were renowned all over the County. These dinners followed the Farmers' Race for a silver cup annually.

When out with the Hambledon a farmer named Boys accosted "Nimrod." He said of the gentlemen following the hunt : "They breaks the fences, but they never mends them." "Nimrod" naturally expostulated. "Oh," said the farmer, "there is one way of mending them. What do you think of a leg of mutton and a good bowl of punch ? " He was alluding to "Squire Villeboy," as he was commonly called, and his famous race and dinner afterwards which had been duly reported in the Hampshire paper. The dinner was at 4 p.m. and at 10 p.m. the chairman proposed " Good night, safe return home and to our next merry meeting."

At the five Hunt balls given annually Mr. Villebois was always steward of the first. He kept seventy couple of hounds in kennel with a large entry of 22-24 couple. The pack was divided into large, averaging 23in. and small, averaging about 21in. There were no coarse hounds and they had a character of their own, bred for nose and pace. Mr. Robert Vyner in his *Notitia Venatica* compares Mr. Villebois to Squire Osbaldeston, " both being allowed to be first-rate judges in every way connected with hounds and hunting." The two types differed considerably, being bred for different conditions. On December 22nd, 1822, Mr. Villebois brought out a special pack, for "Nimrod's" interest and a few friends. It consisted of $16\frac{1}{2}$ couple all got by one stallion hound " Pontiff," and four bitches, who were also out.

The Squire's hunt servants were exceptionally good. Both John Major, and Richard Foster, who came in 1815, were first-rate huntsmen. The first had an unfortunate habit of drinking which the Squire did not approve of, but he killed 40 brace of foxes. Will Biggs succeeded him and then Foster, a fine horseman as well as a fine huntsman. "Nimrod" says that he had very good hands and a close seat and was the best man to get quickly through a cover that he had met with, unless it were Mr. Smith,[11] formerly of the Craven Hounds. Foster was one of the best huntsmen ever seen in the County, but he was, however, unfortunate in never killing more than 39½ brace of foxes. John Jennings and Sawyer, who came in 1815, were both first-class "whippers-in." "Actaeon," writing in 1849 of a former visit to the H.H., says that Foster and Sawyer quarrelled and never spoke to each other for three years except formally on hunting business, but hunted together and killed their foxes as if they had been the best of friends. The sport shown can be briefly summarised from contemporary accounts :—

December 6th, 1817.—A fox found in Woodmancote Holt ran through thirteen parishes and was killed after three hours at Weston Park. A hunt of 30 miles is given as the distance covered by hounds.

December 20th, 1817.—From Abbotstone a fox was killed in Farnham Chase after a 40-mile hunt as hounds ran.

In December 1819 a fox from Black House ran over the Warren to Rowhay to ground at Stoke Park after a hunt of three hours and ten minutes. This hunt took place after the meet at Hinton House where Mr. Tom Smith made his picture of the H.H. The story of this picture is as follows :—

The Hunt was painted coming away from the meet at Hinton House. This was the first painting of a complete Hunt that was ever made and which inspired Ferneley to paint the Quorn. Mr. Tom Smith rode over from Hill House, Hambledon, with Mr. G. Richards on a dull frosty day. On reaching the opposite hill a sudden flash of sunlight lit up the whole picture and Mr. Smith determined to paint it from memory. This he did after dinner on that very night, the first Tuesday in December 1819, finishing the picture at 5 a.m. next morning and never touching a horse or figure again. Many people wished to have the picture engraved, but Mr. Smith was too retiring to allow this to be done. Finally, Lady Gage, whose husband, son, and brother-in-law were all in the picture, drove over to Mr. Smith's home when he was away in Scotland, and asked to see the picture.

[11] Mr. Tom Smith, master of the Hambledon, 1824–29, 1848–52 ; the Craven, 1829–33 ; the Pytchley, 1840–44.

The picture was produced for her inspection and she drove off with it and had it engraved by Turner in London, leaving a message for Mr. Smith, which was not delivered. Mr. Smith afterwards stayed at Melton and found Ferneley engaged on a picture of the Quorn Hunt. He asked to see it, and told Ferneley he was surprised to see a picture of a whole hunt. Ferneley said, "There never was but one of a whole hunt ever painted." Mr. Smith asked where it was to be seen. He was told to go to Watson's in Vere Street and Ferneley said he had taken other artists to see it and they all agreed that it was the first one ever done of a whole hunt, and was done by a Mr. Smith. Mr. Smith was, of course, much flattered.

Following is a list of the large number of members and prominent supporters shown in the picture :—

Mr. W. Long of Preshaw (1812).

R. Foster (Huntsman).

The Rev. C. Manisty.

Sawyer (Whipper-in).

John (Whipper-in).

Mr. Smithers (Bramdean).

Mr. J. T. Villebois, M.F.H. of Harmsworth (1796).

Col. The Hon. J. C. Onslow of Upton House (1815).

The Hon. and Rev. F. North (afterwards Lord Guildford,) Old Alresford Rectory (1798).

Mr. R. Norris of Basing Park (1811).

Mr. Christopher Cooke of East End House, Alresford (1806).

Mr. George Delme of Cams.

Mr. W. Greenwood of Brookwood (1807).

Lord Rodney of Old Alresford House (1803).

The Rev. David Murray of Ropley Cottage (1813).

Capt. Bridges of Hermitage.

Mr. P. Henry Delme of Cams (1820).

Mr. T. Scotland

Admiral Gage.

Mr. R. T. Heysham of Hinton House (1813).

Hon. W. Gage of Westbury House (1818).

Lord Gage of Westbury House (1812).

The Rev. R. Lowth of Hinton, author of " Billesden Coplow Poem " (1803).

Mr. George Butler, Bramdean (1817).

Mr. A. F. Nunez, Warnford Park (M.F.H., Hambledon, 1816–21).

The Rev. H. Johnson.

Capt. Arthur Shakespeare.

Major R. Barrett, Cheriton (1816) (M.F.H., The H.H., 1837–42).

Mr. Powlett Powlett (178–), Lainston House (M.F.H., H.H., 1795–1802 ; Hambledon, 1807–13).

Mr. Paulett Mildmay's servant (Mr. H. Paulett Mildmay of Dogmersfield) (1812).

Mr. Charles Graeme, New House, Alresford (178–).

Mr. Thomas Butler of Bury Lodge (1st Master of the Hambledon Hunt).

Mr. Robert Barrow (?).

Mr. R. T. Heysham, jun., Hinton House.

The Rev. G. R. Richards.

Mr. Thomas Smith (M.F.H., Hambledon, 1825-29, 1848-52), the painter of the picture.

Capt. Standen.
Capt. Price.
Capt. George Greenwood, Brookwood.

Mr. Alderman Silver.
Mr. Joseph Sibley.
Major Gilbert.
Mr. W. Collyer.
Mr. Savage Beare.

Capt. Hawkshaw.
Mr. Michael Rivers.
Mr. W. Wilkinson (gave site of kennels at Ropley to Hunt).
Mr. Gilham.
Mr. Richard Bayley.
Mr. W. Lowth.
Mr. John Lowth.
Capt. Mills.
Mr. John Dunn.
The Rev. E. Dampier.
Mr. Lloyd (1814).
The Rev. S. L. Sainsbury of Froyle (1814).

N.B.—The dates in brackets after names are the dates when the gentlemen became members of the Hampshire Hunt Club.

" Nimrod " paid a visit to the H.H. in 1825 and he gives his experiences of seven days in which he saw one beautiful burst of 40 minutes, two fine runs, one of 2 hours and 27 minutes, and the other of 1 hour and 37 minutes, killing both foxes ; he missed one very fine run through going to London, but returned to partake in the 14-mile point of January 11th, 1825, from Black House over a very severe country. The fox was killed in a pantry of a house at Town Hill, three miles from Southampton. The end of this great hunt was the subject of a picture painted by Mr. Collyer of Chilland, himself a good horseman. Sawyer, the whipper-in, and Mr. Scotland were first up, and the former, in discussing the hunt, said : " I think we all came down that day."

It is a matter of interest and worthy of record that on the 18th November, 1822, Mr. C. S. Apperley, who wrote under the name of " Nimrod," cleared successfully the deer park pailings at Hackwood in a hunt across Lord Bolton's Park. This feat has not again been accomplished as far as it is known. It gives added weight to " Nimrod's " opinions on other horsemen. He mentions the following gentlemen as good horsemen and going well to hounds :—The two Mr. Knights of Chawton, the two Captain Greenwoods of Brookwood, Mr. Scott of Rotherfield, Mr. Baring jun. of the Grange, Mr. Frederick Heysham and Mr. George Butler, brother of the 1st Master of the Hambledon Hunt (member H.H., 1817). The Squire's brother-in-law, Major Barrett, was rather past being a thruster, but was faultlessly turned out and most useful in keeping everything straight in the hunt. Mr. David Murray of Ropley Cottage (member 1813) also is praised for his perfect turnout. Others receiving

F

most honourable mention are Mr. Smithers, a farmer of Bramdean, " as good a sportsman, and as good a judge of hunting
as the County of Hampshire can boast of " ; Mr. Wilkinson of
Alresford, the generous donor of the ground on which the
kennels stand at Ropley, was a great enthusiast.   It is said that
a fox was never found without a " Halloa " from him at some
point in the run.   Mr. Wilkinson had been a very well-known
publican on the Great West Road.   Mr. Wyse, another keen
supporter, was still an active coachman.   He drove the Southampton coach arriving at Popham Lane in the morning, had his
day's hunting on one of his own hunters, and drove his down
coach on in the afternoon.   This enthusiast always carried a
spare stirrup leather round his horse's neck.

On October 4th, 1833, at the Swan Inn, Alresford, two items
of interest appear in the minutes : (1) Mr. Villebois was fined
for appearing in a waistcoat without the Hunt button ; (2) A
piece of plate was presented to Mr. Villebois by the members
of the H.H. as a memorial of their esteem and regard.

The " father of the H.H." was Mr. Charles Graeme, who
came to live in Hampshire in 1785.   A keen sportsman, kind
and courteous to all, he was a most popular Hon. Secretary
from 1805.   He moved his residence several times.   In 1789
he lived at the old house at Rotherfield, then he moved to New
House, Ropley, before buying Dean House, Kilmeston.   Finally,
he moved to Alresford, where he died in 1833.   His son, Mr.
W. T. Graeme, of Highfield, Winchester, succeeded him in his
secretarial duties.

Another sporting character of some renown was the Rev.
Robert Lowth, son of the Bishop of London, and Rector of
Hinton.   He was elected a member of the Hunt in 1803 and
attained celebrity as the author of the Billesden Coplow Poem
published in the *Sporting Magazine* in 1800.   Mr. Lowth saw
most of that famous hunt, though poorly mounted.   He
modestly refers to his own performance as follows :—

> An H.H. who in Leicestershire never had been,
> So, of course, such a tickler ne'er could have seen.
> Just to see them throw off, on a raw horse was mounted
> Who a hound had ne'er seen or a fence had confronted.
> So, with scrambling and dashing and one rattling fall,
> He saw all the fun up to Stretton's White Hall ;
> There they anchored in plight not a little distressing,
> The horse being raw he, of course, got a dressing.

Some of his brother parsons thought they would show him up to the Bishop of Winchester, the Hon. and Rt. Rev. Brownlow North. They tried to shock the Bishop, saying Mr. Lowth was going to ride a match at the County Races. " Is he, indeed," said the kindly Bishop, " Is he, indeed ! Then I bet half-a-crown that he wins." It is not known whether Mr. Lowth won this match, but he won the Hunt Cup on Worthy Down in April 1809. Mr. Lowth was also a good whip and frequently drove to and from Chiswick, where he owned another house, with his four-in-hand.

The Duke of Wellington usually hunted with the Vine and with the Bramshill Pack, but his presence with the H.H. at Popham Lane is once mentioned. On that occasion his seat appeared so very ill-adapted to hunting that Mr. Wilkinson politely suggested taking up his stirrups a couple of holes if he intended to follow the hounds. His seat was of the " tongs across the wall " type, which is borne out in Calvert's picture of the Vine Hunt.

Mr. Villebois died on April 12th, 1837, to the great regret of all who knew him. He was buried in Old Alresford church-yard. His huntsman Richard Foster, who died in 1858, lies near his old master. His end was somewhat typical of his life. On a bitterly cold Good Friday he could not be induced, despite his weakness, to break his fast.

Major C. R. Barrett, 1837-42.

Major Charles Reid Barrett, the Squire's brother-in-law and a former officer of the 11th Dragoons, succeeded him in the management of the Hunt. Unfortunately the fine pack of hounds were left by Mr. Villebois to his youngest brother Frederick Reid Orme Villebois of Benham Park, Master of the Craven, and so formed the basis of that pack, as on the death of Mr. F. R. O. Villebois in 1851 he left the hounds and horses and £1,500 to the Craven Hunt. Actually the Club purchased, in May 1837 for Major Barrett, 48 couple of the Craven hounds for £650. These hounds did very well in Hampshire. The kennels were moved from Harmsworth to Cheriton, Major Barrett loaning the Club the site, and the Club paid for their erection. The new master retained R. Foster as huntsman till 1840. Jack Shirley, afterwards murdered by poachers at Raby Castle when 1st whip to the Duke of Cleveland, was then huntsman.

A good hunt took place on the opening day in 1840 from Cheriton Wood through Sutton and Bighton Woods past Woodridden and Godsfield, killing in the lake of the Grange. As usual Mr. Edward Knight of Chawton, Mr. R. Scotland, Mr. H. Taylor and Mr. Wilkinson of Alresford, were well to the fore.

During Major Barrett's tenure of office the Royal stag hounds visited the H.H. country on December 8th, 1841, meeting at Popham Lane. The hind, when uncarted, ran four miles down the London Road nearly into Basingstoke. When hounds were checked she ran on by Sherborne St. John and chiefly by lanes to Pamber, Tadley and Silchester, being taken finally between Mortimer and Stratfieldsaye, after a not very brilliant hunt of 2 hours and 45 minutes. Prince George of Cambridge, Lord Adolphus FitzClarence, Lord George Bentinck and Lord Dorchester were among the field.

After Major Barrett's resignation three short masterships followed.

Mr. A. Onslow, 1842-45.

Mr. Augustus Onslow was the son of Colonel the Hon. T. C. Onslow of Upton House. Jack Shirley stayed on for the first year being succeeded by Will Cox. Never was better sport shown and several good hunts are recorded.

On December 7th, 1842, hounds found at Hockley and ran through Fully and Hampage over the Warren to Preshaw by Beacon Hill to Riversden, skirting Blackhouse and Brookwood by Bramdean to Hinton, where they whipped off in the dark. Very few were up. Mr. Edward Knight and Mr. Coulthard of Burkham both had bad falls.

On December 9th a fox from Micheldever Wood, was forced over Worthy Park, on by the Race Course and Crawley Belts, past Flowerdown and Littleton, away again by Lainston House to Parnholt where he beat hounds.

On December 24th hounds were more lucky and finally killed their fox after 2 hours and 10 minutes, from near Chawton, through Ropley and Chawton Park to Langrish Farm, Greatham. Seven were up at the death and the Squire of Chawton got the brush.

In 1843 great hunts continued, a thirteen-mile point from Chilton Wood to Crabwood on February 8th, and on December 9th from Easters to Preston House and back to his death in Humbly Grove, the point being eight miles.

During Mr. Onslow's mastership two pictures of the Hunt were made in 1845. One, by the Rev. Peter Aubertin from a sketch made by Mr. James Batten Coulthard, shows the Hunt crossing the River Wey by Neatham Mill, near Holybourne. The other, showing the Hunt at a meet at the Grange, the seat of Lord Ashburton, was painted by Mr. G. B. Spalding. Prints of both appeared in Mr. Schwerdt's book of the Hampshire Hunt.

In 1846 new kennels were built at Ropley on the one-and-three-quarter acres presented by Mr. Wilkinson.

Captain M. E. Haworth, 1845-47.

Captain Martin E. Haworth of New House, Ropley, was the first amateur huntsman in the H.H. country. A combined ball took place on February 12th, 1846, at St. John's Rooms, Winchester, with the Hambledon and Hursley Hunts. This was followed by a meet at Cranbury Park of seven couple of each pack. Squires, the Hambledon huntsman, took charge and, after a quick find, they killed after 55 minutes, Squires securing the brush. The field then adjourned to the house, and were again hospitably entertained by Mr. Thomas Chamberlayne, the owner. The hounds ran well together, the H.H. and Hambledon bitches being rather quicker at casting themselves after a check than Mr. Cockburn's dog-hounds.

In 1846 the H.H. again had a " pantry hunt." On this occasion the fox was found in the Beauworth coverts, and went through Durwood, at the best pace over Kilmeston Down, by Westwood and Shorley, over the Warren, through Rosehill Park into Mr. Lowndes' pantry at Marwell. Despite damage to china and glass, the owner and his wife treated the occurance with great good humour. Captain Haworth was a good houndman in kennel and a good huntsman in the field and also a good horseman. Tom Clark turned hounds to him. His resignation, caused by rising expenses, was generally regretted. He had brought his hounds from the country he previously hunted around Chudleigh in S. Devon.

Lord Gifford, 1847-50.

Robert Francis, 2nd Baron Gifford, now became master. Born in 1817, Lord Gifford was in his prime and so able to show good sport, being both keen and knowledgeable from his previous experience in the Ludlow (1841–42) and V.W.H. (1842–47) countries. During Lord Gifford's mastership the supply of foxes was never better. The chief fox preservers were Mr. Charles Bowyer, Farleigh and Nutley ; Mr. F. J. E. Jervoise, Herriard; Sir Thomas Miller, Holybourne and Froyle ; Mr. H. L. Mulcock, whose Beauworth coverts were always well stocked though the owner did not hunt ; Colonel W. Greenwood, Brookwood ; Sir Edward Doughty, Tichborne ; Mr. Stephen Terry, Dummer ; Mr. T. M. Wayne, South Warnborough. Lord Gifford had 60 couple of hounds which he hunted himself.

In 1848 "Actaeon" paid him a visit on February 24th when hounds met at Farleigh House.   He mentions one or two things of interest. The five hunt horses each wore a " white front to the bridle," presumably a white brow band, to distinguish them at a distance from the field.   He says this was necessary owing to the large number of men riding to hounds in caps.   The fox, after two hours of woodland hunting, was killed in a pond at Dummer, close to the lawn of Dummer House. Squire Terry's son, a good sportsman like his father, entertained them all to a good luncheon.   As it still poured with rain and it was very cold, this was found very acceptable to all.   "Actaeon" did not seem to have enjoyed his day and talks of " large cheerless districts of bad-scenting ploughed land and never-ending woodlands."

On one occasion in 1847 the H.H. Hounds and the Bramshill Hounds met and with no fuss Jem Shirley gave up control and turned hounds to Lord Gifford and the fox was killed.   Sir John Cope's hounds had found in Dogmersfield and the H.H. in Sutton Common, and they met in Gravelly Wood.   It was not certain which fox was killed.   Both had been viewed into cover by the same man.   The Bramshill Hounds had hunted their fox about one hour and the H.H. had hunted their fox about 20 minutes.

In 1849 Lord Gifford's hounds showed a very fast hunt from a turnip field at Hatch Warren Farm, near Cliddesden.   The fox raced away up wind over the open country and across the London road to North Waltham, turning right-handed into Bull Bushes, near Oakley, where, according to the *Sporting Magazine* of the period, a fresh fox suffered " martyrdom for his more gallant kindred."   This good gallop was 1 hour and 20 minutes.

Lord Gifford resigned in 1850 and returned to his own country of Herefordshire, and the management was given to a committee for two years. Lord Gifford became again Master of the V.W.H., 1854–58, succeeding Mr. Henry Villebois.

A Committee, 1850–52
(Messrs. E. Knight, J. W. Scott and F. J. E. Jervoise.)

A committee now took over the management with Mr. Edward Knight of Chawton as Chairman, one of the finest horsemen and keenest sportsmen in the County. Mr. James Winter Scott of Rotherfield Park and Mr. Francis Jervoise Ellis Jervoise of Herriard Park, two of the largest covert owners, served as members. Mr. Napper's hounds, lately the "Findon," were bought and William Summers came with them as huntsman. He had a wide experience of hunting, starting with the Surrey Staghounds, then serving the Duke of Cumberland, Mr. Waring of the West Kent, and then, for 13 years, he served with Mr. Richards and Mr. Napper of the Findon. Good in kennel, cheery in covert and wise in the field, he was one of the best huntsmen who have been in the County. On one occasion when huntsman to the Hursley, in drawing a gorse apparently blank, there were shouts of "Ware Hare," and much cracking of whips, when hounds were going on the line of a hare just viewed away. Summers implored silence and sat motionless till his favourite old hound had taken up the cry. The "That's fox, that's fox! Forward! Away!" and a very fine hunt indeed resulted, finishing with a kill and nearly a column in *Sunday's Bell*. No fox had been seen, but one had stolen away, and Summers had the sense to trust his hounds rather than the field who are only gifted with eyes and not with noses.

Mr. R. Pearse, 1852–55.

Mr. Robert Pearse of South Warnborough Lodge now gave up his harriers which he had hunted very successfully between Alton and Odiham for a couple of seasons and took the mastership. He improved the pack with drafts from Lord Fitzhardinge's hounds and his huntsman Charles Roberts proved himself a good man. John Hickman and Dan Berkshire were his whippers-in. He had a good knowledge of hunting and when he retired Lord Ashburton presided over a dinner of 98 members and farmers given in his honour.

Mr. E. Knight, 1855–56.

Mr. Edward Knight of Chawton House, who has so often been referred to as a first-rate sportsman, now took control with

Joseph Orbell as huntsman. His period of office was a very short one unfortunately.

The *Hampshire Chronicle* give in 1879 at Mr. Knight's death the following sentences :—"An intelligent and keen sportsman and an unrivalled horseman, he will long be remembered by those who had the pleasure of following him when he hunted with the celebrated H.H. Hounds. He was the principal founder and President of the N.E. Hants Agricultural Association which owes its prosperity greatly to the active interest he took in its management."

Much more is written of this very fine example of an English country gentleman. He lived at Chawton from 1826 till his death. His Kentish home, Godmersham, was sold in 1874. His father Edward Austen succeeded to both the Hampshire and Kentish estates of Mrs. Thomas Knight in 1799. He took the name of Knight on the death of Mrs. Knight in 1812. Jane Austen, the famous authoress, was the aunt of Mr. Edward Knight, M.F.H.

Mr. E. Tredcroft, 1856-62.

Mr. Edward Tredcroft of Warnham Court, Horsham, followed Mr. King. He lived at Alresford during his mastership and received a guarantee of £1,150. For a reason which is not now known, his huntsmen had very short tenures. George Kennett was his first, a native of Cheriton, Henry Nason, who had been with Mr. Wall's harriers and the Linlithgow and Stirling, came next and then Will Stansby, each for one season only. Finally, Mr. Tredcroft hunted hounds himself on alternate days with William Fisher.

An amusing incident occured during Mr. Tredcroft's mastership. On March 23rd, 1858, at a meet at Brookwood Park, a strange well-turned-out lady was present at the meet with her groom in attendance. Both were well mounted but kept somewhat wide of the field. Hounds found at once in Blackhouse and ran through Joan's Acre, across the Dene, by West Tisted to Merryfield, killing in a covert beyond. The lady had a bad start but led the second flight, taking everything as it came. She sustained one fall over some stiff rails, but remounted at once and went on as well as before, catching hounds at Merryfield and was in at the death. She had attracted much admiration and caused much curiosity. Inquiries addressed to the groom produced only the vague information that she was " a stranger to these parts, but she is staying at Pelham Place."

Mr. Tredcroft was unanimously applauded in deciding to give the fair unknown the brush. This he proceeded to do with his best bow and complimenting the lady on her riding. A loud laugh came from " the lady " from under a thick veil and hat, veil and curls were swept off revealing Mr. Algernon Lempriere, son of the Admiral, who was the owner of Pelham.

On his resignation Mr. Tredcroft was entertained at the Swan Inn, Alresford, to a farewell dinner by his supporters, Mr. Charles Miller taking the chair, the vice-chair being taken by one of Hampshire's finest sportsmen, Mr. Frederick Baily of Brown Candover. This old sportsman had a silver drinking cup mounted inside a fox's mask given to him by Mr. Tredcroft and inscribed as follows : " Found by the H.H. at Goaley Wood on Saturday, March 18th, 1848, and killed at Farnham Holt, 2 hours and 25 minutes." Mr. Baily came to Brown Candover in 1846 and had to give up hunting in 1889 owing to his leg being broken in three places. The author has heard that Mr. Baily attended a cub hunting meet at Bentley Station some 18 miles away at six a.m., stayed during all the hunt, rode back to a quick lunch, changed horses and rode off to Winchester Market, some 12 miles, a performance which would not often be repeated nowadays.

Mr. H. W. Deacon, 1862-84.

Mr. Henry William Deacon now took over the mastership, living at Ropley Cottage, and ended the series of short periods of office. In 1853 Mr. Deacon bought Mr. Morgan of Woodovis pack and hunted the Lamerton country. He hunted hounds himself with Mr. James Deacon to whip in and showed good sport till 1859, when he resigned owing to the disgraceful slaughter of foxes in certain parishes. He had lived at Holwell, near Tavistock, in Devon.

Mr. Deacon had also ridden successfully both in flat races and in steeplechases. He soon showed that he thoroughly knew his business and his quiet kindly manner made him very popular generally. His consideration for the feelings of others was remarkable and is well shown by the following story.

Mr. J. A. Eggar relates in his reminiscences of hunting how, as a boy, he followed Mr. Deacon when making a cast after a check. The master saw him, but said nothing. Later on, when alone, he quietly explained that he was wrong. His kindness was never forgotten by Mr. Eggar. Mr. Deacon would not " lift " hounds, but encouraged them to work out the scent themselves and when a scent was there they could gallop. One day he killed his third fox under Green's Coppice, near Upton Grey, and wanted to draw again. It was the scent of a lifetime, but the members were against another draw and Mr. Deacon forbore.

There were many good hunts and Mr. Deacon killed 41½ brace of foxes in the year 1868, a record as far as it is known in the H.H. country and only equalled once. His first huntsman was Will Fisher, but he was followed in his second season by Charles Pike who, after riding second horseman to Captain Haworth, had been with the Old Berkshire and Cotswold. George Loader was his 1st whipper-in. Alfred Summers, afterwards a good huntsman, was his 2nd whipper-in. Mr. Deacon then hunted hounds for nineteen seasons with great success. The farmers supported Mr. Deacon and a large number hunted. Some of the most prominent were the Eggars of Bentley, James Taylor of Kilmeston, Owen Richards of Bighton, George Judd of Bishop's Sutton, Frederick P. Baily and Atkins of Candover, H. Fitt of Cheriton, John Turville of Hartley Park, Robert and Richard Hetherington of Ropley, John Godwin of Tichborne, who was to be well known for many years, James Stubbs of West Tisted, probably one of the last men in England to dine in common with his workmen sitting " beneath the salt " on the beautiful old Tichborne banqueting table at the old Manor House, William Lipscombe of Sevington, W. Penn of Woodmancote, T. Cordery of Wield, and Baily Whitear of Shroner House. It was said of Mr. Deacon " he could ride through any of the farmers' houses without them crying " Ware Crockery ! "

Mr. J. A. Eggar gives a few hunts which he remembers.

On December 23rd, 1880, he had a three-hour hunt. Mr. Montague Knight of Chawton, Mr. Vernon Knight and Mr. James Stevens, both of Farnham, with Dickey, 1st whipper-in, were the only ones with hounds. It was the only occasion in twenty-two years in which Mr. Deacon went home without his hounds.

On November 20th, 1881, a fox from Sheetlands ran by Mapledurwell, Butterwood, Andwell, Newnham, crossing the River Lodden and was killed at Sherfield. Only Mr. J. A. Eggar and Mr. A. White were with hounds after the River Lodden.

Another good fox, on February 5th, 1876, from Henwood, in Herriard Park, was lost at Bentley Station after a fifteen-mile point. Again on April 1st another Henwood fox was marked to ground in Sutton Wood, near Alresford, after two-and-a-half hours and making a point of seven or eight miles.

Mr. Deacon after 1867 used to tender his " annual resignation," as it became termed, always wanting rather more money to keep things going, but finally a fire in his stables decided him really to resign as the expenses of rebuilding stables for fourteen horses and buying eight new ones was too much for his resources.

On Mr. Deacon's retirement he was entertained at luncheon at the Town Hall, Alresford, where a fine service of plate to the value of over £600 was presented to him from 250 members and friends in the Hunt. Mr. Montague Knight was Chairman and Mr. F. P. Baily Vice-Chairman. The retiring master was referred to as an " angel in top boots." For three years Mr. Deacon had kept a huntsman, but finding that he was only " highly successful in losing foxes " he hunted hounds himself to the general satisfaction of all concerned for nineteen years. In his speech at the luncheon in thanking the farmers he alluded to their proverbial hospitality. He said he could not drink a glass of wine at mid-day ; if he did he was just as likely to go to Reading as to Ropley. He therefore took to drinking milk and " in the first two years had drunk enough milk to float a man-of-war and it was a great wonder to him that he had not long since been converted into a cheese." He also said that when he started only one gentleman, Mr. Scott, preserved and then everybody did, but they had all got on well together. In thanking the ladies he asked " how could he swear among so many lovely faces."

A very curious incident was related by a son of Mr. Christian of Bighton Wood to Mr. Eggar. He told him that he had been at Mr. Deacon's funeral at Ropley, the church being about a mile from the kennel. He said as the coffin was lowered into the grave the hounds burst into " Full Cry." It was a still day in December. Mr. Deacon was undoubtedly one of the best masters and huntsmen who ever hunted in Hampshire.

A. H. Wood, 1884-88.

Mr. Arthur Hardy Wood, who rented Froyle Place and later Arlebury in Alresford, after good work as Hon. Secretary, now became master for four years and filled a gap most usefully. Mr. Wood was the third son of Mr. John Wood of Theddon Grange. He was born in 1840 and died in 1923. Records of the sport of these years have not been discovered except for one unusual hunt.   Mr. Wood once found at Herriard and ran into the back door of a house at Old Basing.   Mr. Wood hunted the fox himself from under the kitchen table out of the front door and he was killed in the street.   Afterwards he had the pleasure of paying the doctor's bill for a " miscarriage " which unfortunately occurred to the lady of the house.   The guarantee in Mr. Wood's case rose to £1,800.   Mr. Wood, however, was only willing to hunt the country three days a week until the second week in January.   The Club preferred to continue with four days a week throughout the season.

A Committee, 1888-89
Messrs. F. Coryton, M. Knight and F. M. E. Jervoise.

A committee consisting of Messrs. Frederick Coryton of Liss Place, Mr. Montagu Knight of Chawton and Mr. Francis Michael Ellis Jervoise of Herriard now took control, hunting four days a week.   Mr. Knight dropped out after one season, but remained throughout his life a most ardent supporter whose coverts were always sure finds.   He also kept up the family reputation and could go down the Farringdon or Greatham Vales as well as anybody in the County.

F. Coryton and F. M. E. Jervoise, 1889-95.

The Squires of Liss and Herriard kept control for six years, officiating on two days each.   Mr. Jervoise was descended from Sir Thomas Jervoise of the Moat, Britford, Wilts, who married the heiress of Sir Richard Powlett, knight, of Herriard in 1601. He was born in 1844 and died in 1903.   Mr. Coryton was the second son of Mr. George E. Coryton of the Manor House, Greatham, a member of an old Devonshire family formerly of Coryton and afterwards of Pentillie Castle.   Mr. Coryton was born in 1850 and died in 1924.

Alfred Summers was their huntsman, a very cheery woodland huntsman with a fine voice in covert, but latterly somewhat ponderous to mount suitably.   Summers was seventeen years huntsman with the H.H. and nineteen with the Hursley.   He died a Brother of St. Cross aged 91 in 1937.

Both masters were large farmers as well as large landowners and keen sportsmen.   Mr. Coryton's brother William, of Pentillie Castle, was master of the Dartmoor Hounds for fourteen years ; he also founded the East Cornwall Hounds and hunted them for fifteen years at his own expense.   His son Augustus was a popular Hon. Secretary from 1920 to 1934, and again assumed this onerous post in 1948 on the sad death of Mr. John Highmoor. During this mastership some good sport was enjoyed.

Cub hunting on October 24th, 1889, hounds ran from Herriard to Ropley in 55 minutes without a check, but lost on the railway line and on the 28th ran an old fox 2 hours and 30 minutes over the vale from Binsted and killed him at Broxhead. On January 7th, 1890, after running a fox from Plash Wood to ground in a dell and another unsuccessful hunt, hounds found a third in Marylane and ran to ground in the same dell as in the morning. They then found in Brownfields, and ran for an hour and threequarters till the huntsman's horse was dead beat in a ditch, and Mr. Coryton hunted the hounds, but finally had to whip off in the dark without killing.

In the 1890–91 season hounds were stopped by frost from December 11th, 1890, to January 24th, 1891, the longest frost for many years.

On February 2nd, 1892, a fine hunt took place from Avington Park. This good fox was found in Hampage Wood and ran through Ovington Park to Sevington, across the water meadows to Cheriton, skirting Cheriton Wood, through Old Park and Bramdean Common to West Tisted. Running through the farmyard, he ran on to Ashton Wood where a fresh fox complicated matters. The hunted fox crawled into a hole in Basing Park in front of Guy, and saved his brush after providing a ten-mile point through seven parishes.

These joint masters were responsible also for starting the H.H. Shire Horse Society in 1891. It was dissolved during the First World War in 1916 and during that period the twenty-seven stallions had covered 6,286 mares, getting 70 per cent. in foal and greatly improving the local breed of carthorses now giving way unfortunately to petrol-driven engines of all sorts and sizes.

Annual shows were held, the first at Herriard Park, Mr. Coryton being Chairman and Mr. J. A. Eggar, a great supporter of both the H.H. and the Garth, acted as Hon. Secretary. Some £80 worth of prizes were distributed each year. Mr. W. G. Nicholson's challenge cup was won outright by that staunch foxhunter and good horseman Mr. Herbert Chalcraft of Binsted, a representative of a very ancient yeoman family, members of which, originally called " atte Calveroft " in Bramshott parish, can be traced in the 14th century, many of whom have been great supporters and one of whom is still a farmer member of the Hunt.

Visit of the Royal Staghounds, March 23rd, 1889.

The Royal Staghounds, under the Earl of Coventry, John Harvey Huntsman (a native of the Isle of Wight), met at Mr. Hunt's house, Headbourne Worthy Manor Farm, and were most hospitably entertained. The stag was uncarted near Worthy Down, half a mile from the Race Course. Some 6,000 people attended the meet. The masters of the local packs all attended—Mr. F. Coryton (H.H.), Messrs. Russell and Pember (Vine), Mr. A. E. Deane (Hursley), Mr. Harvey (Hambledon), Mr. Shrubb (Tedworth), also the veteran ex-masters Mr. H. Deacon, Mr. A. H. Wood and Colonel S. Nicoll. Among the large crowd of followers were also Mr. Tom Merington of Crondall and Mr. Harry Day of Stockbridge. "Lord Clanwilliam" was the stag uncarted and he went away over Mr. Garrett Moore's training ground, on past Littleton and Northwood, past Lainston House across Wyke Down, over Teg Down and along Oliver's Battery, into the valley crossing over Compton Down, Twyford Down to the top of Morestead Hill, going at a rare pace in the open. He then ran over Longwood Warren to the Devil's Punch Bowl, past Godwins Down nearly to Hockley House, but turned right-handed to Lane End and West Wood. Here he beat hounds ; actually he went on to the Warnford Estate where he was viewed at 2.45 p.m. His further adventures are related below.

On March 30th, 1889, the H.H. met at Medstead Green. Finding near Hattingly, hounds ran past Gaston Grange into Chawton Park where the pack divided, one lot killing their hunted fox with Mr. Coryton the master. Whilst he was breaking him up, Alfred Summers was blowing his horn and his hounds were running with a great cry. They left Chawton Park towards Medstead and Bentworth, past Ashley Farm to Lower Wield, thence on to Park Copse, and over Preston Down to the Lower Farm, Preston Candover. Here the stag " Lord Clanwilliam "[12] aforesaid took soil in the village pond and thoroughly ducked the adventurous two or three couple who first tackled him. He was moved from the pond by a few stout hounds and trotted up the village street, and seeing an open door, actually that of the hen house in the butcher's yard, in he went, and Mr. John Thorp, the butcher, quickly shut the door on the

---

[12] This stag apparently liked a change from the old beans and oats of Swinley Paddocks as on another occasion " Lord Clanwilliam " was also left out during Lord Ribblesdale's mastership. Uncarted at Maiden Earley, he ran hounds out of daylight by Easthampstead. A fortnight later, after being harboured in one of Lord Downshire's coverts, he ran back nearly fence for fence the way he had run a fortnight before, and was taken a field away from the one where he had been uncarted.

hounds. The hunt was about eight miles in 33 minutes and though a pleasant and very fast gallop no one was with the leading hounds and Summers purposely kept the rest of the pack with him, off the scent, when he realised that he could not stop the leaders. Both Summers and Guy had a good start but the pace was too hot to whip off. A sad case of rioting but rather an amusing incident.

Lord Ribblesdale recounts in his book *The Queen's Hounds* (master, 1892–95) that he also paid a visit to the H.H. country when he ran a deer from Aldershot to within a mile of Bishop's Sutton and took the deer (called " Bartlett ") on a down near the Grange, Northington. H.R.H. The Duke of Connaught was out and went well. The master and his second horseman quietly drove the deer along to the nearest farm in the Candover Valley where he could be temporarily housed. This hunt must have been about an 18-mile point from the description given and probably at least 25 miles as hounds ran.

Mr. F. Coryton and Lieut.-Col. R. Knox, 1895-99.

Mr. F. M. E. Jervoise now resigned and his place was taken by the Hon. Secretary, Lieut.-Col. R. Knox. Good sport continued and friendly feeling. One run deserves recording on February 8th, 1896, from a meet at Marsh House, Bentley, the home of a good sportsman and member, Mr. F. Thresher Giles. Both masters were out, Colonel Knox in control. A fine dog-fox broke from Wall Field over the meadows to Irelands, and crossed the Welches meadows at a great pace, leaving Jenkyn Place on the right, over the hop fields to Penley, Gravelly Wood and nearly to Crondall, where the fox was headed. He then turned right-handed through Lea Wood, Dick's Wood, Barley Pound, to Dippenhall, and then on to the Willey coverts and Fish Pond. After a slight check hounds ran on to Northbrook crossing the road, river and railway to Wrecclesham, over the Portsmouth road and Manley Bridge, into Glenberrie, Rowledge, recrossing the Portsmouth road to Lodge Enclosure and the Straits. After leaving the Holt, hounds hunted on past Wheatley to Piplins to Reynolds Hanger and across the Kingsley Meadows to Binswood, over Shortfield Common into Wolmer Forest. Turning left-handed by Hogmoor Pond and Broxhead House, he ran over Broxhead Common leaving Sleaford Farm on the right, to the Kingsley iron works, crossing the road into Stephens Wood, leaving Wheatley Farm on the left, up the valley to Binsted Post Office where he was lost.   A gallant fox who well deserved to preserve his brush.   The distance was not less than 22 miles.   They found at 11.30 a.m. and lost at 3.10 p.m.   The pack hunted splendidly ;   the huntsman Alfred Summers had a nasty fall but stuck to his post.

H.H. Point-to-Point Races.

On Wednesday, March 22nd, 1899, at the end of this mastership the first H.H. Point-to-Point Races were run at Berry Hill, Farringdon.   The races were not actually from point to point, but a few flags were placed on prominent objects which had to be passed on the correct side, otherwise riders took their own line.   The *Hampshire Chronicle* of March 25th, 1899, reports these as " in every respect a thorough success," but unfortunately does not give the results in detail.

During the Nineties the chief thrusters of the Hunt were Mr. Arthur Seawell of Marelands and Mr. Eyre Lloyd of Preston Candover.   The latter on his favourite mare could never resist jumping a gate.   Unfortunately another horse of his, a wild rushing animal called the " Yellow Peril," caused his undoing by a severe neglected fall into a road injuring his spine.   Mr. Reginald Nicholson, though living just out of the country, was a hard-riding member and gallant point-to-point rider. Mr. Montague Knight of Chawton was also always well up and carried on the family tradition of good horsemanship. Before the 1914 war the chief among many sporting farmers and keen supporters were Mr. Tom Bridger of Greywell, Messrs. Austin Chalcraft of Will Hall and Tom Chalcraft of Alton, Mr. Bertie Chalcraft of Wyck, and Mr. T. Cole of Well, Mr. A. Copper of Froxfield, Mr. J. A. and F. Eggar of Farnham and Bentley, Mr. John Godwin of Tichborne, Mr. H. Gray of Abbotstone, Mr. George Langrish of Wick, Messrs. J. F. and J. B. Mills of Bishop's Sutton, Mr. Tom Mitchell of Hartley Park Farm, Mr. J. Pain of Stratton, Mr. Seward of Herriard, Mr. H. Stratton of Chilcombe, Mr. W. Twitchin of Holybourne, Mr. B. Warner of Hawkley who luckily is still able to enjoy a hunt near his home.   Most of these good sportsmen have passed on, a few leaving representatives to uphold their names, but it is sad that names which have been known in the County since mediaeval times.   Chalcraft (*atte* Calvecroft), Godwin, Langrish are no longer present in the hunting field.

When the 20th century opened, the country was at war with the Boer Republics and many a good foxhunting man was absent fighting and some did not return.   Barbed wire greatly

Mr. Thomas Ridge of Kilmeston Manor,
M.F.H. 1749-95.

Mr. J. T. Villebois,
M.F.H. 1803-37.

Mr. H. Deacon,
M.F.H. 1862-84.

Mr. F. Coryton, Master and Joint Master, 1889 - 1909.
Mounted on "Solomon" at Bramdean Cross Roads.
From a painting by Frank Calderon.

Some members of the H.H. at Rotherfield Park about 100 years ago.

increased after the South African War had ended in 1902. Motors had only just appeared and made no difference to hunting for some years. Shooting syndicates became prevalent, wanting big bags and introducing strangers into the County with no interest in its legitimate sports. This change was largely due to agricultural depression. Rents were very low and shooting rents were often more remunerative than farming land with wheat at under 30s. a quarter and oats at 12s. or 13s. a quarter. Many landlords found themselves at a heavy loss and many were forced to let their houses or their shooting and sometimes both. In the H.H. country, with the well-known local joint-masters, all went well and sport was fairly good, though the fixing of meets before Christmas became rather more difficult owing to shooting arrangements having to be taken into consideration.

Mr. F. Coryton and Mr. A. T. E. Jervoise, 1899 - 1909.

Mr. Frederick Coryton was well known to all as a good sportsman and farmer and a popular landlord. Mr. Arthur Tristran Ellis Jervoise came to live on his brother's estate at Herriard Grange. Courteous to all, a good horseman, and with the most unruffled temper, he could not have been more popular. Knowing the country and its inhabitants from boyhood, he was an ideal master in every way. Albert Guy from 1st whipper-in succeeded Alfred Summers as huntsman and was quicker in the field and more successful. Guy had faithfully served the Hunt since the days of Mr. Deacon, a good horseman and excellent hunt servant. He carried the horn from 1896 to 1902 when Jack Cooper succeeded. Cooper was a dashing horseman and for a short time was very successful ' Soon, however, the perpetual lifting of hounds and hunting " halloas " made the pack flighty and unreliable.

The following good hunt deserves recording and it will be seen that considerable success in killing foxes was achieved. On February 21st, 1905, a very good hunt took place from Dean House, Kilmeston, the residence of Mr. C. Naylor, a regular follower. A brace of foxes were soon on foot in West Wood and unfortunately a single hound got away on one, but Cooper picked up the line in Shorley with the body of the pack and ran by Beauworth, Rabbit Copse and Durdans. Crossing the road here, he ran over Gander Down and on to Longwood Warren, over Hancomb Bottom, racing over the downs at a great pace. This fox now went through Hazeley Farm buildings at a somewhat slower pace, by Colden Common and the Brickfields ; he crossed

G

over Crowd Hill, where he was viewed by the 1st whipper-in. He met his end in a hedgerow at Stoke Park, Bishop's Stoke. A nine-mile point in one and a half hours. Miss Higgens received the brush and Mr. Coryton kept the mask. Not many of the field survived to see the finish, but Mr. Montagu Knight, Messrs. Percy and Hubert Shelly, Colonel Slingers, Mr. Naylor, Mr. Thornton and Mr. Stares, John and Wilfrid Godwin and the brothers Mills were all up; and among the ladies, Mrs. Aubertin, the Hon. Mrs. Fred Baring, Miss Christie and Miss Legge. Another fox was found and soon killed in Brockwood.

The season 1904–05 was probably the best of all Mr. Coryton's seasons. In 78 days' regular hunting, hounds killed 33½ brace of foxes and 19½ brace were marked to ground. Hounds were stopped by frost 17 days. In 1900–01 20 brace were killed in 76 days, 13½ brace to ground. In 1903–04 26 brace were killed in 85 hunting days, 24½ brace to ground.

Jack Cooper left in the season 1906–07 and Harry Payne succeeded him and hounds followed his horn about the rides and would not draw. Payne, however, was a sick man and became blind soon afterwards. Mr. Coryton relied chiefly on the Bicester, Dartmoor and Woodland Pytchley Packs for drafts.

In 1907 the Hunt presented Mr. Coryton with his portrait, mounted on Soloman, his favourite grey hunter, with the hounds at the sign post on Bramdean Cross Roads. Mr. Montagu Knight, Chairman of the Hunt Club, made the presentation in a most appropriate speech. A gift of plate and a grandfather clock were also given, together with the picture. The ceremony took place at Chawton House, the Chairman's residence. Both masters resigned.

Mr. G. P. E. Evans, 1909-15.

Mr. George Patrick Elystan Evans now came to the country as master and amateur huntsman. Mr. Evans had hunted beagles as a boy of ten at his home at Hatley Park, Cambridgeshire, and by lending four couple of his best hounds to Eton had been permitted to hunt with the Eton Beagles as a lower boy. Mr. Evans was born in 1872 and was master of the Cambridgeshire Hounds, 1893–94, and joint-master, 1894–1903. In 1904 Mr. Evans went as master of the Tickham to help Mrs. Rigden, whose husband had suddenly died after thirty years in office. Mr. Evans had done a great deal to improve the Cambridgeshire pack, introducing freely the Belvoir blood to get pace and quality. In the Tickham he maintained the high standard achieved by that fine sportsman Mr. A. E. Rigden. Coming to the H.H. in the prime of life, Mr. Evans soon made his influence felt. He knew all about shooting and was a good shot himself and thoroughly understood the running of big shoots. He would help a good keeper and he could expose a vulpicide. To ensure a good supply of foxes he took several useful coverts in the country and ran them himself as syndicate shoots. He also introduced the best of blood into the kennels. He soon showed the results of his good work and the number of foxes killed rose at once. Mr. Evans had a wonderful power over animals, and his kennel discipline was of the highest order. He could show the pack, or any single hound in it, without any of the staff being present and not a crack of a whip. Even his pigs were taught to sit up and beg. In the field Mr. Evans was forcible in his language, but tried his hardest to avoid unnecessary damage to crops or disturbance of live stock. Mr. Isaac Bell in his Fox Hunter's Log Book, describes Mr. Evans' command of language as follows : " He had a good vocabulary for any who pressed hounds ! Until I had hunted with the Cambridgeshire I thought Lord Willoughby de Broke had a good flow of language but I soon discovered that compared to George Evans his was but Basic English."

One story of Mr. Evans with the H.H. is given where no bad language was used. One day an elderly and greatly respected member arrived at a covert in a hunt before the master and hounds, having ridden a point accompanied by some ladies who relied on his well-known knowledge of the country and hunting. Mr. Evans, in his most polite manner, says, " Of course, Mr. ——, you can go wherever you like, but for G—d's sake don't take your harem with you." The member was a pillar of the church and was not amused. There are many stories which could be told of him, but his outbursts were soon passed and concealed a very kind nature. Sport was uniformly good and much was done to make the country rideable.

As in Mr. Deacon's day, the annual meetings during Mr. Evans' mastership were never got through without a good deal of reference to financial problems. Mr. Evans used to say that " he was an expensive luxury," and doubtless he was, but the whole standard of the hounds and hunting was greatly improved and the problem of the shooting syndicates safely dealt with by one who knew as much of that side as any record bag maker. When warned off, as he very occasionally was after the First World War, generally by farmeresses, they seldom withstood the master's personal visits. Frequently a brace of pheasants sent, or, better still, taken quickly to the right quarter prevented an angry letter concerning open gates, cattle hopelessly mixed, or other sad incidents of this nature.

Some of Mr. Evans' good hunts will be given very briefly. In his first mastership a fox found in Woodmancote Holt ran through Hogsdown, Farleigh and Herriard, hounds changing foxes in Honeyleaze : hounds then ran on through Upton Grey, Hoddington and Froyle, finally killing their fox near Bentley Station : a point of about 14 miles and probably over 20 miles as hounds ran. Another, after a frost, with 43 couple of hounds out. The find was at Temple, and hounds ran through Hartley Wood and Binsted Wyck about noon ; after this no one saw a hound till 3 p.m. when Mr. Evans found them " to ground " in Spollicombe. The pack had actually killed at Peacombe about 12.30 p.m. and had then been halloaed on to another fox by the keeper and had hunted by themselves round all the Froyle coverts till they drove this second fox to ground. Every hound up. Another useful hunt from Horsden Common ended in a kill on the lawn at Bramshill House, about a $7\frac{1}{2}$-mile point. Foxes had been made to cover considerable distances, and quickly too, if they wished to preserve their lives. By allowing the Longmoor Draghounds to hunt fox regularly in Alice Holt and Chawton Park, these big woodlands were kept properly disturbed and Mr. Evans could find his foxes more quickly in small coverts, and also the fox population was kept down legitimately to its proper level. One year five litters were bred in Chawton Park by that grand sportsman Mr. Montagu Knight of Chawton, Chairman of the Hunt Club for many years. This good sport was ended in 1915 when Mr. Evans, who had been a Captain in the 60th Rifle Militia, and also a Major in the Bedfordshire Yeomanry, again resumed a military life and served as a Staff Captain in France.

Committee, 1915-19.

Mr. F. Coryton was elected Chairman of a Committee of Management and hunting was carried on two days a week with Will Orvis as huntsman. Orvis was quite good in kennel, but not a very dashing horseman, and frequently spoilt a good run by casting away from an obstacle which appeared somewhat solid. The interruption of the war years played considerable havoc with the carefully-thought-out and most scientific system of hound breeding inaugurated by Mr. Evans. However, thanks to Mr. Coryton and Hon. Secretary Mr. J. F. Complin of Holybourne, the Hunt carried on quite well. Mr. Complin was a good farmer and had always been most useful in adjusting poultry claims and many small troubles in his area at market. A heavyweight and not addicted to jumping, he was very keen and managed to get about the country quite well, mounted on the most massive of horses.

Mr. A. P. Robinson, 1919-21.

Mr. A. P. Robinson of Norwich succeeded for two seasons, during which he showed some useful sport. He went away with the leading hounds and by hard riding made his foxes travel and killed a fair average. Unfortunately, on the business side, affairs were not left in a satisfactory condition.

Major A. C. Bovill, D.S.O., M.C., 1921-23.

Major Anthony C. Bovill, D.S.O., M.C., who had served with harriers, now took the horn, with Orvis as kennel-huntsman and 1st whip. He was an accomplished horseman, but was not quick over this difficult country. He was apt to wait for his tail hounds when a fox was found, and so foxes got too much of a start and sport deteriorated, hounds losing their keenness through lack of blood.

During Major Bovill's mastership two unusual hunts took place worthy of record. One was a cub hunt on a blazing hot day at Sutton Wood on October 15th, 1921. The day was more fit for tennis than hunting. A brace were on foot and often viewed but there appeared to be no scent whatever and hounds could not hunt. About 11 a.m., however, Alresford Pond was drawn and an old fox went away on the far side, hounds running very fast and with a good cry. They ran by Sutton Wood, skirting Bowyer's Grove, to the Gullet, where a slight check ensued. The master and the author were alone with them. Away again, unaided, past Hook's Wood and Medstead, through Red Wood, over the Alton Road by the Abbey, past Spenser's Grove to ground in Chawton Park Beeches. About a 9½-mile point, very fast over a completely blind country. Few horses were fit for the gallop. The weather was blazing hot throughout, yet the scent seemed perfect throughout the run.

The other unusual hunt was from a meet at the Golden Pot on March 24th, 1923. Finding a brace at once in some turnips near Hawkins Wood, hounds ran through the Warren and Pountney Copse to Close Down Wood, through Humbly Grove, to ground in Deans. Again finding in Brick Kiln Common, hounds ran through Great Park, by Holdings Corner to Humbly Grove, Little Park and Privett to the grounds of Hoddington House, the home of Lord Basing. Happening to be with hounds running full cry into the garden, there was suddenly dead silence. The author went towards the house and heard a deep baying coming from beneath the ground. Finding an open cellar, workmen being engaged in putting in a new hot water system, the author found the pack jumping up at a hole in the wall about five feet up. A careful tour of the house was made with one old hound called " Dorking " and the 1st whipper-in who had arrived. Pad marks were seen in places. Suddenly, going along a corridor, old " Dorking " jumped up and gave tongue. As it was obvious that the fox was not on the window sill, the author suggested " Dorking " must be standing on him. The fox was found underneath the boards. How he got there was a mystery, unless some old flue had been opened for pipes to be pulled through.

Major Bovill went as joint-master to the Isle of Wight Hounds for 1924-25 and continued as master 1925-32.

Lieut.-Col. C. G. Mangles and Captain R. Orred, 1923-24.

Lieut.-Colonel Cecil Gardiner Mangles, M.C., late of the 20th Hussars, son of Mr. Frank Mangles of Shalden Lodge, now took the horn, Captain Roland Orred, tenant of Farleigh House, assisting him as field master. Colonel Mangles was very keen and, before the First World War, with Mr. Jack Darling, had a very useful pack of beagles which they hunted wherever they could get permission to do so. He had the advantage, too, of having lived in the country and hunted in it as a boy. As a huntsman, however, he was not successful and the number of foxes killed dwindled, with the invariable result that the number of foxes dwindled, too. Captain Roland Orred proved an excellent field master, well mounted and courteous to all, but unfortunately decided to resign after only one season.

Lieut.-Col. C. G. Mangles and Capt. J. B. Scott, 1924-25.

Colonel Mangles continued with Captain Jervoise Bolitho Scott of Rotherfield Park as joint-master and field master. Captain Scott was one of the largest covert owners in the Hunt and his coverts always held foxes. An ex-officer of the 7th Hussars, he was always well mounted and he loved a good hunt and a good ride. Unfortunately, sport did not improve and Lieut.-Colonel Mangles resigned at the end of the season. From

Hampshire he became joint master of the Essex and Suffolk Hounds in 1928 and continued in that county with various joint-masters until 1936, finding it a very much easier problem to show good sport there than in Hampshire. Will Orvis continued as kennel huntsman and 1st whip.

Captain J. B. Scott and Mr. G. P. E. Evans (2nd mastership), 1926-27.

Capt. Scott agreed to continue as joint master with Mr. Evans again as joint-master and huntsman. Captain Scott supported the Hunt most nobly financially and by his generous help and that of other members, some very valuable hounds were purchased. Sport rapidly improved and it was to the great grief of the country when Captain Scott decided to retire at the end of the season.

Mr. G. P. E. Evans and Mr. J. M. Hastings, 1927-32.

Mr. Evans now took Mr. John Maurice Hastings as joint-master. Mr. Hastings had been joint-master of the Vyne since 1929. Each master hunted hounds two days a week, keeping their own packs.

Sport generally continued to keep a good standard. On November 1st, 1928, a curious incident happened. After meeting at Abbotstone Down, a fox was found that had been hunted several times and always got to ground in Godsfield Copse. On this occasion the master and Will Scott, his 1st whip and kennel huntsman, had spent the previous day stopping every kind of hole in Godsfield, including the badger-earth. The fox took two or three turns round Godsfield Copse, but finding no refuge open took to the open over Chilton Down and the Candover road, then back to Wield Wood where he was killed and found to have a double brush, one rather dark and one tan coloured, with a fine white tip. Rowland Ward, who mounted it for Mr. Evans, had never heard of or seen such a formation. When running he appeared only to have a very fine and rather unusually bushy brush.

On April 25th, 1929, Mr. Evans married Diana, daughter of Stuart Smith, Esq., of Hall Place, Ropley, a senior member of the Hunt Club. The wedding in hunting dress was very largely attended and the ceremony was followed by a meet of the hounds. About 250 mounted followers attended the meet and 500 motor cars were counted in the park. Sport was not good; a fox was run to ground in Chawton Park and a second fox beat hounds. To the great regret of all who knew her Mrs. Evans died after an operation in 1930.

A remarkable hunt took place from Herriard Church on March 2nd, 1931. Finding in Hen Wood, hounds raced away at once over the Park and Grange Farm and through Preston Oakhills without a check, over the road to Down Wood and Bradley Wood, when the hounds were brought to slow hunting. " Halloa'd " away by Pitters Wood, hounds ran on to the Wilderness. During this time one of the boldest riders in the Hunt, Mr. Frank Halliday, M.V.O., and his nephew, now Lt.-Col. C. A. T. Halliday, O.B.E., Royal Hampshire Regiment, had been alone with hounds. The Hunt staff came up at the Wilderness. The fox was soon " halloa'd " away from College Wood, swinging right-handed over the open to Barton Copse and Wield Wood and out again past Park Copse and over Preston Down nearly to Preston Candover village, crossing over the Wield road, through Preston Grange gardens, over Shapley Hill to the Yew Tree, where the fox was viewed by the master, dead beat, with a couple of hounds snapping at him, dodging round a hay stack. Here, unfortunately, a fresh fox got up and was "halloa'd" away by Will Scott, the 1st whipper-in. Horses were very beat and no one who had ridden the hunt was fit to do much more when hounds again went away through Bradley Wood. The master found hounds eventually, having killed near Ellisfield. Some 30 miles had been covered and though the point was not exceptional the pace and hound work were quite outstanding.

The following appreciation of Mr. Evans from an unbiassed American, Mr. A. Henry Higginson, ex-M.F.H. of the Middlesex Hounds in America, and master or joint-master of the Cattistock Hunt (1930–1939) and joint-master, South Dorset (1942-1945), in this country, may be of interest :—

In December, 1928, Mr. Higginson visited the H.H. and stayed with Mr. Evans. Frost prevented one day's hunting, but he had a day at Hartley, meeting at the house of that good and most hospitable sportsman, Mr. Tom Mitchell, at Hartley Park Farm. Hartley Park Wood was the draw, a roughish place. Mr. Higginson says " Evans hunted hounds himself, and is an excellent, if a noisy, huntsman." He had not been much impressed with hounds in kennel, but he says " they were a most workmanlike and excellent hunting pack in the field. . . . I was greatly struck by hounds' work. It was first class in every respect. They drew well, stuck to their line well, and have plenty to say about it when they find, and also during the hunt itself." He mentions as the best dogs out old " Dalesman " (Carmarthen) and " Bully " (Sir E. Curre). The criticism of " noisiness " is not quite fair on Mr. Evans, though perhaps natural in one coming from an open country. In big woodlands a huntsman must be heard both by the hounds and for the sake of the field. With Mr. Evans the field had no excuse for riding in the master's pocket as he could be well heard and his mastery of the horn left not the slightest doubt as to what he meant, whether "Away," "A find," "Riot," etc., Hounds, too, knew just what was meant, having most musical ears. To hear Mr. Evans blow " Gone away " was the best panacea to banish the cares and troubles of this world.

Mr. G. Evans, Mr. M. A. Hastings and Mr. B. Hamilton, 1933-34.
Mr. G. Evans and Mr. B. Hamilton, 1934-35.
Mr. and Mrs. G. Evans, 1935-37.

Mr. Evans now took in other joint-masters to assist him. A very good hunt in a deep and difficult country came from a meet at Hawkley on November 11th, 1933, after all had been most hospitably entertained by that fine sportsman Mr. Benjamin Warner. Hounds found in Grove and ran very fast towards Temple right-handed to Blackmoor Wood where he was killed, Hounds found another fox in Blackmoor Wood who was run. again very fast, round the Moor and back into the Park when he was killed. Finding again in Temple, hounds ran a circle round Le Court back to the Moor where he, too, met his end. Yet another fox was found outside Blackmoor Wood and ran almost the same circle round Temple, Oak Hanger, Le Court, and he, too, was killed in the Park. Two brace above ground in the same day is seldom heard of in Hampshire. It speaks volumes for the huntsman, the hounds, and, last but not least, for the covert owner, the late Earl of Selborne, who provided three of the foxes. Lord Selborne rode well to hounds, though his important public duties had made his appearances in the field very rare in later years.

On October 30th, 1934, the last day's cub hunting, a cub was found outside the Gullet and ran towards the Wilderness, turning left-handed through Wield Wood where he was killed. Found in the Wilderness and ran a circle round before going away through Bighton Wood, Lower Lanham, Godsfield, past Preston Grange, back to Wield Wood and killed in the open between Woodridden and Bighton. This finished a wonderful cub-hunting season when 23 brace of cubs were killed. Seventeen brace also were marked to ground and only three brace dug out. This was the best cub-hunting season Mr. Evans ever had and no better has ever been recorded.

Mr. Evans had married again in 1934, Mrs. Lawrence.

Mr. Evans' long study of the breeding of hounds brought its reward in the creation of a first-rate hunting pack with great drive. They had excellent noses and a fine cry. This was achieved by judiciously introducing Sir Edward Curre's strain. This great hound breeder had succeeded in uniting the best qualities of the English and the Welsh foxhound.

Mr. Evans in 1935 had a great success at Peterborough. "Dashwood," by "Oakley Gordon" (31) out of "Darling" (29), won the first prize for unentered doghounds, "Rarity," by "Tiverton Simon" (26) out of "Rachel" (29), won the first prize for brood bitches, and also the Championship Cup. This bitch would speak to the line on a tarmac road and often put the pack right. Her statue, beautifully executed, formed part of Mr. Evans' parting presentation (see opposite).

At the Aldershot show Mr. Evans won every class, both for dogs and bitches. The pack were not, however, a show-bench pack, but good in their work with plenty of drive, wonderful noses, and it was a pleasure to hear their cry.

The stallion hound much used to create this level good hunting pack was Carmarthen "Dalesman," a hound of great character who knew whether a fox was in covert in the most marvellous way. He would not leave Mr. Evans' horse unless a fox was there. If he was there "Dalesman" would find him, and he was a first-rate killer. "Bully" was another hound of great hunting powers. The pack cast themselves beautifully and could find and account for their foxes with any pack in the County.

Sir Edward Curre did not choose his sires for looks alone. His favourite, Stevenstone "Sanfoin," proved his exceptional worth when hunting with that pack; hounds checked by a river, "Sanfoin" jumped in without a second's hesitation, swam across and killed his fox single-handed in the meadows beyond *and brought him back across the river*. The four Burrow "Whipcord" was another strain of great value, bringing the best blood of Lord FitzHardinge's hounds. Mr. Evans pursued the same ideas as Sir Edward except that he made no attempt to produce a white pack which was so desirable on the Welsh mountains, but must have meant drafting many a good hound.

" RARITY."

Champion Bitch, Peterborough and Aldershot, 1935
(for type it may be of interest to compare with " Jasper " facing page 145).

THE H.H. AT ROTHERFIELD PARK, 1936.

Reading left to right.—Mr. Prichett, Jack Packman (2nd whipper-in), Capt. J. B.
Scott, Mrs. Evans, M.F.H., Mr. G. P. E. Evans, M.F.H., Mr. Henry Warner
(amateur whipper-in), Bert Chandler (2nd horseman), Will Scott (1st
whipper-in and K.H.).

Mr. H. A. Andreae, M.F.H., with Brigadier M. W. Selby Lowndes and Jack Kealey and hounds. Moundsmere Manor in the background. From a painting by Captain Lionel Edwards, 1950.

Mr. G. P. E. Evans and Lieut.-Col. M. R. F. Courage, D.S.O., 1937-39.

Mr. Evans was joined by Lieut.-Colonel Miles Ralph Ferguson Courage, D.S.O., of Preston House, an old Gunner officer, a keen sportsman and polo player. Will Scott hunted hounds. Will Scott was a hard Northumbrian and had been 1st whip and kennel huntsman for ten years. Not a good horseman and difficult to mount suitably, he was determined to be with hounds and with or without a fall, he always got over somehow and attained his object. With a pack at their best, Will Scot killed 41½ brace of foxes his first season and maintained very good sport. On May 2nd, 1939, Mr. Evans retired and Colonel Courage carried on alone, at first with Will Scott as huntsman.

Lieut.-Col. M. R. F. Courage, D.S.O., 1939-44.

In 1939 the Second World War broke out and everything became more difficult, even more difficult than in 1914-18. Colonel Courage, however, managed to carry on through the many difficulties and the Hunt owed a great debt to him for undertaking such an arduous task. In 1941 Charles James took the horn, but was not successful in the field and sport deteriorated owing to his lack of enthusiasm. During Colonel Courage's mastership much was done to improve the kennels and two new cottages were built.

Mr. H.A. Andreae, 1944.

Mr. Herman Anton Andreae of Moundsmere Manor took over the mastership, keeping James as huntsman at first and Jack Kealey for one season, 1946-47. Mr. Andreae was a great yachtsman and well known as one of the best helmsmen sailing in the " J " Class. A very busy man, he had not had much time to devote to hunting, on which, however, he was very keen. He generously took the hounds at a nominal subscription of only £250 per annum, thus allowing the Hunt Club finances to be soon put in a very prosperous state by the able Hon. Secretary, Mr. John Highmoor. He allowed Mr. Evans to remain in the huntsman's cottage at Ropley to superintend the hounds, horses and general kennel management. The country was hunted three times a week and gradually a fourth day, though officially a bye-day, was added and kept up as long as possible.

In 1947-48 season Brigadier M. W. Selby Lowndes, D.S.O., late R.A., came as huntsman and deputy-master. His career is so varied and unusual that it deserves a record. His father, grandfather and great-grandfather were all masters of foxhounds, their period of office covering nearly 100 years from 1806–1900. The Brigadier himself has hunted the fox, the hare and the jackal in England, Italy, Palestine, India and France. He has been master and huntsman of the following packs :—1911-14, the Handley Cross Harriers in the East Kent country, a private pack ; 1918-19, the R.A. Hounds, Italy ; 1919-21, Vale of Acre and Sarona Vale Hunts, Palestine ; 1923-25, Nowshera ; 1925-27, Lucknow Hounds in India ; 1929-32, the R.A. (Bordon) Draghounds (two days a week for one drag). In 1932-34 he was amateur huntsman to the Tedworth, in 1934-35 to the Wilton and 1935-36 he was deputy master to the Clifton-on-Teme, returning to the Wilton as amateur huntsman again in 1937-39. In the early days of the war before Germany staged her offensive, he hunted the Lille beagles in France ; the pack was destroyed before the evacuation. After the war, 1946-47 he was master of the Newmarket and Thurlow before coming as amateur huntsman for the H.H. in 1947. Brigadier Selby Lowndes can certainly be said to be keeping up the great sporting reputation of his family. Sport was greatly improved and when the country is more rideable Brigadier Selby Lowndes will probably prove a most successful huntsman. The supply of foxes is good and will improve the more hounds can kill. Hounds hunt well and in 1948 and 1949 were again successful at both Peterborough and Aldershot.

" Reptile," by " Ranger " (41) out of " Dainty " (38), was 1st in the brood bitches, following this success up in 1949 at the Aldershot Hound Show by being 1st and Champion in the same class. " Cosy," by " Challenger " (44) out of " Comedy " (45), and " Wagtail," by " Roisterer " (43) out of " Willing " (46), won the unentered bitches (couples) class at Aldershot in 1949, and in the unentered dogs class " Trimmer " and "Trimbush," by "Tramples" (46) out of " Harmless " (45), were winners and also reserve to champion—a great achievement for unentered dogs. These successes show that despite the war years and all their difficulties, the H.H. have kept their standard well and it is also obvious that Mr. Evans, who still manages the hounds for the master, has not lost his cunning.

On Friday, October 28th, 1949, Mr Andreae entertained at Moundsmere Manor thirty-eight members and farmer members of the Hampshire Hunt. The dinner was to mark the bi-centenary of the Hampshire Hunt, and this purpose it well accomplished. Mr. Andreae, after the loyal toast had been drunk, spoke shortly of the pleasure it gave him to welcome his guests. He spoke of the H.H. as the " Happy Hunt " and long may it be so. General Sir George Jeffreys, Chairman of the Hunt Club, mentioned something of its past, and that his memories went back to being blooded by Mr. Deacon ; he thanked the Master and Mrs. Andreae for their great hospitality. Brig.-General Hope gave a short sketch of the history of the Hunt and Captain Holmes thanked both the Master and Mrs. Andreae on behalf of the farmers. The health of both Mr. and Mrs. Andreae was drunk with musical honours. As this dinner marked a definite stage in the long and continuous life of the Hunt and the war precluded an earlier celebration in 1945, it is perhaps fitting to give the names of those present, as though some important covert owners and farmers and unfortunately the Honorary Secretary, were absent, those present were all keen supporters and most helpful in keeping foxes to hunt, their land to ride over, walking puppies and maintaining general good will in very difficult times.

General Sir George D. Jeffreys, Major F. H. T. Jervoise, G. W. Harrap, Esq., G. Evans, Esq., Brig.-General J. F. R. Hope, Colonel J. B. Scott, H. K. Goschen, Esq., Lieut.-Colonel M. R. F. Courage, J. W. Simpson, Esq., H. A. Andreae, Esq., M.F.H., Lieut.-Colonel J. A. T. Bower, Lieut.-Commander H. K. Andreae, R.N.V.R., A. R. L. Aylward, Esq., Captain A. J. M. Holmes, Major C. J. P. Ball, Major H. A. Pelly, Lieut.-Colonel H. J. Nicholson, Lieut.-Colonel J. D. Floyd, Major-General Ll. I. G. Morgan-Owen, L. L. Pike, Esq., Captain S. W. Roskill, R.N., R. R. Edgar, Esq., Brigadier M. W. Selby-Lowndes, Major J. A. F. Barthorp, A. D. P. Adams, Esq., J. N. McClean, Esq., J. F. Montagu, Esq., G. R. A. Dolby, Esq., G. B. Barnes, Esq., F. Butler, Esq., B. Butler, Esq., K. Clarence Smith, Esq., John Gray, Esq., G. D. Hunt, Esq., H. Warner, Esq., Lieut.-Colonel J. D. Bibby, R. A. Shortis, Esq.

The following nobleman and gentleman were guests of the Master :—Lieut.-Colonel The Lord Dorchester, one of the best covert owners in the Hunt, and J. Nitch-Smith, Esq.

Amongst those prevented by illness from attending was W. H. Ings, Esq., one of the best sporting farmers in the Hunt.

Mr. Andreae's generosity and sportsmanship in carrying on the mastership during a very difficult period and when suffering great physical pain and disability received recognition by a party given in his honour on 3rd August, 1950, at Burkham House, the home of General Sir George Jeffreys, the Chairman of the Hunt Club. At this party, his portrait mounted on "Black Velvet," painted by Captain Lionel Edwards, was presented to him by the Chairman on behalf of the members and subscribers to the H.H. A silver horn and a handsome book containing the names of all subscribers were also presented.

The puppy walkers have been splendid during the difficult war years and their invaluable care and keenness still continues and produces excellent results.

In recent years Mr. Bryan F. Butler of South Warnborough, a farmer member of the H.H., has earned an international reputation in show-umping contests. His well-known horse "Tankard" won the *Daily Mail* Cup in 1948 and the King George V Cup in 1949. In 1949 Mr. Butler also won the Oxford Gold Cup on "Bruto" and the Harringay on "Tankard."

SONGS OF THE HAMPSHIRE HUNT CLUB.

By The Rev. C. Powlett.

Draw near, ye frail mortals of every degree,
Who heartily sigh and complain,
We'll find you a medicine, without any fee,
Shall quickly alleviate your pain.
    Would you drive away care,
    To the Wheatsheaf repair,
    Where mirth and good humour embrace,
    Our Hampshire Hunt join,
    While young mirth and old wine
    Enliven the joys of the chase !

The squabbles for party and contest for power
We leave to the great ones at court,
The fox-hunter wishes to charm the dull hours
With vigour to keep up the sport.
    Here the soldier forgets
    His old wounds and his debts,
    The sailor, his rocks, sands and storms,
    The priest his solemn face,
    The doctor his grimace,
    The lawyer his pleas and grave forms.
        Would you drive away care, etc.

A soldier[1] accomplished appears in our front,
Whose valour no danger can check ;
With the same eager spirit he leads on the hunt
As Wolfe led him on at Quebec.
    Here he meets with new toils,
    Other conquests and spoils,
    War and hunting pursue the same ends ;
    Yet his laurels fresh bloom
    In the field a like doom,
    On Montcalm, sly Reynard attends.
        Would you drive away care, etc.

A chieftain[2] intrepid now crowds to the van,
His canvas wide spread to the gale ;
With the ardour displayed on the sea of Japan,
He gallops o'er mountain and vale.
    All the horrors combined,
    Of fire, water and wind,
    Ne'er could check him in glory's bright race ;
    Steering still the same track,
    He disdains to look back,
    When Joe[3] gives the signal for chase.
        Would you drive away care, etc.

[1] The " soldier " was General Shirreff of Upton House Old Alresford, father of Admiral Shirreff of Ropley Cottage, member of the old club.

[2] " Chieftain " was Vice-Admiral Sir Hyde Parker, 5th Baronet of Milford Hall, Suffolk. Commander-in-Chief at the victory of August 1781 over the Dutch off the Dogger Bank. Member of the old club.

[3] Joe Hall, huntsman.

A sportsman[4] came next, who in plain English style,
French manners and foppery defies,
His countenance spoke him a man without guile,
The truth you might read in his eyes.
When he points out the way
We with pleasure obey,
And cheerfully follow his call;
O'er the fences we bound,
But if some reach the ground
We laugh at the Cockneys who fall.
                Would you drive away care, etc.

Of tithes and oblations no longer intent,
The parson[5] came hobbling along,
To forward the sport ever anxiously bent,
Though feeble and lost in the throng,
His weak muse and his horse
Have alike run their course,
Long hackney'd, exhausted, and lame
Yet the veteran entreats,
In return for past feats,
Your favour he humbly may claim.
Then to drive away care
He'll to Vernon's repair,
Where wit and good humour embrace,
The Hampshire Hunt join,
While young mirth and old wine
Enliven the joys of the chase!

———

Free from care, from pain, from sorrow,
Haste to Thorny Down to-morrow;
There shall our steeds outstrip the wind,
Whilst time and age creep far behind.
No long vigils of love we keep,
Nor evening's cups protract our sleep;
But e'er the sun has reached the skies,
Fresh as the morn we gaily rise.
                Then free from care, etc.

See, from France yon petit maître!
Thus exclaims the puny creature:
" Comment, sortir avant l'aurore
Sans dejeuner? Tis a great bore."
No trifling fops can ever know
From the brisk chase what pleasures flow;
Joys above those of power and wealth—
Vigour of mind and rosy health.
                Then free from care, etc.

[4] Thomas Ridge of Kilmeston Manor, M.F.H., and President of the old club.

[5] The Rev. Charles Powlett, b. 1728, died 1809, eldest natural son of Charles, 3rd Duke of Bolton, K.G., by Mrs. Lavinia Bastwick (née Fenton) whom he married October 20th, 1751, Rector of Itchen Abbas and St. Martin's, near Looe, in Cornwall, author of the songs, member of the old club.

The mushroom cit who rolls in riches,
Curses the gates, the woods and ditches.
" What ! for a warmin," vilely cries,
" Wenture your necks and wound your eyes ? "
But we will teach the wary Jew
We've our douceurs and premiums too :
Bacchus at night the sportsman warms,
And Venus gives us all her charms.
 Then free from care, etc.

The woods and hills with joy resounding,
Every heart with pleasure bounding ;
What transports in our bosoms glow,
When first we hear the " Tally-ho ! "
Bridegroom and Batchelor lead them on ;
Soon they give way to Turpin's son ;
Now to the head young Herod strives,
Old Windham roars and Wilful drives.
 Then free from care, etc.

Checked by the sheep-cots in the valley
Men of weight gain time to rally ;
Mopping his front and double chin,
Each heavy blue[1] comes puffing in,
Juniper hits it down the way,
Magpies and crows his point betray ;
Through the wet mead and chalky soil
The villain runs his tainted foil.
 Then free from care, etc.

Distressed at length he gains the village
Where of late he roamed for pillage ;
Midst his old haunts he finds no friend,
And Joe's who-whoop proclaims his end.
My rhymes are done ; once more excuse
Your ancient laureate's limping muse,
And here in Dian's joyous court
Drink in full cups the noble sport ;
Then free from care, from pain, from sorrow,
Haste to Thorny Down[2] to-morrow.

---

[1] The Hunt changed from blue to scarlet in 1799, retaining blue for evening wear.

[2] Thorny Down, near Brown Candover, now the property of Major C. J. P. Ball, D.S.O., M.C., of The Manor House, Brown Candover : a member of the club and staunch fox preserver.

CHAPTER V.

NEW FOREST HUNT.

1781–98	Mr. V. H. Gilbert, Lambs Corner (afterwards called Bartley Manor House).
1783	New Forest Hunt Club started at Romsey.
1784	Created the Official Lord Warden's Hounds and given the Royal Button of the Lord Warden.
1800–02	Mr. J. Compton, Minstead Manor.
1802–08	Committee : Lord Cavan, Mr. C. Mitchell, Mr. Williams.
1808–14	Mr. J. Warde, Foxlease.
1814–28	Mr. S. Nicoll, Lyndhurst.
1828–38	Mr. W. Wyndham, Burnford House, Bramshaw.
1838–42	Mr. C. W. Codrington, Burnford House, Bramshaw.
1842–53	Captain L. Sheddon, Elcombs, Lyndhurst.
1853–54	Mr. T. Theobald, Forest Lodge.
1854–60	The Rev. E. Timson, Tatchbury Mount.
1860–69	Captain W. Morant, Brockenhurst Park.
1869–74	Mr. W. C. Standish, South Stoneham and New Park, Brockenhurst.
1874–78	Sir R. Graham, Jessamine Cottage, Lyndhurst, and Fritham Lodge.
1878–85	Mr. G. A. E. T.-G.-Meyrick (afterwards Sir George), Hinton Admiral.
1885	Country divided, East and West.

EAST.

1885–86	Major Browne, Hall Court.
1886–89	Mr. F. Bradburne, Lyburn.
1889–94	Mr. S. Pearce, Loperwood Manor.
1894–95	Mr. H. M. Powell, Wilverley Park.

WEST.

1885–91	Mr. J. Mills, Bisterne.
1891–95	Sir J. H. Thursby, Holmhurst.
1895	The country was then reunited.
1895–99	Mr. H. M. Powell, Wilverley Park.
1899–1900	Mr. C. Heseltine (afterwards Lieutenant-Colonel, O.B.E.), Walhampton Park.
1900–05	Mr. H. F. Compton, Minstead Manor.

1905–07	Mr. H. M. Powell (second mastership), Wilverley Park.
1907–11	Mr. W. de P. Cazenove, Langley Manor.
1911–13	Mr. J. A. Cooke-Hurle, Jessamine Cottage, Lyndhurst.
	Major E. F. Cooke-Hurle, Northerwood Farm, Lyndhurst.
1913–14	Major E. F. Cooke-Hurle, Northerwood Farm, Lyndhurst.
1914–15	Major H. T. Timson, Tatchbury Mount.
1915–18	A Committee (Mr. E. L. Wingrove, Field Master).
1919–	Sir G. L. T.-G.-Meyrick, Bart., Hinton Admiral.

LORD WARDEN'S MANIFESTO ON HUNTING IN THE NEW FOREST.

ADVERTISEMENT.

No hounds are to be permitted to hunt in the New Forest except the Lord Warden's and (if he should choose to come) the Duke of Richmond's, but in the month of April, *viz.*; from the 1st till the 30th, both days inclusive.

That no pack be suffered to go out more than three times in one week, and, *to prevent confusion, it is agreed that the Lord Warden's are to hunt Monday, Wednesday and Friday.* Mr. Groves[1] to hunt Tuesday, Thursday and Saturday, and no more than two packs of hounds to be in the Forest at the same time. Any strange pack must give way for the time, that there may be no more than two packs at one time.

The earths are not to be stopt till half-past-four in the morning, and no hounds to be thrown off before five.

The earths during the month of April not to be stopt, but by the keepers or their servants.

The keepers have orders not to suffer any fires to be lighted on the earths, nor any person to stand on the earth to keep out the foxes ; no tarriers to be taken out or foxes dug in the month of April.

The following letter was also sent by Colonel N. Heywood, Deputy Warden and Equerry to H.R.H. The Duke of Gloucester, addressed to Mr. Grove :—

SOUTHAMPTON.
January 27th, 1784.

Sir,
The keepers and others in the New Forest represented to His Royal Highness The Duke of Gloucester the great scarcity of foxes at present in the county, he thinks proper to revise some regulations that were agreed to with the Duke of Richmond and Lord Eglinton when they had liberty to bring their hounds in the Forest. He wishes also to add

[1] W. Chaffyn Grove of Waddon and Zeals, M.P. Shaftesbury 1764, Weymouth 1768, M.F.H., hunted round his estates and in Cranborne Chase.

a little to the regulations, as the necessity appears greater at this time. As your hounds have occasionally been in the Forest, he commands me to send you a copy of the regulations, and he hopes, as the Forest Hounds will strictly adhere to them, there will be no objection on your part. *The Lord Warden has given his name to Mr. Gilbert's hounds, and for the future he will look upon them as the established pack of the country*, but does not mean to prevent your hounds coming out under the enclosed regulations.

I have the honour to be, Sir, etc.

To Mr. Grove.

New Forest Foxhounds.

Mr. V. H. Gilbert, 1781-98.

The first Master of Foxhounds in the New Forest was Mr. Vincent Hawkins Gilbert of Lamb's Corner, afterwards called Bartley Manor House. Everything was very well done and earned the approval of the famous Mr. Peter Beckford of Steepledon, Dorset. The latter does not mention Mr. Gilbert by name in his famous book *Thoughts upon Hare and Fox Hunting*, but often refers to him, and letter XV alludes to Mr. Gilbert's method of stopping the field pressing on his hounds. He begins by shouting " Hold Hard!" as loud as he can. If anyone should persist after that he begins, moderately at first, saying : " I beg, sir, you will stop your horse " ; " Pray, sir, stop" ; " God bless you, sir, stop " ; but rising, in the case of a persistent offender, to " God damn your blood, sir, stop your horse ! "

In 1783 a club was established at Romsey, but the meetings were altered in May 1790. Mr. Gilbert appears to have been a man of action and an entry in his diary reads " Horsewhipped one White for being impertinent and beating the hounds." He discharged Woods, his first huntsman, in July 1781 for neglecting the hounds, but allowed him to come back in October, " having made proper submission and asked pardon." In May 1790 he was finally discharged. He then engaged Tull for the season 1791–92, Fox for the season 1792–93, and Tom Sebright in 1795. Woods was somewhat of a miser and about £1,000 was found in his cottage when he died in 1820, £39 of which was in silver.

Mr. Gilbert regarded his best run as one from Burley Beacon, killing his fox at Hasely Heath after a run of four hours. All the chief residents of the Forest supported him—Lords Wallingford, Poulett, Hinton and Euston, Sir Thomas Tancred, Sir Thomas

Mr. V. H. Gilbert, M.F.H., 1781-98, Founder of the New Forest Hunt.

Mr. H. M. Powell, Master, New Forest Hunt, 1894-99 (East portion 1894-95), 1905-07.

Heathcote, Sir Philip Jennings-Clarke, Messrs. A. Drummond, Warton, Yalden, Compton, Morant, Sloane (afterwards Sloane Stanley), Eyre, Foyle, Serle, Grove, LeBroque, Reynolds, and the well-known name of Mr. Brocas, also the Deputy Ranger, Colonel Heywood. Mr. Compton of Minstead Manor and Mr. Eyre of Warrens and Mr. John Morant of Brockenhurst Park have still descendants holding their estates. Mr. Gilbert kept his hounds at Northerwood Park, occasionally taking them to Cranborne.

The badge on the New Forest Hunt button is of great interest and antiquity. It is a Royal badge worn by the keepers and other servants who wear the Crown livery in the Forest. The stirrup was presumably chosen from that known as Rufus' stirrup in the Verderers' Hall (actually 16th century). The reason of its adoption by the New Forest Hunt was that in 1784 in the edict given by the Lord Warden, laying down who should hunt and when hunting should take place in the Forest, the New Forest Hunt was adopted as the Lord Warden's hounds. Also, on January 27th, 1784, Colonel Heywood, Equerry and Deputy Ranger to the Lord Warden, H.R.H. The Duke of Gloucester, states in a letter to Mr. Grove of Fern, Wilts., who also hunted in the Forest, " The Lord Warden has given his name to Mr. Gilbert's hounds." As the Lord Warden's hounds the Hunt could wear the ancient Royal badge. This is the oldest and most interesting button now worn in Hampshire. The H.H. button, the only other Royal button, was probably not given until 1795, and could not have been given before 1788.

Mr. Gilbert died in 1798 aged 80 years and was buried at Eling Church on October 9th.

Mr. J. Compton, 1800-03.

He was succeeded by Mr. John Compton, the Squire of Minstead, but he did not take office till 1800. Tom Sebright remained as huntsman. His son, Tom Sebright, used to say he learned his fondness for hunting when running with Mr. Villebois' hounds near Romsey as a boy. He lived with Mr. Musters and was whipper-in to Squire Osbaldeston, and for forty years was huntsman to Lord FitzWilliam. The father was quite a huntsman of renown in his day. The "Druid" said that he showed all the science of " a master forester."

The country was not hunted between 1798 to 1800. It is interesting that exactly a hundred years later another Compton of Minstead Manor stepped into the breach in 1900 when the two brothers Heseltine volunteered for the South African War. Mr. Compton only remained in office for three years when a committee succeeded.

A Committee, 1803—08.

In this year a committee of " all the talents " took control. They were Lord Cavan of Eaglehurst, Mr. Charles Mitchell and Mr. Williams. During their years of office King George III used to stay at Cuffnells, Lyndhurst, generally on his way to and from his house at Weymouth. His rooms remained unchanged in furniture and hangings until the Second World War.

Mr. John Warde, 1808-14.

The famous Mr. John Warde, called " The Father of Fox Hunters," became master in this year. Mr. Warde had started as a master of Harriers in 1770, hunting hare around his seat at Squerries in Kent. He soon changed to foxhounds and left Kent in 1776 ; subsequently he was master of foxhounds in Oxfordshire, Northamptonshire and Warwickshire, before bringing his great knowledge and experience to the Forest. His kennels were first at the King's House and then at his home at Fox Lease. His hounds were renowned for their size, one stallion hound measuring 27in., and they were known as " John Warde's jack asses." However, they were also remarkable for perseverance, steadiness and nose. There is little doubt that the breeding of such large hounds with great bone and fine ribs was of service to the modern foxhound. Mr. Warde had a terrible disaster in 1814 when madness broke out in his kennels and forty couple of hounds were lost.

Mr. Warde was always ready for a joke and made everybody cheerful around him. On one occasion, however, he was not very successful. A very rich gentleman lived in the Forest and hunted, but no one was ever asked into his house. Mr. Warde determined to get something to eat and drink out of him. On this occasion the gentleman had returned home before hounds found, but when they did find, an excellent run resulted ending in a kill. Passing his house, Mr. Warde resolved to try for some hospitality. The footman first said his master was at dinner. John Warde would not take this for an answer, and was shown into the dining room where the gentleman was dining with three servants in attendance. The run was duly recounted and after going over it again two or three times and regretting the gentleman's absence, still nothing was offered, neither bite nor sup. He gave up in despair, but just as he reached the door turned and said : " Will you allow your footman to bring me a glass of small beer ! " It is not related whether he ever got even this cheap refreshment.

In correspondence he was short and to the point. On being asked for the character of a whipper-in he replied : " Dear Sir, I beg to say if J. B.——had been worth keeping I should not have parted with him. Yours truly, John Warde."

On leaving the pack in 1814, John Warde became Master of the Craven Hounds being altogether M.F.H. for 56 or 57 years.

The Peterborough Show probably owes much to Mr. Warde's summer shows at Squerries as these were the first shows for foxhounds ever held.

Abbey was his huntsman and Neverd and Zack Goddard his whippers-in, of whom, Neverd accompanied his master to Berkshire.

Mr. S. Nicoll, 1814-28.

Mr. Samuel Nicoll succeeded to the mastership and hunted hounds himself. His kennels were at Sir Charles Burrard's house at Lyndhurst. At first Joseph and George Grant were his whippers-in and then Joe Peckham turned hounds to him. Nimrod describes Joe Peckham as taking his fancy very much " a good rough-looking fellow, born in the Forest, and about as hard as one of his native oaks." He kept about forty couple of first-class hounds, breeding about half and getting the young draft from the Duke of Beaufort yearly. His bitch pack earned great renown and one season are said never to have missed their fox. Both he and his staff were very well mounted and he was a great kennel manager.

Mr. Nicoll showed he was a man not to be trifled with on his first day in the New Forest. Some of the field were wantonly pressing on the pack after he had begged them not to do so. He then soundly abused them, to the utter astonishment of one offender at any rate, who expressed surprise that Mr. Nicoll should use such language to a committee man. " The committee be damned," said Mr. Nicoll, " you are not worth damning singly, so I'll damn you all in a lump." " Nimrod," when he paid the Forest a visit in 1825, is quite enthusiastic as to the establishment in general. He was generally courteous in the field, but on one occasion a Southampton butcher, by name Alison, aggravated him beyond endurance by continually over-riding hounds. " Upon my word, Mr. Nicoll, I don't understand this, sir ; I did not come out to be damned," said the butcher. " Then go home and be damned," replied Mr. Nicoll.

Mr. Nicoll's ready wit was well known and a reply he made to Lord Cavan is typical. A covert had been drawn blank and Lord Cavan came up to say that two hounds—" Petticoat " and " Harlot "—were running back in covert. " That is impossible, but it shows what your mind is running on."

In order to train his young hounds to ignore " haunch " Mr. Nicoll kept a deer at his kennels. He had a notably fine voice and his cheer always acted as a wonderful stimulant to his hounds. No day was too long for him and often he had to find his way home in complete darkness. Joe Peckham was then a great help to him as he knew every Forest path and Mr. Nicoll used to catch hold of Joe's whip lash. Joe kept some very fine pigs. They looked so well, the master one day told him, that he was taking the hound meal. " Lord have mercy on you, master," said Joe, " it all goes down the hounds' throats." Unfortunately for Joe, Sir John Cope came to stay with the master, who, looking out of his window when dressing, saw a man going down a hedge with something on his back. The man was followed and overtaken and he proved to be Joe with two bushels of meal. The culprit was discharged, but the master could not do without him and had to forgive him and take him back into his former service.

In summer Mr. Nicoll was a keen yachtsman and his small yacht *The Louisa* was well known in the Solent. One day the Yacht Club was excited by a strange signal apparently being flown from the yacht. Telescopes were used in vain and a boat was sent to make enquiries. The answer was " No. 2 pair of trousers hung up to dry."

Mr. Nicoll's dress was not his strong point at any time. His hunting boots were about the same colour, tops and bottoms, and badly cleaned as well. One day the master was to draw some coverts on the outskirts of the Forest newly acquired by a rather particular gentleman. Lord Lisle asked Mr. Nicoll to make a point of turning out smartly as " first impressions are everything." The master turned up in a very old coat of purple hue, very old boots and breeches and an ancient white hat. This he flattened down on arrival, saying " First impressions are everything, my Lord." Joe Peckham on this occasion wore a very stained kennel coat and had a boot on one leg and a gaiter on the other.

In a good hunt one day from Bramshaw, Mr. Nicoll again showed that he was no respecter of persons when annoyed. Hounds ran by Paultons and then through Sir Thomas Heathcote's coverts at Embley and on to Broadlands. At Embley no one was allowed in the coverts and the gates of Broadlands were locked and hounds could not scale the park wall. Mr. Nicoll ordered Joe Peckham to get off and burst the door open and let the hounds in after and then remarked " This is fox hunting with a vengeance. We are first prohibited by a baronet and then locked out by a lord." However, Lord Palmerston, the owner of Broadlands and a very good sportsman, took it all in very good part and asked the master and the field to lunch with him and all ended happily. It is not recorded if Mr. Nicoll killed his fox, but no doubt he was properly accounted for.

" Nimrod " was astonished at the way the Forest heavy-weight Mr. George Harbin of Fritham, weighing 20 stone, got over the country and displayed all the activity of a 10-stone man.

Among his many supporters Mr. John Pulteney of Norther-wood was one of the best. Lords Montague of Beaulieu, Hedley, Cavan and Lisle, Messrs. Andrew Drummond of Cadlands, the Rev. John Lukin, William Sloane Stanley of Paultons, George Eyre of Warrens and Robert Eyre of Cadnam, Chudley Haynes and Sir Hussey Vivian were all keen followers. Sir William Hoste also, renowed whether he hunted in the Forest, the Hambledon or the Shires, Admiral Aitcheson, Mr. Henry Combe Compton[2] and the Rev. E. Timson who was fitting himself for his mastership later on, also the Rev. W. Wilder of Eling, very knock-kneed and no beauty, but went very well to hounds.

In 1825, when hounds were running across New Park, near Brockenhurst, Mr. Nicoll warned Sir Bellingham Graham, who

[2] Mr. H. C. Compton had a house at Quorndon and left a good name behind him both as a sportsman and a gentleman. When at Eton he and George Osbaldeston walked to Ascot and back to see one race run between school hours. He was three years junior to Osbaldeston.

was staying with him, that he must come to a gate as they had a deer fence in front of them.   Sir Bellingham, a thruster from the Shires, however, rode straight on and Mr. Tom Smith followed.   Sir Bellingham's horse " Beeswax " got over the palings and ditch, but his horse pecked badly on landing. Mr. Tom Smith on " The General " cleared palings and ditch perfectly.   Sir Bellingham offered him 250 guineas for his horse, but Smith wisely refused, though he had only given 45 guineas three months before.   He never had reason to regret his refusal and afterwards refused still more for him in the Pytchley country.

On December 7th, 1827, *Aesop* records that the Staghounds met at Mr. Henry Coombe Compton's Manor House at Minstead and drew Boldre Wood, Furze Brake, where a stag was found which went to the border of Beaulieu Manor and then turned towards Brockenhurst.   The stag was secured at the head of the mill by the active assistance of Major Rose and Mr. C. Vivian. Among the big field were Rt. Hon. Sir George Rose and General Sir Hussey Vivian and several officers also followed the hounds. It is not stated what pack of staghounds—presumably they would be the Royal pack.   The stag does not appear to have been harboured and roused by the tufters in the orthodox way, but " found " like a fox.   The report given in *Aesop* (p. 181) is probably inaccurate in wording.   At that date unauthorised packs would not have been allowed.   " Nimrod " met the well-known Rev. William Butler, the rector of Frampton in Dorset, in the Forest.   He told him it was the fortieth successive April he had hunted there.   " Billy " Butler was always good humoured, wet weather or fine, good sport or bad, and was greatly liked by all, including the Prince Regent.

Mr. Nicoll resigned at his tenth season in 1828, selling his pack for 1,000 guineas to Lord Kintore who hunted the V.W.H. country.   Mr. Stephen Terry, the diarist, alludes to him as follows : " Nicoll, very clever, given to jocularity, his ardour and language in a burst run most animating."   Mr. Nicoll added poetic talent to his abilities as a huntsman and his poem " The New Forest Hunt " is given at the end of the chapter.

The Hunt also had the reflected honour of owning " Justice " the sire of the famous Beaufort " Justice."[3]   The late Lord Bathurst said in his book *The Breeding of Fox Hounds*, " The

---

[3] This famous hound and his son ' Jasper ' were bred by Mr. Wyndham of Dinton, the father of the next master.

' Justice' blood probably flows in three out of every four fox-hounds of the present day."

Mr. Nicoll apparently did not receive all the support that he required though he continued to show good sport. Just before resigning he had a parting shaft of wit at his detractors. A hound called " Gratitude " was ridden over by a follower. Mr. Nicoll, with his eye on the grumblers, said : " For God's sake, don't kill ' Gratitude,' it is already reduced to a hound's name." " Nimrod " was always high in his praise. He says " His seat was good and his strength of arm was of use to his horses in assisting them over bog and quagmire of that—to me—infernal country." " Nimrod " was never complementary to Hampshire whether North or South. Mr. Nicoll's sons took his eye. His remarks on Sam, aged 12, are given in the Hursley chapter, and he says of the youngest, aged seven, " in his scarlet coat and hunting whip, he and his pony are allowed to be quite unique."

Mr. W. Wyndham, 1828-38.

Mr. William Wyndham of Dinton House, Wiltshire, now became master, living at Burnford House, Bramshaw, during his years of office. Mr. Wyndham was born in 1796 and married in 1831 Ellen, daughter of the Rev. Samuel Heathcote of Bramshaw Hill, Hants. He succeeded to the family estates at Dinton in 1841. He was J.P., D.L. and Member of Parliament for South Wilts. The family had held Dinton since 1689, but it was sold in 1916 by his eldest son who had inherited Orchard Wyndham in Somerset on the death of the last Lord Egremont's widow in 1876. Mr. Wyndham died 1862.

The kennels were moved to Bramshaw, which move was deplored by the sporting correspondent " Nim South," who said there was nothing now to do on a rainy day. In Mr. Nicoll's day the kennels had been a great meeting place for all sportsmen on non-hunting days.

Mr. Wyndham hunted hounds himself having learnt much from his father who had a very smart pack at Dinton with which he had hunted much of the South and West Wilts and Wilton countries. His servants were William Butler and Henry Gillett, afterwards huntsman to Captain Sheddon. Sam Powell, 2nd horseman and whipper-in, and Sharp from the Hambledon also served him. The Royal Buckhounds visited the Forest during Mr. Wyndham's mastership. At their first meet at

Lyndhurst in 1836 about 2,000 people turned out to see them. Among the more notable were the Duke of Beaufort, M.F.H., Lords Bateman, Cavan and Uxbridge, Lord Adolphus Fitz Clarence, Mr. Wyndham M.F.H., Mr. Sam Nicoll, ex-M.F.H., Sir Edward Hulse and Mr. H. C. Compton from the Forest. Mr. J. T. Villebois, M.F.H., Mr. Donnithorne Tayler, M.F.H., Mr. John King, M.F.H., Sir John Cope, Bart., M.F.H., Sir John B. Mill, Bart., M.F.H., Mr. T. A. Smith, M.F.H., Mr. James W. Scott, M.P., from the other packs in the county, and J. W. Erle-Drax, M.F.H., and the Rev. H. Farr Yeatman, ex-M.F.H., from Dorset and Mr. G. B. Hankey, M.F.H., from the Surrey Union. Mr. C. W. Codrington, soon to succeed Mr. Wyndham, was also present and many other well-known sportsmen. Whether the sport was up to the standard of so distinguished a field is not recorded.

In 1838 the Earl of Errol again brought the Royal Buckhounds to the Forest. Their first meet was at Bolton's Bench. Lords Kingston and Portman were out with Mr. Wyndham, M.F.H., Mr. John King, M.F.H., and the redoubtable Rev. Billy Butler looking very cheerful as usual, this being his fifty-third successive spring meeting in the Forest.

One of Mr. Wyndham's supporters was " Dicky " Wyse, referred to also as a great supporter of the H.H. (p. 66). This old stagecoachman once arranged to swop horses with Mr. Jack Hewett, a sporting butcher from Southampton who used to horse a couple of coaches. The conditions were that neither should see the horses. Wyse's horse was a roarer and Hewett's had a bad spavin. Hewett soon discovered his mount's failing, but said nothing ; the next day, however, Wyse passed his shop on three legs, returning from a hunt. He said in passing " No friendship in horse dealing, Mr. Hewett, no friendship in horse dealing ! "

On another occasion a hunting parson who had a bald head and was very plain in feature and knock-kneed said to Wyse " That is a very ugly horse you are on." " Yes, sir," said Dicky blandly, " and I should say beauty was not by when you were dropped."

Mr. Wyndham felt he ought to devote more of his time to Wiltshire and handed over house and kennels to Mr. Codrington his brother-in-law in 1838. He hunted the South Wilts country then at his own expense until 1848. His pack which were rather

slow and lumbering but good line hunters were then sold for
£400. His brother Francis succeeded him, collecting a pack
of exactly opposite type and showed good sport there for the
next ten years.

Mr. C. W. Codrington, 1838-42.

Mr. Charles William Codrington succeeded his brother-in-
law as master, living at Bramshaw. He had considerable
experience of hunting and despite his great weight (he rode
22 stone when in the Forest) he had hunted hounds quite
successfully. From 1814–24 he was Master of the Old Berkshire
Hunt. In 1814 he married the eldest daughter of Mr. Wyndham
of Dinton. He also founded the South Wilts Hunt with
kennels at Sutton Veney. Jem Treadwell had served him
as 2nd whipper-in with the Old Berkshire Hunt and now
ably assisted him in Wiltshire. Mr. Codrington had a great
knowledge of all matters connected with hunting and kennel
management and a marvellous memory for hound pedigrees.
In the sixteen years he served Mr. Codrington, Treadwell
learnt much, but he was not destined to show his abilities in the
Forest. In 1836 the pack was sold to Mr. Hall of Holbrook
House and again in 1837 to Mr. J. V. Farquharson of Langton
House, called the Meynell of the West, Treadwell accompanied
the hounds. Mr. Codrington bought Sir Walter Carew's
hounds from Devonshire and hunted the Maiden Bradley,
Black Dog Woodlands with them, Mr. Wyndham agreeing to
bring his hounds from the New Forest to cub hunt at Dinton
and to leave sufficient for his brother Francis to hunt that
country two days a week. In 1838 Mr. Codrington engaged
George Whitmere as his huntsman and brought David Edwards,
known as " Humpy David " as whipper-in. This man was
afterwards with Mr. T. A. Smith in 1842 and then with Mr.
Montague of the South Berks where he was a great success.
Mr. Codrington was known as " the Great Western " and
Mr. Stephen Terry says " his horses seemed uncomfortable under
him, he constantly chiding them." This is, perhaps, hardly
to be wondered at with 22 stone on their backs. Mr.
Codrington, however, showed good sport and some of his
hunts have been recorded.

On November 20th of his first season a fox from Lyndhurst
ran through the New Park enclosures, running very fast over the
open at Heathy Ditton, leaving most of the field inside the

enclosure. Mr. John Drummond, Major Gilbert and the Rev. E. Timson were noted as having ridden well up to hounds.

The *Sporting Review*, Vol. III, of 1840 gives two other good hunts, a precis of which is given. In November 1839 a fox from No Man's Land, near Bramshaw, took the field a hunt of nearly three hours, and was killed at Grimstead, two or three miles East of Salisbury. " Humpy David " only was near them at the end and he had to ask their line on several occasions. This meet gave a point of about twelve miles and double that distance as hounds ran. The other hunt chronicled was from Wilverley Post on the 28th of December, 1939. Hounds found in Holmsley Enclosure and the fox took them over Picket Plain to Picket Post, skirted the Rowe Enclosure, passing through Broomy, over the open to Ashley. He then continued over the heath as if for Studley Head, but he was headed and a check occurred ; hounds again hit his line and ran into him in the open after 1 hour and 50 minutes. Mr. H. C. Compton and his brother Captain C. F. Compton, R.N., Lauchlan B. Mackinnon, R.N., Colonel Robbins and the hunt staff only were up at the finish.

Six couple of hounds of Mr. Codrington's hounds were sold for £600, a great price at that time and a proof of his knowledge of their breeding. He died in 1842, much regretted by all his friends and supporters.

Captain L. Sheddon, 1842-52.

Captain Lindsay Sheddon, formerly an officer of the 17th Lancers, was elected master on October 15th, 1842. There were no hounds, horses or servants, or even kennels, in the country. This did not daunt Captain Sheddon and he got drafts from the Quorn to start with, and boldly advertised the opening meet for November 15th. The 5,000 fallow deer in the Forest did not improve matters with hounds unbroken to deer. In 1843 Captain Sheddon bought the Hursley Pack and afterwards relied on Mr. T. A. Smith's drafts. Henry Gillett was his huntsman, formerly 1st whip to Mr. Wyndham with the South Wilts Hunt. Walks were very few in the Forest at this time which prevented breeding to any extent. Kennels were built at Furzy Lawn, one mile from Lyndhurst. Mr. H. C. Compton gave the land and several members subscribed £50 each. He was able to show Mr. Wyndham during a short visit to his old haunts a really fast hunt from near Ringwood, killing in the open near Woodlands—a 12-mile point in 1 hour and

5 minutes. Mr. Wyndham said it was the finest hunt he had ever seen. Sport was very good and a series of long, straight hunts were enjoyed and two or three hunts giving 10 or 12 mile points were recorded.

Ladies are first mentioned as hunting with Captain Sheddon, possibly encouraged by the fine riding of his wife. Lady Rose Lovell, Mrs. Robbins, Mrs. Rowley and Miss Gore (afterwards Lady Edward Thynne) were all keen followers and good horse-women. Many gentlemen were elected to the Hunt Club during his mastership, no less than 43 being elected after 1842. Good sport continued until Capt. Sheddon's last day, when a fine hunt from Brockenhurst concluded a very successful term of office in 1852.

In 1847 a painting of the N.F. Hunt at the Yew Tree, Lyndhurst, was made in water-colour by Admiral Sir Charles Burrard of Lyndhurst (1793–1870). Northerwood House stands up well in the background and the whole makes a very charming picture, but there is no attempt at portraiture. This is, how-ever, the only painting of the N.F.H. that is known.

Mr. Tom Smith was again the hero of an incident in the New Forest in the early 1840's. The Royal Staghounds met at Stoney Cross in Lord Rosslyn's mastership (1841–46) intend-ing to take a particular old stag which had been doing much damage to cottage gardens. When roused the stag went away well and hounds raced after him followed by some 500 horse-men. Mr. Smith let everybody pass him and watched hounds closely as they entered some covert ; he saw the same leading hounds emerge that he saw enter, but only two couple came out, the others having apparently got on to another line. Mr. Smith halloed as loud as he could, but only four or five followers came to his halloa. He went on with his two couple for eight or ten miles to an enclosure called The Frenchs. Here Mr. Smith found the stag laying in some high bracken with his antlers right back. He whipped him up and he again went away for some four or five miles. He jumped the enclosure palings and kept near his hounds, now reduced to one couple. He saw the stag take soil in a stream and, sitting on the bank, he again halload loud and often. A forest keeper arrived and he was sent to fetch Charles Davis, the Royal huntsman. A whipper-in came and, at last, the master, Lord Rosslyn. He asked who had gone away with the two couple. Seeing Mr. Smith, he then said . " Mr. Smith, you must have been the person." Mr. Smith pleaded guilty and was told that he ought to have stopped them. " Stop them," replied Mr. Smith, " I might as well try and stop the Thames. I had enough to do to keep within sight of them." Lord Rosslyn again marked his disapproval and Mr. Smith said " When I want a character I shall not come to your lordship for it." The antlers were sawn off when the stag was taken and offered to Mr. Smith, but after his altercation with the master he would not accept them. The stag was taken to Swinley Paddocks at Ascot. This incident is referred to again on page 186.

Mr. T. Theobald, 1852-54.

Mr. Theobald Theobald of Sutton Courtney, who lived at Forest Lodge, Lyndhurst whilst master, now took control for a brief period. He had previously hunted the country between Bath and Warminster. His huntsman was Smith, formerly huntsman to Lord Folkestone's harriers. Mr. Theobald Theobald afterwards lived at Sutton Courtney, Berkshire, and was master of the Craven Hounds, 1858–62. He was sixth son of Thomas Theobald of Winchester, born in 1808 and died in 1884.

Rev. E. Timson, 1854-60.

The Reverend Edward Timson of Tatchbury Mount, a member of an old Forest family, took over the mastership and brought hounds from Cornwall to his own home at Tatchbury Mount, moving the kennels from Furzy Lawn. For one season only Sam Powell hunted the hounds. He was succeeded by John Donnicomb and he again by William Hawtin from the Bedale. Mr. Timson showed some excellent sport of which the following hunts are examples.

On February 10th, 1857, hounds found in Mr. Stanley's plantations and hunted steadily up to Crow's Nest. They then raced their fox for 40 minutes by the telegraph to Eyeworth Wood by the Royal Oak and Fritham to Holmhill and Puck Pitts, where this good fox was marked to ground. Donnicomb hunted the hounds very well.

Another fine hunt took place on November 19th, 1859, from Stairsley owned by that great preserver of foxes, the Duke of Buccleugh. The fox ran through King's Copse, over Hertford Heath, along the Ipley River to Ferney Croft and the Deer Leap to Langley Manor, by the Marchwood coverts to Denny Wood, where hounds were whipped off after 20 miles. The following gentlemen were noted as being well to the fore in this hunt :

Sir Henry Paulet, Bart., Captains Heath, Martin and Buckworth
Powell, and A. Gore, Messrs. Palmer, Shrubb and Carter among
others. Few followers were at the finish when hounds ran out
of scent. The huntsman was always well in his place and
Captains Timson and Gore, Messrs. Palmer, Shrubb and Carter
stayed with hounds throughout this long hunt.

Captain W. S. Morant, 1860-69.

Captain William Samuel Morant, youngest son of Mr. John
Morant of Brokenhurst, succeeded and hunted hounds himself.
The Morant family had prospered in Jamaica in the 17th century
and his great grandfather Edward had been M.P. for Lymington
and other places. His grandfather and father had lived at
Brokenhurst Park, which is still owned by the family. Kennels
were moved back to Furzy Lawn ; William Hawtin continued
with the hounds as kennel huntsman, providing a son also a little
later as whipper-in. During Captain Morant's time the hunt
uniform was changed to scarlet coats with green collars and
green waistcoats, the old button being retained.

Mr. W. C. Standish, 1869-74.

Mr. William Cecil Standish of South Stoneham House now
brought his own hounds from the Hursley of which pack he
had been master since 1862. Mr. Standish resided also at
New Park, Brockenhurst. Presumably he would use the
kennels at Furzy Lawn when distance to the meets made this
an advantage. Mr. Standish also hunted hounds himself,
Summers being his kennel huntsman. Hounds were kenneled
at Mr. Standish's house. On his retirement, due to ill-health,
hounds and horses were sold at Furzy Lawn kennels. The
former fetched £1,350 and the latter averaged 120 guineas,
which well showed that Mr. Standish and his staff had been
well mounted. Mr. Standish had started the Pau hounds in
the 40's when staying abroad as a young man.

Sir R. Graham, 1874-78.

Sir Reginald Henry Graham, 8th Baronet of Norton Conyers,
near Ripon in Yorkshire, son of the famous Sir Bellingham,
succeeded Mr. Standish. Sir Reginald bought the Craven
Hounds, 70 couple for £500, thus Mr. Villebois' blood must be
strong in the country still. Mr. Henry Chaplin also gave him
18 couple from the Blankney. For two years he lived at
Jessamine Cottage, Lyndhurst, and after his marriage in 1876 at

I

Fritham Lodge. He had foxhunting bred in him and was a friend and pupil of Lord Henry Bentinck. He used the Blankney in consequence for building up his pack and also the Craven. After Jack Goddard left in 1875 Charles Hawtin then acted as kennel huntsman and 1st whipper-in ; he died in 1877 and was buried at Emery Down. Alfred Mandeville then whipped in in his place. Jim Reynolds was 2nd whipper-in. Sir Reginald had been master of the Cotswold, 1871–73, a bad accident causing his resignation. His father, Sir Bellingham, had been master of the Quorn, Atherstone and Badsworth, as well as the Hambledon for three months. Sir Reginald described the Forest country as "the most difficult to hunt" from a huntsman's point of view that he knew, but he also said that, given a scent, hounds ran as hard as he had seen them run anywhere. He remarked, too, that in spring the Forest often carried a scent when the ground was baked dry and hard. This is probably accounted for by the heather retaining a body scent and partly, no doubt, by the state of a dog fox at this season.

The Duke of Beaufort visited the Forest for two days, bringing his hounds on April 15th, 1875. A huge field turned out to see the Duke kill a fox on the first day, but he was not so fortunate on the second day. Sir Reginald's bitch pack soon achieved a reputation and were known as " The Fast Ladies."

Sir Reginald's best days with the N.F.H. appear to have been : the first, with his " Fast Ladies," on February 14th, 1876, after heavy snow, he got to the meet at 1.30 at Brockenhurst Bridge. He found at once in the Park and ran *via* Boldre, Stockley, Frame, Pigbush, back through Woodfidley and Denny and caught his fox by Denny Lodge. This was a hunt of 55 minutes at racing pace without a check. Sir Claud de Crespigny and Sir Reginald were alone at the kill. This was the fastest hunt Sir Reginald ever saw in his long and varied career.

On March 11th of the same year a stout fox went away from New Copse through Perry Wood, sharp right across the railway to Whitley, back through New Copse, Lady Cross, Frame, Hawk Hill and on to Beaulieu Heath, heading for Norley across the farm on the fox was rolled once on the Heath within fifty yards of Norley Wood. This hunt was an hour and a half. The pace very fast from Hawk Hill, and the ground was very heavy. The dog pack was out on this occasion, only six of the field were up at the kill : besides the Master, Lord Henry Scott, M.P., Sir Claude de Crespigny, Messrs. Powell-

Montgomery, Duplessis, Emms. The 2nd whipper-in, Prinner, was also up. The 1st whipper-in, Charles Hawtin, had to stay in the kennels owing to the death of William Andrews, the kennelman. On November 6th, 1877, another red-letter day occurred. The meet was at Ower and a fox was soon found at Embley. After being raced about the large coverts the fox was pushed out towards Pauncefote Farm, left-handed to Greenhill, down the meadows towards Romsey. He was headed by a mob of foot people and hounds raced him up the meadows to Great Bridge, pulling him down by Timsbury Mill. The Master, Alfred Mandeville, who had replaced Hawtin who had died that year, the 2nd whipper-in and Mr. S. Carter of Totton alone represented the field.

In the 1874-75 season Sir Reginald killed 19 brace of foxes in 96 days, frost stopping hunting on 12 days. In the next season 1875-76 he killed 23½ brace of foxes in 89 days. Sir Reginald, in his *Foxhunting Recollection*, writes : " I have nothing but the most pleasant recollections of those happy hunting grounds in the New Forest, and in spite of ' Time,' who steals our hours away, my thoughts can still linger in a vision of those delightful spring mornings when I drew Matley Bog, and did not draw in vain." Sir Reginald was a true sportsman and could appreciate the beauties of wild hunting. He was not only a hunting man, but had served with the 14th Regiment in the Crimea, 1854-55, and was afterwards Captain in the Rifle Brigade in 1856. He was a J.P. and D.L. for the North Riding and a J.P. for the West Riding of Yorkshire and so had a busy life. It was regretted that his term of his mastership was not longer.

The Chairman of the Hunt in Sir Reginald's time was Sir Henry Paulet of Testwood, a sound and tactful sportsman. Among the best supporters were Mr. Henry Compton of Minstead, called by Sir Reginald " that model country gentleman " ; General Parker, an old Life Guards man, who found the fast ladies a bit too fast for him ; Captain Buckworth Powell of Foxlease, an old Grenadier ; Lord Normanton of Somerly ; Mr. Bradburne of Lyburn ; Captain Timson of Tatchbury, an old Carabinier ; Captain Morant ; Messrs. William and John Everett ; Lord Londesborough ; Lord Eslington, afterwards Lord Ravensworth ; Captain Martin Powell, the Hon. Secretary for so many years : " never was there a better Hunt Secretary " was Sir Reginald's comment, and a great little sportsman called Mudge who trotted about happily when well over ninety and greatly enjoyed himself.

Mr. G. A. E. T-G-Meyrick, 1878-85.

Mr. (afterwards Sir) George Augustus Elliot Tapps-Gervis-Meyrick of Hinton Admiral, Christchurch, afterwards 4th Baronet, took over the mastership when only 23 years old. He hunted five or six days a week and in every month except in June. The Deputy Surveyor, the Hon. Gerald Lascelles, ensured a good supply of foxes and no expense was spared to make everything go well. His Tapps ancestor in the 18th century had married Catharine, the eventual heiress of the Gervis, and Clerke families, acquiring the Hinton Admiral estate among other properties, and his father assumed the name of Meyrick under the will of his great-grandfather, the last male representative of the ancient family of Meyrick of Bodorgan in Anglesea, an estate possessed for a thousand years without sale. This family also had the blood of the ancient Welch Kings in their veins. He built a little hunting box by the kennels for his convenience during cub hunting and bought most of Sir R. Graham's bitches and hunted hounds himself. Taking over all the outlying parts of the N.F. country which had been loaned to other hunts, he had great distances to cover, but, with both himself and staff splendidly mounted, and youth on his side, no distance was too great. His lavish expenditure was a strain on even his considerable resources and when asked who was to succeed him he replied " I don't know. As far as I can see there are only two men who could afford to—my saddler and my corn merchant." Mr. Meyrick, in addition to Sir Reginald Graham's bitches, purchased large drafts from other packs, especially from the Grafton. He always had a very large pack in kennel.

On Mr. Meyrick's resignation the country was divided and so continued until 1895. From 1905 till his death in 1928 Sir George was Chairman of the Hunt Club and very liberally supported it.

Major Browne, 1885-86 (East).

The Forest proper was hunted by Major Browne of Hall Court for one season. He brought his own small bitch pack. His sons somewhat astonished the Hunt by wearing red coats and bowler hats ! The Hon. Gerald Lascelles was empowered by the Committee to buy a pack of hounds at Rugby. With the assistance of George Carter of the Fitz William, he bought about 25 couple of bitches, half from Mr. Meyrick's pack and half from the Burton. He also bought some doghounds of Mr. Mark Rolle's pack, but finding them unsuitable, exchanged them for others more suitable. This founded the present pack, now owned by the Hunt Club.

Mr. F. Bradburne, 1886-89 (East).

Mr. Frederick Bradburne of Lyburn then took over the Eastern portion. He engaged John Dale as huntsman. A popular master and well known to the country.

Mr. S. Pearce, 1889-94 (East).

Mr. Stanley Pearce of Testwood became master of the Eastern portion, with Will Povey as huntsman. On one occasion during his mastership his hounds clashed with the Western pack, hunted that day by the kennel huntsman, Sam de Ville, at the Rifle Butts near Lyndhurst. Both huntsmen showed great jealousy and made a great deal of noise screaming at their own hounds. The combined pack ran on about three miles by the Brockenhurst Road into New Park when Allen, the huntsman of the Buckhounds, rushed out of kennel blowing his horn incessantly. Povey's 2nd whipper-in asked Allen to stop as it was giving him a headache. Luckily, after a turn round New Park, the fox was killed to a double who-whoop.

On another occasion Mr. Pearce had an unfortunate termination to a hunt when a fox found in Langley, near Lyndhurst Road Station, was lost at Cadlands ; it was, however, afterwards found out that the fox had been shot in the mud at low tide.

Hunt point-to-point races were started during Mr. Pearce's mastership, and are still continued.

Mr. H. M. Powell, 1894-99 (East).

Mr. Henry Martin Powell, of Wilverley Park, Lyndhurst, took the mastership, retaining Povey as huntsman of the dog pack whilst he hunted the bitches. Mr. Powell's father, Lieut.-Colonel William Martin Powell, after serving in the 6th Inniskilling Dragoons, had become Adjutant and eventually commanded the Hampshire Yeomanry ; he had added to his military duties 30 years of good service as Honorary Secretary to the Hunt previous to 1887. Mr. H. M. Powell relied much on Grafton blood, but bred his own puppies as well. Despite an outbreak of mange among the foxes in the Forest he showed good sport. Mr. Powell had reunited the country on Sir John Thursby's resigning the Western portion in 1895. A good hunt is recorded by Colonel A. H. Cowie, R.E., a keen supporter, on January 5th, 1897. Finding at Busketts Lawn, hounds ran hard through Minstead Manor, over Acres Down and Fritham Plain into Holly Hatch through Broomy, back past Ocknell, over the open in Slufters, Milkham, Roe Wood and Picket Post, then to Crowe Chapel where he was killed in the open, after a hunt of 1½ hours and a point of some 10 or 11 miles—about 20 miles as hounds ran. The scent was first-rate and hounds could not leave the line. Frank Hutchins acted as his 1st whipper-in and kennel huntsman.

Mr. J. Mills of Bisterne, 1885-91 (West).

Mr. John Mills of Bistern had previously hunted a fine harrier pack and as Mr. Meyrick's hounds were going up for sale in April he again got his harriers into condition and his huntsman, George Seers, hunted fox with them. On the first day they found a fox in Wilverley enclosure and hunted *through hares*, running to Beaulieu Heath. Seers became a fine huntsman of foxhounds with great control and knowledge of woodcraft.

Sir J. H. Thursby, Bart., 1891-95 (West).

Sir John Hardy Thursby, 1st Baronet, of Ormerod House in Lancaster and of Holmhurst, near Southampton, now took the Western portion, allowing his son George, later to be master of the Buckhounds, to hunt the pack. It was during his mastership and when his son George Thursby was not out, that the clash of the two Forest packs mentioned on the previous page occurred.

Mr. C. Heseltine, 1899-1900.

Mr. (afterwards Lieutenant-Colonel) Christopher Heseltine of Walhampton Park became master and his brother, Mr. (afterwards Major) Godfrey Heseltine, hunted the hounds, but on both volunteering for the South African War, the Hon. Secretary, Mr. Wingrove, acted as master, with Frank Hutchins, the 1st whipper, doing duty as huntsman. Mr. Wingrove was a great-nephew of the Rev. Edward Timson of Tatchbury Mount. He lived to be the *d'oyen* of Hunt Secretaries and was a great pillar of support to the Hunt at all times. Major Godfrey Heseltine, after serving with the Carabineers, was master of the Walhampton Basset Hounds from 1910-15 and 1920-32. He was also a most successful master of the Ootacamund Hunt in Southern India, 1906–10 and 1917–19, and did much to improve that country and make it more possible to ride over; the passages he had made over the very deep and dangerous bogs are still a monument to his energy. This hunt is one of the two at present surviving in India after the British withdrawal from that country.

Mr. H. F. Compton, 1900-05.

Mr. Henry Francis Compton of Minstead Manor became master and hunted one pack himself while Jones, from South Staffordshire, hunted the other. Mr. Compton was a good judge of foxhounds and believed in the Dulverton blood, founded much on one of the Duke of Beaufort's Peterborough Champions " Rustic." Tom Newman, who hunted the Badminton dog pack, had complete faith in this hound who was as good in his work as he was handsome. Mr. Compton was M.P. for the New Forest Division, 1905–06, J.P. and D.L., a Verderer for 47 years, and Chairman of the Hunt Club for 15 years. A great figure in Forest life, he died in 1943 ; his wodow now owns the estate.

Mr. H. M. Powell, 1905-07.

Mr. Henry Martin Powell again became master and carried the horn as successfully as he had done before.

Mr. W. de P. Cazenove, 1907-11.

Mr. Walter de Pradine Cazenove of Langley Manor, Totton, became master. Jones still remained as huntsman and showed good sport. Mr. Cazenove was a member of the Hunt Club for 29 years and died on December 1st, 1946. Though not so quick as his predecessor, he accounted for many foxes during his mastership. From 1897–1900 Mr. Cazenove had been master of the Wilton Hounds. There he had proved himself a successful breeder of hounds and the Wilton greatly benefited as his successor bought the pack in 1900. In 1903 the dog pack went to the New Forest, the bitches remaining with the Wilton. Mr. Cazenove had also been master of the Woodland Pytchley, 1901–03.

Mr. J. A. and Major E. F. Cooke-Hurle, 1911-13.
Lieut.-Colonel E. F. Cooke-Hurle, 1913-14.

Mr. John A. Cooke-Hurle and Major Edward Forbes Cooke-Hurle of Northerwood Farm, Lyndhurst, became joint-masters for two seasons, but Mr. J. A. Cooke-Hurle resigned in 1913 and left his brother in sole control. He was recalled for service in 1914 in the First European War. Mr. John Cooke-Hurle had previously been master of the Lamerton Hounds in Devon from 1907–10 and then joint-master with his brother Edward for one more season until coming to the Forest.

Major H. T. Timson, 1914.

Major Henry Thomas Timson of Tatchbury Mount, grandson of the Rev. Edward, M.F.H. 1854–60, being stationed at Romsey, tried to combine Army duties with the mastership of the Foxhounds. He made his metamorphosis from soldier to master of hounds at the Vine at Ower and changed back again before his return to Romsey. Major Timson had already experience as joint-master of the Buckhounds, 1908–10. His " double life," however, became known to " authority " and had to be discontinued.

Committee, 1914-19.

A committee then took charge, Mr. Wingrove again acting as master. With Mr. O. T. Price, an ex-master of the Buckhounds, as a very keen and able assistant. Fred Cooper was huntsman and despite all the many war-time difficulties hunting was continued.

Major (afterwards Sir G.) L. T-G-Meyrick, 1919 to date.

Major (now Sir) George Llewelyn Tapps-Gervis-Meyrick, D.L., of Hinton Admiral, born in 1884, now succeeded to the mastership in the prime of life ; in 1928 he also succeeded his father as 5th Baronet. He has become a well-known judge of hounds and for over 30 years has kept the Hunt going in the style to which he was accustomed, despite the advent of the Second World War in 1939–45.

Jack Candy, from South Dorset, was 1st whipper-in and kennel huntsman until 1942, a real lover of hounds. Jack Candy died rather suddenly in November 1942 to the great regret of his many friends.

Fred Perry,[4] who had been huntsman to the Albrighton Hunt for 16 years, was luckily living in retirement at Bank, near

---

[4] Fred Perry started his sporting career in 1896 as stable boy with the Spring Harriers on the South Downs. He was then 14 years old In 1898 he came for one season to the New Forest Buckhounds. In 1899 he went to the Vine Hunt and stayed until 1918 as 2nd and 1st whipper-in. In 1909–12 he was 1st whipper-in to the Albrighton Hunt with Major C. G. Mayall. On Charles Morris's retirement in that year he was promoted to be huntsman and carried the horn sixteen seasons, retiring in 1933.

SIR GEORGE Ll. T.-G.-MEYRICK, Bart., M.F.H., 1919 to date.

Double Kill.
Sir George Meyrick, M.F.H. (*right*), and Mr. O. T. Price (*left*).

THE NEW FOREST HUNT AT RUFUS STONE.
Reading left to right.—Sir G. Meyrick, F. Perry, Major P. P. Curtis, M.C.

Lyndhurst. He now came forward to carry on alone to the end of the Second World War, when he was joined by his son Ralph on coming out of the Army, the father acting as 2nd whipper-in to his son. This family combination still carries on despite Fred Perry's age of 69 years (1950). The Forest is now hunted regularly twice a week. Many of the difficulties created by the war still exist. Barbed wire and a mess of aerodromes and camps, trenches still open and becoming more dangerous through being hidden by brambles, rides deeply cut and drains stopped by the haulage of some 400,000 tons of timber. Despite all, the Hunt goes on and generally some 25 to 30 followers turn out. For the Hon. Secretary's lawn meet at Annesley Cottage over a hundred turned out mounted in the season 1848–49.

Hounds are a useful, good-looking pack, with a great cry. They are not shown but bred for use ; fresh blood lately has been supplied by the Carlow Pack with very good results. Hounds have been very often robbed of their reward by bad earth stopping. It is to be hoped that this very important duty may again be carried out by the Forest Keepers. It is a misfortune that the recent Deputy Surveyors have not hunted.

The 1949–50 season proved the best since 1938–39. The pack were in great form and, as the earth stopping improved considerably, killed more foxes. The staff remained unchanged and Sir George Meyrick carries the horn for his thirty-first season.

Of the present followers of the Hunt the master's wife must take first place and his daughter Susan, wife of Mr. Peter Green, M.C., heir to Minstead Manor. Mr. Green lost a leg in the Second World War and was believed to be killed, but happily was repatriated after a memorial service had been held in his memory. Lieut.-Colonel G. D. E. Meyrick, M.C., 9th Lancers, a first-rate horseman, has not hunted in the Forest during recent years. Brig.-General E. W. M. Powell, C.B., C.M.G., D.S.O., a permanent member of the Club and indefatigable worker for the good of the Hunt, has not recently ridden, but still helps in every way. General Powell was master of the United Hunt for nine years and the Meath for three years. Mr. O. T. Price, ex-master of the N.F. Buckhounds, is still, at over 80, a most prominent follower and with his hardy grey hunter totalled 101 years in the season, 1948–49. He is a mine of Forest and hunting lore. Both he and Mrs. Price on foot seldom go home till hounds go home. Miss Rachel Pulteney well represents her family.   Her brothers, Major W. K. C. Pulteney, a Trustee and member of the Hunt, and Captain M. J. Pulteney, also a member of the Hunt, both used to go well.   Major William Pulteney is now again able to hunt regularly but his brother is unable to ride since the war. St. Austin's has been sold. The Secretary and his wife, with three expert daughters, winners of many prizes, and two keen sons coming on, would provide a small field of their own if times were more favourable and all could be mounted. Of more recent supporters, Lieut.-Colonel and Mrs. T. F. K. Howard and family, Lieut.-Colonel A. W. G. East, Miss Priscilla Hunt, Captain and Mrs. Philip Dodgson and family all are staunch supporters. Mrs. Payne seldom misses a a hunt and could not be keener. There are, of course very many more. Two members, Messrs. C. Dallas and J. G. Duplessis, who now can only support and no longer hunt, have been members of the Hunt Club since 1885. Major-General Sir Richard Lee, K.C.G., C.M.G., of Woodlands, a permanent member, and his wife have had to give up hunting owing to age and ill-health, and another permanent member, Lieut.-Colonel Jack Jeffreys, unfortunately no longer appears in the field. All were good men to hounds in their time.

Sir George's best sport seems to have been in the early 1930's. A run from Blacksmith's Bog, by Bramshaw Wood, Lyburn, Longcross Pond, Linwood, Malwood, The Bentleys, Holm Hill, Milkham, Roe Wood, Pinnick, to Marrow Bowls Hill where they lost, covered over 20 miles of country and gave a $9\frac{1}{2}$-mile point.   Another hunt from the same bog in 1933 finished at Ironshill Lodge, near Lyndhurst Road Station, a point of $6\frac{1}{2}$ miles.   Another very good hunt took place from New Park to Rhinefield, Oatfield, Wilverley Enclosure and Holmsley to ground in Cuckoo Hill.   This gives a 10-mile point and probably over 20 miles as hounds ran.   A very good gallop was enjoyed, too, in the cub-hunting season from Ipley over Beaulieu Heath and Norley Pylewell when they lost their fox between Pylewell Park and the sea, about a $7\frac{1}{2}$-mile point.

Hon. Secretaries.

The Hunt has been lucky in having very few changes in Hunt Secretaries. The first known is Lieut.-Colonel William Martin Powell of Brooklands, who was a Captain in the 6th Inniskilling Dragoons and became Adjutant of the Hampshire Yeomanry in 1854, and continued his duties till 1881—a wonderful and unusual record. He then was promoted Major to command, 1881–84. He was Hunt Hon. Secretary from 1853–87. He died in 1909 at the age of 87. In 1888 Mr. Ernest L. Wingrove, son of Mr. Drummond Wingrove of Langley Manor, Totton, succeeded him and remained in office till 1932, dying in 1941, having twice acted as Field Master or acting Master during war periods. Mr. Wingrove was famed for his tact and friendliness to all visiting sportsmen. In 1932 Mr. George C. Ferguson of Coppithorn Hill, Copythorne, took over until the season 1938–39. He lost his life in the H.M.S. *Prince of Wales* on December 10th, 1941, as Lieutenant-Commander, R.N.V.R. In May 1939 Major P. P. Curtis, m.c., of Annesley Cottage, Lyndhurst, an old 15th Hussars officer, took over the duties which he still carries out very efficiently. Major Curtis had lived in the Forest as a boy and known it in the intervals of soldiering for some 40 years. In the First World War Major Curtis was a Brigade-Major and G.S.O. II in much heavy fighting. After the war he distinguished himself as an amateur steeplechase jockey.

———

NEW FOREST HUNT.

By S. Nichol, Esq., 1810 (M.F.H., 1814–28).

November the nineteenth, despising the weather
Some sportsmen at Dibden assembled together ;
After waiting awhile for John Warde and his hounds
They were quieted at once by the heart-stirring sounds
Of " Try for—Yoi ! Wind him ! Creep up to him, boys,"
Hush ! Hush ! We shall head him ; don't make such a noise
Now observe how they draw ! Look at Spinster, the jade—
Hark ! Hark ! She has found him ! Hark, Spinster, my maid !
Like lightning she's joined by the rest of the pack,
" Tally ho ! Gone away ! " is hollered by Zach.[1]
Then over the road, 'cross the main earth he breaks
And by Sir John Keane's house the enclosure he takes,
And Ipley Farm bridge the first point that he makes,
But here headed, he turned up the lane thro' the flood
Running over the bottom for Langley Great Wood.
Here he's headed again, but not dreaming on death
He now gallantly faces the wide open heath.
When riding and hollering, elated with joy,
To the right we leave Matley, to the left the Decoy ;
At the very best pace up the hill we ascend
And run straight o'er the open to Denny Lane end,
To the right of the Lodge, thro' Etherise flying,
On entering Woodfidley we thought he was dying.
But still onward again the hounds eagerly push
And pass through at top speed, the enclosure Blackbush.
Here the veteran Bos.[2] never minding his neck
By his riding too hard, brought the hounds to a check.
But Solon, esteemed the most excellent hound,
By his shrill squeaking tongue made the cover resound,
And others quick join him, like pigeons in flight
For when Solon speaks to it he's sure to be right.
Away forward they strain to Whitley Lodge plain
When old Farmer New reynard's headed again
And reluctantly forced, being pressed by the pack,
To retrace in a circle the same country back.
And still farther yet, his heart never failing,
He makes for the corner of Pickering's pailing,
Turning up to the left reaching Ramnor's great hill,
The hounds get behind, tho' assisted by Will.
Just here with hard riding the horses were spent,
And the pack shortly brought to a cold hunting scent,
But that's nothing to them, for what's seldom the case,
They can hunt a low scent and yet run the best pace.
With hounds that in hunting so brilliantly shine,
Such as Alfred and Hotspur, he still kept his line.
While slowly advancing Zachariah[1] cries " Hark ! "
He's now hollered again right away to New Park.

[1] Zachariah Goddard was 2nd whipper-in.
[2] Mr. Boscawen, a hard-riding old gentleman.

Then away to the holloa we instantly trot
And with eagerness ask if he's " hunted " or not.
" Quite done," was replied, " and he shortly must tire,
For his tongue's hanging out, and he's covered with mire."
With a fair scent through the Park we proceed
And keep gaining upon him quite up to Queen Mead.
Across Over Green Flat, now he's pressed by the hounds,
Straight away for the corner of Brockenhurst Grounds.
The pack here he hoped by his cunning to bother,
Up one side the hedge, down the ditch on the other.
By this shifting and dodging we thought him our own
But away to Rhinefield Alfred tells us he's gone.
Through the vile yew enclosures (some more of the sort
When planned by Glenberrie, will ruin our sport.
Let me tell the wise lord, if not too affronting,
They will ruin the public as well as the hunting).
But I'm now off my scent, so I'll quickly hark back
And leave this dull lord to return to the pack.
To the left up the bottom like lightning they fled,
As they stream up the hill " only see what a head ! "
Was exclaimed by John Warde, " Now again how they press
Sure no hounds in the kingdom such powers possess."
Here no man could tell which hound worked the most
As they strove all alike towards Wilverley Post.
But not liking the open, he turned for some gorse,
When the hounds were again overrode by old Bos.
Though this error my friend commits in the field
For hard riding and keenness to no man he'll yield.
Now they hit it once more into Hinchelsea break
And stout as the day, made the whole cover shake.
Sure alas ! at this sport was misfortune our guide
For with friend we observe the whole pack to divide—
On different scents—some went this way, some that,
Some ascending the hill, some crossing the flat.
From this direful disaster we found it in vain
To recover the scent of our old friend again.
Thus finished a chase of three hours or more,
Such a chase as scarce ever I witnessed before.
Then homeward we walked as but few chose to trot,
For almost all the horses their gruel had got.
Now snug in my cottage, of good generous port,
A full bumper I drink to John Warde and the sport.
Then the Balls and the Routs of Southampton remove
'Tis of port and good humour we sportsmen approve.
May to Lyndhurst repair some more friends of the chase
And tea and the Tabbies be banished the place !

(*Copied from a manuscript commonplace book at New Hall, Bodenham, Salisbury.*)

"CROWN AND STIRRUP."

(New Forest Foxhounds.)

At cover late, I heard, the other morn,
The bitches running, and the doubling horn.
They've found! "Hike Holloa!" Will has seen him break!
Some loiter; some reflect which line he'll take,
But RIDE, you boys, who wish to see him die!
The pack race to it, settle down, and fly.
RIDE like the devil, else it's all in vain,
You might as well go straight back home again.

    *   *   *   *   *   *   *   *

How are the mighty fallen! Put to rest
By forty minutes of the very best!
Let's see who now the striving pack can view.
Not many—those that can, good men and true.
First Harry Powell,[3] in his place, of course,
Well carried by that stout old whalebone horse;
And close to him his trusty henchman Frank[4]
(For that he has his good black mare to thank).
Pulteney[5] and Matcham,[6] though they both wear "specs,"
Riding as if each had a brace of necks.
Compton[7] from Minstead, on his second nag,
From find to finish I know he'll never fly.
Wingrove,[8] the Sec., who's worth his weight in gold—
Would that these sportsmen never could grow old!
Mount them alike on hunter or on hack,
By hook or crook they will keep near the pack.
There's Turpin[9] hustling on his gallant grey;
"Morny"[10] and Lascelles,[11] Tuck,[12] too, on the bay;
Brown[13] on his new quad; Timson,[14] Heseltine[15]—
These are the boys who with the pack can shine!

    *   *   *   *   *   *   *   *

Dallas[16] we miss; and I'll bet 10 to 1
In former days he used to see the fun.
The Colonel's[17] sure to turn up at the finish—
Yes, never will his love of sport diminish.
We seek in vain the old Doctor's[18] cheery face.
The fox in his beat held the foremost place.
Alas! to happier hunting grounds he's gone.

    *   *   *   *   *   *   *   *

But "forrard!" lads; the pack keep driving on—
"Forrard! Hark Forrard!" See! from scent to view
The bitches racing—"Tally Ho! Leu! Leu!"
"Who Whoop! they've got him! Who Whoop! of earthly things
Hunting's the king of sports, and sport of Kings!"
      Who Whoop!

(Written by Colonel Alec E. Cowie (late R.E.), January 1897, Member 1901–11.)

PREFACE.

Milton and Chaucer both are dead and gone,
The classic Avon mourns the departed " Swan."
Why regret these ? When Matcham[6] still remains
To sing of hunting o'er New Forest plains.

At Bramble Hill there dwells a bard,
His hat is flat, his name is Matcham,
He reels off verses by the yard ;
I can't think how his brain can hatch 'em.

R. W. B.[19]

April 19*th*, 1898.

I.

With careworn face, lean form, and haggard eye,
The Master[3] of the Foxhounds first rides by ;
Sadly his thoughts o'er many subjects range
From poultry bills to owners, keepers, mange—
As through his troubled mind wierd visions stray.
Gloomy forebodings of the next blank day—
A wretched scapegoat on whose head is piled
A heavy load of criticism wild—
If scent is bad, meets wide, and horses lame,
Or foxes scarce ; tis he alone to blame,
And after reddest of red letter days,
He gets the scantiest medium of praise.
What wonder then he shuns the babbling crowd,
Its ceaseless chatter, and its laughter loud,
And with a heart, heavy and cold as stone,
Surrounded by his hounds, jogs on alone ;
Finding, when gloom and wrath his bosom fill,
A never failing safety valve in " Will."
But every cloud, we're told, bright silver lines,
Behind the darkness that the sun still shines,
As you may note, if you are standing near,
When " Frank's "[4] shrill holloa strikes upon his ear,
How instantly transformed our Master seems,
How with fresh life and joy his visage beams,
Spurring his willing horse ; swift as the wind
He leaves his sorrows, and his cares behind.
Pleasure and hope his fears and troubles calm,
His echoing horn chaunts a thanksgiving psalm ;
Then as he hears from many deep-toned throats
Come pealing forth the gladsome opening notes,
And as he sits and marks with kindling eye
The distant hounds as to the horn they fly,
And sees the pack go streaming o'er the plain,
Then Henry Powell is himself again.

2.

'Tis with awe and deep humility I take my pen to write,
I feel guilty of audacity infernal,
Choosing for the subject of the lines I now indite
The Father of the Hunt, the gallant Colonel.[17]
When an urchin I was told "the boy is father to the man,"
But nowadays we travel so much faster,
And in this case seem to hit on quite a different plan
For the Colonel is the father of the " Master."
When he's hunting it's notorious, he " hangs a splendid boot,"
And of elegance, and ease, gives the impression ;
None so qualified as he, to teach the young idea to shoot
Or to " hunt " would be the more correct expression.
Horses, saddlery and " turn out " he'll severely criticise,
But the things that most annoy him, and are hateful in his eyes,
Are a snaffle, and a bridle decked with buckles.
Who so deeply versed as he is, in the many varied ills
That horseflesh (more's the pity) is the heir to.
There is not a vet (their treatment as a rule is " cures or kills ")
Who can give him any points, that I will swear to.
He knows every inch of country, and the run of every fox ;
And his usual hunting lunch consists in picking
(I apologise most humbly if the rhyme I'm making shocks)
The drumstick of a pheasant or a chicken.
Now I hope and trust sincerely, before my story ends,
That for years to come the Colonel may be seen
When not hunting, criticising all the horses of his friends
From his old familiar station on " Goose Green."

———

3.

And now let "Ave Caesar " be our cry,
Although I trust we're not " about to die,"
We must salute the Forest's uncrowned King,
And, raising high our voices, his praises sing.
'Tis but the duty of the humble Vassals
And tenants of the mighty Gerald Lascelles,[11]
Despotic Ruler, Autocrat Supreme,
Whose word to question none would ever dream ;
Though in these democratic days, it's true,
He has been bearded by a brazen few,
A sect who love contentions, squabbles, fights,
Stiffnecked, and stubborn as the Israelites.
Upon their sacred rights he dares encroach,
And is to them a " hissing and reproach."
The while they rave, and clamour, and abuse ;
Their frenzy he with calm indifference views ;
Though as a blazing fire their fury flares,
Like Gallio, for such things he nothing cares—
A many-counselled man he might have been,
Such an archbishop as we've seldom seen ;

How well his manly figure would adorn
The Apron, and the snowy sleeves of Lawn;
He might have been an Admiral of the Fleet
Or on the woolsack proudly ta'en his seat;
Or had his thoughts towards war, and bloodshed turned,
Doubtless a Marshal's Baton he'd have earned;
He might have been a great Prime Minister
With schemes like Machiavelli, Deep and Sinister.
Too great the task, for him, a choice to make
Among so many, which road he would take,
On which to sit, among so many stools;
Kismet decided—over as he rules—
A shrewd, experienced judge of Horse and Hound,
A better sportsman nowhere can be found.
On Falconry, by all the world it's known
As an authority he stands alone.
Profound his knowledge both of beasts and men,
He owns the ready writer's facile pen;
Possesses ready wit and winning smile,
A voice that from the tree a bird could wile.
A tongue that could persuade one wrong was right,
That light was darkness, or that black was white.
None can its charm and eloquence resist,
He's also " something of a naturalist."

———————

4.

The greedy buck had drunk his fill
From some green pond or gurgling rill;
Then comfortably down he laid
In the enclosure's grateful shade.
He'd not have had so big a drink
If he had paused a while to think,
For as he raised his antlered head
He heard the sound of doom and dread
Breeze-bourne to his affrighted ear,
The deep note of the fierce " Mounseer."[20]
Nearer it draws—unnerved, distressed,
Cold terror clutches at his breast—
He dares no longer resting stay;
Holloas proclaim " He's gone away ! "
Soon on the poor doomed creature's track
Is laid the liberated pack;
Trembling, he flies through sunny glades
And ancient Beechwoods' gloomy shades,
Seeking some friend to take his place,
He struggles on in piteous case.
Useless his trembling limbs to strain
O'er boggy ground, and heathery plain,
Dead beaten he can do no more,
The hounds are on him—all is o'er.

K

The moral is all creatures oughter
Abstain from drinking too much water.
I would not be a deer, I tell 'ee,
Pursued by Mister Festus Kelly.[21]

5.

Here comes a face (a portly form it crowns)
Never disfigured by ill-humoured frowns ;
That cheerful still, no matter what befall,
Ever benevolently beams on all.
Sure 'tis our " Sec."[8] whose jovial, hearty air
Will from the gloomiest bosom banish care ;
Peace and content where'er he goes he'll bring,
And always seems as happy as a king ;
And never, I am sure, has he been heard
To speak an angry or an unkind word.
With cheery laugh, and heart quite free from guile
He greets us all with broad expansive smile,
And we may truly say that in his case
For once " The right man is in the right place."
He at Hunt meetings often may be seen
Calling attention to the Rule Fourteen.
Urbane, and courteous : ever suave and mild.
One " draw " there is whereby he may be riled,
When of his stewardship called to give account
And asked to name the " Fund's " exact amount,
No one, as he, when e'er he gets the chance,
So energetic in the mazy dance ;
But though a great admirer of beauty
He ne'er lets pleasure interfere with duty ;
And with his honeyed tongue and easy tact
Contrives from all subscriptions to extract.
So well he's known, 'tis needless here to state
His horse, like his opinion, carries weight.
Long may he flourish, for 'tis very plain
" We ne'er shall look upon his like again."

6.

You can talk of the bravest of heroes
From Richard the First down to Ney,
They would make a poor show across country
With Pulteney[5] to show them the way.
How pale they would grow, and still paler,
Beginning to funk, and to shirk
If they had to play follow-my-leader
When he sat down to cut out the work ;
And how they'd be picked up in pieces,
Broken collar-bones, legs, arms and necks,
The result of their trying to follow
The mild-mannered man in the specs.

He regards neither danger, nor distance ;
There is no one so fearless and keen,
Be the pace what it will, or the country ;
Wherever the hounds go he's seen.
The miles he has ridden, the places
He's jumped, I'm afraid to relate.
If one fence more than all his soul loveth
It's a strongly-made, high and locked gate.
I am certain his deepest affliction,
Worse even than laming his horse,
Is if hounds come to draw at St. Austin's
And there isn't a fox in the gorse.
Without doubt his idea of a heaven,
Bands, halos, harps, wings—and all that,
Is jumping forever large fences
On the tireless ghost of old " Pat " ;
And lest ceaseless saltation in safety
At length peradventure might pall,
He'd prefer as a chance and excitement
To take now and then a bad fall.

7.

Oh ! Young Lochinvar he came out of the West,
And in all the wide border his steed was the best ;
Without crabbing the horse of the Young Lochinvar
I will bet Compton's[7] " Satan " is better by far.
When the " Socman of Minestead " is well on the ride
There isn't another can live by his side,
For " Satan " has still got to learn how to fall
And his master rides paces like A. Nightingall.
When the time for our Point-to-Point races comes round
At the finish the pair well in front will be found,
While the rest struggle home in a woe-begone tail,
Clacey leads back the winner once more to scale.
Harry Compton's the boy for diversion and fun
With beagles, or terriers, with rifle or gun ;
But the sport next his heart is with horse and with hound
And a fox at the Manor can always be found.
He is cheery and friendly and courteous to all,
He'll ride hard to hounds, or dance hard at a ball.
That he's quite our " show man " we all freely confess,
And we'll hope that his shadow may never grow less.
He's a chairman, a " beak " and a Verderer too,
His friends they are many, his enemies few ;
I believe he has all that a man can desire,
So here's luck and long life to the young Minstead Squire.

8.

Who next appears ? Upon the well-bred grey,
Beaming on all, with jest and laughter gay ;
Always brimful of merry quip and talk—
You need not ask—of course it's " Piggy Palk,"[22]
Quick witted, cheerful, who so fond as he
Of *risqué* talk, *bon mot*, and *repartee* ?
A boon companion, full of chaff and banter,
His favourite pace, a Rotten Row-like canter.
But we must leave him, and his merry laugh ;
Here in a dog-cart comes his better half,
No need has she of clumsy motor car,
For " Blacky " in the shafts is better far.
Keen her enjoyment of all sport and fun,
Of every fox she seems to know the run.
Judgment and instinct, both must have a share,
For at the finish she is always there.
It has been whispered that some sportsmen say
" Oh ! What a second horseman thrown away."

9.

B stands for Blathwayt,[19] bold and bad,
Of wrath a most capacious vessel,
Who never strives ('tis very sad)
With mankind's enemy to wrestle.
With gold-rimmed specs., and aspect mild,
He might pass for some harmless curate,
But Oh ! his language when he's riled,
I'm sure that you could not endure it.
It's not so much the things he'll say
(His repertoire is poor and scanty),
But said in his most vicious way,
They'd terrify a wild Ashantee.
There's nothing can his love efface
For sport in every form and fashion ;
The wild New Forest deer to chase,
His great, his chief, his ruling passion.
'Tis there alas ! that you will find
His nature's darkest side apparent,
The vampire yearnings of his mind
For gore becoming most transparent.
Scent may be bad, and hounds divide,
His ardour nothing can diminish ;
Like the wild huntsman, he will ride
O'er rough and smooth, from find to finish ;
And when the end is drawing near,

And round their prey the hounds are baying,
He gives a wild exulting cheer,
His fierce, triumphant joy betraying,
Eager to take his victim's life,
And its carotid vein to sever,
He pushes in with glittering knife
And puts an end to it forever.
After his butcher's work is done,
Quite satisfied with gore and glory,
He turns, to magnify the run,
Empty his flask, and tell some story.
Yet when not ravening for blood
(This is his nature's oddest feature)
No cow that ever chewed the cud
Could be a kindlier, gentler creature.
On any subject he'll converse,
The most abstruse, or the most trivial;
No ruffian he—quite the reverse—
His tastes and habits most convivial.
'Tis sad that in this genial friend,
Whose jokes one's sense of humour tickle,
The rival instinct thus should blend
Of Mr. Hyde and Dr. Jekyll.

———————

10.

'Tis of Captain Richard Turpin[9] I am now about to sing,
A task that I perform with greatest pleasure;
Though I fear I can't describe him as " an artless little thing,"
I may safely call him " quite a perfect treasure."
He is fond of wit and humour, has " a most engaging way,"
Takes no part in petty squabbles, fights or quarrels,
And the only thing about him I regret that I must say
Is " His manners are much better than his morals."
So courteous, mild and affable, so gentle he appears,
I feel sure he ne'er would give you the impression
That man of war and bloodshed he has been in former years,
And to fight for Queen and country, his profession.
He dearly loves a story, and he dearly loves the chase,
He's in our New Forest Hunt a great believer,
And the runs as he describes them, both for distance and for pace,
Put to shame the Quorn, the Pytchley and the Belvoir.
Now old " Roderick's " but a memory, he rides a gallant grey
(When it meets a German band it's rather tricky);
He's a shining light in Lyndhurst, where we hope he'll always stay
For we never could get on without our " Dicky."

II.

In the New Forest wide, there are so many ride
That the names of them all I can't mention,
As was, I may say, when commencing this lay,
My original plan and intention.
I have said what was true of each man that I knew,
Unbiassed by fear or affection,
And now that 'tis done I must hope there's not one
Who objects to this moral dissection.
If there's ought that offends that I've said of my friends,
Great my sorrow, and deep my remorse is,
Though I cannot but fear, some will say with a sneer,
" His rhymes are as lame as his horses."
As I must be exact, I shall just state the fact
That we, as a Hunt, are not " dressy,"
But as all the world knows, out of place are fine clothes
In a country so muddy and messy.
There are ladies galore, always well to the fore,
A goodly and gracious procession,
But bolder than I would the man be who'd try
To mention them all in succession.
Always right in the front, at the top of the Hunt,
Jack Powell[23] to go is a " one-er,"
And no marvel, for he is a gunner.
And another brave man, always well in the van,
So slim, and so smart, and clean shaven,
Heseltine[24] you will note, in an up-to-date coat,
And, by jove ! he's no funker or craven.
Brother " Chris "[15] by his side, always ready to ride,
No one fonder than he of a flutter ;
Through the hairiest place, with a grin on his face,
He goes, as a knife goes through butter.
Splashing round like a frog, there is " Hope " in a bog,
Big and black, more or less as it chances,
For sometimes, we know, he can't choose, but must go
Wherever his wayward horse fancies.
You will find any day, in the thick of the fray,
Reynolds, Forman[25] and Gambier[26] hustling.
At a deuce of a pace, as if riding a race,
May see Admiral Murray[27] go bustling,
Always cheery and keen, in the front he is seen ;
Of a Hunt Challenge Cup he's the holder,
And if truth must be told, while we're all growing old
The Admiral grows younger, not older.
Then the way " Downman "[28] goes is what nobody knows,
For ten to one " on " is the betting ;
When we're all beat and done at the end of a run
He'll appear with his horse still curvetting.
There is yet one more pair, who will surely be there,
Regard not banks, timber or water,
No matter their size, they've no fears, in the eyes
Of " Clowes "[29] and his brave little daughter.

" Bradford,"[30] too, you may spy, always ready to buy
Our screws, or sell one to a client.
With the hounds any week you have not far to seek
Ere you come on the sport-loving " Bryant."
You will find not a few representatives too
Of the Forces who guard and defend us
By land or by sea or wherever they be,
All riding with keenness tremendous.
And a great many more, but I told you before,
And I do so again, though with sorrow,
If I mentioned each one, I should never have done
Though I wrote until this time to-morrow.
The first wish of my heart till I have to depart,
And extinguished are life's dying embers,
Is " Luck and good sport of the very best sort
To the New Forest Hunt and its members."

---

[3] H. M. Powell of Wilverley Park, Master 1894–99, 1905–07. **Member of the Hunt** for 53 years and reunited country 1895. Died November 25th, 1943.

[4] Frank Hutchins, 1st whip and kennel houndsman to Mr. H. M. Powell.

[5] Mr. Keppel Pulteney of Northerwood Park and St. Austin's, Lymington. A member for 52 years. Died December 8th, 1944.

[6] G. E. E. Eyre Matcham of New House. A member for 41 years. Died July 10th, 1939. Writer of third poem.

[7] H. F. Compton of Minstead Manor, Master 1900–05. Member for 51 years and Chairman from 1928 to 1943. Died April 15th, 1943.

[8] Ernest L. Wingrove of The Oaks, Ashurst, Lyndhurst, Hon. Secretary 1887–1932. Member for 58 years. Chairman of Committee and Field Master 1916–18. Died 1941.

[9] Captain Richard Turpin, a gay sportsman who lived in a cottage outside Lyndhurst on the Beaulieu Road.

[10] Mornington Cannon, one of the most famous jockeys of his day. A regular follower and subscriber to the New Forest Hunt.

[11] Hon. Gerald Lascelles, C.B., third son of 4th Earl of Harewood, Deputy Surveyor of the New Forest 1880–1915. A great supporter of all sport and excellent administrator. Hon. Member 1880. Born 1849, died 1928.

[12] " Tuck," a sporting farmer from near Christchurch, well known in his day.

[13] Probably C. Berney Brown of Sway, Lymington. A member 1891–99 and keen supporter.

[14] Major H. T. Timson of Tatchbury Mount, Master 1914–15.

[15] Lieut.-Colonel Christopher Heseltine, O.B.E., of Walhampton Park and afterwards of Brambridge Park. Master 1899–1900. A member for 53 years. Died June 13th, 1944.

[16] Charles Dallas of Eastley, Wooton. Still living. Member from 1885.

[17] Lieut.-Colonel William Martin Powell of Brooklands, 1824–1909. Hon. Secretary 1853–87. Died 1808.

[18] Probably Doctor R. G. Freeland of Brockenhurst. A member for 29 years. Died September 27th, 1943. Dr. Freeland was not on the telephone and continued to drive round his patients in a dog cart.

[19] R. W. Blathwayt of Boldre. Born 1850, succeeded to Dyrham Park, Gloucestershire.

[20] Probably a hound well known at the time.

[21] Edward Festus Kelly, Master of N.F. Buckhounds 1894–1901, of Northerwood Park. Born 1854.

[22] Colonel Hon. Edward Arthur Palk of Little Testwood, Totton. Born 1854 4th son of 1st Baron Haldon.

[23] Brig.-General Edward Weyland M. Powell, c.b., c.m.g., d.s.o., of Brooklands. M.F.H., United, 1910-19, Meath 1919-22. Born 1869.

[24] Major Godfrey Heseltine, Master of Ootamacund Hounds and Walhampton Bassett Hounds. Born 1871, died 1932.

[25] Jack Forman of Setley House and New Park. Died 1900.

[26] M. Gambier of Buskett's Corner. Member, 1896-1921.

[27] Admiral Murray of Poulner, Ringwood. Member 1895. Killed hunting 1901. A memorial bridge erected to his memory in Withybed Bottom, near Lucas Castle, South of Stoney Cross.

[28] C. B. Downman, a member for 53 years. A permanent member. Died 1939.

[29] Colonel Clowes of Bartley Close, Totton. Member 1897-99.

[30] Bradford, a well-known horse dealer at Brockenhurst.

The illustration opposite, painted about 1875 by Miss Lucy Standish (daughter of W. C. Standish, M.F.H., New Forest, 1869-74), is reproduced by kind permission of the owner, Brig-Gen. E. W. M. Powell, c.b., c.m.g., d.s.o.

In those days there was a certain amount of friction between the Foxhounds and the Deerhounds.

Lyndhurst Church can be seen on the left above the milestone. It is called " The Lyndhurst Coach, meeting a storm."

No. 1. LORD NORMANTON (alongside driver) : " I think your leaders are rather unruly. I hope you have got them well in hand."

„ 2. LORD H. SCOTT (behind driver) : " What a storm before us."

„ 3. LORD NELSON (next to No. 2) ; " Had we not better get down."

„ 4. SIR HENRY PAULET (driver), Chairman of N.F.H. : " Yes, my Lord, I have the team well in hand ; as for the storm, it will lay the dust."

„ 5. MR. BRUNKER, with the horn.

„ 6. MR. CUMBERBATCH, with crown on his head, Deputy Surveyor of the New Forest : " Let them kick, they can't do any harm."

„ 7. GENERAL PARKER, Castle Malwood (next No. 6) : " I think, Powell, you had better put on the brake."

„ 8. CAPTAIN LYNDSAY SHEDDEN (behind General Parker) : " Quite right, General, it will steady them."

„ 9. CAPTAIN M. POWELL (in uniform), Adjutant, Hants Yeomanry Cavalry, and Secretary, N.F.H. : " I have got it on as far as it will go, General."

„ 10. LORD LONDESBOROUGH, Northerwood (inside coach) : " Guard, Guard, let me out, it is very hot inside."

„ 11. MR. ESDAILE (running beside coach), Burley Manor : " C'rect card, my Lords, please read it. It is very dusty down here."

„ 12. Near Wheeler, CAPTAIN POWELL MONTGOMERY, Wilverley Park.

„ 13. Off Wheeler, MR. H. COMPTON, Minstead Manor.

„ 14. Near Leader, MR. LOVELL, Hinchelsea, Master, Deerhounds.

„ 15. Off Leader, SIRL REGINAD GRAHAM, Master, N.F.H.

The Lyndhurst Coach, meeting a storm.
(for description see opposite).

CHAPTER VI.

THE VINE HUNT.

MASTERS OF THE VINE HUNT.

1795–1824	Mr. W. J. Chute, The Vyne.
1824–26	Mr. A. Pole, West Ham House.
1826–27	Mr. C. E. Beaver, Overton.
1827–45	Mr. H. A. Fellowes, Hurstbourne Park.
1834–35	A Committee.
1835–36	Mr. Donnithorn Taylor.
1845–48	A Committee.
1848–49	Sir R. H. C. Rycroft Bart., Manydown Park.
1849–51	A Committee.
1851–52	Rev. E. St. John, Church Oakley.
1852–54	Capt. A. Mainwaring, Worting House.
1854–58	Lord Portsmouth, Hurstbourne Park.
1858–59	T. Walker (alias Marsh).
1859–66	Mr. A. E. Whieldon, Quidhampton.
1866–68	Sir Bruce Chichester, Manydown Park.
1868–88	Rt. Hon. W. W. B. Beach, P.C., M.P., Oakley Hall.
1888–93	{ Mr. G. H. Pember, Tangier Park. { Capt. A. G. Russell, Ewhurst Park.
1893–96	Capt. A. G. Russell, 2nd mastership.
1896–1900	Mr. G. H. Pember, 2nd mastership.
1900–01	Capt. A. G. Russell, 3rd mastership.
1901–03	Mr. E. B. Podmore, West Ham House.
1903–13	Sir R. N. Rycroft Bart., Dummer House.
1913–15	Lady Portal, Laverstoke Park.
1915–19	A Committee.
1919–23	Mr. R. H. Gosling, Ashe.
1923–26	Mr. A. W. H. Dalgety, Overton.
1926–29	{ Mr. A. W. H. Dalgety, Overton. { Mr. R. S. Gilbey, Hyde End Farm, nr. Newbury.
1929–32	{ Major C. F. Garrard, Stanten House, Kingsclere. { Mr. John M. Hastings, Mill House, Old Basing; and { Malshanger.
1932–38	Sir N. E. O. Rycroft, Bart., Dummer House.
1938–40	Capt. W. Fox, Adbury Park (killed in action).
1940–41	Mrs. J. H. Walford, Beaurepaire Park.

1949   Lieut.-Col. J. H. Walford, D.S.O., The Old House, Wolverton.

N.B.—The Hunt closed down in May, 1941. Six couple of hounds were kept by the Craven Hunt and bred from. In 1946–49 the South Berks hunted some of the Vine country, using the Vine hounds as far as possible.

Mr. W. J. Chute, 1795 - 1824.

The founder of the Vine Hounds was Mr. William John Chute of the Vyne and Pickenhall Hall, Norfolk. Born in 1757, he succeeded his father Mr. Thomas Lobb Chute in 1791. Possibly, during his father's lifetime, and certainly, at a very early date after he came into the property, Mr. Chute founded a pack of harriers. His first huntsman is believed to have been named Cowley. Nothing is known of him except that he resolutely objected to some faddist who had induced Mr. Chute to try feeding his hounds on meal alone—" cat lap " as Cowley described it. The wise huntsman knew that hounds were carnivorous animals and fed them surreptiously with raw horse-flesh until this whim had passed.

A tradition exists that Mr. Chute founded his harrier pack on one owned by Mr. Erle. A picture, now at the Vyne, shows Mr. Erle in a scarlet coat with a white collar with a hunt servant in a blue coat with a red collar and another servant in mufti holding a horse. Bailey's Magazine of 1874 states that the horse was an old cropped mare bought from Mr. Dale of Pot Bottom Farm near Laverstoke. The Dale family are stated to have had this picture for many years and at that time (1874) the picture was at the kennels of Longford Castle. Nothing, however, is known of Mr. Erle and it is probable that he was not a Hampshire man.

The exact date when Mr. Chute changed his pack to a regular pack of foxhounds is not absolutely certain. It is given differently by the various authorities of the early 19th century. There is one fact which probably determines the date, the date on which H.R.H. The Prince of Wales left Kempshott, April 1795. Mr. Terry of Dummer House gives the famous run with " Spanker " as an Easter Tuesday, 1794, at the latter end of April. This run determined Mr. Chute to become a foxhunter. He would wait, undoubtedly, with his unfailing courtesy till the Royal pack had left the district and then take over country formerly spasmodically hunted by

Mr. T. L. Sclater-Matthew of Tangier, Mr. William Poyntz of Midgham and H.R.H. The Prince of Wales.

It can be reasonably assumed that the 1795–96 season was his first season as M.F.H. The country that he hunted has not changed very greatly during the years and remains roughly about 20 miles square. On the north were the Craven and the Rev. Ellis St. John afterwards the Bramshill Hunt (now South Berks and Garth), on the west partly H.H. and country afterwards Tedworth then hunted by various packs, Lord Craven or Mr. Smith of Cruxeaston and Mr. T. Smith of Tedworth. On the east Lord Stawell and then Mr. Russell afterwards H.H. and, Garth. On the south H.H. then and now. Many changes have taken place with such large coverts as Wherwell Wood, Doyleys and Doles, between the Vine and Tedworth and adjustments have been made from time to time elsewhere.

The Spanker Hunt is given in the Diaries of Dummer and is worthy of record as it was the cause of the foundation of the Vine Hunt. In 1792 a litter of cubs had been bred in a drain at the Vyne under the drawing room (presumably an old Tudor barrel drain then disused). The litter had been moved to Carpenter's Down and had been chivied by the harriers from time to time. Mr. Chute had been presented with a foxhound called " Spanker " by Mr. William Poyntz, and he was anxious to try what Spanker could do, so, with a keen foxhunter like Mr. Stephen Terry in his house, a hunt was arranged rather late in the day on Easter Tuesday, 1794. Will Biggs was told to bring Spanker and nine couple of harriers. A fox was soon found in Carpenter's Down and he ran through Sherborne Wood towards the Vyne, but suddenly headed away across the Aldermaster road and over the downs. Here a shepherd viewed him a long way in front of hounds. This seems to have been the only view, but he must have layed down somewhere as Spanker, who had been half a mile ahead of the harriers throughout, is said to have coursed him for the last 300 yards before he reached an earth in Chilton Wood (formerly a large covert running from Lilly's Copse towards Breach and stretching in part from the Chilton to Dummer Lane to the Preston-Candover—Dummer lane). Spanker could be heard baying deep in the earth but Mr. Chute could not dig ; he was not even a M.F.H., and Spanker had to be left.

This hunt must have represented a point of at least nine miles and took three and a half hours. There is no wonder that Mr. Chute aspired to be a foxhunter.

Five days after this hunt a note came to Mr. Terry from the huntsman to say that Spanker had not returned to kennel. Mr. Terry collected half a dozen men and they worked at the earth for several hours before digging up to the hound, alive but quite a skeleton, with the dead fox between his paws. Mr. Terry took him home in a borrowed cart, well bedded with straw and he was well looked after at Dummer House. The hound recovered and hunted for another two seasons. This hunt seems to have settled the foxhunting project and Mr. Chute deputed his brother, the Rev. Thomas Vere Chute, to buy eighteen couple of foxhounds from the Charlton Hunt. "Sexagenarian" thinks Mr. Chute hunted fox as early as 1791–92 and finally gave up hunting hare in 1794-95. "Aesop" gives 1796 as the start of foxhunting proper. He retained six couple of harriers, but they were always a nuisance and could not run up with the foxhounds. Mr. Chute had always a preference for a small hound with a good nose, like the Egremont blood. His portrait well shows what he was like about the time of his founding his pack. A fair, round face, good humoured and intelligent. He was most affable to all he met out hunting and many people preferred having a middling day with him rather than a better day with others. His humour was of a somewhat whimsical nature and as he got older his eccentricities were more pronounced. Sturdily built but never a great horseman or well mounted, he could well stand long days in the saddle. He was not fond of jumping but preferred to dismount in good time and, catching his horse by the tail, allowed the horse to pull him over an obstacle. He spoke French fluently and could write reasonably good Latin verse. His taste in books and music was naturally good ; he ate sparingly but was most particular what he ate ; his bread and butter had to be spread by a maid, never by a man. He liked good port wine in moderation and abhorred claret, saying that old Bush, his butler, " could make as good stuff as *that* out of the washings of his port wine glasses." A strict Churchman and a staunch Tory, he was a fine type of a cultured 18th century gentleman in no way affected by the lax standards of the Regency Bucks. He represented the county in Parliament from 1790 till 1820 with a short interlude in 1806 when the Whigs were in power after Pitt's death. He did not wrangle in Parliament or in the field, in fact, he was never heard to use a coarse expression, but he was able to make a suitable and witty reply to his Radical neighbour, Sir John Cope. This worthy baronet sent Mr. Chute a note saying that he had a litter of five dogs in that year's entry, whose names had all pretty much the same meaning for they were Placeman, Parson, Pensioner, Pilferer and Plunderer. Mr. Chute's retort was quick and extremely apt ; he told Sir John that he could show him a litter of which the names were equally synonymous, being Radical, Rebel, Regicide, Ruffian and Rascal.

Soon after he started his foxhounds he had a long run from St. John's to Chawton Park. Mr. Chute got into trouble getting out of Bradley Wood. He slipped while leading his horse and the horse trod on his thigh. Mr. John Portal of Freefolk said " Egad, I thought we were going to lose our *member*." " Did you ? " said Mr. Chute, rubbing his leg. " Well, I can tell you I thought I was going to lose *mine*."

He never was a conventional master of hounds. His kennel management was most casual but effective. Mr. George Tattersall describes the kennels (now pulled down) as follows : " Where was a more miserable hole in the shape of a kennel for foxhounds than that in which the Vine pack was lodged in the late Mr. Chute's time." There was no grass yard and in summer the favourite hounds roamed at will in the gardens. The casual methods adopted were well shown in June, 1822, when Sir John Cope, Mr. J. T. Villebois and some other hunting men came over to see the brood bitches and whelps. One old bitch had chosen the copper hole in the brew house to whelp in. She very soon evicted a youthful member of the party who had been told to get her out. Hounds were bred to a definite idea, however, in accordance with the motto over the kennel door—" Multum in Parvo." They were, as a type, rather long in body but deep and muscular, the back rather arched, good forelegs and feet and splendid loins. A picture of New Forest " Jasper," a favourite stallion hound, hung in the lodging room. The picture is still at the Vyne and is reproduced facing page 145. At the back of the picture painted by Mrs. Chute, is written these lines composed by Mr. Chute :—

" Hic bene apud memores veteris stat gloria gentis,
Hinc plus quam solito robore vulpes eget." [1]

Characteristically Mr. Chute used to say that " as great families have the portrait of their distinguished ancestor, the judge or the general or the statesman, in their room, he did not see why the dogs should not have their family picture also. " Jasper " was said, by the Rev. J. E. Austen-Leigh, to

[1] The late Mr. Chaloner W. Chute in his *History of the Vyne* translates these lines freely as
" Here see the glory of an ancient breed
Which urges foxes to their utmost speed."

have been bred by Lord Egremont, but this hound obtained
his name and fame from Mr. V. H. Gilbert who presumably
bought him when master of the N.F.H. The Stud Book
unfortunately does not go back quite far enough for this hound's
pedigree.

Hounds hunted usually five days a fortnight, but they hunted
just as the master wished and it was very difficult sometimes to
find out where the hounds would meet on any day. This was
a common failing in nearly all private packs. They seldom
advertised their meets. The results of this casual method are
well shown by a letter, still preserved at the Vyne, written by
the 1st Duke of Wellington after a long and fruitless hack vainly
trying to find hounds :—

"*Strathfield Saye. March* 23. 1820.

My dear Sir,

I went out this morning to meet your hounds, having ordered my
horses to Clarken Green, as I had settled with your huntsman. I went
on as far as Dean, but could not find my groom, and I then returned
to Clarken Green, thinking it probable that he had gone to the covert-
side. From Clarken Green I went to Ebbworth (Ibworth), and not
finding or hearing anything of you or my horses, I have returned home.
I regret this exceedingly, particularly, as I feel you will have waited for
me. I shall be much obliged if you will let me know on what days
and at what places you will go out next week.

Ever yours most faithfully,

WELLINGTON."

The Duke writes very politely after a most annoying morning,
being a great supporter of the local packs and himself an ex-
master of hounds. His pack hunted during the Peninsular War
from Portugal to Toulouse. After the peace this pack " une
meute des meilleures races d'Angleterre " was offered to the King
when the Duke became Ambassador at Paris. When called
again to power in November, 1834, the King's letter reached
Stratfieldsaye at 6 a.m. The Duke was up and about to go
hunting. He counter-ordered his horses and posted up to
London at 8 a.m. to temporarily assume nearly the whole
government of the country, which he carried out with his
usual punctual and decisive efficiency till Sir Robert Peel arrived
from Rome some three weeks later. The Duke then became
Foreign Minister. The Government was not appreciated at
the Elections, but this did not give the Duke a sleepless night.
He told his neighbours that he would not miss his hunting in the
autumn of 1835 "whatever way the cat jumps in this quarter."

Luckily, in a letter to his brother, Thomas V. Chute, then a
captain in the Hampshire Light Dragoons stationed at Lewes,

we have an authentic account of an 18th century hunt. The hunt took place on November 20th, 1798. This letter was in the possession of the Rev. J. E. Austen Leigh and runs as follows :—

" The Vyne.   Wednesday.

Dear Bro :

Such a touch yesterday as never seen before in my time.   At ½ past twelve (a hard frosty morning) found his honor of immense size in the long copse in Spring Lane in Pamber forest, with a pretty little drag.   Will talio'd him across ye lane, but hounds would not come to halloo, however, with a very bad scent, only 2 or 3 dogs owning it, hunted him by Timber gate and to ye Turnpike road, for Lee Copse, and back through ye forest, by Gander brook, along ye hollow copse on left of Spring Lane.   This took ¾ of an hour, recovered him in ye copse next ye mill, on right of Lord's Lane, came off at his brush, ye same track back, but came to picking thro' ye Forest, till we crossed ye Turnpike, and then prettily for Lee Copse, Tadly |Place, |and down to Witch Lane, where I believe he stopped again, for he was only 2 or 3 minutes before them over West Heath, where the water flew beautifully whilst they caught it carrying a head, and took a burst to Hanington Scrubs, where we overtook them.   I think you will say, pretty well, but it is nothing to what I have to say.   Going thro' Macreth's copse on this side the water, I stopped to get Will's mare over the rails, and so lost the fine run over ye Lawn and to ye top of his shrubbery, when I overtook Curtis, and heard ye curs going into ye Dean's Woods, down ye hill and thro' ye wood into second long field, across ye gap into ye heavy stoney field that was turnips last year, up to ye barn.   Here I stopped Black Mare for wind, but she soon recovered, and spun up ye steep stony lane for Hanington, where I overtook them going into first scrubs all together, but rather slack.   He turned then into ye green lane again, at this end of the second scrubs, to ye end of it, and then bore for Canon Park, hunting it across fallows, in ye open, curs recovered their wind and laid on again, but came to a fault by overrunning it in a path (from Hanington Scrubs to ye end he seemed at a loss as he could not find a gap and run down the hedges instead of topping them and not going straight).   Here a halloo on ye Warren showed Will's stupidity, for instead of going as he ought up to the man with hounds close by him, he encourages them to spread, by which means away they go after rabbits, and then on forward where the man pointed for the chance of getting ye scent, so we were left at a loss where to find it, back to ye man and then forward again, and at last, casting beyond the Warren, we got on again slowish, but pretty hunting over North Oakley Down, thro' Nutley, Kingsdown to Quidhampton, back of Lefroy's[2] house, cross over ye Turnpike at ye hill beyond Lefroy's to ye cottage in ye lane, and up ye lane thro' ye copse.   I believe this is Burydown, next to Ash Park, left Bramdown, ye large wood to ye left (I don't know which is which of Burydown, Bramdown and Burleigh) and took ye open country at back of Overton, turned to ye left (large fields) thro' Quidham, Southleys, and across to Laverstock Wood, where ye sun

[2] The parsonage of Rev. Isaac Peter George Lefroy, 1745–1806, Rector of Ashe and uncle to Thomas Langlois Lefroy, the early lover of Jane Austen.

down, all animals moving, we had 2 or 3 scents and so called away,—
had there been light I think we must have killed, curs not tired and fox
ran four hours and a half, and frost against us in the hill.   Curtis dished,
Black Mare worth any money, Vanity (Ld. Eg.) incomparable, ye old
hounds kept us back very often.

Yours, in haste,

W. Chute."

There are many points of interest.   Hounds worked up to
their fox by the drag of his night's adventure.   Curtis, the landlord of the Angel Inn at Basingstoke, seems to have been the
sole follower.   The old harriers, riotous and slow, spoiling
the hunt.   How not to take hounds to a " Halloa ! "   Mr. Chute
only knew the country to the Turnpike road, the Freefolk wood
country was H.H. and freely poached by various visiting packs.
The point of about 11 miles and hunt of four and a half hours
shows a leisurely performance, with time for horses and hounds
to get their wind but obviously some very good hound work
by a few foxhounds despite old babblers and some flighty
young hounds.   Will Biggs was the huntsman, obviously not a
very good one, though he is said to have looked very like a
fox.   He went to Mr. Villebois at Harmsworth as feeder later
on.   " Macreth " refers to Sir Robert Macreth, a rich Indian
merchant whose " lawns " and " shrubberies " at Ewhurst were
passed in the hunt.   He and Rumbold had started life as
servants in a London hotel.   Macreth was senior in service,
but Rumbold made more money.

A story of the transitional period between hare and fox
shows Mr. Chute's whimsical humour well.   The harriers often
hankered after their old quarry and two strangers were com-
menting rather loudly on the rioting and were overheard by
the master and the whipper-in.   The latter started to rate the
offenders.   " You scoundrel," said Mr. Chute, " what do you
stop those hounds for ?   You know we can catch a fox any
day, and we have not had a hare in the house for a month.   If
you had left those hounds alone we might have had a hare for
the party to-morrow."   His cub-hunting, too, was very
characteristic.   He was very soon bored by the huntsman
trying to teach the young entry to hunt in covert and would
take hounds off to find an old fox.   Certainly he was not the
stereotyped M.F.H. but distinctly individual, a mixture of
shrewdness and weakness, but invariably good tempered.

His next huntsman was Phil Gosling who did good work
in getting the pack into better discipline, but he did not survive

Mr. W. J. Chute of the Vyne,
M.H. 1791-95, M.F.H. 1795 - 1824, Founder of the Vine Hunt.

New Forest " Jasper," painted by Mrs. Chute.

Regarded as chief ancestor of the Vine Pack said to have been bred by Lord Egremont, but obtained his fame and name from Mr. V. H. Gilbert, M.F.H., New Forest Hunt.

His Grace The 1st Duke of Wellington, k.g., with the Vine Hounds

(from a print found in the writing desk of the 1st Duke at Apsley House by the present Duke, by whose kind permission it is reproduced).

for long. His place was taken by George Hickson, his whipper-in, the most renowned of Mr. Chute's servants. Hickson was a neat, good-looking man with excellent sight and hearing. He hunted hounds quite well, but was sometimes extremely rude to his good-natured master. Will Burket came as whipper-in. On one occasion George Hickson was deposed for a short time and a man called Cane was introduced. This was not a success and when Cane asked for leave of absence during a frost, he was told that he could go but that he need not return. Hickson was back again when the frost broke. The change was explained by Mr. Chute in a witty sentence : " *Cane* did not kill a fox because he was not *Able*." This saying was capped by the Reverend Thomas who said that his brother was delighted to find himself again " Cum canibus sinĕ Canē."

His huntsmen wore a twisted bugle on a strap over their shoulder, a more melodious instrument, but not so handy as the straight horn.

Two examples are given of the freedom of speech allowed to George Hickson. The master had bought a rather better horse than usual called " Whiskey " and George was allowed to hunt him for one season. The master then took him for his own use. After he had done this, in a nice hunt from Summer-down through Manydown by Tangier, hounds began to really run in the Park and Mr. Chute was left. Hounds ran by Long Coppice and North Oakley to Nutley, where a large fallow brought hounds to their noses. The master caught up here and began asking all sorts of questions of George whose attention was riveted on the hounds just feathering. Mr. Chute at once commenced to bombard his huntsman with questions— " George, where have you been ? What hounds have been ahead ? Which have been doing it ? George, why don't you answer me ? " At last the huntsman, driven to desperation, replied : " You have gone and taken away my best horse from me. Why don't you ride up and look for yourself, if you want to know what hounds are about."

The next occasion was in Black Wood, always a neutral covert with the H.H. Mr. Villebois was out and the Master wished all to go well before that rather austere critic. However, all did not go well, and much rabbiting and riot took place with the young hounds. George could, however, hear one reliable hound, " Larkspur," throwing his tongue on the drag of a fox, intent on listening, he was again pestered with questions : " George, is that right ? What hound is that ? Will it do,

L

George ? " At last George said, quite exasperated : " How can I tell unless I listen ? And how am I to listen if you keep chattering so ? Do be quiet for a minute. You make a worse noise to-day than ever you did." Mr. Chute's insistence was due to a nervous desire to show Mr. Villebois sport, but he probably realised that his servant spoke under great provocation and George Hickson remained for many a year at the Vyne, finally acting as coachman to Mrs. Chute after Mr. Chute's death.

In his last season Mr. Chute had the luck to show the great " Nimrod," Sir John Cope, Mr. Blackall Simmonds from the Bramshill Hunt, Mr. Edward Knight and Mr. E. Gage from the H.H., a very good hunt from Pamber Forest with a kill in Hackwood Park. An eight-mile point showed his pack to great advantage. About this time another momentous event occurred. Mr. Chute was induced, after a great struggle, to allow Fox the hairdresser to remove his pigtail. Mr. Fox won the battle only by demonstrating that only five hairs remained, all the rest was ribbon. This must have been one of the very last pigtails in the county.

Among the prominent followers of Mr. Chute's hounds who wore his button (very like the present members' button) were first and foremost the 1st Duke of Wellington, Mr. John Portal of Freefolk, Mr. William Portal of Laverstoke, Mr. J. L. Sclater of Tangier, Mr. Bigg-Wither of Manydown, Mr. Charles Harwood of Deane, Mr. William Wickham of Bullington. Some very keen and knowledgable black coats, Rev. Henry Pole of Wolverton, who had hunted his father's harriers, Rev. Edward St. John of Ashe, Rev. John Orde of Winslade, the taciturn Rector of Baughurst and, of course, the Rev. Thomas Vere Chute who was a better sportsman than his brother and usually hunted from Christmas till the season ended. From Basingstoke came the Curtis' father and son, already mentioned. Some of the May family, generous benefactors to the town, Mr. Warne the lawyer, Charles Lyford the surgeon, and several of the Tubbs family, very prominent farmers.

Mr. Chute's health seemed to give way rather suddenly after the spring hunting. He died in London aged 67 in 1824 regretted by all who knew him. With him, too, passed away something of a more leisurely and more cultured age never to return. The hounds became the property of his brother Thomas who also inherited the estates. The hounds were offered to Mr. John Portal but refused. Finally, Mr. Abraham Pole, brother of Sir Peter Pole of Wolverton Park, consented to take over the mastership.

Mr. A. Pole, 1824-26.

Mr. Abraham Pole bought West Ham house and built kennels there. A sum of £800 was raised by a few of the gentlemen in the county for his initial expenses. He obtained the services of Richard Adamson as huntsman who had valuable experience with Mr. Musters and Lord Scarbrough. Adamson soon proved himself a first-rate woodland huntsman. The Duke of Beaufort helped with some good hunting hounds and by a couple of valuable stud hounds ; one of these was a badger pied hound and the pack soon lost its uniform black and white appearance. Mr. Pole had some good horses, far better than Mr. Chute's, but he felt he was only a stop-gap and gave the hounds back to the gentlemen of the county in the spring of 1826. Adamson killed 14 brace of foxes this season, but there were fourteen blank days.

Mr. C. E. Beaver, 1826-27.

Mr. Charles Everett Beaver of Overton now took over, but only for one season. An old officer of the 34th Regiment and the 11th Light Dragoons, he had always been keen on hunting. He was a good jockey and rode thoroughbred horses to hounds. He would have had knowledge of hunting from early days with the Quarley Hunt and Adamson showed good sport, yet for some reason the arrangement was not satisfactory and only lasted for a year. Sport was about the same as during the previous year.

Mr. H. A. Fellowes, 1827-34.

Mr. Henry Arthur Fellowes of Hurstbourne Park now came to the rescue. Born in 1799, he was the son of the Hon. Newton Wallop who had assumed the name and Arms of Fellowes on succeeding to the estates of his maternal uncle Henry Arthur Fellowes of Eggesford in Devon. Father and son did not agree very well, though both were devoted to hunting. He was probably glad, therefore, to come to Hurstbourne to look after affairs generally for John Charles, the 3rd Earl of Portsmouth.

He wisely retained Adamson as his huntsman. The control of the Hurstbourne estate, coupled with his own vigour of mind, soon made the Hunt go well. Mr. Fellowes became a most efficient and popular master of hounds and greatly improved the pack. Adamson was a very good horseman who kept with his leading hounds and so could help them if it was necessary.　The supply of foxes improved and 24 brace and sometimes more were killed.　Mr. Robert T. Vyner, the author of *Notitia Venatica* has much to say about the pack which he visited in 1834.　He mentions that they had been bred from drafts of the old Egremont blood and crossed by stud hounds from the Duke of Beaufort's and Mr. Assheton Smith's kennels : he found, however, much of " the original character of the old foxhound of days gone by, which is visible in no other established pack—an inclination to be rough, and, as it is termed, sour about their muzzles and chaps."　He explains that roughness does not mean like Welsh hounds, for " though the hard and ferocious character of the foxhound is stamped on them, a better shaped, more powerful and truly sporting pack does not exist in the world."　He mentions that Mr. Musters' last pack were chiefly descended from the Vine hounds, *e.g.*, " Voucher," " Broker," " Lionel," etc.　He calls them steady from all kinds of riot, quick and yet patient, very determined and particularly suited for their country which he calls " a cold, flinty and cheerless tract, with immense woodlands."

In 1824 Mr. Fellowes had to give up the management to a committee for reasons of health.　The committee consisted of the Rev. E. St. John and Mr. W. Hicks Beach, (later Colonel W. Beach).

A Committee, 1834-35.

The committee handed the management over to Mr. Donnithorne Taylor, assisted by Mr. Harris.

Mr. D. Taylor, 1835-36.

Mr. Donnithorne Taylor was given a contract for a certain definite sum of money subject to notice to terminate the agreement by either party to be given on February 1st.　When February 1st came, notice was given but Mr. Taylor did not wish to go.　He was, however, firmly requested to leave.　On March 15th 1836, Mr. Taylor gave a parting dinner to some sixty farmers at the Poyntz Arms, Overton.

Mr. H. A. Fellowes, 1836-45.

Mr. Fellowes resumed control to the general pleasure, and Adamson still carried the horn.　This good man had deteriorated considerably owing to drinking too much and he left in 1842. Will Boxall came as huntsman for one season and had to go because of illness.　John Press then came, to be succeeded by John Dale, a farmer's son from Southington.　He had been passionately devoted to hunting all his life. He served two years with Will Bone and Philip Tocock as his assistants.

On December 17th, 1839, Mr. Fellowes had a good hunt of one and a half hours from Bramley, killing in a bedroom of a house belonging to Mr. J. Newnham of Silchester. A number of good hunts took place from Sherborne Wood, Chinham, Bramley Frith and Manydown.

A curious instance of a hound's homing instinct is given by Mr. R. T. Vyner. A fine bitch called "Frenzy" was sent him in 1834 from the Vine kennels at Overton. As soon as she was let out, she returned home through four counties, a distance of about 100 miles. She was sent back at once by Adamson and duly whelped. As soon as her whelps were weaned she again returned to Overton. On being again sent back to Mr. Vyner, she was tied up in a stable by the carrier about ten miles from her destination. During the night she bit through the cord and she made her third return journey to Overton. This time her pertinacity was rewarded, and she was allowed to remain in peace.

During Mr. Fellowes' mastership in 1844 the picture of the Vine Hunt in Hurstbourne Park was painted by Mr. Henry Calvert. The 1st Duke of Wellington figures prominently dressed in correct hunting costume, with two of his sons, the Marquis of Douro and Lord Charles Wellesley mounted, his daughter-in-law driving a pony chaise with Baron Newmann ; the Master and Miss Mary Fellowes ; some distinguished strangers are mounted, the Archduke of Austria and the Earl of March ; some visitors from the Bramshill Hunt, Lord Dorchester, Mr. Francis P. Piggott, J.P., Mr. Blackall Simmonds, Capt. Frederick, presumably from the Hursley, and a good many of the local notabilities—Colonel W. Beach and his boy, Master W. W. B. Beach, afterwards Master of the Vine Hunt and Father of the House of Commons ; Sir Michael Hicks-Beach, Bart, and his brother, Mr. W. Hicks-Beach ; Mr. Charles Bridges ; Capt. Brown ; Mr. William Chaplin ; Mr. Chapman ; Captain Cunnyngham ; Mr. Curtis ; Mr. A. P. Greville (dismounted) ; Mr. Darby Griffiths ; Mr. William Holding ; Mr. and Mrs. Lees ; Mr. John Portal ; Mr. Robert Rawlins ; Sir Richard Rycroft, Bart. (afterwards Master of the Vine Hunt) ; the Rev. Edward St. John and his son, Mr. Edward St. John ; Mr. George Twynam ; Mr. John Wickham ; 1st Whipper-in, Will Bone, and 2nd Whipper-in, Philip Tocock, and the Duke's groom, John Mears. The picture is an unusually good one and was described in *The Times* as " impressive, important and even dignified." Despite this, John Dale, the huntsman, so much disapproved of the attitude the painter had given him that he would never have the print hung in his room as long as he lived. He is shown riding his favourite horse " Omnibus." The artist has undoubtedly been unkind to the black-coated gentlemen of the Hunt, many of whom were very keen supporters. The Rev. J. Evans of Ashe was well known with the N.F.H. as well as the Vine, the Rev. Champion of Steventon, Rev. M. Harrison of Oakley, Rev. H. Pole of Wolverton, Rev. R. Pigott of Ellisfield in the H.H. country and several others were prominent as also were some very keen farmers, Mr. Twitchin of Hannington, Mr. Pain of Woodmancote, Mr. Webb of Bullington and others. One character in the picture deserves special mention—Mr. Chapman, steward at the Vyne. He knew the lair of every fox and he was even allowed to speak to hounds by name, but as he never jumped a fence, however small, he did not trouble the huntsman much after the find. Mr. Calvert deals more kindly with some of the prominent members than the correspondent to *Bailey's Magazine* who describes the Duke's usual costume as unique, " a red dress coat, white trousers, made of that horrible invention moleskin, cut short to do duty for breeches and of course bagging at the knees, boot-tops brownish and both badly cleaned." Mr. John Portal's coat is said to be " a very long, once red, coat, which reached down to the calves of his legs." The Squire of Dummer, Mr. Stephen Terry, is spoken of as with a coat and hat to match Mr. Portal's, " the former purple in colour."

Perhaps these old sportsmen could have shown the way to the critic, despite their aged coats. In 1845 Mr. Fellowes resigned and he was entertained to dinner at the Poyntz Arms, Overton. Sir William Heathcote of Hursley presided at the dinner.

A Committee, 1845-48.

A Committee now took over with Sir Richard Rycroft as chief manager. Will Cox from the H.H. came as huntsman and his brother George came as whipper-in for three years. John Dale left for the Renfrew and Lanarkshire Hunt.

Sir R. H. C. Rycroft Bart., 1848-49.

Having been at the head of affairs for three years, Sir Richard Henry Charles Rycroft, 3rd Baronet of Calton, Yorkshire, the tenant of Manydown Park, now took the mastership. He suffered misfortune very early by losing Will Cox, his huntsman, through a severe accident. His only whipper-in, James Treadwell, was dismissed for making an impertinent remark to an important subscriber. Charles Barwick succeeded him. In spite of these difficulties Sir Richard had some good sport.

On March 4th, 1848, a fox from Pamber Forest raced through Silchester, Bramley, Sherfield, Hartley Wespall and Stratfield Turges and was killed at Bylands. Another good hunt took place from Waltham Trimleys through Blackwood, Dummer Down, Woodmancote Holt and Thorney Down. This stout fox then crossed the Candover Valley and was killed at Upper Lanham after one hour and fifty minutes, probably covering at least 12 miles of country.

One notable supporter of the hunt in these days from 1845 onwards was an old Waterloo veteran, Mr. John Currie of Southington, who had a silver plate in his head but was very keen.

Sir Richard resigned owing to the many annoyances he had had during the year.

A Committee, 1849-51.

Again a Committee took charge of the affairs of the Hunt. It consisted of Mr. Edward St. John, Mr. Melville Portal and Mr. W. Beach. They carried out some improvements in kennel and Will Cox was still huntsman.

Mr. E. St. John, 1851-52.

Mr. Edward St. John of Church Oakley took control and he showed better sport than had been recently shown. A fine horseman and with hunting in his blood, the Vine might have benefited greatly had not the shires lured him away. He had a hunting-box at Bitteswell, near Lutterworth, and was well known with Mr. Tailby's hounds, the Pytchley and the Atherstone. His hunt servants were Will Cox, Charles Barwick and young George Hickson.

Captain A. Mainwaring, 1852-54.

Captain Arthur Mainwaring of Worting House, fourth son of Sir Harry Mainwaring of Over Peover in Cheshire, now became master. His father had been master of the Cheshire, 1818-37 and he should have known something of the duties of an M.F.H. He obtained the services of George Turner from Lord Southampton as huntsman. As usual, the Duke of

Wellington was appealed to to help the hunt.   He was now an old and very busy man, and not quite so munificent as in 1824. His letter, lent to the author by the late Mr. Ellis W. H. Beach of Dean House, is given in full.   The letter was written to his grandfather.

" London.   April 27th. 1852.

Sir,

I have had the honor of receiving this morning a letter dated the Vine April 26th signed by yourself, in the name of Mr. St. John and yourself, appointed a committee by the Vine Hunt to communicate with me on the subject of the Vine Hounds.   I have besides received a letter upon the same subject from Mr. St. John dated 6th April.   It appears that the gentlemen of the C^y (county) care very little whether it is hunted or not by the Vine Hounds.

There is no person who cares so little about the subject as I do. I am seldom in the county during the hunting season and have little leisure time to enable me to go out with the Hounds.

I have not the honor of any acquaintance with Capt. Mainwaring.

I will subscribe one hundred pounds for the season 1852–1853 if £370 as stated in the paper submitted to me by Mr. St. John is sub-scribed by the gentlemen of the county.

I will be responsible for no more than one hundred pounds.

I have the honor to be,

Your most obedient servant,

WELLINGTON."

The end of the letter is distinctly more encouraging than the earlier portions.   The Duke was then 83 years old and he died five months later on September 14th.   £100 was a generous gift by one who disclaimed interest, and its proportion to the very modest total of other subscriptions mentioned is remarkable.

Besides the Duke, the chief supporters of the Hunt at this time were Lord Charles Wellesley, Lord Lymington, Lord Calthorpe of Elvetham, Hon. T. G. Baring (afterwards the 1st Earl of Northbrook), Sir Richard Rycroft, Captain C. Bridges, Messrs. W. H. Beach, W. S. Chaplin, W. L. Chute, E. St. John, Darby, Griffiths and Oldfield, and General Shubrick often came out from Andover and rode some very good horses.   His instructions to his dealer, by name Bean, were precise and to the point, if somewhat terse.   On one occasion they were: " Bean, start instanter to the North, inspect all blood stock from two years old, and report accordingly."

On January 12th, 1854, Lord Bessborough brought the Royal Buckhounds to Popham Beacons.   He stayed with Lord Ashburton at the Grange.   The country was half covered with snow and the sport was apparently not very good; the stag was taken in Freefolk. Scent is often good under these conditions, so the stag was probably very unenterprising.

Captain Mainwaring went back to his native county in 1854 and was master of the Cheshire Hounds from 1855–58. He did not prove so successful as his father had been.

The Earl of Portsmouth, 1854-58.

Isaac Newton, 5th Earl of Portsmouth, of Hurstbourne Park, succeeded his father in 1854 and at once reassumed the family name of Wallop. To the general satisfaction he took the mastership of the Vine Hounds. A man of great energy and of a very cheerful nature, he not only did everything to show sport, but also founded the North Hants Hunt Club to promote good fellowship. The club was Lord Portsmouth's creation and his own idea and it did not survive long when his lordship was ordered away from Hampshire's cold winds back to Eggesford, his Devon property. His hounds made a great name in the West Country, where he continued to hunt until 1890 with great success.

His loss to the Vine country was very great. A picture was painted of his huntsman George Turner holding mask and brush and blowing his horn, with two hounds, " Bardolf " and " Bobadil " jumping up at him. Frank Goodall, the 1st whipper-in, is in the distance. Arthur Hedges, afterwards huntsman to the Puckeridge, then 2nd whipper-in, does not appear in the picture.

Lord Portsmouth took 50 couple of hounds with him to Eggesford where they were hunted by John Dunn at first and then by Dan Berkshire. Twenty couple he sold to Mr. George D. Wingfield Digby of Sherborne Castle, Dorset, and George Turner went with these hounds to the Blackmore Vale.

The names of the club members are given, as though the club did not have a long life, it represents the chief sporting landowners of North Hampshire 100 years ago :—The Marquis of Ailesbury, Savernake; Mr. Robert Allfrey, Wokefield Park; the Hon. Thomas G. Baring, M.P., Stratton Park; Mr. Thomas Baring, Norman Court; Mr. Thomas Best, Red Rice House; Mr. Slingsby Bethell, Hackwood Park; Mr. John H. Brewer, Garlogs; Captain C. Bridges, Overton; Earl Bruce, Savernake; Earl of Carnarvon, Highclere Castle; Mr. W. L. W. Chute, The Vyne; Mr. Henry B. Coles, Longparish; Sir W. Cubitt, Penton Lodge; Mr. N. Cumberledge,

Crookham ; Lord Dorchester, Greywell ; Mr. Ralph Etwall, Andover ; Mr. William Etwall, Longstock House ; Mr. William Everett, Abbotswood ; Hon. D. Fortescue, M.P., Andover ; Mr. Henry Fowle, Andover ; Mr. Henry Fox, Adbury Lodge ; Mr. W. T. Graeme, Winchester ; Mr. Allan B. Heath, Andover ; Mr. G. J. Huddlestone, Tunworth ; Mr. H. J. Hunt, Kempshott ; Mr. F. J. Ellis-Jervoise, Herriard Park ; Mr. W. Kingsmill, Sydmonton House ; Mr. George Lamb, Worting ; Colonel W. Lascelles, Andover ; Captain Arthur Mainwaring, Worting House ; Mr. R. W. G. Mount, Wasing Place ; Mr. H. S. Oldfield, Beaurepaire ; Mr. W. J. Pearse, South Warnborough ; Mr. Francis Pigott, M.P., Heckfield ; Sir John W. Pollen, Bart., Redenham House ; Mr. W. S. Portal, Church Oakley ; The Earl of Portsmouth, Hurstbourne Park ; Captain W. Prowse, Andover ; Mr. John Quicke, jun. ; Mr. R. S. Routh, Farleigh House ; Mr. Nelson Rycroft, Wootton St. Lawrence ; Mr. George Sclater, Hoddington House ; General Shubrick, Andover ; Mr. Charles J. Slocock, Newbury ; Mr. Thomas Assheton Smith, M.F.H., Tedworth House ; Rev. E. W. St. John, Ashe Park ; Mr. Edward Tredcroft, M.F.H., Alresford ; Captain Tyssen ; Mr. Tyrwhitt Walker, Bossington House ; Sir Joshua Walmesley, Wolverton Park ; Captain R. P. Warren, Worting House ; Mr. Arthur E. Whieldon, Quidhampton ; Mr. George Willes, Hungerford Park.

Walker, alias T. Marsh, 1858-59.

Mr. Thomas Walker, alias Marsh, a relation of Sir Watkin Wynn's huntsman who had been master of the North Herefordshire Hounds in 1856 and had nearly brought ruin to both the hounds and the country. It is curious that this adventurer should twice have been able to add M.F.H. to his assumed name. The only good point recorded of him was that he was a devil to ride. When out with the Vyne he was recognised as an old stud groom of Sir Richard Sutton's, by name Walker, and was addressed by that name. Marsh stoutly denied his identity, but much worse was to follow. On January 30th, 1859, Marsh turned out a bagged fox by the kennels, one hind leg having been cut off, it was said, by his order. Twenty-six couple of hounds were put on the line, Marsh following on horseback. The hounds soon put the wretched animal out of his misery. On February 25th Walker, alias Marsh, was tried by the Bench at Kingsclere. Mr. Melville Portal of Laverstoke was in the chair. The charge was " Causing a fox to be cruelly tortured

on the morning of Sunday, January 30th, contrary to the pro-
visions of 12 and 13 VIC C 92." William Searle, the 1st
whipper-in, gave evidence. The Bench technically could not
convict, the fox not being a " domestic animal." The Chairman, however, expressed the feelings of the Bench on this outrage
to public decency and morality and strongly denounced the gross
cruelty shown. Notices were at once served, prohibiting Walker
from drawing their coverts or entering their lands, by all the
chief landowners in the country. The office of master was
therefore soon vacant.

Mr. A. E. Whieldon, 1859-66.

Mr. Arthur Whieldon of Welton Place, Northamptonshire,
had bought the West Kent hounds which were really a portion
of Mr. J. J. Farquarhson's famous Dorset pack and engaged
their huntsman Humphrey Pearce before he had a country or
kennels and no meeting of the Vine hunt had taken place.
Mr. Whieldon had begun well by being blooded as a very small
boy by Squire Osbaldeston when he killed a fox from Dodford
Holt in his father's park.   Afterwards he and his brother George,
when at Winchester College, kept some harriers and hunted
hare before breakfast on Twyford Down.   His brother was
afterwards Squire of Wyke Hall, near Wincanton. Mr. Whieldon
had hunted regularly in Northamptonshire with the Squire,
Sir Harry Goodricke, and Mr. George Payne.   He had learned
hunting principles from very good sources.   He was accepted
gladly by the Vine Hunt and he showed a better sequence of
sport than any other Hampshire pack for the period.   As his
huntsman said of him, " There's no Mary Ann about my
master."   Some account of his first hunts are given.

Of many good days the following deserves recording as a
remarkable performance.   On 29th November, 1862, hounds
found a stout fox in Lord Portsmouth's ozier beds at Tufton,
raced over the meadows through Hurstbourne Park into
Wherwell Wood.   Mr. Whieldon, his two whippers-in and
two of the field were with hounds.   The fox was forced right
through this enormous covert of 4,000 acres without a check or
turn and he took the open again by Lower Clatford, after four
miles of woodland.   He then crossed the river leaving Red
Rice on the left and hounds ran into their fox dead beat below
Abbots Ann in the Tedworth country, after one hour and
twenty-five minutes with every hound up.   Curiously enough

the Tedworth had met at Red Rice and said they had no scent.
The only others of the field who rode out this splendid hunt
were Captain Harvey and his brother Henry, Messrs. George
Brooks, George Rawlins of Bullingdon, and Benjamin Bovill
of Farley. The distance was about 13 or 14 miles.

Another great hunt took place from a meet at Elvetham on
the 29th December, 1864. This hunt was almost entirely in
the Garth country. The fox broke over Wildmoor and ran
through Tylney Park and Blackwood. He afterwards crossed
Murrell Green, leaving Bramshill to the left and finally this
stout fox met his end near Blackwater, after a run of nearly
three hours. The point was about 18 miles and the hunt
some 26 miles. Hounds killed when darkness was falling at
5 p.m. The master's second horse was quite beaten and he
had to borrow another to jog his weary way home—30 miles
to the kennels at Overton, which he safely reached at 10 p.m.
Nowadays this journey over Hartfordbridge Flat, with blazing
motor cars travelling at speed, would be a real nightmare.
While hounds were running in full cry over the Flat they met
Mr. Garth's hounds jogging along with Robert Tocock and
Tom Sweetman in charge, to take up their quarters at the inn
there. These fresh, eager hounds could not be stopped from
joining in and for a time both packs ran together. The hunt
servants were eventually able to stop the Garth hounds, presumably at some short check, and the Vine pack finished their
run by themselves, but with several fresh followers from the
Garth Hunt who came out to the cry of hounds. Another
good hunt in the afternoon took place from Great Deane Wood
past the Vyne to Stratfieldsaye, where hounds killed without
a check. A curious incident happened one day in the fir
plantations at Aldermaston. The master was galloping through
the wood when his horse put his foot in a rabbit hole, throwing
Mr. Whieldon against a tree where he lay stunned for some
time. Luckily some kind followers searched for him and they
saw a white object on the ground. Approaching nearer they
found an old bitch called " Cordial " lying by the master and
licking his blood-stained face. This hound had been a present
from Lord Portsmouth to the master : such devotion is most
remarkable. Another hound named " Bounty " distinguished
herself in the lake at Ewhurst Park. The pack were swimming
after a fox in view, when the fox sank exhausted in deep water.
Old " Bounty " dived and brought up the dead fox and swam
with him to land.

During this most successful mastership only one angry complaint was made by an old dame who had lost some poultry. On his return home Mr. Whieldon wrote the following note, enclosing a sovereign: "A sovereign remedy for lost fowls. N.B.—One dose quite sufficient." The dose was enough and the old dame always met the master with a smile and a welcome, and also with a fox on the farm as well.

Covert owners helped by cutting rides through the biggest woods, Mr. Melville Portal setting an example by cutting a wide ride straight through Freefolk Wood. Browndown, Deane's Wood and Great Deane Wood were also attended to by Mr. Harwood and Mr. Terry.

During Mr. Whieldon's mastership he had not a blank day. Among his many supporters were Mr. John Arundel of Brimpton and Mr. George Brooks of Monk Sherborne. This sportsman fed his pet litter with partridges when rats and rabbits failed. His most prominent farmer supporters were the Twitchins, father and son, a name to be long well known in sport (they were then at North Oakley), John Bailey of Bear Mill, Beckingham Ashe, Stephen Burdass of Freefolk, Francis Budd, M.H. of Cliddesden, J. Hooper of Litchfield, Meate of Overton, and G. Webb of Hannington.

Mr. Whieldon was well supported also by the Church. The Rev. Charles Pettat, Rector of Ashe and Dean, took the keenest interest in the kennels and others came from Newbury and the edge of the H.H. Country.

His hunt servants were Pearce, who stayed till 1861, but drink became his undoing; George Southwell succeeded him, a very good hunt servant in kennel and in the field. He had had previous experience in the Cottesmore, Southwold, Craven and Tiverton countries. Henry Purdue, whipped-in, who used to run after hounds in Lord Portsmouth's time. Mr. Whieldon had done a great deal to put sport in the Vine country at a high level. On March 4th, 1862, he was presented with a silver horn at the Town Hall at Basingstoke. No previous master of the Vine had been so honoured.

Sir Bruce Chichester, 1866-68.

Sir Bruce Chichester was then living at Manydown Park. For his first season George Southwell hunted the pack and James Stacey carried the horn the next season. Stacey afterwards hunted a pack in Portugal. Sir Bruce retired through ill-health.

Rt. Hon. W. W. B. Beach, P.C., M.P., 1868-88.

The Rt. Honourable William Wither Bramston Beach, P.C., M.P., D.L., of Oakley Hall and Keevil Manor, Wilts, now succeeded to the mastership.   A large landowner and one who had hunted with the Vine from boyhood, no choice could have given greater satisfaction.   He appears in Calvert's picture as a boy in Eton jacket.   Mr. Beach was not a hard rider, in fact it is said that he seldom exceeded a trot, but he enjoyed the sport and was courteous to all and popular in the county.   He represented North Hampshire in Parliament from 1857–85 and West Hampshire from 1885 to 1901, becoming latterly " Father of the House."   It is said that during this long period he never inflicted a speech on his fellow-members : on one occasion, however, he asked for a window to be closed.   James Stacey continued as huntsman and proved competent.   Rather over 40 couple were kept in kennel and hounds hunted three days a week.   Henry Strike was 1st whipper-in.   Stacey had served with many packs, starting with Lord Petre in 1833, Mr. Drax 1840. He then learnt a good deal with Harry Ayres with the Berkeley, and served the V.W.H., the Old Berkshire, the Cottesmore, Mr. J. J. Farquharson, Lord Henry Bentinck, then with Mr. Ramsay for eight years, six years as huntsman, returning to England at his master's death to serve one year with the Cambridgeshire before coming to the Vine with a ripe experience of 34 years with ten different packs of hounds.

In 1887 subscriptions decreased and the Committee of the Hunt had difficulty in raising the £1,200 per annum promised to Mr. Beach.   The Committee also found the country hunted inadequate for three days a week and the Hon. Secretary, Mr. A. Gordon Russell, approached the South Berks Hunt as to taking back some of the country loaned to them.   The new boundary proposed was from Pineapple Brimpton, the Furze Bush, Aldermaston, then straight to Buttersland Farm and thence south along by the Fair Oak Lilly Mill to Sherfield.   Some difference of boundary was proposed by the South Berks through their Secretary, Captain Knight, and the matter was dropped in 1888.   A very unusual and somewhat interesting case appeared at Newbury County Court on August 11th, 1887.   A farmer, Alfred Vince of Ram Alley Farm, Kingsclere, sued the master for £50 damages alleged to be suffered by him through depreciation of his flock from fright caused owing to the huntsman Perry taking his hounds twice through a sheep fold near Dairyhouse covert.   Hounds were in perfect control and the shepherd took a hurdle out to let them through and the deterioration was not immediate but noticed a month later. Judge Lushington gave the case for Mr. Beach. Apparently all was peacefully and privately arranged afterwards and Mr. Vince appears among the first lot of farmers to receive the Hunt button next year. The Committee then appointed to deal with this case was Colonel Bickerstaffe, the Earl of Carnarvon, H. Harris, Esq., W. H. Kingsmill, Esq., General W. Lukin.

Mr. Beach received the general support of landowners and farmers. Though he could not devote a great deal of time to the routine duties of a master of hounds owing to his public duties, it was a great advantage to the country to have a settled management for twenty years. Mr. Beach started by keeping very careful accounts, but soon gave up the bother of totalling them. Expenses were not heavy, never exceeding £1,500: for some years they were a good deal less. Hound meal came down during his period of office from £18 a ton to £11 a ton. Hay fell from £7 a ton to £4 a ton; oats from 30s. a quarter to £1 a quarter. Wages remained the same; his huntsman received £10 a month, others from £2 a month to £5. 10s. 8d. a month, the latter perhaps the stud groom.

Subscriptions did not vary much until his last years when they declined. The chief financial supporters were the Duke of Wellington, the Earl of Carnarvon, Sir Nelson Rycroft, who gave £100 per annum each; Mr. John Hargreaves and Mr. Henry Harris gave £50 each. Some yearly expenses may be of interest in comparing them with the inflated prices of modern days. His saddler's bill was about £10, blacksmith's about £20, tailor's about £40. Mr. Evans of Basingstoke provided all the men's clothing; the last of the family only went out of business in 1948. Expenses generally did not alter very much until the First World War.

On his retirement Mr. Beach received his portrait, given by the Vine Hunt, the Earl of Northbrook taking the chair and making the presentation.

Mr. A. G. Russell and Mr. G. H. Pember, 1888-93

Mr. Alexander Gordon Russell, eldest son of General Lord Alexander George Russell, G.C.B., tenth son of John 6th Duke of Bedford, then renting Ewhurst Park from the 3rd Duke of Wellington, and Mr. George Herbert Pember of Tangier Park came as joint masters, with H. White as huntsman.

In May, 1883, the Hunt decided to increase the Committee to 24 members which would seem a rather unwieldy body. The Committee were permitted to wear the Hunt button with powers to grant this privilege to other subscribers of £20 and upwards by ballot. Farmers being permitted to receive this privilege without subscriptions. The proposition to form a Hunt Club was defeated. Wherwell Wood was loaned to the Tedworth Hunt in July of this year. In November, 1888, 14 ladies, the wives and daughters of members of the Committee, were granted the Hunt button, as also were 23 farmers and four other gentlemen. Some of the farmers' names were well known in Hampshire sport for many years—Messrs. B. Barton, G. Beckingham, Albert Booth, G. K. Budd, John Butler, Charles and William Clift, Edward and John Cooper, William Ilsley, Richard Portsmouth, John Pain, John Rowden, Styning, Andrew, Edwin and Tom Twitchen, S. Wentworth and S. Wickham.

About this time four blackcoats took a prominent part in the Hunt affairs, the Rev. A. G. Barker, the Rev. W. Marriner, the Rev. J. Scott-Ramsay and the Rev. F. W. Thoyts. The Mayor of Basingstoke, Major (afterwards Colonel) John May, attended Hunt meetings which were usually held at the Town Hall, Basingstoke by his permission. He was a very generous and public-spirited gentleman whose name is perpetuated by May's Bounty, the fine sportsground presented to the town. Colonel May also kept a pack of harriers for four or five years. Other prominent supporters were Melville Portal, Esq., Colonel Portal, General Sir Pollexfen Radcliffe, Sir Nelson Rycroft, A. W. Thornton, Esq. In December of the same year, 1887, the names of G. H. Pember, Esq., and Dr. Reginald Maples were added; both of these gentlemen gave great service to the Hunt, the latter for many years. Mr. Beach's resignation was received with much regret but both the new joint masters were well known in the Vine country.

As Mr. Russell was now to be joint master for the ensuing season he had to resign the Hon. Secretaryship which onerous post was taken by Mr. Arthur Lamb of Basingstoke who held it from 1888 until 1896.

Mr. A. G. Russell, 1893-96.

Mr. Alexander Gordon Russell, tenant of Ewhurst Park, now assumed sole control and appointed Tom Attrill, a former

The Rt. Hon. W. W. B. Beach, p.c., m.p., M.F.H. 1868-88.

His Grace, The 4th Duke of Wellington, k.g., g.c.v.o., on " Nimrod."

Sir R. N. Rycroft, Bart., M.F.H. 1903-13.

whipper-in, as his huntsman. A testimonial was presented to Mr. Russell and to his daughter at the opening meet of the next season at Tangier Park.

Mr. G. H. Pember, 1896 - 1900.

Mr. George Herbert Pember again came forward at the wish of the Hunt and succeeded Mr. Russell. Mr. Russell offered to act as Hon. Secretary for the season as Mr. Lamb had retired and died almost immediately afterwards. The master brought in Will Haynes as huntsman who came from the Ledbury Hunt. Dr. Maples had helped Mr. Lamb as Assistant Secretary, which office he had added to his many duties as doctor and general pacifier of claims on the Hunt.

In October, 1896, Mr. B. Gartside gave the shooting of Sherborne Wood to the Hunt, a very sporting gesture which was most gratefully received.

Mr. F. G. Barker, now Colonel Barker, c.b.e., Chairman of the Garth Hunt, became Hon. Secretary in succession to Mr. Russell in 1897. In 1901 he handed over to Mr. R. C. Blencowe as his militia regiment were embodied.

Captain A. G. Russell (3rd Mastership), 1900-01

Captain Russell again took control for one season with Tom Attrill carrying the horn. The chief cause of Captain Russell's resignation was that the 4th Duke of Wellington wished to live at Ewhurst Park on succeeding to the title on his brother's death in 1900.

Mr. E. B. Podmore, 1901-03.

Mr. E. Boyce Podmore took West Ham House and not only took over the mastership, but also kept a pack of harriers for his small son " Bob." The boy, aged about ten, hunted his hounds with some success and his father whipped-in to him. Mr. Podmore hunted the foxhounds himself with Tom Attrill as whipper-in and kennel huntsman. Mr. Podmore took the Cotswold country for one year after leaving the Vine. His son died at this time and Mr. Podmore did not again hunt hounds. Mr. Podmore died in 1928, aged 67.

Sir R. N. Rycroft Bart., 1903-13

Sir Richard Nelson Rycroft, 5th Baronet of Calton, Yorks., who lived at Dummer House, now took the mastership, to the great pleasure of the country. Sir Richard was born in 1859

M

and had always been a keen sportsman. He was a D.L. of the county and had served in the Rifle Brigade and with the Imperial Yeomanry in the South African War and also commanded a squadron of the Hampshire Yeomanry.

Tom Attrill hunted the hounds and looked well after them in kennel. In the field he became rather slow latterly for his hard-riding and energetic master. The field was considerably enlarged by a keen contingent of Aldershot officers who became regular supporters of the Hunt on Saturdays. Sport continued to be quite satisfactory though there were some doubtful places where no litters were safe.

Sir Richard bred many horses but never was lucky enough to breed one up to his weight as a hunter. Sir Richard was able to get a Vine Hunt Club started to try and encourage more general interest in the Hunt. At a meeting at Malshanger, then the residence of Sir Wyndham S. Portal, Bart., on April 6th, 1903, a club was formed of landowners or tenants of property in the Vine country. The subscription was £20, except for non-resident landlords who could join for seven guineas. Sons or brothers of members who had no separate establishment could also join as honorary members for seven guineas. The wives, daughters and sisters of members were given the privilege of wearing the Hunt button. The evening dress was laid down as a scarlet coat with white facings, black collar with Vine leaf embroidered at the corners. A Committee of the President, Hon. Secretary and six members was arranged for. The President was the 4th Duke of Wellington and the Hon. Secretary was Mr. R. C. Blencowe, and the original Committee besides the President and Hon. Secretary were Rev. A. G. Barker, Major-General W. Lukin, Messrs. H. Welch Thornton, W. J. Walker and M. A. Booth. The farmers' representatives were Mr. W. Clift and R. Cooper. The master was an *ex-officio* member of the Committee. The President was a mainstay of the Vine Hunt until his death. The Rev. A. G. Barker, a great sportsman of the race of squarsons which now seems extinct in the county. Mr. Harry Welch-Thornton was very keen but, becoming a sufferer from horse asthma, had to give up hunting and driving his team. He sold Beaurepaire Park and retired to Devonshire and became master of the Culmstock Otterhounds from 1906–31, so he still could enjoy the cry of hounds which he loved so well. Mr. W. J. Walker, the tenant of Wolverton Pack, was a great sportsman and a firm supporter of the Hunt till his death. All the members were not great hunting men, but many of the non-hunting men attended the meetings and the club did good in arousing more general interest. One original member, Mr. J. L. Longstaffe, was a most sporting London solicitor. With his long flowing grey beard he was a well-known character with the Vine and the H.H., enjoying every minute of his day's outing. Two of the original nine honorary members elected became popular and efficient Hon. Secretaries—Major (now Colonel) F. G. Barker had already served from 1897–1900 and again took office from 1907–09; Colonel (afterwards Brigadier-General Sir) Bertram Portal carried on from 1909 till 1913, when he became field master and handed over his secretarial duties to Mr. C. L. Chute. Mr. W. Holding succeeded Mr. Blencowe in 1906, but ill-health forced him to resign the next year.

A good hunt of one hour and forty-five minutes took place on February 2nd, 1903. A fox from Summer Down took hounds very fast through Great Deane Wood, Firth Wood, left-handed into Warren Bottom, on towards Ibworth to Deane Wood by Hannington, back to Warren Bottom, by Great Deane Wood to Little Wood; the fox was then viewed under Clerkengreen Arch into Oakley Park, hunted through the grounds and keeper's cottage to East Oakley, crossed the railway over Homesteads Ltd. into Fardown and was killed nearby nearby.

On January 31st, 1905, a four-hour hunt took place when scenting conditions were bad and frost had prevented hunting for a fortnight. A fox got away from Paul's Wood almost before hounds were in covert, but they got on to his line over Northfields across the railway line to the kennels. He crossed and recrossed the line again and then went past Ashe Rectory, through Ashe Park, past the house, over Cheesedown Farm, into Oakley Park, where a check occurred. He was picked up again in Smalls and crossed the Winchester Road, over Hatch Warren Farm to Sullingers, Short Wood and Inn Wood, across to Nutley by the Grove near Dummer Grange and killed near the Alresford road by Nutley village. This gave a point of nine and a quarter miles, a fine performance under difficult conditions.

Sir Richard says in his diary that a day from Maynards on March 3rd, 1906, was the best day he ever had in Hampshire. They ran towards Sherfield, left-handed to Ross Copse, over Sherfield Farm, across Bullsdown Brook, raced by Bullsdown Copse, through Bramley Camp, by the Lodden, Longbridge

Mill, Hartley Common Wood towards Heckfield, through Reeves to Pithams and then out of the master's knowledge of place names, but hounds killed.

A very good hunt occurred on December 24th, 1909, from Silchester to Stratfieldsaye, back through Tubbs Gully, nearly to Carpenter's Down into Sherfield Manor, Ragg Copse and gave up by Bullsdown, hounds running from 11.15 a.m. to 3.40 p.m. over heavy ground and working beautifully over the cold ploughs.

On February 26th, 1910, a fox was shaken down from a tree near Devenish and was accounted for. Another was found in Frith and gave a fine run of an hour and fifty minutes, being killed at Cufauld, some casualties occurring in the Bulls-down Brook. The master always went straight ahead and latterly sometimes went away with about five couple of hounds, leaving Attrill to come on with the rest. The author remembers a hunt on February 10th, 1912, when about five couples ran without a check from Ewhurst over a rather trappy country past the Pine Apple, Brompton, to ground in a copse opposite King John's Hill in the Craven country. A gallant officer told him he had taken twelve tosses and appeared to have thoroughly enjoyed them. The yearly tally was generally 13 or 14 brace including cubhunting, and in the last years of Sir Richard's mastership this dropped to six brace.

Sir Richard was a most popular master and did his utmost to show sport. In addition to farming some 3,000 acres he took an active part in all county affairs where his sound judgment was of great value. When hounds were running his broad-shouldered figure with coat wide open and a bunch of violets in his button-hole was a most characteristic figure at the van of a hunt.

Lady Portal, 1913-16.

Lady Portal, wife of Sir William Wyndham Portal, 2nd Baronet of Laverstoke Park, now became the first lady master of the Vine. Her brother-in-law, Colonel Bertram P. Portal, C.B., D.S.O. (afterwards Brigadier-General Sir Bertram Portal, K.B.E.), and Sir Wyndham Portal became field masters. Sir Bertram was generally in charge and he knew everybody in the country from his work as Honorary Secretary. These duties were taken over by Mr. C. L. Chute of the Vyne who obtained the assistance of Dr. R. Maples in his work. Dr. Maples was afterwards able to carry on when Mr. Chute proceeded on active service. He already was in charge of the Poultry Fund. Everything started very well. Lady Portal added 20 couple of hounds to the existing 35 couple and obtained the services of Ernest Jones as huntsman. In her first season 27½ brace of foxes were accounted for, a considerable increase on the usual tally and one which probably has seldom been equalled. In 1915 Lady Portal, owing to war difficulties and her numerous duties resigned but continued to act as master for another season to some extent.

A Committee, 1916-1919.

A Committee consisting of the Duke of Wellington, President of the Hunt Club, Mr. W. J. Walker and the acting Hon. Secretary, Dr. R. Maples, now assumed control. Dr. Maples was a most indefatigable worker as well as very keen follower. Dr. Maples, besides looking after the poultry and acting as Hon. Secretary, also acted as field master after Lady Portal resigned. The Duke was the largest landowner in the county and his Ewhurst, Wolverton and Hannington properties were all in the Vine country and the supply of foxes was always certain. The Duke also supplied foxes on his Stratfieldsaye estate to the South Berks and to the Garth, but as he lived at Ewhurst Park himself the Vine were his particular interest and he was a most regular follower as long as he could possibly ride. For the last few years he was physically unable to ride and followed in a motor car. Owing to Mr. C. L. Chute's absence on active service Dr. Maples took over the duties of Hon. Secretary in 1915. This Committee ably steered the Hunt through the remaining difficult war years.

Mr. R. H. Gosling, 1919-23.

Mr. Robert Henry Gosling of Ashe Park succeeded the Committee. Mr. Gosling had been master of the Garth Hunt for seventeen years. He was an acknowledged expert in hound breeding and was asked to judge at the Peterborough Show. Ernest Jones continued as huntsman. Mr. Gosling got together a good pack of hounds after the difficulties of the war years, but the staff were hardly well mounted enough to keep with hounds when they were really running. Wire after the war increased but it was still quite possible to get to hounds in the woodland Saturday country.

A very fast hunt took place in Mr. Gosling's last season after a meet at Beaurepaire House on 19th January. The first

fox, from Quarry Copse, was hunted slowly by Little London
and given up on the edge of Pamber Forest.   George, the 1st
whipper-in, was hunting hounds.   The next fox, from Bramley
Firth, went well away through Rampiers, over Silchester Camp,
past Mortimer West End and through the Hundred Acres.
Hounds hunting beautifully through the fir woods.   The first
check occurred on the cross-roads by the S.E. corner of Aldermaston Park.   One bitch hit the line, but there was only
one broken pale in the Deer Park palings where a hound could
get in.   No hunt staff being present, it was difficult to get
hounds in as they could not jump the Deer Park palings. About
five couple, however, entered and rolled their fox over in the
park fairly beaten as the rest of the pack were brought round
by the first gate.   Unfortunately they put up a deer and prevented the proper rites being performed on the fox and a good
mask was lost.   The hunt was eight miles as fast as a good horse
could gallop and hounds were unassisted until the cross-roads
and park palings were encountered.

On the 2nd February hounds had a very good hunt from
Birdalls by Beaurepaire and Cranes where the fox was headed
and ran back by Morgastens and the Vyne Park Copse where a
short check occurred, on to Bramley Frith, over the railway into
South Berks country.   Hounds ran the old London—Silchester
road for a short time, left Mortimer on the west and were only
two minutes behind over Beech Hill.   Here, after two hours
and a quarter, unfortunately the fox was holload, some hounds
got their heads up and saw a hare.   Here, too, George came up
and, forgetting his horn, galloped to rate these hounds and the
fox lived. A great deal of country had been covered and only one
check had occurred till the unfortunate ending.   Most of the
hunt was fast and provided a considerable variety of obstacles.
Hounds hunted very well, but had not been cured of riot. If,
however, no holloaing had taken place they would undoubtedly
have killed their fox.

Mr. Gosling left a good-looking level pack of English
foxhounds.

In 1923 Dr. Maples resigned the Hon. Secretaryship both
of the Hunt and the Poultry Fund after very strenuous and
difficult years of good work.   Mr. Charles Illingworth of
Bramley took over both duties.

Mr. A. W. H. Dalgety, 1923-26.

Mr. Arthur William Hugh Dalgety came from a county
family settled for about a hundred years at Lockerley Hall, near

Romsey. He was an old 9th Lancer officer and an enthusiastic sportsman and a keen houndman. During his mastership he lived at Overton by the kennels. As always, the Duke of Wellington was the greatest friend and supporter to the new master. Only once was there a disagreement which is worth relating. In October the Duke wrote suggesting a day in late November for his best covert shoot. The master naturally arranged to meet seven or more miles away. Hounds chose to run a six-mile point straight into the Duke's shoot. Hounds were stopped and taken home at 2.30 p.m. Next morning at 11 a.m. a clatter of horse's feet round the stable yard and a liveried groom presented a courteous note asking the master to see the Duke as soon as he could. That evening the master went over to Ewhurst and received his only rebuke, not, however, for running into the shoot, but for the effrontery of his stopping hounds.

In 1926 Mr. Dalgety was joined by another keen young sportsman Mr. R. S. Gilbey, but Mr. Dalgety continued to hunt hounds.

Mr. A. W. H. Dalgety and Mr. R. S. Gilbey, 1926-29.

Mr. Rupert S. Gilbey lived at Hyde End Farm, near Newbury. Sport improved and Mr. Dalgety rode up to his hounds. Mr. Dalgety had two good hunts in 1928. One, to celebrate Leap Year, on February 29th, finding at 3 p.m. at Haywood and running by Sydmonton, over Litchfield Down and over Beacon Hill, killing at Hollington—a nine mile point. The other from Nutley Bottom on March 25th, within a mile of the Vine kennels and killed on Lady Craven's estate about a mile from the Craven kennels. This hunt was about a seven-mile point and ten miles as hounds ran. Not content with hunting the fox, Mr. Dalgety kept a small pack of deerhounds with which he hunted deer as opportunity arose. He killed several fallow buck from Sir Alfred Herbert's woods near Whitchurch. In 1929 this partnership ended and Mr. Dalgety went as master of the Southdown Hunt where he has remained in control for the next twenty years, sometimes alone and sometimes with a joint master. He has also not forgotten the deer, having been joint master of the New Forest Buckhounds on two occasions, 1936–38 and 1944–47.

Mr. C. H. Illingworth took on the duties of Hon. Hunt Secretary in 1923 and remained in office until 1945, giving great help to the Hunt generally and being a regular follower.

Major C. F. Garrard and Mr. J. M. Hastings, 1929-32.

Mr. Charles F. Garrard lived at Stanton House, Kingsclere, and hunted hounds alternately with Mr. John Maurice Hastings who lived at first at Mill House, Old Basing, and afterwards at Malshanger.

Fred Roberts was 1st whipper-in and kennel huntsman to the masters.

Sir N. E. O. Rycroft, Bart., 1932-38.

Sir Nelson Edward Oliver Rycroft, Baronet, of Dummer House now became master. He was the fourth generation of his family to be master of the Vine hounds. His father Sir Richard, his maternal grandfather, the Earl of Portsmouth, his great-grandfather, Sir Richard, had all proved themselves as good masters of hounds. Mr. Henry Fellowes, too, another very popular master, was his great-uncle. No one worked harder to make the country rideable by putting up hunting gates, chicken coops and unbreakable railway sleeper jumps in the wire which had greatly increased. He also tried very hard, and with some success, to reclaim much of the Tuesday down-land country which had ceased to be hunted for lack of foxes. Unfortunately some blank days in this country were still endured. New kennels, which were badly wanted, were built at Sandford Farm. His huntsman, Fred Roberts, did all he could to show sport and was popular with followers, farmers and keepers. Two amateur whippers-in ably assisted him, Major Claud Booth and Mr. James King, who was succeeded by Mr. H. Brown. Good sport was maintained and hounds generally accounted for 13 or 14 brace of foxes, hunting two days a week. On several occasions hunts giving six- or seven-mile points were enjoyed, but hounds were sometimes defrauded of a kill in these hunts.

On February 10th, 1934, a good day followed a meet at Bramley. Finding in the Frith, hounds ran fast to Pamber Forest and after a turn round the forest ran out by Howes Farm over the stream past Gosling's Farm to Silchester Walls and marked to ground where the fox was killed by terriers. Then from N. Copse another fox was run to ground in the South Berks country by the Great Western Railway. The next fox, found in Devenish, ran by Butlers Land to the Mount back through the Walls, Scrubbs, to Three Ashes, on by the forest through the Plantation by Blackwater and Cranes to Sherborne Wood. The leading hounds were seen just behind their fox by Rooksdown pointing for Worting Wood.

Sir Nelson's best season was 1935-36, but the records have unfortunately been lost.

In 1934 the Hunt suffered an irreparable loss in the death of the 4th Duke of Wellington, their President. A tale, typical of this great sportsman, may be related here. At a Committee meeting of the Hunt Club in 1933 held at Ewhurst, the Duke produced a bottle of his best port wine saying, " I am the happiest man in England ; I have had foxhounds on my property every day in the week except Sunday." His health was drunk with enthusiasm. Few landowners in England could say as much. Presumably the Vine, South Berks, Garth and the Craven must all have been on his estate. Mr. Charles L. Chute of the Vyne succeeded the Duke in the Presidency of the Hunt Club.

Captain W. Fox, 1938-40.

Captain William Fox of Adbury Park, near Newbury, now became master and also carried the horn. He had had previous experience as amateur huntsman to Lady Curre's famous pack He brought Harry Guold with him as 1st whipper-in and K.H. Captain Fox had served in the 60th Rifles and Seaforth High-landers and on the outbreak of war in 1939 he was called up and joined the 2nd Battalion Seaforth Highlanders, with whom he was killed in 1940. During Captain Fox's absence on service, Mrs. Walford assumed the duties of acting master with Harry Gould as huntsman. A very keen sportsman, Captain Fox's loss at this time was a very serious blow to the Hunt.

Mrs. J. H. Walford, 1940-41.

Mrs. Walford (*née* Miss Diana Myrtle Ralli) was the eldest daughter of Sir Strati Ralli, Bart., M.C., of Beaurepaire Park. Mrs. Walford made her home with her parents as her husband had also rejoined the 2nd Battalion Seaforth Highlanders. Mrs. Walford had to give up the mastership for reasons of health and the pack became dormant. Financial stringency forced the sale of the kennels. Six couple of hounds were kept with the Craven and these were bred from to keep a nucleus for future years.

In 1945 Mr. C. L. Chute of the Vyne resigned the Presidency of the Club and Mr. Charles Illingworth resigned the Hon. Secretaryship after 22 years of very valuable service. Sir Nelson

E. O. Rycroft became President and Major J. C. Humphrey of Island Heron, Wolverton Common, took over the duties of Honorary Secretary. Both of these gentlemen are still in office. From 1946–49 the South Berks hunted some of the Vine country adjoining their own and used the Vine hounds, which they had taken over from the Craven, as far as possible when they hunted this country.

Lieut.-Colonel J. H. Walford, D.S.O., 1949-

Lieut.-Colonel John Herbert Walford, D.S.O. and bar, of the Old House, Wolverton, after a distinguished military career in the 60th Rifles and Seaforth Highlanders, now retired from the Army and became master under very difficult circumstances. Temporary kennels were built at Hannington which proves a good centre for hunting the country. Colonel Walford is hunting the whole country as it was hunted before the war. Much of the country has been unhunted and it is impossible to produce first-rate sport everywhere and at once. Hounds, however, have been well received and prospects next season are good.

Several useful hunts took place about Christmas time in the season, 1949–50. On Christmas Eve a five and a half mile point from Kingsclere Down to North Lodge, Sandleford Priory; on Boxing Day a good hound hunt of about eight miles from Little London to ground in the South Berks country and a very good children's day from the master's house on January 17th. Thirty members of the Pony Club with five instructors turned out and saw the first fox marked to ground; after this Sandford Wood provided a good fox who gave them a fast five and a half mile point to Aldermaston Court where hounds were stopped. Nimrod Capell carries the horn and Tom Nottingham is whipper-in. Capell is a son of Ben Capell of Belvoir fame, and the son also has hunted the Belvoir hounds and then the South Atherstone, 1930–36, and the South Staffordshire for six seasons before coming to the Vine. Both Colonel Walford's family and his wife's are well known in the county at Arlebury, Wolverton and Beaurepaire, both are popular and very keen. They have worked very hard to get the country and the hounds in proper order and it is to be hoped that their efforts will meet with success and that every assistance will be given them. More farmers are hunting than formerly, but at present few landowners have been out.

CHAPTER VII.

THE HAMBLEDON HUNT.

Masters of the Hambledon Hunt.

1800–04	Mr. T. Butler, Bury Lodge, Hambledon.
1804–06	Colonel J. Cook, Soberton.
1806–07	[1]*Major-General T. de Burgh (afterwards Lord Clanricarde)*, Belmont (afterwards Warnford Park).
1807–16	Mr. W. Powlett-Powlett, Lainston House (West).
1813–14	Mr. John Delmé, Cams (East).
1814–15	Mr. Joseph Eyles, East Meon (East).
1815–16	Rev. G. Richards, North House (East).
1816–21	Mr. A. F. Nunez, Warnford Park.
1821–22	Sir B. R. Graham (for three months and Mr. G. Osbaldeston—finished season), Hill Place.
1822–23	Mr. J. Walker, Purbrook Park.
1823–25	Mr. C. Shard, Hill Place, Droxford.
1825–29	Mr. T. Smith, Hill House, Hambledon.
1829–41	Mr. J. King, Corhampton.
1841–48	Mr. W. J. Long, Preshaw.
1848–52	Mr. T. Smith, Fir Hill, Droxford.
1852–56	Mr. G. Wall, Warnford.
1856–59	Mr. W. J. Long (second mastership), Preshaw.
1859–68	Captain W. H. Poulett (afterwards 6th Earl Poulett).
1868–71	Colonel J. Bower, Studwell Lodge.
1871–72	Captain Sullivan (killed).
1872–74	Mr. W. J. Long (third mastership), Preshaw.
1874–89	Mr. W. Long (jun.), Preshaw.
1889–94	Mr. T. W. Harvey, Purbrook Park.
1894–1900	Hon. F. A. Baring, Meonstoke House.
1900–07	Major W. P. Standish (West), Marwell Hall.
1900–07	Mr. H. S. Whalley Tooker (East), Hinton Daubnay.
1907–15	Captain W. P. Standish (whole County), Marwell Hall.
1915–21	{ Major W. P. Standish O.B.E., Marwell Hall. { Mr. S. Hardy, The Spain, Petersfield.
1921–26	Mr. S. Hardy, The Spain, Petersfield.
1926–29	Major E. F. Talbot-Ponsonby, Hill Place, Swanmore.
1929–33	Major J. Blake, Monckton House, Alverstoke.

[1] The hunt was then a harrier pack.

1933–35   Mr. G. Joynson.
1935–39   Mr. J. P. Long, West Lodge, West Meon.
1946–49   Captain P. Vivian, R.N., Hill Place Cottage, Swan-
              more.
1949–   Lieut.-Colonel J. H. Hulbert, Fir Hill, Droxford.

The Hambledon country is about 18 miles North to South by 20 miles East to West. " Nimrod " describes it as " a rough uncouth country, abounding in woods and forests, but the best in Hampshire for hounds."   " Gelert " calls it " the best country south of London."   Actually, if the difficulties of modern times, broken-up estates, barbed wire, bungalows, ploughed-up commons and downs can be forgotten, it then had more country carrying a scent than most of its neighbours.   No expense or energy now can bring back its former state when hounds could be really followed over its strongly-fenced vale from Bishop's Stoke, Durley, Bishop's Waltham to Wickham.   Despite all difficulties it remains a very pleasant country to hunt in and it is easier to see something of hound work in the open than in most of the Hampshire packs.   It has suffered severely lately in the break-up of estates, Westbury, Basing Park and Cor-hampton among others having come under the hammer.   In a previous chapter Mr. T. Land has been referred to as having hunted parts of the Hambledon country in the 18th century. The author does not think, however, that his greatest admirer would have said that he had an established country. He was a tenant of Winchester College and owned no land and he had no permission at any time to hunt in the Forest of Bere, then still a Crown Forest.   Colonel Thomas de Burgh had hunted fox around his home at Belmont, but he gave his hounds to the Prince of Wales in 1793.   Some landowners were members of the H.H., but that pack could not give all the sport desired and so " a meeting was held for the purpose of establishing a pack of foxhounds in the vicinity of Hambledon, as it was the desire of many gentlemen fond of rural sport to have the amusement of that noble diversion, foxhunting, as there was at that time no established pack of foxhounds convenient to the gentlemen resident in that neighbourhood to enable them to partake of that noble diversion."

Mr. T. Butler, 1800-04.

As a result of this meeting a hunting club was formed in the year 1800. Mr. Thomas Butler of Bury Lodge engaged " to collect a pack of foxhounds which should consist of not more than 30 couple nor less than 20 couple, to provide for their maintenance and every expense at his own cost, with also a kennel and such persons as he might think necessary to their management." Members were unlimited in number, but had to become subscribers by the first day of meeting and should pay the annual sum of ten guineas to Mr. Butler. Hounds were to go out on five days a fortnight or oftener if Mr. Butler was agreeable and weather permitted. " No weather should stop hounds from going to the meet unless the snow should be one foot deep at the kennel door." Hounds to be at the covert at 9 a.m. from the 10th October to the 5th April. Mr. Butler arranged the meets and it was arranged to dine monthly during the hunting season. Further, " No French wines to be called for on the forfeiture of five pounds ; and the bill was to be called for at 8 o'clock." No mention of frost preventing hunting is made and it is of interest that the anti-French, war-like spirit existed in the matter of wine. Will James, Mr. Land's old huntsman, was again huntsman to Mr. Butler and should have known how to kill a fox. Thomas Carter of Soberton, and Foster of Hambledon were his assistants.

It is pleasant to recount in these days of change that Major-General Stephen Seymour Butler, C.B., C.M.G., D.S.O., a direct descendant of Mr. Butler, still lives at Bury Lodge and both he and his two sons are keen horsemen and supporters of the Hambledon Hunt. Mr. Butler only had the hounds for three seasons, but he and his brother George rode well to hounds for many years and Mr. Butler also kept a pack of harriers. Mr. Butler died in 1858.

Major J. Cook, 1804-06.

He was succeeded as master by Major (afterwards Colonel) John Cook who was born in 1773, his father being a merchant of Christchurch, Hants. As a very young man he hunted harriers near Wareham in Dorset and he acquired some reputation as a slayer of hares before he came of age. He entered the 28th Light Dragoons, but did not attain military fame on the battle field. He was master of the Thurlow country from 1800–04, marrying Miss Elizabeth Surtees of Dinsdale-on-Tees. This branch of the Surtees family have the same motto and crest as that of Hamsterly which produced the famous Robert Smith Surtees, who has delighted so many readers with his inimitable sporting novels. During his Hambledon mastership Will Neverd was his huntsman who afterwards served Mr. John Warde for many years. After leaving the Hambledon in 1807, Colonel Cook hunted the Roothings in Essex. He was equally successful there " in making the foxes fly by day and the corks by night " at the Dunmow gatherings. He was a strict master in the field, but a most popular and convivial one out of office. In his remarkably able book *Observations on Fox Hunting*, he names the three necessities for success in fox hunting. They are as true now as when he wrote them

(1) " Blood is so necessary to a pack of foxhounds, that if you are long without it, you cannot expect sport ; many say that the art of fox hunting is keeping your pack in blood."

(2) " Whatever you do, never turn out a bagman. . . . . What chiefly contributes to make fox hunting so far superior to other sports is the wildness of the animal you hunt, and the difficulty in catching him."

(3) " Next to turning out bagmen, lifting of hounds is the most prejudicial. They should seldom be taken ' off their noses.' Nothing is gained by it in the end ; hounds that are seldom lifted will kill more foxes in the course of a season than those that frequently are."

In 1813 he had to give up his hounds for financial reasons but on receiving a military appointment he again got together a pack in a corner of Staffordshire. His family, however, proved too expensive and he soon had to give up his hounds. In 1828, when stricken with a fatal disease, he returned at the request of his old friend Mr. Nicoll and carried the horn in the New Forest and kept everything going well in Mr. Nicoll's enforced absence. He then returned to France where he had settled at Honfleur and died in 1829.

(?) *Major-General T. de Burgh*, 1806-07.

Major-General Thomas de Burgh is given as master by various authorities for the season 1806–07. He had given his fox-hounds to the Prince of Wales in 1793 ; when he returned from abroad he had a pack of harriers. Phil Gosling carried the horn and Sawyer turned hounds for him. He may have hunted a fox with them to amuse his friends, but he certainly did not hunt the country regularly. This interlude may have accounted for the green coats worn in Mr. Powlett's time.

Mr. W. Powlett Powlett (West), 1807-16.

Mr. William Powlett Powlett lived at Lainston House, near Winchester, and hunted the West Hambledon country. He resigned this country to Mr. Nunez in 1816. He occasionally stopped for hunting at North House, near Broad Halfpenny Down, also at Meonstoke Rectory and Midlington House, Droxford. Mr. Powlett Powlett has already been somewhat described on page 59 when master of the H.H. Sawyer, his first whipper-in, described him as " a radical sort of a gentleman." He would never advertise his meets and if he were out of temper he would not say where he was going. He was nicknamed " Pontius Pilate." Will Reeves was his huntsman, but was not too well mounted and nor were Sawyer and Ned Gosling, the whippers-in. Mr. Powlett in 1811 attained notice in the *Sporting Magazine* for blowing up a correspondent calling himself " The Foxhunter Rough and Ready " for going past him in Lord Temple's rides. The correspondent thought he gave him a good excuse for losing his fox. " The gentlemen sporters " were reported as not " riding cruel fierce " in the Hambledon country with a few exceptions. Lord Lisle and a green-coated farmer by name Goodman were both thrusters, the latter selling a horse by his prowess for £170 for which he had given only £17, called a " slow little prad." Mr. Probyn, too, is mentioned as going along bravely. Mr. John Sadleir Moody of Southampton is also honourably excepted. He was Hon. Secretary to the Hunt for many years.

The first notice of the Hambledon Hunt Cup being run for on Soberton Down was May 6th, 1807, won by Mr. Dillon's bay mare. In the next year Mr. Powlett gave a cup won by Mr. Wooll's horse. The Dining Club used to meet from time to time at the Red Lion, Fareham, and the George Inn, Hambledon. Sir Robert Calder of the Holt, Mr. Richard Goddard, Mr. F. King, Mr. Moses Hawker of Cattisfield, Sir Thomas Champneys of Exton and Mr. Thomas Thistlethwayte of Southwick were stewards of these meetings of which Mr. Powlett was President.

"Aesop " states that the Hambledon Hunt at this period wore green coats in the field. They were even called " The green baize Hunt," the cloth, obtained from the Committee, being of poor material. Colonel G. Wyndham of the Drove bought Mr. Powlett's hounds and Luke Freeman was his huntsman.

Mr. J. Delmé, 1813-14 (East).

Mr. John Delmé of Cams, a keen supporter, kept a pack for one season. Smith was huntsman, afterwards a game-keeper, a very unusual change of role. Mr. Delmé died when dressing for hunting and the pack was sold at Tattersalls with the servants in deep mourning. Sawyer, the 1st whipper-in, entered the service of Mr. J. T. Villebois.

Mr. J. Eyles, 1814-15 (East).

Mr. Joseph Eyles of East Meon hunted the East Hambledon country for one year, which had not been regularly hunted since Colonel Cook's time. Mr. Eyles' brother Richard kept a pack of harriers at Berely House. Mr. Eyles died on 4th March, 1815. Old Will James was his huntsman and he continued with his successor. The kennels were at East Meon.

Rev. G. Richards, 1815-16 (East).

The Rev. G. Richards of North House, Hambledon succeeded, but only for a year. On December 4th, however, the Hamble-don had a great hunt from Stoke Wood through Chidden, Combe Wood, over the top of Butser and Holt Down, through Ditcham, Up Park, North Marden, and killed on Trayford Down. Hounds were still kennelled at East Meon. He was described by Ned Gosling as a " good sportsman, and knew all about hunting well."

Mr. A. F. Nunez, 1816-21.

Mr. Nunez of Warnford Park now took over the Hambledon country proper, moving the kennels from East Meon to Warn-ford. Mr. Nunez was a very heavy weight but he rode first-rate horses and, with Ned Gosling (son of Phil Gosling before-mentioned) as pilot, he did very well. Madness broke out in the kennels during Mr. Nunez's time and 13½ couple had to be destroyed, a very serious loss ; but in those days sometimes a whole pack had to be destroyed from this cause.

On January 13th, 1819, a very good hunt was enjoyed from Basing Park by New Copse, Tisted Common, Colemore, Priors Dean, Oakshott, over Old Litton to Ashford, up the hangers to Old Warren Copse, to Colemore village, when he was killed " in very high style." Two hours without a check.

Mr. Nunez's weight was once made the subject of a some-what rude joke by a French count by name Sauveur who was living at the Swan Inn at Alresford. He was fond of hunting and a good violin player. One day hounds found in the ozier beds at Warnford and ran up old Winchester Hill. The count spurred past the master saying " Come along Old Fat Gut." The master had taken the hill quietly and at the top cantered past the count, whose horse was completely blown, saying, " Come along Old Cat Gut," which deservedly silenced the count.

Mr. Nunez had a stiff test for hunters he thought of buying : they had to canter with him from the bottom to the top of Beacon Hill—no bad test of wind, muscle and condition.

Mr. Nunez had first Will James, then Will Reeves, and, finally, John Neal as huntsmen. Reeves did not prove satisfactory to the subscribers. Mr. Nunez died in 1829.

Sir B. R. Graham and Mr. G. Osbaldeston, 1821.

Sir Bellingham Reginald Graham, 1st Baronet of Norton Conyers, near Ripon, Yorks., came in November to Hill Place and started the season. It is said that, when treating for the country, on being told the subscription was £700, he remarked : " That will barely keep me in spur leathers." The famous Squire Osbaldeston who had resigned the Quorn finished the season. The Squire could ride, but walked with great difficulty owing to a bad injury to his leg. Foxes were scarce and his hounds were too fast for a plough country, being used to Leicestershire grass. As usual, however, the Squire persevered, and with Dick Burton and Tom Sebright, they killed three and a half brace of foxes in 14 weeks. At a check when he was able to come out, the Squire would cast with half the pack and Tom Sebright with the other half. A novel way of casting but obviously a saving of time. His wonderful loquacity caused some amusement. It was, however, but a part of his immense, and even superabundant, vitality. When Sir Bellingham Graham went as master to the Quorn he asked Mr. Tom Smith to stay with him for the opening meet at Kirby Gate. They had a very good hunt in the course of which Mr. Smith took a complete somersault over a fence and an enormous ditch, avoided by the rest of the field who knew it well. Later on, the master and Sir James Musgrave were trying to lift a gate, in some very high palings, off its hinges. Mr. Smith, in no way daunted by his fall, jumped the palings and was alone with hounds when they killed. Sir Bellingham offered him the brush, saying, " Tell the Hampshire lads I can kill a fox here though I did not kill many among them."

N

Mr. J. Walker, 1822-23.

The Squire's short reign was soon over and he went back to Leicestershire recovered from his injury. He was succeeded by Mr. John Walker of Purbrook Park, a rich Yorkshireman, keen on the Turf and Road. He and his brother horsed the Bognor coach for some years; he also was a member of the Benson Driving Club. He hunted hounds himself, with Hugh Jermyn to turn hounds, but soon tired of fox hunting and devoted himself to coaching and racing. He was succeeded by Mr. Shard. Mr. Walker sold his hounds to Sir Bellingham Graham who had left the Quorn and sold his hounds to Squire Osbaldeston.

Mr. C. Shard, 1823-24.

Mr. Charles Shard had hunted the country around Danebury, Clatford and Wherwell, formerly hunted by Mr. Powlett when he lived at Little Somborne. He moved to Hill Place, Droxford, and kennelled the hounds at Warnford in Mr. Nunez's kennels. John Sharp was his huntsman but proved unsatisfactory and John Major came who killed more foxes than had been known for some time. They had a great hunt of three hours and five minutes on March 10th, 1824, meeting at the Waterloo Inn, finding in Plants Coppice, they ran past Southwick House, through Pinsley Wood, then, after an hour's hunting in the Southwick coverts, the fox was forced over the open through Old Park Catherington, Stoke Wood, Old Winchester Hill, crossing Soberton Down into the Forest of Bere to his death at Sheepwash. The distance covered was some 30 miles and only five or six horsemen were up besides John Major. During this hunt hounds were never lifted to a halloa.

Ill-health prevented Mr. Shard from continuing as master to a four-day subscription pack, but he generously gave 40 couple of most useful hounds to the Club on his resignation.

Mr. Shard was a good judge of horseflesh as well as a good huntsman. Lord Maryborough[2] gave him 500 guineas for a dappled grey which he rode at Ascot in the Royal Procession as Master of the Royal Buckhounds in the reign of William III.

Some of Mr. Shard's exploits as a master of staghounds will be seen in chapter XII.

[2] Afterwards Earl of Mornington.

Mr. T. Smith, 1824-29.

Mr. Tom Smith, sometimes called " Gentleman Smith " or " Hambledon Smith," was born and bred a Hampshire man. As he attained so much celebrity as a sportsman, writer and artist, some sketch of his career may be of interest. He was the eldest son of Thomas Smith of Shaldon Manor, near Alton, who farmed on a considerable scale and was also a good and keen horseman. In Mr. J. T. Villebois' hunt with his harriers from Preston Copse to Amory Wood, mentioned on page 60, Mr. Smith (senior) was alone with the master at the kill. There were twelve children and a moderate income and therefore Mr. Smith was not accustomed to the luxuries which were enjoyed by his equally famous namesake Mr. T. Assheton Smith. His father encouraged his boy to hunt and take interest in animals. He was allowed to pursue his father's hares with a very " Bobbery " pack. This gave young Tom much pleasure and he felt quite a M.F.H. He also from very early days followed his father with Mr. Russell's hounds, learning their names from old Will Harrison, the huntsman. He also followed the H.H. when hunting nearby. He hunted whenever he could, but also took to studying wild animals and also taught himself to be a very promising draughtsman. His Etonian career was a very short one and he finished his education at a school at Holybourne. The fear of invasion was acute in those days and his father raised a company of local volunteers, being joined by young Tom as ensign 1807–14. After the peace in 1814 the family moved to their new home called Shalden Lodge which his father had built. On his father's death " Young Tom " soon had all the affairs of the large farm upon his shoulders and he undertook them most efficiently and with considerable ingenuity. He showed his mechanical skill by inventing a six h.p. threshing engine. Wheat was at a high price and by working double shifts he succeeded in threshing his mother's wheat and selling it at from £45 to £48 a load before the price dropped to £12 or £13 a load. He greatly improved a locally invented turnip drill and started a new and successful system of restoring old pastures. Whatever he did, he did with the greatest energy. On one occasion, when a Vice-President of the Winchester Agricultural Society, which was holding its show at 11 a.m. on the morning after a ball at the Bull, near Guildford, young Tom determined to be at both functions. He rode 18 miles to the ball, danced till 4 a.m., and then rode 40 miles to Winchester and attended the opening of the show.

A lucky love affair gave him a chance of broadening his hunting experiences. Mr. James Ward, a member of the H.H., offered to take him to Lyndhurst and mount him with John Warde's famous hounds. On arrival, Mr. Ward's affections overcame him and he quickly returned to his sweetheart, young Tom's sister. Tom Smith was left with three good hunters, grooms, boots and breeches and scarlet coat to do what he liked. He soon attracted the notice of the old master who often asked him to dine, especially after a good day. John Warde used to say afterwards, " I entered Tom as a puppy." This was not quite true as he was already well entered, but he must have learnt much from the " Father of Foxhunters."

On taking the Hambledon hounds he only received £600 a year subscriptions and 30 couple of hounds. He made the pack up to 40 couple for the next season, but the lack of adequate funds was always a great difficulty which makes his outstanding reputation the more creditable. His early days as master were not propitious. He allowed John Major to hunt hounds. Only one fox was handled in six weeks. Mr. Smith told the huntsman he must kill a fox. John Major, possibly fortified with drink, said, " You had better hunt hounds yourself." The master sent him home at once and soon found a fox in North Coppice. After a ring or two, he got him well away and hounds ran well, then there was a sudden stop the other side of a thick hedge. Mr. Smith, full of zeal and much elated, broke through the hedge to handle his first fox and found a dead sheep ! Hounds, after being well rated and flogged, were taken home. The master dreamt of hounds rioting in all directions and the incident got on his nerves. Even when the shepherd called to thank the huntsman for killing a poor giddy sheep that had caused him " a mort of trouble," the young master felt his hunting career ruined. A very successful day followed, luckily, and many others were to follow. Mr. Smith had the services of old Will James as kennel huntsman who had been with Mr. Land in the 18th century.

After a visit to the kennels in 1825, " Nimrod " recounts an interesting conversation with the old huntsman, well showing the trials that huntsmen have to endure. The old man said " His hounds went out seventeen times without killing a fox First it was my fault, then it was the hounds' fault, then they were too fat, then they were too thin. At last, one morning hounds all fled from my horse's heels like mad things ; the moment they got to a covert, found their fox directly, and killed eighteen of the next nineteen foxes." Carping critics might well remember this tale when impatient on a bad scenting day.

Mr. Smith kept his hounds at Hill Place in kennels built by Sir Bellingham Graham. He lived with his wife at Swanmore House and when she died moved to Exton House. His reputation was made by an outstanding hunt in his first season.

On Monday, January 18th, 1825, a fox was found at Oliphants about 1 p.m. He went away fast by the Markwells, skirting Lady Holt Park, through Ditcham, over Hasting Down to Up Park, passing through a herd of deer without faltering. Hounds then hunted over Telegraph Hill, through the long chain of West Dean Woods, the fox keeping to the rides throughout, and on to Chalton Forest, passing near the Drove where a slight check occurred for the first time owing to a flock of sheep. Soon recovering the line, they ran on over the Downs towards Petworth, skirting Burton Park, running the bottom to Graffham, up the hill and had their fox completely beaten in a large covert nearby. One gentleman actually dismounted to take the fox as he thought. This occurred two hours and forty minutes after the find. At this critical moment a countryman halload away a fresh fox on the Down. Hounds had their hackles up and could not be stopped. They were finally stopped near Potscomb Wood, some 35 miles from their kennels. The following gentlemen saw the hunt through : Messrs. E. Morant, G. Butler, Hale, Captain Georges, whose gallant grey mare " had the best of it," the Hon. William Gage, Messrs. Richards, Hill and Norris. Colonel Wyndham hospitably entertained them all at the Drove, where he kept his harriers.

In his second season Mr. Smith well showed his tough physique following a meet at St. Margaret's, near Titchfield. The fox swam the broad river between the village and Southampton Water followed by the hounds, the master and Captain Yorke ; when they felt their horses sinking they slipped off and swam for the far bank, but did not steer their horses. " General," the master's horse, at first swam for the open sea at Spithead, but turned into a creek and got stuck in the mud. The other horse followed the master's horse dutifully. However, the master recovered his horse and killed his fox on the common. Some carriages had stopped to watch on the common and Mr. Smith was asked if he were not very cold and wet. He replied, " Neither, but I have some water in my boots." Holding up his foot, water poured out as from a bucket and steaming !—on January 18th this appears a high tribute to Mr. Smith's circulation.

Another rather interesting incident occurred when Mr. Smith was staying with Mr. Fleming of South Stoneham. Hounds found at Bitterne, ran to Bursledon, turned by Botley and ran back to ground at Bitterne. Everybody had had enough except Lord Palmerston who wanted to see the fox dug. The master was loathe to do so, knowing the sandy soil in which a fox could dig as fast as they could. He did not wish, however, to affront Lord Palmerston and started to dig. They continued by the light of lanterns and had their fox at 10.45 p.m. The future Prime Minister then rode 14 miles back to Broadlands quite happy, as he had qualified his horse for the Hampshire Hunt Cup having seen three foxes killed—usually a more sensible proviso than the modern qualifying system for a Point-to-Point.

Prominent supporters of hunting at this time were Admiral Colpoys, Sir William Hoste, well known in Leicestershire and as good with hounds as on the sea, Mr. George Butler, Mr. E. Gale Morant, Mr. E. Hale, Captain Georges, Rev. G. Richards, Major Ridge, son of the old Squire of Kilmeston, and Captain Close; both these latter gentlemen had served many years in India.

In his last season, on December 19th, Mr. Smith had another good hunt from West End through Allington, Durley, Stroud and Cleverly Woods, by Corhampton, Preshaw and Exton crossing the River Meon at Warnford and hounds killed their fox after a run of 17 miles. Out of a field of about a hundred a dozen finished—Messrs. Moody, S. Taylor, Captain B. Green, Colonel George Greenwood of Brookwood Park, Mr. C. Brett and Captain Sullivan were among the lucky ones.

In 1829 Mr. Smith resigned and took the Craven country for four seasons. There he distinguished himself as a horseman by his famous jump of Elcot Park Wall, 6ft. 2in. on the take-off side with an 8ft. drop on the landing side.

After hunting the Craven hounds til 1833, Mr. Smith enjoyed a rest, hunting where he wished till he became master and huntsman of the Pytchley from 1840–44. It was apparently there that he wrote *The Life of a Fox*, though dated by the author from Hill House, Hambledon, 10th June, 1843. This unique book shows his great knowledge of the habits of the wild animal. It is given local interest by " Wily," his first narrator saying that he first drew breath " in a breeding earth carefully chosen by my mother in a well-known covert called Park Coppice, situated in the centre of the Hampshire Hunt." This covert has always been a good find and is now most suitably owned by Mr. Herman Andreae, the master of the H.H. (1949). It is not, however, in the centre of the H.H. country by any means.

The *Life of a Huntsman* was written after he had finished his Pytchley mastership. In this book he gives a huntsman's qualifications—" health, memory, decision, temper and patience, a good ear, voice and sight, courage and spirits, perseverance and activity, and with these he will soon make a bad pack a good one ; if quick, he will make a slow pack quick ; if slow, he will make a quick pack slow." Both books are full of sound common sense and his method of casting must have caused the death of many a fox. It is the only definite diagram of a cast ever made and the reasons for his method are thoroughly sound and convincing.

The sketches in his books, in *Sporting Incidents in the Life of another Tom Smith* written by a friend, and his pictures of the H.H. and the Craven Hunt prove his capacity as an amateur artist. His mechanical skill and inventive capacity ranged over a wide field and his sketch and model of a locomotive armoured battery had the warm approval of the Prime Minister Lord Palmerston, and Queen Victoria saw the model at Osborne with interest. The Ordnance Department, though polite, were not interested. In 1866 it aroused public interest when exhibited at Southampton. His greatest feat of hunting skill was probably the killing of 90 foxes in 91 hunting days in the Craven country, a feat not at all likely to be repeated. Mr. Nicoll of the N.F.H., no mean judge, called him " a heaven-born huntsman." Mr. Codrington, also a most knowledgable master and huntsman, said of him, " If I were a fox, I would rather have a pack of hounds behind me than Tom Smith with a stick in his hand."

Mr. J. King, 1829-41.

Mr. John King of Fowelscombe brought his foxhounds from Devonshire and so was known to his many friends and admirers as " King of the West," he had also a famous pack of harriers which he had sold to Mr. Yeatman of Stock House, Sherborne. He was an all-round sportsman, a good shot and a good fisherman and very keen on hunting the fox and the otter. He hunted only bitches in two packs, one of 22 inches or 23 inches and one of 21 inches. In 1831 the Hambledon Hunt Club was re-established with Mr. Delmé Radcliffe of Shawford House as Hon. Secretary, and a song composed by him was sung at their dinner on January 4th, 1831. It was called " The Hambledon Hunt " and is given at the end of the chapter.

As the author of the *Noble Science* in 1839 and as a M.F.H. himself, Mr. Radcliffe earned great fame. The famous Rev. John Russell once shook him by the hand at Goodwood Races and said he would have walked there from Dartmoor to shake hands with the author of the *Noble Science*. Mr. Radcliffe only acted as Secretary for one year but had left his mark, and his good work in getting the Hunt Club together again gave Mr. King a good list of cheerful subscribers.

In 1833 Mr. King killed 17 foxes in 16 hunting days, a noteable feat in that woodland country. Mr. King hunted hounds himself, but suffered from a bad fall and from indifferent health. He had a most able assistant in John Squires who started huting at nine years old in Devon. Squires was a first-rate horseman and nothing stopped him. He was subsequently huntsman in 1841 and stayed in the Hambledon country till 1848, being as good in the kennel as in the field.

Among Mr. King's hard riders and keen supporters were Sir Jervoise C. Jervoise of Idsworth, Mr. J. H. Campbell of Exton, Mr. George Orred of Rooksbury, Lord Vaux, 2nd Life Guards, the well-known sportsman and sailor, Captain (afterwards Admiral) Sir Henry Keppel of Droxford, General Coles of Woodcote, Mr. H. P. Delmé of Cams Hall, Mr. Thomas Butler of Bury Lodge, Mr. George Butler of Millbrook, Lord Lisle, who died in 1834 falling from his horse in a fit, Messrs. J. S. Moody (Hon. Secretary 1839–43), Mr. Thomas Ridge, S. S. Taylor, of Upham (Hon. Secretary 1843–59) and the Rev. Lukin of Nursling.

On November 12th, 1833, the pack had a good hunt in thick fog and very deep going from Allington to Durley, going fast and killing in 52 minutes. There were many falls and some hard riders had more than one.

On February 6th, 1835, in another good hunt, they ran from near Bordean, by Froxfield, Hawkley hangers, across the open to Woolmer Forest where the fox was taken alive in a pond and deservedly turned loose.

On December 14th, 1836, the hounds again distinguished themselves, running a fox from near Highden Wood over Butser Down to Harting Down; after several miles over the

MR. THOMAS BUTLER, M.F.H. 1800-04, M.H. 1823-34.
Founder of the Hambledon Hunt.

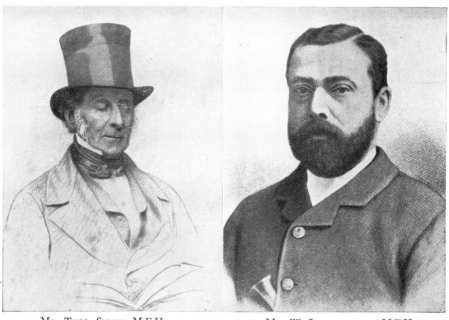

MR. THOS. SMITH, M.F.H.,   MR. W. LONG, JUNIOR, M.F.H.,
1825-29 and 1848-52.   1874-89.

Downs a sheep dog caused a check. The fox turned over the vale towards Rogate and hounds raced on for four miles at a pace no horse could live with, killing after one hour and fifty minutes near Midhurst. The distance was 17 miles. Admiral Jervis, the hero of the battle off Cape St. Vincent, having lost his hat early in the day, also sustained a heavy fall riding at a gate post. Ill-health made Mr. King resign in 1841 after a most successful mastership.

Mr. W. J. Long (jun.), 1841-48.

Mr. Walter Jervis Long, eldest son of Mr. Walter Long of Preshaw, now succeeded as master, with John Squires as huntsman. He received good support and good sport was shown.

In 1846 Mr. Long had two good hunts, the first from Allington, by Brambridge and Colden Common, through Twyford Park and on by Morestead, hounds killing their fox rising the hill on Chilcomb Down—11 miles in one hour ; the next from Wallops Wood, after a most punishing hunt of three hours, hounds had to be called off. Squire's horse was utterly beat and he was mounted by Mr. J. Clarke Jervoise of Idsworth.

Mr. Long always rode well up with hounds. He was quiet and courteous, and deservedly popular with his field. From 1829–49 no less than eighty-eight members were elected to the Hunt Club well showing the great popularity of Mr. King and his successor. The ancestor of the present master was among them, Mr. George A. Hulbert of Stakes Hill Lodge.

Mr. T. Smith, 1848-52.

On Mr. Long's resigning the mastership, Mr. Tom Smith again assumed control until 1852. He showed good sport as was to be expected after the added experience of hunting the Craven from 1829-33 and the Pytchley from 1840-44. The latter pack he took with Lord Cardigan's financial backing. His horses only cost him from £20 - £60, somewhat below the average price in " the Shires." The Club bought Lord Chesterfield's hounds for £400 after 20 couple had been chosen for Lord Ducie. (It is reported that these were afterwards hung as incorrigible rogues.) He quickly discharged his huntsman and 1st whipper-in for disobedience and so faced his immaculate and critical field at Crick with a hunt staff consisting of the old feeder and a young stable boy, both in very shabby old clothes With a poor pack of hounds and no staff he showed an excellent run of 58 minutes and killed.   Lord Cardigan was the only man near the master at the kill.   He said, " Capital, capital ! I'll give you a character."   Alluding to what Mr. Smith had told Lord Rosslyn in the New Forest (page 112), Lord Rosslyn was out on that day.   On two occasions afterwards he completely cut down the hard-riding Pytchley field, killing his fox on each occasion.   On the second occasion another local sportsman, Mr. J. Wheble of the Bramshill Hunt, afterwards M.F.H., South Berks, 1853-55, alone accompanied Mr. T. Smith over the big brook.

On March 24th, 1851, a fine hunt is recorded from Idsworth. Hounds found near Chalton Mill and went straight by Blend-worth and Horndean Holt.   They raced to Havant Thicket and turned right-handed to Bedhampton Park, by Lea Park, through Crookhorn to Belmont, and on till stopped by the sea, when, after running through some gardens, he was killed at Stakes. Mr. Smith and Mr. Alfred Dyson were always to the fore and the only others who could face the deep and strongly-fenced country were Mr. Hulbert of Stakes Hill Lodge, Mr. Sartoris, 16th Lancers, Mr. Shaw and Mr. Stares.

In his last year with the Hambledon Mr. Smith killed 29½ brace of foxes, hunting three days a week.   His last day was given a special notice in the *Hampshire Chronicle* of Saturday, March 27th, 1852, as " Saturday (a good-bye day) at Broad-halfpenny Down at a quarter before eleven."   This notice puzzled his supporters as Saturday was usually a bye day and not published.   However, some 150 horsemen turned out to see what was in store for April 3rd.   The day was not ideal, a hot sun, baked earth and an east wind.   The master drew quickly through Highden Wood, Tegleaze Gorse and Wood without finding.   At Stoke Down Gorse not a hound spoke for an hour but the master appeared confident of finding.   At last a favourite bitch appeared interested.   Mr. Smith cheered her on and into the furze he went himself.   " Destiny " threw her tongue now and other hounds quickly responded.   Know-ing, as foxes do, the lack of scent, the old fox had laid absolutely quiet in his lair and would not have moved except for Mr. Smith's perseverance and quick observation of his hounds.   Keeping the pack together, the fox was finally driven through part of the field and away down wind over the open down.   The fox soon turned sharply left-handed over the parched up fallows, but his relentless huntsman kept to his line through Wallop, Stoke and Brookes' Woods and there, failing in an attempt to run back to Stoke Down, he pointed for Waltham Chase, running over Soberton Race Course down; over this fine turf hounds raced and the field galloped like a cavalry charge. Hounds rolled their fox over after fifty minutes at the southern end of the Race Course. A good sporting end for Mr. Smith's last day as master. Few men, in the difficult conditions, would have been able to have even found this fox, let alone roll him over in the open. About 150 members and friends in the Hambledon country combined in a presentation to Mr. Smith. After retirement he was not allowed to rest and he continued to show his versatile talents.

While serving as High Sheriff of the County in 1858 he considered that the wretched housing conditions were responsible for a great part of the heavy list of crime at Assizes. He therefore founded a building society to increase all cottages to have three good bedrooms. He also drew admirable plans for cottages—one for £70 contained living room, washhouse, three bedrooms and a wood shed, and was quite pleasing in appearance. Another suggestion of his was to aid recruiting for the Army; it was to have all elementary schoolboys taught drill. This suggestion was very well received by H.R.H. the Duke of Cambridge. A further suggestion of his at an agricultural dinner at Alresford was acted on six months later. He urged all farmers to learn rifle shooting so that a mounted troop of foxhunters could be formed whenever needed. The 1st Hants Light Horse were founded and the old master was their "guide" and earned the Government efficiency grant. During his second mastership Mr. Smith had the assistance of Charles Champion as 1st whip and K.H. Champion was father to the famous Zetland huntsman and grandfather to the huntsman of the Cheshire Hounds.

Mr. G. Wall, 1852-56.

Mr. George Alfred Ellis Wall of Worthy Park, Winchester, who had just given up the Hursley Hounds, took over the mastership. He lived at Droxford during his mastership. At first Charles Champion, and then Henry Nason, was 1st whipper-in and Will Fisher 2nd whipper-in. He was a heavyweight but a good horseman and well mounted. He obtained drafts from the Cottesmore, Mr. T. A. Smith and the Hursley, keeping from 40 to 46 couple of hounds in kennel. He showed good sport, carrying the horn himself.

The following hunts are taken from his diary. Several more good hunts were reported in *Bailey's Magazine*, etc.

On Friday, November 4th, 1853, a brilliant hunt took place from a meet at Owslebury Down. Two coverts were drawn blank, but a good fox was found in Black Down. He ran straight through Preshaw Park, through Durwood and Black Down, over the open to Rowhay, by Greenhill, through the covert on to Deeps, over Wintershill Common and back skirting Ashton village, over the small enclosures by Stephen Castle's Down and the doghounds killed him in a hedgerow close to Cleverley Wood. This good hunt took an hour and fifty-four minutes at a good pace throughout.

On Saturday, January 6th, 1854, from a meet at Wickham Gate, the dog-pack again provided what Mr. Wall describes as a brilliant run. Hounds found at once in Ayling's Copse and ran through High Wood, over the meadows to the common and nearly to Wickham village, across the road by Wickham Gate, over a fine country to Close Wood, then over the water meadows, through The Liberties, skirting West Lodge, into Rooksbury Park. Hounds ran through the garden by the Observatory down to the entrance lodge where hounds killed him as he was trying to scale a wire fence. This run was one hour and twenty-three minutes without the slightest check. For some reason only seven people were out to enjoy the hunt.

Several of his followers seem to have been interesting characters. Mr. John Harvey of Upham, a steeplechase rider, is said to have mounted and ridden a savage bull. Caleb Owton of Owslebury, who kept a pack of harriers also, rode a famous mule. Some of his neighbours tried to thwart Mr. Owton on one occasion by locking the lower half of the stable door. The mule simply jumped out of the top half and his owner rode away to the discomforture of those who were watching. Tom Cordery of Hazeley was very keen; the name is well known in Hampshire sport. Mr. William Standish of Upton Cottage, Bursledon, was a keen supporter as he should have been; he was afterwards master of the Hursley and New Forest Hunts.

On his retirement in 1854 some sixty of the leading sportsmen of the county entertained him to dinner at the Red Lion Hotel, Fareham.

The Wickham Steeplechases were started in Mr. Wall's time, run over Mr. Bovill Smith's farm.

Captain Wilder, 1856.

Captain Wilder succeeded to the mastership in April, but died in July of that year.

Mr. W. J. Long, 1856-59.

Mr. Walter Jervis Long of Preshaw again stepped into the breach with Orchin as huntsman. Deafness, however, prevented Orchin continuing as huntsman and Thomas Hills took the horn. In 1858 Mr. Long had to go abroad for his health and Mr. Thomas Wynne Hornby of Upham acted as field master for him, acting also as honorary kennel huntsman.

Captain W. H. Poulett (succeeded as 6th Earl Poulett, 1864), 1859-68.

Captain William Henry Poulett, late Captain of the 22nd Foot, took over the mastership and everything possible was done to show sport. Hounds hunted six days a week and frequently the master and Cox, the huntsman, were out with different packs on the same day on opposite sides of the country. The country was considerably enlarged by taking in a large slice of Sussex, country formerly hunted by the Duke of Richmond.

Alfred Munns was huntsman in 1859, but Will Cox succeeded to the horn the next season. On March 1st, 1861, what *Bell's Life* described as " quite an old-fashioned run " was enjoyed from near West Dean House. They had two hours and ten minutes over twenty-two miles of the stiffest Sussex country and killed in the open. The huntsman's horse having cast a shoe, the master took over his duties with great success.

Captain Poulett succeeded his uncle as 6th Earl Poulett in 1864 and inherited the family estates at Hinton St. George, Crewkerne, Somerset. During his mastership, Lord Poulett moved the Hunt Steeplechases to Waterloo where a very successful meeting was established, the master acting as starter. Lord Poulett long maintained some connection with Hampshire by becoming Hon. Colonel of the 2nd Battalion Hants Rifle Volunteers. He started his military career as Lieutenant in the Buffs (2nd Foot) in 1845. After Lord Poulett's death in 1899 followed the famous law suit and it was not until 1903 that his only son by his third wife succeeded in establishing his right.

Lord Poulett was a good whip and had ridden flat races. He owned several good chasers, " The Lamb " being twice successful at Liverpool and ran beautifully a third time under top weight but could not quite win.

Colonel J. Bower, 1868-71.

Colonel John Bower of Studwell Lodge, Droxford, now became master, but not on so lavish a scale. Hounds hunted three days a week only. This old sportsman was blooded in Fife, aged five, in Waterloo year, and remained an upright vigorous figure till over 90 years of age, hunting a short-tailed cob. His family came from Kincaldrum in Angus. He was the father of the Hunt and took the chair at all Hunt meetings for many years and lived to be 100. John Hollings who had whipped-in for the Quorn and Mr. Tailby, was his huntsman.

Captain D. Sullivan, 1871-72.

Captain Desmond Sullivan became master and hunted the country four days a week, but he suffered a fatal accident after the end of his first season. His father kept staghounds and both he and his wife were good riders to hounds.

Mr. W. J. Long, 1872-74.

Mr. Walter Jervis Long again, for the third time, became master. He had succeeded to the family estates of Preshaw and Muchelmey in Somerset on his father's death. Tom Phillips was his huntsman, a very experienced hunt servant. He had been with Lord Dacre, the Duke of Buccleugh, the South Berks and the Calpé Hounds. He had also hunted harriers in Sussex and in Ireland.

Mr. W. Long, 1874-89.

Mr. Walter Long, eldest son of Mr. Walter Jervis Long, took over from his father and carried the horn himself with the greatest success. In one season he killed 66 brace of foxes, a big bag for the country. This shows how well he hunted hounds and how well, too, he was supported. Walter Newman, his 1st whipper-in, hunted hounds two days a week. Owing to a bad fall and ill-health Mr. Walter Long gave up the mastership to the regret of all in 1889.

Mr. T. W. Harvey, 1889-94.

Mr. Thomas W. Harvey of Purbrook took over the master-ship with Walter Newman as his huntsman. He was keen and popular but living on the southern outskirts of the hunt proved a strain which, together with increasing deafness, brought about his resignation.

Hon. F. A. Baring, 1894 - 1900.

The Hon. Frederick Arthur Baring, second son of the 4th Baron Ashburton of the Grange, Alresford, Hants, now assumed control. He lived at Meonstoke House, opposite the kennels, during his mastership. Mr. Baring took over Mr. Harvey's huntsman and whippers-in, but carried the horn himself on the east side of the country. Mr. Baring was a very keen houndman and took great interest in their breeding. His interest in hounds after giving up hunting was continued in his interest in retrievers. He was often to be seen with a couple of retrievers watching the work of hounds many miles from his home. Though a first-rate shot, he gave up shooting but always retained his retrievers and would pick up with great pleasure for his relatives and friends.

The hunt that Mr. Baring remembers as outstanding took place on a most unpromising day and is best described in his own words :—

" March 12th, 1897.—Met at Butser Hill, self hunting the small pack. A regular hurricane blowing at the meet. Trotted back to the shelter of Highden Wood ; just outside the wood Percy Seward holload a fox out of a hedgerow, getting on the line at once, hounds raced back to Butser, finding the wind too much for him he turned right-handed, hounds running very fast down to the Portsmouth road, which they crossed just above the cutting. Racing over Mar Down, they crossed the railway line into Ditcham and close to the house came the first check ; holding them on round the house, they hit the line, and, running down the hanger, crossed on to Harting Down. On this very poor soil much foiled by rabbits they could only just hold the line and crossing to the end opposite Up Park, two fields away, they came to a dead stop and try as they would they couldn't recover it, but I was loath to give it up. I had noticed one hound trying very hard to take a line along a track across the fields towards Up Park. It was neck or nothing, so, picking them up, I galloped across two fields, luckily found a gate into the park, and cast them right-handed. Hitting the

line at once they ran fast across the park out by the Golden
Gates and then as hard as they could go along North Marden
Down, the heather seeming to hold a really good scent.   At the
end of the down they checked ; as I sat watching them swing
their cast, the fox jumped up under my horse's feet and ran into
a covert known as the 'German Lyth,' where they caught
him.   An eight-mile point, ten as hounds ran."

After Mr. Baring's retirement the country was divided into
East and West portions.

East.
Mr. H. S. Whalley Tooker, 1900-07.

Mr. Hyde Salmon Whalley Tooker of Hinton Daubnay,
Horndean and Norton Hall, Somerset, took over the eastern
side of the country.   He retained Jack Newman, who had
twenty-six years of experience in the country, as his kennel huntsman, and his brother, Mr. Francis W. Tooker carried the horn.
Foxes were scarce owing to an outbreak of mange which had
affected the whole country, but with the support of both covert
owners and farmers the supply was soon adequate.   The
masters of both East and West portions were keen on shooting
and treated covert owners with every consideration.

West.
Captain W. P. Standish, 1900-07.

Captain William Pery Standish of Marwell Hall and Scaleby
Castle, Cumberland, now commenced his twenty-one years of
mastership and joint-mastership by taking the western portion
of the Hambledon country.   Born in 1860, he had been brought
up with hounds, his father, Mr. W. C. Standish, having been
master of the Hursley 1862–69 and the N.F.H. 1869–74.   Captain
Standish had retired from the East Yorkshire Regiment and
succeeded to the family estates in 1893.   He soon took up
county work as J.P. and was High Sheriff in Cumberland in
1902.

His start as M.F.H. was under most adverse circumstances.
Foxes were few and both mangy ones and three-legged ones
are mentioned in his diaries.   His staff and hounds were new
to him.   Fred Mitchell started as his huntsman and the first
two seasons were disappointing, only $8\frac{1}{2}$ brace killed with four
blank days in his first season and $10\frac{1}{2}$ brace killed with seven
blank days in 1901–02 season.   Captain Standish then promoted
Fred Bell, the 1st whipper-in, and sport improved even though

Bell had the misfortune to break his collar bone in December 1902.

Some useful fast hunts are mentioned of thirty-five minutes and fifty minutes and the tally rose to 21½ brace in the season.

An amusing incident occurred with one prominent supporter, the well-known cricketer and athlete Mr. C. B. Fry. Mr. Fry's keenness sometimes overcame his discretion, and he was apt to press hounds too closely; huntsmen naturally did not approve. On one occasion hounds suddenly checked just beyond a five-barred gate. The leaders of the field and hunts-man drew up to watch them cast. Mr. Fry[3] came up rather late, and without a second's hesitation, charged the gate. He was not very successful on this occasion and his horse remained balanced on top of the gate with two legs on each side. Bell then said in a very heartfelt manner and most respectfully, "Oh, Mr. Fry, how I wish that they played first-class cricket all the year round in England." A roar of laughter from the field greeted this very tactful rebuke.

Captain Standish continued his uphill struggle and obtained better support as time went on, though in the 1906–07 season four blank days are again noted. An average of over 34 brace of foxes was killed in his last three seasons of the divided country.

Captain W. P. Standish, 1907-15.

After Captain Standish reunited the country sport consider-ably improved and no more is heard of blank days. Two good hunts took place from a meet at Soberton Down on February 19th, 1908. The first fox was found in Stoke Wood and hounds ran fast by Tegleaze to Winchester Hill, across the valley to Henwood and Duncombe Hangers, then passing by the game farm over the hill to Combe Wood. Here, after a run of an hour and twenty minutes, hounds divided and were stopped. The next fox from Tegleaze Gorse, ran through Combe Wood to Hyden, where he went to ground. Tegleaze Gorse soon provided another old dog-fox which, after a ring round Combe Wood, went away by Hermitage and Park Farms, through Hambledon Hangers, out by Gliddens and Dock Yard Copse to Denmead, where he was rolled over in

[3] Mr. C. B. Fry was resolute in whatever he did. As a cricketer he scored 3,445 runs for Hampshire in 65 innings, once scoring 258 not out. His average of 57·41 must be almost a record for the period. He twice headed England's batting averages and his work and his wife's work in saving the *Mercury* training ship in 1908 should be remembered by all. Mr. Fry has just given up this fine work. Hundreds of successful merchant seamen and Naval ratings owe their success in life to him.

the open after a run of an hour and fifteen minutes.   This year, though 45½ brace of foxes were accounted for, the master was not appreciative of scenting conditions.   Only four days are noted as good, 32 as fair, 19 as bad, and 13 days as very bad.

Sport continued to improve and George Roake who had carried the horn since 1907 proved a quick and efficient hunts-man.   Well mounted and a good horseman, he could ride well up to hounds and the country was still rideable.   Big estates still existed, some very well fenced, downs were downs and very pleasant to gallop over, in fact, the country had not altered very much since the days of the great Tom Smith.   Portsmouth and its environs were creeping out, but the Waterlooville country was still a pleasant ride and the Portsdown Hills were not yet invested with bungalows !

The improvement in the sport was shown by the number of foxes accounted for.   In 1909–10 51 brace, in 1912–13 55½ brace, in 1913–14 52½ brace.   In 1914 George Roake had a very good hunt when the master was absent ; he describes it in a letter to the master written on 13th November, 1914, the hunt taking place on the 12th November.   Roake began at Butser where the ranges were busy ; Butser Hill was blank. He then drew the Lythe downwind and foxes were found in all directions.   The pack split up in five divisions and it took Roake an hour to get hounds together.   Hounds then found at once in Hales Copse, ran up towards Ramsden and back to the copse where he got in ; hounds were held on and soon a fresh fox was viewed away over the road nearly to the Seven Stars, but he turned back left-handed through the Langrish coverts, right-handed over the Petersfield road and then through Mr. Sylvestre's coverts, and, being headed, to Strawberry Hanger, where the earths were stopped.   Then he raced to Boredean Hill, turning through Brickyard Copse, crossed the road by the Seven Stars and ran the old lane, turning up to Ramsden in view and was raced to ground at the top end of Hales Copse.   This was a hunt of an hour and fifteen minutes during which hounds were not cast and not once assisted in any way.   Roake apparently was very pleased with his horse's performance, by name "Slocock," who " got where the others could not."   At the express wish of an important member of the field this fox was got out and killed at 5.30 p.m. after two and a half hours' work.

The master had to be much away, but received very cheerful letters from Roake as to the sport.   Though the hunt related does not appear to be of a very wonderful nature, it shows a fine supply of foxes and yet another old dog was killed at 6 p.m.

The master's military duties made it necessary for him to look around for a joint master to help him. Captain Standish was working at a Remount Depot and soon was promoted Major and Assistant Commandant of the Depot, 1916–19. Mr. Sam Hardy of The Spain, Petersfield, came forward as joint master in 1915.

Major W. P. Standish, O.B.E., and Mr. S. Hardy, 1915-21.

The 1915–16 season proved a record one. In 115 days' hunting no less than 69 brace of foxes were killed, 38 brace in regular hunting, and 15 brace were marked to ground. The master's notes on scent were now very different. Thirty-one days were noted as good, 6 as very good and 5 days were partly good. No signs of austerity appear as yet. In fact, a note from a Wiltshire farmer dated 14th July, 1916, offering whole cheeses, 60 to 80 lbs., or truckle cheeses of 12 to 15 lbs., *ad libitum*, at the market price of 11 pence per lb., seems to indicate anything but starvation. In the next year, however, the submarine campaign made affairs look very different. It was the shadow of coming austerity probably which made the master make a rough estimate as to the expenses of hunting two days a week. It is undated but is among the March 1916 entries. The items may have some comparative interest against modern days. Huntsman, £125 per annum ; Whip, £80 ; Kennelman, £65 ; boy, £39 ; Stud Groom, £80 ; seven horses and the flesh cart horse at 30s. a week ; 70 quarters of oats for hounds at 45s. ; 1 ton rice, £21 ; 1 ton meal, £25 ; coal, £100 ; straw, £60 ; 1 ton biscuits, £19. The whole comes to £1,395, not an extravagant amount.

Sport soon shows a decline when reductions had to be made. In 1917–18 the tally dropped to 34 brace and the next year to only 19 brace. By 1920, however, it had again recovered a little to 27 brace.

On his retirement after a long and successful mastership, including a bad start and all the war years, Major Standish was presented with his portrait mounted on the " Snob," a reproduction of which appears facing page 196. Major Standish died on November 11th, 1922, to the great regret of all who knew him. His daughter Monica (now Mrs. J. S. Atkins), always a keen and most promising follower, now carries on the family's hunting tradition as joint master of the Atherstone (South) since 1943.

Mr. S. Hardy, 1921-26.

Mr. Sam Hardy now carried on after his joint master's death, keeping George Roake as huntsman. His real interest was probably in his handsome team of hackneys, but he enjoyed hunting in his own way, though by no means a thruster in the field. He was always cheerful and courteous to all, but gave his huntsman too complete a control of hunting and kennel management. Mr. Hardy spared no expense but Roake deteriorated when left so much to his own devices and sport was far from being as good as under Major Standish's management. His smart phaeton and pair, only rivalled by that of Mrs. W. G. Nicholson of Basing Park with her blood horses, always added interest to the meets. Mrs. Nicholson (daughter of the Rt. Hon. W. B. Beach of Oakley Hall, twenty years master of the Vine Hunt) remained one of the most staunch supporters of the Hambledon till her death, and very frequently hunted also with the H.H.

Major E. F. Talbot-Ponsonby, 1926-29.

Major Edmond Frederick Talbot-Ponsonby of Southwood, Tiverton, Devon, and Hill Place, Swanmore, Hants, took over the mastership. An old Gunner officer, Major Talbot-Ponsonby had been master of the Kildare Hunt for ten years, 1911–21. He hunted hounds himself with William Deakin as 1st whipper-in and kennel huntsman. Major Talbot-Ponsonby's father, C. W. Talbot, had lived at Langrish House, Petersfield, as well as Inchquin, Co. Cork, to which property he had succeeded on the death of the 3rd, and last, Lord Ponsonby in 1866, and Major Talbot-Ponsonby had married the youngest daughter of Mr. William Nicholson of Basing Park, and so was no stranger to the Hambledon country and he had considerable experience of hunting.

Sport was well up to the average, but the master found the cold scenting conditions and big woodlands were very different from small Irish gorses and sound pastures. Both he and his staff were well mounted.

Major J. Blake, 1929-33.

Major Jack Blake of Monckton House, Alverstoke, now became master. No better man could have been chosen. He

Major W. P. Standish, o.b.e., of Marwell Hall on " Snob," M.F.H. 1900-21.
" Chanter " (1916) " Weathergage " (1920) " Frenzy " (1919)

MAJOR JACK BLAKE, M.F.H. 1929-33.
The present Chairman of the Hambledon Hunt.

knew the country from boyhood, and had been a most efficient
Hon. Secretary for some years.   Well known and popular with
all classes, he was assured of willing support.   His 1st whipper-
in and kennel huntsman Sam Nash became a casualty before
hunting started and George Tongue succeeded him with Walter
Gupwell as 2nd whipper-in.

It was not a good scenting season and no hunt of great
interest occurred, but good average sport was enjoyed.   Seventeen brace were killed, 28½ brace were marked to ground.   The
last hunt of the season, on April 14th, produced a very hard
day, running all the time and marking three to ground and
having two other fast hunts spoiled by cold showers.

The next season was considered the best for many years,
scent was better and hounds killed 22½ brace and marked
26 brace to ground.   Several very useful hunting days were
enjoyed.   On November 8th from Marwell Hall, slowly by
Fishers Pond to The Vineyard, when the fox was raced to
Keeps and Austins Copse over the open to Greenhill and
Longwood over Owslebury Down, checking on the main road.
Soon put right, they ran to Wells Copse where another fox
saved his brother and led the field to Upham, where he too
found relief and handed over to a successor who was lost.
Hounds ran hard for over two hours and deserved a victim.
On February 25th they had their revenge by again finding
possibly the same fox and running by Fishers Pond, to Park
Hills, towards Deeps to the fir plantation, back to Park Hills
and the fir plantation.   He was killed after a hard one hour and
twenty minutes, hounds never leaving him despite others afoot.
Another fox from Twyford Park ran to Down Farm, Morestead,
and Colden Common and back to Twyford Park.   After another
run in the country he was killed after a good hard hunt of one
hour and ten minutes.   February 4th from Southwick village
also produced a nine-mile ring, followed by an hour and ten
minutes without a check to ground with hounds right on his
brush.

The season 1931–32 was also one of good sport, though
cub-hunting was late and disappointing, starting very wet,
followed by fifty days of drought.   On November 28th Preshaw,
as usual, provided a good hunt of an hour without a check and
ended in a kill.   On January 30th from Upham House a fox, found
in Grasteds, after a six-mile point in one hour and twenty
minutes, was killed at Wickham.   On February 3rd Southwick
foxes provided one and a half hours' good hunt with a kill and

a good two hour hunt to follow, covering a lot of country. The season yielded 18½ brace killed and 25½ brace to ground.

The master's last season was his best for scent and therefore sport was above the average. A memorable cub hunt took place on September 22nd from Broadhalfpenny Down. Hounds raced a straight-necked cub for an hour and finished with a 12-foot drop into the road from a wall before being pulled down in the village street at Hambledon. Hounds were so shaken that the pack missed its turn to hunt. Again on October 3rd an old fox from Limekiln Copse gave an excellent one and three-quarter hour hunt over eleven miles of country and saved his brush as hounds were stopped at Henwood. In December four good hunts took place. On the 17th, after an unenterprising fox had been killed, the Moors held a brace ; one of the brace provided a good five-mile point in thirty-five minutes, being marked to ground at the foot of Whiteways Lane. Christmas Eve at Morestead Pond started badly with a policeman saying hounds were in a prohibited area (Foot and Mouth disease). An obliging fox finished the conversation by breaking the right way to Owslebury and Deeps, and after a quick double hounds raced him by Roughay and pulled him down in Firs after an hour's good hunt. The next fox went all round the Upham country and was nearly caught in the village, but just escaping, he took refuge in a rabbit hole and was soon evicted. Boxing Day at Meonstoke also produced a good day for all but the foot people out for a holiday. The fox from the Fir Hanger went away to Beacon Hill, Wheely Down, by Joan's Acre and Blackhouse in the H.H. country, on by Hinton House, through the churchyard to the water meadows, by Shorley and then by Beauworth cross-roads to Hockley House where shooting was in progress and hounds were stopped, probably eight or nine miles as hounds ran, in an hour. December 31st from the Alma produced a very busy day and a straight four-mile point in twenty-five minutes, but all three foxes hunted were marked to ground. February 22nd produced a seven-mile point from Wickham Common to Waterlooville. Hounds may have changed as the wire made it impossible for the master to keep with them. Another good day was enjoyed on March 11th from Upham Pond. The first fox was killed after a two-hour hunt in Redlands. Another, from Upham Copse, gave a good fifty minutes' run, being killed in the middle of Owslebury village. The season's tally was 20½ brace killed and 35½ brace to ground.

To the very general regret of all Major Blake resigned and such good sport has not yet again been seen. His interest in hunting has not in any way decreased and for the last few years he has been Chairman of the Hunt, succeeding Major Reginald Nicholson of Bereleigh in 1946.

Mr. G. Joynson, 1933-35.

Mr. Gerald Joynson, though very crippled, had previous experience as M.F.H., having been master of the Clifton-on-Teme Foxhounds, 1928–32, and also the Isle of Wight Foxhounds, 1932–33. His brother Mr. Brooke Joynson whipped-in to him. Both knew their business. After leaving the Hambledon, Mr. Gerald Joynson was master of the South Staffordshire, 1935–36 and his brother master of the Stainton Dale for that year. They joined as joint masters of the North Hereford, 1936–38. Mr. Joynson continued for the next season as master before obtaining another joint master for 1939–40. From 1946–48 Mr. B. Joynson was master of the Cowdray. Mr. Joynson was greatly helped by his brother in the field who acted as pilot for him. The family were alluded to by Mr. Michael Berry, now joint master and huntsman of the Woodland Pytchley and formerly a well-known hunting correspondent, as the " much travelled Joynson brothers."

Mr. J. Long, 1935-39.

Mr. Jack Long of West Lodge, West Meon, succeeded to the mastership with E. Haynes as his 1st whipper-in and kennel huntsman. In September 1939 Mr. Long joined the Army and was posted as " missing " and then " presumed killed " in 1941.

A Committee, 1939-45.

The management of the Hunt was undertaken by a committee, with Major Jack Blake as acting master. Hunting was carried on only for the 1939–40 season and then suspended. The hounds were sent in August 1941 to North Cornwall and in 1944 to the H.H. On each occasion E. Haynes went with them. On May 1st, 1946, they returned to the country.

Captain P. Vivian, R.N., 1945-49.

Captain Paul Vivian, R.N., had started a private pack of a few couple of hounds in Stockheath Camp, Havant, in 1943. On being demobilized, he lived first at Hill Place Cottage, Swanmore, and then moved to West End House, Hambledon.

A great debt of gratitude is owed to Captain Vivian for getting hunting going again in the country in adverse circumstances and with a very small subscription. No day was too long and he worked extremely hard, but was not rewarded by very good sport. Jack Andrews and Mrs. Vivian assisted him as whippers-in in 1948–49 season. Admiral B. C. Watson, C.B., D.S.O., of West House, Hambledon, acted as Hon. Secretary.

Lieut.-Colonel J. H. Hulbert, 1949-

Lieut.-Colonel John Harvey Hulbert, an old Gunner officer, of Fir Hill, Droxford, has taken the mastership. He lives where the famous Mr. Tom Smith lived during his second mastership and his great-grandfather is mentioned on March 24th, 1851, in a select half-dozen horsemen who rode a very good hunt of two and a half hours from Idsworth to Stakes mentioned on page 186 during Mr. T. Smith's second mastership.

It is hoped that sport will again reach the standard that Mr. Tom Smith always showed.

Lieut.-Colonel J. H. Hulbert's first season was not a lucky one. His huntsman Jack Andrews did not prove successful in killing foxes and the master took the horn himself towards the end of the season with some improvement. Colonel F. W. Jagger of Lower Farm Warnford took over the duties of Honorary Secretary.

Support is good and with Mr. J. Moore Stevens as amateur huntsman the future is promising. Mr. Moore Stevens has five years' experience as joint master and huntsman to the West Somerset (Quantock Farmers) Pack.

In 1950 a considerable honour came to Miss Jane Chrystal of Meonstoke House when her 10-year-old " Remus " won the exacting Badminton Olympic Trials, a three-day event including a steeplechase over 40 obstacles. Captain Terry Collins rode this clever horse.

———————

THE HAMBLEDON HUNT.

* By Mr. F. P. Delmé Radcliffe, 1831.

Now the frost is all gone, and we're happily met,
To debate on the true science over our wet,
Fill a bumper all round, let us jovially sing
Hurra ! for the Hambledon—Long live our King ![1]

Chorus—Fill up your glass, every man ;
　　　　He is an ass who won't hunt when he can.

We are all truly loyal, for every one knows
A fox-hunter is loyal wherever he goes ;
And I'm sure round this table we all are agreed,
We've a King well adapted for taking the lead.

To such a King's honour it greatly redounds,
That his rein chiefly tends to direct him to hounds ;
But as Kings are not *subject* alone to my pen,
I'll now give you a touch at a few of his men.

To begin with, a scion of such a good stock,
Prince Dick[2] is a varmint young chip of the block ;
He will face any fences at his father's command,
So let's hope that his days may be long in the land.

As the pride of our country, by all 'tis confest,
That our Greenwoods[3] in winter appear to be best ;
Either Colonel or Captain, whatever they ride,
Will get over a church and the steeple beside.

From Hill Place comes George Butler,[4] unlikely to fail
In maintaining his place on the hill or the vale ;
On his old Irish horse he would ne'er be too late
At the right side of stake-and-bound hedge, stile, or gate.

Next skimming the furrow you'll see Major Ridge,[5]
If he comes to a brook he'll not look for a bridge :
Such a sportsman as this is not easily beat,
And I trust he'll get over whate'er he may meet.

* Frederick Peter Delmé Radcliffe, the author of the poem was a cousin of Henry Peter Delmé. His father Emilius Henry Delmé assumed the name of Radcliffe on his marriage with Anne Melicent Clarke, eventual heiress of Hitchin Priory through her mother Anne Radcliffe. Mr. F. P. Radcliffe, succeeded in 1832, born 1804, died 1875, author of *The Noble Science*, M.F.H. Hertfordshire Hunt, 1835-39.

The song appeared in the new *Sporting Magazine* in 1835 as "Written by somebody; published by nobody; for the use of anybody; and dedicated, without permission, to the Gentlemen of the Hambledon Hunt."

[1] Mr. John King, M.F.H., 1829-41, lived at Corhampton.

[2] "Prince Dick," Mr. King's son Richard.

[3] Colonel William Greenwood of Brookwood Park, member H.H. 1838, and of the Hambledon Hunt ; and his brother Lieut.-Colonel George. Both fine horsemen noted by " Nimrod " and other authorities.

[4] Mr. George Butler of Hill Place, younger brother of Mr. Thomas Butler of Bury Hill. A first-rate man to hounds.

[5] Major Thomas Ridge, son of Mr. Thomas Ridge of Kilmeston Manor, M.F.H., H.H., 1749-95. He was a member of the Hambledon Hunt.

On a roaring bay horse in the wake of Sir Frank[6]
You may see Mr. Halkett[7] come over the bank ;
Should he want any wind for the troublesome jade,
He can find a *North Wester*[7] to bring to his aid.

Squire Delmé[8] from Cams is determined for one,
As he fully enjoys it to see all the fun :
Should he chance to arrive rather late with his drag
He can make up his ground on his little brown nag.

He brings brother George,[9] who, all ripe for the burst,
Has resolved in his mind to be nothing but first ;
Sometimes the *Freemason*[10] indulges his whim,
Just to prove that the secret is lasting with him.

And a Bedfordshire Sportsman with only one fear,
Lest the *Guardsman*[11] should ever be found in the rear ;
Just as jealous as George, and as anxious to go,
While he can with the first for the fame of the " O."

And I trust he will go when he gets on his *Socks*,[12]
If that trump William Gage[13] will again find a fox,
Just to lead such a chevy from Henwood till dark,
With a pretty " Who-Whoop " beyond Rotherfield Park.[14]

Now I've sung a great deal, and could sing a deal more,
But perhaps, if I do, you may vote me a bore ;
If I've not told you half of the prime ones you'll see,
Come well mounted to-morrow to cover with me.

So I'll wind up my rhyme, having told you my reason,
With wishing us sport for the rest of the season ;
May we ne'er be prevented a day by the frost,
And all ride the best horses that ever were cros't.

Last, though not least, to the ladies—'twere really too bad,
If I had not a stanza for beauty to add,
To the joy of our hearts, the delight of our life—
God bless all in the country—maid, widow, or wife.

One word more to the farmers I cannot withhold :
May they all ride a gelding to turn into gold,
May they ne'er be annoy'd by bad crops or by Swing,
But merrily thrive, and go hunting with King.

> *Chorus*—Fill up your glass, every man ;
>   He is an ass who won't hunt if he can.

[6] Commodore Sir Francis Collins, c.b.

[7] Son of Sir John Halkett, Bart., of Fareham, who kept staghounds. " North Wester " was a good hunter of his and winner of races.

[8] Mr. Peter Delmé of Cams Hall, 1794–1883.

[9] Captain George Delmé, R.N., brother of the above, both first-rate sportsmen.

[10] " Freemason," a hunter of Captain George Delmé's renowned for his " lasting " good qualities.

[11] " Guardsman." ⎰ Both horses belonged to a member of the Oakley Hunt.
[12] " Socks." ⎱ " Guardsman " won a steeplechase, December 1829.

[13] The Hon. William Gage of Westbury House, a staunch sportsman. Henwood was renowned for pheasants and foxes.

[14] Rotherfield Park, the seat of Mr. James Winter Scott, member H.H., 1821, and member of the Hambledon Hunt. A good horseman and a preserver of foxes.

This song appeared in the new *Sporting Magazine* for November 1834. The author is unknown.

THE SONG.

Now concluded's the Summer, November's set in,
With thoughts fixed on hunting with our King[1] I'll begin,
And gladly inform you what sport you're to expect
With this sportsman—ye Nimrods—where wrong pray correct.
    Down, down, down, derry down.

His return first to health 'tis with pleasure I view ;
How rejoic'd is the country, how cheering to you ;
So I'll spur on my Pegasus, laud to the skies,
That tidings so welcome to the hunt should arise.

If my nag keep the pace it will give me delight,
As a King is the subject propos'd for the night ;
So as rider I'll mount—should the steed be found slow,
My song being ended to the kennel 'twill go.

Not a fault to be found with so splendid a pack
As the bitches of King, nor for tongue do they lack,
Which you'll freely allow when the fox is on foot,
For hanging would follow any one that ran mute.

'Tis a pleasure to cast your eyes over his stud
All adapted for strength, or for strength in the mud ;
In short, ye hard riders, through the season you'll see,
The John King's well appointed to hunt H.H.C.

When th' Squire of Cams Hall's[2] renown'd coverts are drawn,
Let your horse be well bred, and come early that morn,
For there foxes are plenty and stout, bear in mind,
And of hounds you will scarcely lose sight, ere they find.

Well fam'd in our annals, merry Henwood we boast
Not surpass'd for its fox, so the owner we'll toast ;
Come then fill your glasses, I'm right I'll engage,
And with pleasure I'll give you his name William Gage.

When the meeting is fix'd, " Preshaw House," all attend,
For no blank day is fear'd, with so steady a friend ;
Reynard's faithful preserver take place in my song,
And with loud acclamation we'll drink Walter Long,[3]

Come now Warnford, the tribute of praise is your due,
And the park of your name is familiar to you ;
Where an Abbot[4] resides, for good thus inclin'd ;
And though hares are in plenty, a fox you will find.

[1] Mr. John King, M.F.H. 1829–41. He had a bad fall in the season 1832–33.
[2] Mr. H. P. Delmé of Cams Hall.
[3] Mr. Walter Long of Preshaw, High Sheriff 1824. Born 1788, died 1871.
[4] Mr. William Abbott of Warnford Park, member.

I will now give a name, sirs, of Hampshire renown,
Who is lord of the manor of Soberton-down,
Henry Minchin, Esquire, part owner of Wallop,
May he live to hunt long and enjoy oft a gallop.

Here's a health to a friend[5] whom the hunt will confess,
If I give his initials, S.H., you will guess,
Famed for dinners, for foxes, for friendship no less ;
'Tis easy enough then to say his name ends with an S.

Here's our Sheriff for Hants,[6] come fill to the toast,
And the country will tell you we've reason to boast ;
So the Hunt will agree, too, for at table he stood,
Said, " My pheasants at Weston for foxes are food."

I have said much of coverts and foxes, I trow ;
I'll introduce covers very different now—
The covers are Austin's,[7] well famed at the Crown,
In Waltham, where inhabits a Fox[8] of the town.

I've a word for subscribers : in friendship to-day,
The Secretary begs they'll be prompt in their pay ;
For hounds must be attended, I need not add more ;
Here's an end to my song, or you'll vote me a bore.

      Down, down, etc.

---

[5] Probably Mr. Samuel Hawkins of Marwell Lodge.

[6] Mr. Thomas Chamberlayne of Cranbury Park, member, High Sheriff 1835. Born 1805, died 1876.

[7] Mr. Austin was landlord of " The Crown " where the Hunt Club dinners were then held.

[8] Mr. Fox was the Club Banker.

CHAPTER VIII.

THE GARTH HUNT.

Masters of the Garth Hunt.

1810–17   Rev. H. E. St. John, West Court, Finchampstead.

1817–50   Sir J. Cope, Bart., Bramshill Park, Basingstoke.

1850–52   Mr. J. J. Wheble, Bullmershe Court, Reading.

1852–1902 Mr. T. C. Garth, Haines Hill, Twyford.

1902–19   Mr. R. H. Gosling, Manor House, Waltham St. Lawrence.

1919–22   Major L. A. Jackson, Wokingham.

1922–26   Major Sir H. R. Cayzer, Tylney Hall, Basingstoke.

1926–28   Lieut.-Col. Lord Dorchester, o.b.e., Greywell Hill, Basingstoke.

           Mr. H. S. Chinnock, Dinorbin Court, Fleet.

1928–31   Col. F. G. Barker, c.b.e., Stanlake Park, Twyford.

1931–36   Major Sir H. R. Cayzer (2nd mastership).
           Mr. R. H. R. Palmer, Hurst Grove, Twyford.

1936–39   Col. Sir H. R. Cayzer (3rd mastership), created Lord Rotherwick 1939.
           Miss E. Barker, Stanlake Park, Twyford.

1939 (May—Sept.) Miss E. Barker (2nd mastership).
           The Earl of Northesk, Cedar House, Sherlock Row, Twyford.

A Committee, 1939—   .

The acting masters were:—

1939–45   Col. F. G. Barker, Stanlake Park.
           Miss E. Barker, Stanlake Park.

1945–46   Mr. R. H. R. Palmer, Hurst Grove.
           Mr. V. P. Simonds, Hall's Farm, Farley Hill, Reading.

1946–   Miss E. Barker, Stanlake Park.
           Mr. V. P. Simonds, Hall's Farm, Farley Hill, Reading.

Rev. H. E. St. John, 1810-17.

The first gentleman to hunt a pack of hounds in what is now known as the Garth and South Berks country was the Rev. Henry Ellis St. John of West Court, Finchampstead, who started a pack of harriers in 1790. As he was then only fourteen, his father, the Rev. Ellis St. John (1739–1809), must have really founded the pack. Thomas Tocock, a name to be well known in later years, was his huntsman. Mr. St. John came of a remarkable family. His great-grandfather, Ellis Mews of Winchester, married thrice, his first two wives Frances St. John and Martha Goodyear, were both considerable heiresses and through them he became the owner of Farley Chamberlayne, Dogmersfield and West Court. His third wife was also of a well-known Hampshire family, Sarah Cobb (*née* Stukeley), daughter of Sir Hugh Stukeley, of Hinton Ampner House, but she was not an heiress. She was the widow of Rev. John Cobb, warden of Winchester College, 1720–24. His great-uncle, Sir Paulet St. John, has already been referred to on pages 28 and 29, as one of the early foxhunters in the county. Two of his sons, the Rev. Edward, till 1850, and John of Banisters after 1850, hunted harriers at West Court and John also hunted round Winchester. His brother Edward was a great supporter of the Vine Hunt and his nephew Edward was master of the Vine Hunt for a short time. Mr. St. John became more ambitious in 1810 and bought the Duke of Bridgwater's pack of foxhounds and hunted them himself, Joe Paice turning hounds to him. He showed such good sport that he has been compared to the famous Rev. Jack Russell of Devon. Colonel Blagrave of Calcot was high in his praise, saying "We never had really a good series of sport after Mr. St. John, though, of course, his successor had many good runs, there was not the same regular character of sport." The real reason of this was that his successor hunted a very much larger country and probably hounds did not come the gallant Colonel's way so often as formerly. Mr. St. John died in 1841.

Sir John Cope, Bart., 1817-50.

Sir John Cope, 11th Baronet of Bramshill, now undertook the mastership, receiving from Mr. St. John his hounds and hunt servants. Kennels were made for them at Bramshill. The story of his coming into the title is somewhat amusing. Born in 1768, he had been in partnership with a solicitor,

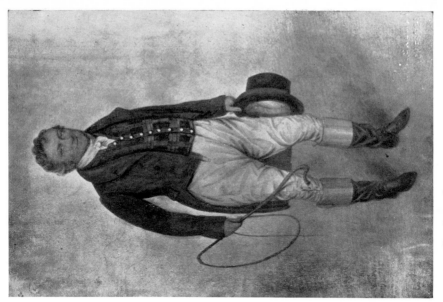

Sir John Cope, Bart., M.F.H. 1817-50.
Master of the Bramshill Hunt.

Rev. H. E. Sir. John, M.H. 1790-1810, M.F.H. 1810-17.
First master of foxhounds in the Garth Country.

Mr. Gerard Wharton, in London. On his brother Sir Denzil Cope's death in 1812 a special messenger was sent to announce the event from Bramshill. Sir John was examining a legal deed in his office when the messenger arrived. The new " Sir John," on seeing the address and glancing at the contents, threw over the deed to his partner, saying : " There, Jerry, hang the Law and now for foxhunting." They were always great friends, however, and Mr. Wharton regularly stayed at Bramshill. Sir John had hunted both with Sir Thomas Mostyn's hounds in Oxfordshire and in Leicestershire. Having broken his thigh in a riding accident, his leg was rather bent in consequence. He was also very short sighted. His keenness on sport overcame all difficulties. To assist him in the field he had a very unusual hunting crop made with an eyeglass fixed where the horn crook joins the whip. Its use on an offending member of the field probably aided his language which was sometimes emphatic. Luckily, in those days there was no wire lurking to undo the short-sighted.

Sir John's hounds were for some ten years of a very distinctive type. High on the leg, very wiry and muscular, with rather long necks. They were very independent and inclined to go wide of the main cry hoping for a turn in their favour. Some critics called them a pack of " skirters," but they accounted for foxes very well in the woodlands. On one occasion Mr. John Warde gave Sir John a day in the Craven country and his hounds killed a leash of foxes, somewhat surprised at their " guerilla " methods. They never came away together from covert and so streamed over the country and were mixed with the field, the horn being a kind of rallying point. After about 1825, however, Sir John used Mr. Warde's kennels to breed from and they became more normal in their methods and the hounds became a fine muscular type who hunted as a pack and still did the enormous distances required of them. After 1843 Sir John gave up some of his outlying country in Berkshire to Mr. Mortimer G. Thoyts of Sulhamstead. Sir John was one of the first masters to try vaccination for distemper, but though he had some success, he found it was not infallible. His hunt servants were well mounted on horses of good breeding and stamina. He liked big hounds in direct opposition to his neighbour, Mr. Chute of the Vyne. They were collected chiefly from Sir Thomas Mostyn, Mr. Nicholl of the New Forest Hunt, and Mr. John Warde. Mr. Chute told him one day, " Nose is everything and you look only for big legs and feet." Some of his hounds' names were very odd as he insisted on using names for his entry that had never been used before in the kennel. After thirty years some were rather difficult for the hunt servants to pronounce.   He worked his hounds hard but they always looked well.   On one occasion, after a very good hunt leaving hounds twenty miles from kennel he drew again, found and killed after an hour and three-quarters.   On another occasion, when the Bramshill pack clashed with Mr. Villebois', a single hound named " Sampson " of the former pack ran far ahead and tackled the fox alone, being so severely mauled that it was a fortnight before he could again come out.   Many good hunts were enjoyed in his large country stretching from Windsor to Basingstoke, including the country round Nettlebed, Caversham and Maidenhead.   Sir John only kept 40 or 42 couple of hounds and 14 horses for the staff, so all had to be fit.

A few examples of his good hunts have been recorded. In December, 1822, hounds found at Fleet and ran to ground on Jays Farm, Pangbourne, fully a 20-mile point.   In 1839, finding a stout fox at Bucklersbury, skirting Yatterden, he ran to Compton and Aldworth, over the Ridge Downs to Unhill Woods and Blewbury, when he was killed after a three-hours' hunt, about 25 miles as hounds ran.   Only half-a-dozen riders got to the end of this hunt.   Another good hunt took place on March 17th, 1848 : finding at Horsden Common, hounds ran to Rye Common, Dogmersfield, along the back gardens of Odiham, over a wall into Mr. F. Cole's grounds ; thence the fox went away to North Warnborough, then to South Warnborough, Sutton Common, High Wood, Froyle, and killed at Gabriels, both Mr. Garth and Mr. Simonds, afterwards master and honorary secretary for many years, being well to the fore in this hunt.   At a meet in 1831 at Hartley Row Gate an interesting description was given by " Nim South "[1] in the *Sporting Magazine* of the Duke of Wellington's appearance at the meet.   He saw a solitary horseman approaching at a snail's pace in the rain.   " He was a man somewhat stricken in years, with a grave and thoughtful countenance."   He wore a plain scarlet frock coat, a lilac silk waistcoat, kid gloves and drab fustian trousers with Wellington boots.   South recognised the unmistakable nose and duly took off his hat to " the greatest man of the day."   The Duke bowed and smiled and chatted in the shed out of the rain.   A stage coach passed by and coach-

---

[1] " Nim South " was the pen name of Robert Smith Surtees of Hamsterley Hall, Durham, 1803–64, author of *Handley Cross*, etc.

man and passengers all took off their hats, receiving the Duke's usual salute of two fingers to his nose. On Sir John's arrival and the rest of the field, he was cordial and intimate with all. They had a very moderate day's sport but South says " I have seldom seen a man with less idea of riding than he has. His seat is unsightly in the extreme and few men get more falls in the course of the year than His Grace. Nevertheless, he seemed to enjoy the thing amazingly, and what with leading over occasionally and his groom's assistance, he did very well."

Another story of the Iron Duke occurred in Sir John's later years when an irate tenant farmer stood in a gap with a pitchfork against the Duke. The Duke argued his age in wishing to go through the gap but to no effect. Horrified spectators asked the farmer if he knew who it was he was stopping. He replied, " Oh, yes, I knowed 'un. Boneyparty couldn't stop him, but *I* could ! " On another occasion one of the Duke's keepers came under suspicion of vulpicide. When the Duke was informed of this he wrote to the master as follows :—" He could hardly realise a man being so cruel and hard-hearted as to kill in cold blood such a noble animal as a fox, but he trusted Sir John's informant had been misinformed." This horror of vulpicide may sound, perhaps, somewhat oddly from a man of the Duke's experiences, but really accentuated the difference between " murder " and honourable death in the chase, or in war.

On Tuesday, 9th November, 1841, Sir John found a fox near Bramshill and killed very near to Windsor Castle, so near in fact, that a royal servant came running out to Sir John whilst he was breaking up his fox, with the news that a prince had been born at Buckingham Palace. Actually Prince Edward was born at 10.50 a.m. that morning. Sir John wrote his name in the Queen's book and made polite enquiries. Shortly after this a hunting crop with a silver fox on the handle was received by Sir John from the Queen. This crop used to hang under the picture of the Hunt in the hall at Bramshill, but lately, together with the " quizzing glass " crop, was in possession of Mrs. John H. Cope of Finchampstead Place, Berkshire. An interesting sequel to this event occurred on 10th November, 1845, when Sir John took his hounds to Cumberland Lodge at the request of H.R.H. the Prince Consort. The *Windsor and Eton Express* of Saturday, November 15th, report the occasion rather quaintly : " The field, which was exceedingly numerous, included the Prince Consort, the Duke Ferdinand, and Princes

P

Augustus and Leopold of Saxe Coburg, who were attended by Major-General Wemyss, Mr. G. E. Anson and several other members of the Royal Household.   A fine fox was unkenneled at Cranborne, which, after affording about half-an-hour's hunting in cover, broke into the open and was killed after a sharp run at Fyfield.   Prince Albert, with his illustrious relatives and some of those of the Royal suite, left the field before the hunt had concluded and proceeded to the Castle to luncheon at two o'clock.   The brush was cut off by Shirley, the huntsman, and given to G. E. Anson, Esq., to be presented, we believe, to the Prince of Wales as a birthday present.   (N.B.—The Prince was four years old on the previous day.)   The horse ridden by Prince Leopold of Saxe Coburg started off shortly after the Prince had left Cumberland Lodge, and, running against a tree (the branches coming into contact with H.S.H.'s head which was slightly cut), threw its rider, but fortunately without the Prince sustaining any serious injury.   H.S.H. immediately returned to Cumberland Lodge and shortly afterwards was sufficiently recovered to mount another of Prince Albert's hunters and join his Royal relatives in the field."   Perhaps it was the recollection of his first brush which caused King Edward VII to wish to be master of the Garth Hunt after the Royal Buckhounds were given up in 1901.

Tom Tocock and Joe Paice first served Sir John as huntsman and whipper-in, with John Major, son of Mr. Villebois' old huntsman, as 2nd whipper-in.   Tocock had the unusual habit of grabbing the pommel of his saddle when jumping, but, despite this unprofessional failing, he remained as huntsman for fifteen years.   After one year with John Major, James Shirley came in 1835 and remained till Sir John resigned in 1850. Robert Tocock (son of Tom Tocock), George and Thomas Sweetman and Thomas Nevitt served as whippers-in at different times.   A rather characteristic story of the master was told by the estate steward at Greywell to Mr. J. A. Eggar, given in his book.   When a little boy, Sir John came riding up near Hartley Wintney and said "Have you seen a fox, boy?" Young Preston said, "I don't know what a fox is but I saw a great red dog with a long tail and his tongue was hanging out." Sir John said, "If you have told the truth there will be half-a-crown for you, but if you have told a lie, you will have this whip."   He gave a toot on his horn and the huntsman and hounds came up ; they soon hit the line and killed in the church-yard on the hill.   Sir John came back to their home and his mother said, " Sir John wants you." The boy ran indoors not wanting the whip. Sir John then said to his mother, " I am not going to give him the whip : tell him I have half-a-crown for him." The boy then appeared and Sir John threw down half-a-crown saying, " Keep your eyes open, boy, and see as many great red dogs as you can."

Among the chief supporters of the Bramshill Hounds were Colonel Blagrave of Calcot ; "Aesop " relates that the gallant Colonel jumped a spiked gate nearly seven feet high on one occasion near Stratfieldsaye. Needless to say, he was not followed. This gallant sportsman died in 1867 aged 89. Others who were always well to the fore were Mr. Hawley of West Green, Messrs. Joseph and William Parfitt of Eversley, Messrs. Blackhall and Henry Simonds, Mr. William Makepeace of Bracknell, Mr. Leveson Gower, Mr. Pigott, Messrs. Bazalette and Dobson of Mortimer, Mr. Patterly, also Mr. George Montague.

Ill-health forced Sir John to resign to the regret of all and he gave his hounds to Mr. Wheble of Bullmershe Court near Reading. Sir John did not long survive his resignation, dying on the 18th November, 1851. Eversley Church was hung with black hangings and was crowded at his funeral. The funeral procession was followed by a single hound. The Victorian gloom of the hangings would hardly have appealed to the departed Squire.

The well-known artist, Edmund Havell (1814-47) painted a picture of Sir John Cope with his hounds at Bramshill House in 1837. Sir John stands on the central steps with his friends, Thomas Peers-Williams, M.P., and Captain Edward Gordon, R.N. This picture is now hung in the National Gallery of British Sports and Pastimes at Derby House. He also painted a picture of Sir John Cope and his huntsman and hounds behind Bramshill House.

Mr. J. J. Wheble, 1850-52.

Mr. J. J. Wheble of Bullmershe Court, near Reading, tried to hunt all Sir John Cope's great country, including the South Berks country which Mr. George Montagu had taken for three seasons and now resigned. He built kennels at his own house but found the country too much for him and Mr. Garth took over the Hampshire portion, Mr. Wheble retaining the South Berks country till 1855.

GARTH.

Mr. T. C. Garth, 1852 - 1902.

In 1852 Mr. Thomas Colleton Garth was unanimously elected as master of the country east of the River Loddon. He had distinguished himself as a keen and good horseman in Sir John Cope's day and was destined to leave a considerable mark on hunting history though not aspiring to hunt hounds himself. He built kennels for the hounds at his house, Haines Hill, near Twyford, Berkshire. In 1853 he bought 30 couple of Mr. Wheble's dog pack, big upstanding hounds of 24½ inches. He also engaged Robert Tocock as his huntsman and his son Henry Tocock and Thomas Sweetman as whippers-in. Henry Tocock was succeeded by George Bartlet from Sir Watkin Wynn in 1859.

The opening meet of the Garth Hounds was held at Haines Hill where a large party partook of breakfast. That the new master was popular was shown by the large numbers of farmers at the meet. Robert Tocock stayed till 1865 when he retired after forty years of hard work in the field, " much worn and torn by falls and rheumatism," as a contemporary put it. Thomas Sweetman then took the horn, having turned hounds to his predecessor for thirteen years and been 2nd whipper-in before that. His reign was not a long one. On 12th November, 1869, at a meet at Greywell Hill, the seat of Lord Dorchester, he dropped dead from his horse. Mr. Garth then promoted Charles Brackley who had learnt his work with Mr. H. Villebois[2] in West Norfolk and with the Bicester, and also had whipped-in for a time to Tom Sweetman. His assistants were Thomas Austen and Henry Povey. Charles Brackley stayed for thirty-five years with Mr. Garth. He was very good in kennel, a good woodland huntsman, quiet and efficient in the field ; he knew his work and killed his foxes consistently. Never a great thruster, with rather a tubby figure, it is related of him on one occasion that after the master and 1st whip had jumped rather a nasty fence together, Mr. Garth called " Come on Brackley, this is the right side." " That's all very well, sir," was the

[2] Mr. Henry Villebois junior, M.F.H., the V.W.H. 1849–54., the West Norfolk 1859–65 and 1875–77 (part of country). He was a nephew of Mr. J. T. Villebois, the master of the H.H. His father was also a good sportsman and celebrated whip.

Mr. T. C. Garth, M.F.H. 1852 - 1902,
from whom the Hunt takes its title.

answer, " but how the dickens am I to get there?" Brackley latterly got somewhat surly and familiar, and even rude on occasions. The master had a good cure for his rudeness by sending him to draw a covert Brackley particularly detested. One of these was Shottesbrooke Great Wood. When the master was annoyed, he addressed his huntsman as " Brackley," when in good humour as " Charles." A good story illustrates the peculiarities of both master and huntsman. Mr. Garth : " Charles, Charles, they're 'ollering, tremendjious on the 'ill." Brackley : " Wot ever's got you—O' course they're 'ollering, they're building a 'ouse on the 'ill, been 'ollering all day." Mr. Garth : " Oh, building a 'ouse are they ; well, Brackley, you get along and draw Shottesbrooke Great Wood." In the covert concerned it was difficult to get to hounds, and around it was a stiffly fenced grass country abhorred by Brackley, as he detested galloping and jumping more and more as he became older. Mr. Garth's lack of " aitches " was presumably a pose or habit and had nothing to do with lack of education. He was the owner of large sugar plantations, precise and neat in dress and very consistent in his attire. Mr. Garth's appearance is well shown in his portrait by " Spy." His trim, clean-cut face with white hair, gave him a rather austere appearance In the field he always wore rose-coloured tops to his boots, neatly secured with leather garters tied in a bow, beautifully cleaned leathers, pale primrose in colour, white leather waistcoat, Gladstone collar and blue birdseye tie, a single-breasted coat with three buttons showing the bottom of his waistcoat, a tall high hat never tilted, and individual in shape. An upright seat on a horse gave him a dignified appearance in the field. He did not, however look " part " of his horse. He rode great distances and never had second horses for either himself or staff. When old and he had become very bent in the saddle, he was sometimes driven home in a brougham when the distance was very great. His Friday country gave him very long rides both to the meets and home, but when once an H.H. visitor, in saying good-night, said, " You have a long ride home, Mr. Garth," the answer was " I shall be home in time to hunt to-morrow." When the meet was at Greywell Mr. Garth used latterly to drive to the White Lion, Hartford Bridge, and then ride on, arriving at about 9.30 a.m. He then ate an enormous breakfast. A new uncut ham was always produced, besides eggs, sausages, etc. He used to say, " I like a lot of ' cawfee ' and tea cakes before 'unting."

As a squire he was most charitable, strictly religious, and a most regular attendant at the two churches in his patronage, Hurst and Ruscombe, every Sunday.

He farmed well and bred many of his hunt horses.

His chief joys in life were hunting and yachting. The summers he spent sailing his own boat, the *Hyacinthe*. In manner he was somewhat reserved and brusque, but this concealed a warm heart. Socially he was not very forthcoming and dancing was not his forte. Two stories are told of him. One, at a dance at Bearwood, his partner stopped and dodged away from him afterwards: " 'Ere, catch my 'orse," the abandoned master is related to have said. Another dancing tale was after a turn with a youthful partner of the rushing type: "A good mover, but pulls terrible 'ard."

The old squire was kind to youth but his house was not a very lively one to stay in. After dinner, he was soon apt to take a nap, in one case, at any rate, not before telling the butler " Give him a glass of port, good lad, good lad, his mother always keeps foxes." This was said to the present Lord Dorchester when staying at Haines Hill as a boy.

In the field Mr. Garth never abused either servants or field. " Please, gentlemen," was his strongest caution to the field, and coming from so respected a character, this was quite sufficient. He liked a lively well-bred horse, but insisted on a staid type of horse for his hunt servants. " Quiet 'osses seldom kick 'ounds," was his principle. He would give a good price for a good horse. At Mr. J. J. Farquharson's sale on June 9th, 1858, Mr. Garth gave 250 guineas for " Crocus " and 200 guineas for " Tom," two of the best hunters in Mr. Farquharson's numerous stud.

Mr. Garth's coverts were always well stocked with pheasants but he did not care for shooting. Once, when pheasants were seen to stream over the master with no shots resulting, a neighbouring gun thought that he must be ill and ran to ask what was the matter. He was answered, " Matter, matter, what do yer mean, matter ? " " Well," said the friend, " why don't you shoot ? " " What," said Mr. Garth, " shoot those beautiful things, those beautiful birds? I like to see them fly but of course they won't fly unless they're disturbed so we have to disturb them, more's the pity."

Mr. Garth bred some very good hounds and kept up Sir John Cope's stamp of big hound. One, by name " Ringwood," was so good that the Marquis of Worcester asked Mr. Garth for the loan of him for use at Badminton.   He was descended from Mr. T. A. Smith's " Bertram " and in Charles Brackley's opinion was the best hound that he ever hunted.

One of Mr. Garth's well-known supporters was the Rev. Charles Kingsley.   Mr. Kingsley was born in 1819 and came to Eversley as Rector in 1844 and remained there till his death in 1875.   He was passionately devoted to hunting, to the country, and to country folk.   Two descriptions of hunts may be given in his own words : " We had a pretty thing on Friday with Garth's, the first run I've seen this year.   Out of the Clay Vale below Tilney Hall, pace as good as could be, fields three acres each, fences awful, then over Hazeley Heath to Bramshill, shoved him through a false cast, and a streamer over Hartford Flat, into an unlucky earth.   Time, fifty-five minutes, falls plentiful, started thirty and came in eight, and didn't the old mare go !   Oh, Tom, she is a comfort ; even when a bank broke into a lane and we tumbled down, she hops up again before I'd time to fall off, and away like a four-year-old, and if you can get a horse through that clay vale, why then you can get them ' most wards,' least wise, so I find, for a black region it is, and if you ain't in the same field with the hounds, you don't know whether you are in the same parish, what with hedges, and trees, and woods, and all supernumerary vegetations."

The next account was in a letter to T. Hughes, Esq. Mr. Kingsley had done all his parish work and was sitting down to his dinner at 4 p.m.   He heard the hounds in his patch of gorse, " so I jumped up, left the cook shrieking, and off.   He wasn't there, but I knew where he was, for I keep a pretty good register of foxes (ain't they my parishioners and parts of my flock ?) ; and as the poor fellows had had a blank, they were very thankful to find themselves in five minutes going like mad.   We had an hour and a half of it—scent breast high as the dew began to rise (bleak nor'-easter, always good weather) and if we had not crossed a second fox, should have killed him in the open ; as it was we lost him after sunset, after the fiercest grind I have had this nine years and I went back to my dinner. The old horse behaved beautifully ; he is not fast, but in the enclosed woodlands he can live up to anyone and earned great honour by leaping in and out of the Loddon, only four more doing it, and one receiving a mucker.   I feel three years younger to-day. . . . .   The whip tells me there were three in the river together, rolling over horse and man !   What a sight to have lost even by being a-head!"

Perhaps it was after this good hunt that Mr. Kingsley felt inspired to write that wonderfully stirring poem the " Ode to the North-Easter " given at the end of the chapter. Mr. Kingsley's prose description of a foxhound is given below. It does not equal the verse : " The old savage ideal of beauty was the lion, type of mere massive force. That was succeeded by an over-civilised ideal—say the fawn—type of delicate grace. By cunning breeding and choosing through long centuries, man has combined both, and has created the foxhound, lion and fawn in one ; just as he might create noble human beings, did he take half as much trouble about politics (in the true old sense of the word) as he does about fowls. Look at that old hound, who stands doubtful looking up at his master for advice. Look at the severity, delicacy, lightness of every curve. His head is finer than a deer's ; his hind legs tense as steel springs, his fore legs straight as arrows ; and yet see the depth of chest, the sweep of loin, the breadth of paw, the mass of arm and thigh ; and if you have an eye for form, look at the absolute majesty of his attitude at this moment. Majesty is the only word for it. . . ."

The chief landowners and covert owners all supported the veteran master, H.M. Queen Victoria and H.R.H. Prince Christian at Cumberland Lodge heading the list. Among others the 3rd Duke of Wellington, the 5th and 6th Marquesses of Downshire of Easthampstead Park ; the 4th, 5th and 6th Lords Calthorpe of Elvetham ; the 3rd and 4th Lords Dorchester and Lady Dorchester, who planted a gorse covert in Butter Wood for many years a sure find ; Lord Eversley and Colonel Walpole of Heckfield ; Mr. Vere Allfrey of Ashridge Wood, whose covert never failed ; Mr. George Barker of Stanlake Park and his son, the Rev. A. G. Barker, the Rector of Sherfield-on-Loddon ; Sir William Cope of Bramshill, where the first Wednesday's meet of the season was always held ; Lady Julia Follett ; Mr. R. H. Gosling, his successor ; Sir George Littledale of Bracknell, a famous explorer who crossed the Pamirs into and across China with his wife, no mean adventure in those days ; Sir Henry St. John Mildmay of Dogmersfield, who always gave the meet for the first Friday in the season ; the Count Marella of Wentworth Park—he and his English countess always gave the meet for the first Saturday of the season ; his countess continued to ride to hounds when over 80 years of age ; the count had to abandon Spain as his revenge on local political opponents who had looted his house and insulted his wife was rather unusually drastic; Mr. W. Howard Palmer of Heathlands, whose son, Mr. Reginald H. R. Palmer, was M.F.H., the Garth Hunt, 1931–36; Sir Charles Russell of Swallowfield; Mr. John Simonds of Newlands, Honorary Treasurer for many years and President of the Hunt Club; his son, Major John H. Simonds, succeeded him as Hon. Treasurer; Mr. William Simonds of Farley Hill, whose eldest son, Mr. Gerald P. Simonds, is master of the Farley Hill Beagles and whose second son, Mr. Vivian Simonds, is now joint acting master of the Garth Hunt; Mr. E. M. Sturgess of Barkham Squares, for many years Hon. Secretary and Secretary of the Garth Hunt; Mr. Sturgess continued to hunt and ride to and from the hunts to a great age; Colonel Van de Weyer of New Lodge, Winkfield, a great supporter and generous subscriber who put up some miles of seven-foot fox-proof fencing to keep foxes out of Windsor Forest and Park.

Other good supporters were Mr. William Cave of Hartley, a very good sportsman and well mounted, always ready to help the master. Mr. William Cordery of Hall's Farm, Swallowfield, rode well to hounds for many years, an enthusiastic sportsman who regularly drove to see hounds when over 90 years old. Mr. Cordery always hunted in a green coat and scarlet waistcoat (both with Mr. Garth's private button " G " as shown on page 212), velvet cap, top boots and breeches. His painting in oils was presented to him by the Hunt and is now in the possession of Mrs. John Simonds. Mr. Frederick Bridger of the Manor Farm, Greywell, always hunted in a black frock coat, top boots and brown cords and a bowler hat, a great supporter of both the Garth and H.H. Two regular supporters in the Friday country were Mr. James Brooks of Odiham, still alive and over 90 years of age, and Mr. James Mulford of Greywell, also still alive.

Till 1885 Mr. Garth took no subscription whatever; after 1885, when his plantations ceased to pay, he took a small subscription. On his retirement in 1902 it was unanimously decided by the Hunt Club to call the hunt by his name, and it has always been known as "the Garth Hunt" since that date.

Mr. Garth had been entertained to dinner by his friends in 1855 and given a silver hunting horn. In 1871 he received a presentation portrait, by Mr. Stephen Pearce, of himself mounted on "Harlequin," his favourite horse, with Tom Sweetman.

Mr. Garth died in 1907, still a bachelor, regretted by all ; a fine type of true sportsman.

Mr. R. H. Gosling, 1902-19.

Mr. Robert Henry Gosling of the Manor House, Waltham St. Lawrence, became master and the kennels were moved from Haines Hill to Benhams St. Lawrence.   Mr. Gosling purchased Mr. Garth's hounds for £700, a very moderate sum.   He was very interested in hound breeding and continued to breed the big hounds traditional in the country.   Drafts were purchased from the Cottesmore, Craven and Cheshire, and particularly from the Puckeridge.   Other sires were used from famous kennels, including the Badminton, and no trouble was spared in keeping the pack up to a high standard.   His dog pack averaged 24in. and the bitches one inch less.   Mr. Gosling was a charming man when off his horse, but was so terrified of his hounds being injured that he was not always quite so charming in the field.   The following tale well illustrates his peculiarities. About 2 p.m. one of his most prominent supporters and a large landowner viewed a fox away from Arch Wood, Dogmersfield. He duly hallaod the fox away and, on the arrival of the master was addressed as follows : " Dunder-headed blockhead, you don't know a fox when you see one ; my hounds can find a fox without your help."   No answer was given, the master was duly saluted and the sportsman went home.   On the following Friday hounds were at Greywell and hounds could not get on to a fox in Butter Wood.   The same sportsman was with the rector of the parish in the big ride and they viewed a brace of foxes across the ride.   They remained silent and a blank day resulted, much to the master's annoyance.   Riding home, Mr. Gosling overtook the sportsman on Hook Common and he was told that a brace of foxes had been viewed and that the rector of the parish could vouch for the truth of the statement. The master asked him why he did not " halloa " and he was reminded of the preceding Friday.   The master did not reply but came in and had a drink when passing the sportsman's home. That was the last unpleasantness between them.

Mr. Gosling was not a thruster in the field and did not care to stay out late.   At this time Prince Christian, the Ranger of Windsor Forest, was a very generous and keen supporter of the Hunt and Colonel Van de Weyer from New Lodge was also very keen, and both were members of the Hunt Committee.

Mr. Gosling first engaged as huntsman Bert Thatcher, brother of the more famous Arthur Thatcher of the Cottesmore. He only stayed two seasons and was succeeded by Harry Chandler in 1905 from the Bedale and he again was succeeded by Joe Lawrence from the Old Berkshire, both of whom knew their work well, but Lawrence was again succeeded by George Tonge. Edward Taylor, however, Mr. Garth's old whipper-in, remained in his place for seven years.

Mr. Gosling had the very difficult war years to contend with and the sad necessity of having to put down many of the hounds he had taken such a keen interest in breeding no doubt nearly broke his heart. During Mr. Gosling's mastership new kennels at Bracknell were built in 1910, modelled on the FitzWilliam (Grove) kennels at Barnby Moor, near Retford, Nottinghamshire.

On Mr. Gosling's retirement the pack was bought by the Hunt Committee and remains the property of the Garth Hunt.

Major L. A. Jackson, 1919-22.

Major L. A. Jackson now undertook the mastership, the first master to be quite unconnected with the county. He hunted the hounds himself with Jack Molyneux, son of Mr. Garth's whipper-in, as kennel huntsman and 1st whipper-in. His first season was far from a propitious one owing to an outbreak of rabies. Hunting was started eventually, late in the season, four days a week instead of three. The master tried to show sport, but was very much worried by the big fields to which he was not accustomed. Good days were enjoyed on January 19th and February 20th. The first was from Home Wood, through Billingbear Park and Charity Wood, to Millers Gorse and Waltham Osiers. Hounds then ran on by Shottesbroke to the Hazes. Here they turned and ran back to Billingbear Park and out to Haines Hill and into Charity Wood again, where they marked to ground in a badger's earth. After a brace of badgers had been bolted, the fox came out and was soon accounted for. This was a hard hunt of one hour and fifty minutes. In the next good hunt Jack Molyneux carried the horn, the master being unwell. Hounds found in Cox Moor and ran first to Horsden Common in the H.H. country, a seven-mile point. This line has been taken on two or three occasions, the reverse way, by the H.H.

In 1920 Wyndham Daniels succeeded Jack Molyneux and began his long career with the Garth Hounds. He had previous experience of ten years with the Taunton Vale as 1st whipper-in and kennel huntsman, carrying the horn for two seasons. From 1914 to 1918 he was huntsman to the South Shropshire Hounds. Before 1902 he had experience of harriers and with the Radnorshire and West Hereford Foxhounds. His advent was of the greatest advantage to the country where he soon showed himself a first-rate sportsman and a very tactful and efficient hunt servant both in kennel and in the field. In the 1920–21 season Daniels hunted hounds two days a week on Monday and Friday, and the master two days, Wednesday and Saturday.

On Monday, February 27th, 1922, from a meet at the old kennels a very good hunt rewarded all who stayed out till 3.30 p.m. Finding in the Hazes the bitch pack ran to the Bigwood and round it twice to the Cut then on by Redstone Farm, Shippetts, Holyport to Fifield, where the fox was viewed two fields ahead. Still hunting on past Deadworth Green and Glewer this good fox was killed in a field the other side of Windsor Race Course about 6 p.m.

The Army Point-to-Point was run at Arborfield this year and H.R.H. the Prince of Wales (now H.R.H. the Duke of Windsor) rode, but unfortunately came to grief over the water jump.

Saunders had been 1st whipper-in and old Edward Taylor, who had served Mr. Garth for fifteen seasons and Mr. Gosling for seven, came back from retirement to act as 2nd whipper-in. In 1922 he again retired to a well-earned rest and took the present joint master, Miss Barker, out on Mondays and taught her much of hunting lore.

Motor cars now tended to stay out with hounds in increasing numbers and became a considerable menace to sport.

Major Jackson retired in 1922 and for two seasons (1922-24) was master of the Cotswold Hunt. From 1930 to 1934 he was master or joint master of the Hursley Hunt. On January 21st, 1922, a fox was killed in the hedge of " Effie's Copse " where the present joint master (1948) of the Garth was duly blooded and given the mask. Miss Effie Barber loaned the mask to H.M.S. *Garth* where it decorated the wardroom during the ship's commission.

Major Sir H. R. Cayzer, 1922-26.

Major Sir Herbert Robin Cayzer of Tylney Hall, Rotherwick, now took over the mastership with W. Daniels as huntsman.

Sir Herbert purchased back the farms which had been sold away from the property and soon the Hunt was brought back to great prosperity. Despite his many business interests as Vice-Chairman of the Clan Line Steamers and his family firm Cayzer, Irvine and Co., etc., his energy and ability soon brought good sport to the Garth. Mr. H. S. Chinnock assisted in the field as deputy-master and his courtesy and help with farmers was much appreciated. Sir Herbert having bought all Mr. M.W. Muir's horses and tackle when Mr. Muir retired from the Cotswold mastership that year, the hunt staff were very well mounted.

Mr. E. M. Sturgess retired after many years as Hon. Secretary at the end of 1921-22 season and Colonel Winwood took over these important duties. The presentation of Mr. Sturgess' portrait, by Cecil Alden, on his favourite grey, with his own covert, Kidgham, as a background, was made at Sir Herbert's opening meet at Stanlake Park. Mr. John Simonds of Newlands, the President of the Hunt Committee, made the presentation. No less than 378 horsemen were counted at the meet and upwards of one thousand people were present which well testified to the late Hon. Secretary's popularity and the general respect and affection in which he was held.

On March 25th, 1924, Daniels broke his collar bone and a very odd arrangement, probably unique in foxhunting annals, was made. The master and his deputy hunted hounds for two hours each alternately. It was lucky for the hounds that the accident occurred late in the season.

The autumn, 1924, was so wet that the opening meet had to be put off for floods, probably the only instance in Hampshire of such a very unusual event. Sport was good as always in a wet season. A very good hunt took place after the Hunt Ball at Tylney Hall on January 9th, 1925. There were nearly 200 followers, a very large field for the Friday country. Hounds found at once in the park and, after a smart gallop, the fox was marked to ground. The next fox, from Wildmoor, crossed the River Lyde, running south of Tylney Hall, past Bridgetts Farm, by Street End Copse, nearly to Sherwoods, crossing the River Blackwater near Mattingley Bridge, thence over Hazely Heath, northwards through Heckfield and into Stratfieldsaye Park. The park palings here are not big, but quite enough for blown horses and were too much for Daniels. The fox was beat and ran roads and gardens by Faircroft and finally beat hounds. A very small percentage of the field had kept with hounds and there were many dirty jackets among the survivors.

Another useful hound hunt took place from East Moor, near Waterend Gate, through Mill Wood, Hang Wood and Butter-wood. Hounds pushed their fox through this large covert and out to the south through Puddings and Sturts, Hen Wood and Priest Wood and on to Ellisfield. Thence they returned to Tunworth and Five Lanes End and finally ran up to their fox in the Fir Belt at the back of Upton Grey Lodge. Very pretty hound work was seen in the large woodlands with some nice bursts in the open. Most of this hunt was in the H.H. country.

In 1926 Sir Herbert found that his Parliamentary and business duties were too arduous for him to continue as master and resigned to the regret of the country generally. Sir Herbert was M.P. for Portsmouth (South). He had also served as a Major in the Q.O. Royal Glasgow Yeomanry and during the 1st World War had commanded the 24th Divisional Mounted Troops from 1915–17. Sir Herbert rode well to hounds and his only difficulty was to find the spare time for the many duties of a master of hounds of a pack hunting four days a week.

Lt.-Col. Lord Dorchester, O.B.E., and Mr. H. S. Chinnock, 1926-28.

Lieut.-Colonel The Lord Dorchester, o.b.e., of Greywell Hill, and Mr. Herbert S. Chinnock of Dinorbin Court, Fleet, now assumed control and had two very happy seasons of good sport, despite crowds and motors. Lord Dorchester was an old 9th Lancer who had seen much military service both in South Africa and in other parts of Africa as well as serving throughout the 1st World War. Before coming into the title he had a very interesting pack of Bassett Hounds, which give the most sport of all methods of hunting the hare ; he was well known also as an all-round sportsman and sporting writer. Mr. Chinnock, being also well known as a local squire and having acted with great tact and courtesy as deputy master to Sir Herbert Cayzer, ensured a popular mastership. Lord Dorchester was responsible for Wednesdays and Saturdays, Mr. Chinnock Mondays and Fridays.

On December 27th, 1926, a good hunt took place from Stokes Farm. The brush was presented to Captain de Buisseggon of the famous " Cadre Noir " who hunted in his smart uniform. This fine horseman was unfortunately killed in action in the 2nd World War.

For this mastership the Hunt Committee arranged to lend the masters £500 free of interest for capital expenditure. This arrangement has proved a boon to succeeding masters in times of increasing financial stringency.

Lord Dorchester had a really fine hunt on January 28th, 1927, after meeting at Bylands. The find was in a rough field by Sherfield Mill and hounds ran fast over the Reading road, up the water meadows east of the River Loddon, running the length of Hartley Wood and out by Hartley Mill and then over the Loddon. Hounds beat the field here, though touch was kept over Sherfield Park by Buckfields, Long Copse, Sherfield Hill, nearly to Carpenter's Down, by Bramley Ordnance Depot, the Bulldown Brook to Bullpits ; thence straight on to Strat-fieldsaye, over the Loddon, past Tubs Gully where the masters and huntsman nearly caught them, into the Pheasantry and out across Stratfieldsaye Park, where this good fox was viewed by the Island. He was killed at the top of the Warren on the edge of Park Pittams. The hunt was one hour twenty-five minutes at racing pace, hounds never being touched and running unattended most of the way. A howling gale blowing all the time. Lord Dorchester heads his diary entry "Take out your hounds on a werry windy day." In this Mr. Jorrock's famous advice was certainly not borne out.

This season was a good scenting season summarised as follows :—5 days nil ; 20 days moderate ; 20 days fair ; 28 days good ; 11 days very good. Eighteen brace of cubs and 30 brace of foxes were accounted for in 84 days. The next season $18\frac{1}{2}$ brace of cubs were killed and $24\frac{1}{2}$ brace of foxes in 74 days. Sixteen days were lost through frost and Foot and Mouth Disease. Sport was good and among the good days was a 14-mile hunt on February 17th, 1928, from Blackwood, after meeting at Mattingley Green, running by Cowfold, Odiham Bridles, nearly to Thorpes, by Highfield, Heckfield Heath, Cold Harbour, Switzerland, Park Pittams, to just short of the Wellington Arms. Here the fox crossed the road *via* Lower Pittams, and again by Odiham Bridles, Blackwood, Street End, Cowford, Twelve Acres to Caesars Reeves, Hartley Wood, Sedgemoor, and killed in the open by Reeves without a real check throughout. A good holding scent on a bright cold day with a rather strong S.W. wind.

Lieut.-Colonel F. G. Barker, C.B.E., 1928-31.

Lieut.-Colonel Frederick George Barker, c.b.e., of Stanlake Park, Berkshire, now took control. His grandfather, George Barker, had been on the committee which elected Mr. Garth in

1851. Colonel Barker had been a foxhunter all his life, his father was Rector of Sherfield-on-Loddon, a keen if somewhat eccentric hunting man. The old gentleman, a notable figure in a tall hat with a very large brim, always carried with him a good luncheon of pork pies and baked potatoes wrapped in a red flannel bag. Colonel Barker knew the Garth, Vine and South Berks countries well. He had been Honorary Secretary to the Vine Hunt from 1896 till 1903 when he was called up with the 3rd Royal Berkshire Regiment, and again from 1907 to 1910. On coming into the family estates he had done everything possible to promote sport with the Garth Hounds and had very frequently had to take control in the field in the master's absence. Daniels remained as huntsman and Percy Roberts came as 1st whipper-in, Charles Miles being 2nd whipper-in. His first season's tally was 37½ brace of foxes. The master started his first season with a broken collar bone which did not mend well. On 5th November in his next season after the opening meet his horse crossed his legs and came down when galloping up a lane and the master broke his leg. Lord Dorchester and Sir Gerald Mildmay of Dogmersfield Park carried on as field masters, Colonel Barker settling the meets. On December 29th the master came out again and saw a brace killed at High Standing Hill.

In 1929 the Hunt lost two of their most staunch supporters, Mr. William Simonds on January 19th and Sir Gerald Mildmay on February 27th. The pad of the last Dogmersfield fox killed was placed on Sir Gerald's coffin. This fox was found in the Arch Wood and killed in Ewshot canteen. Soon after his death this fine estate was sold up in pieces and ruined.

For the 1929–30 season Jack Bonham from Mr. Smith-Bosanquet's hounds succeeded Percy Roberts, who, however, stayed in the county with Mrs. Simonds of Farley Hill, where the Farley Hill Beagles were then kept.

On June 29th Mr. John Simonds of Newlands, President of the Garth Hunt Club, died. He had been Honorary Treasurer also for many years and was succeeded in this post by his son, Major J. H. Simonds, c.b. The death of these three veteran supporters was a loss which was greatly felt by all. It was lucky that a well-known local master was in control to keep everything going well and smoothly.

Fred G Barker
Otay Meet, Stable 1948

COLONEL F. G. BARKER, C.B.E., M.F.H. 1928-31.
The present Chairman Garth Hunt Club, in his sixty-seventh season.

The 1929–30 season opened well with a bag of $27\frac{1}{2}$ brace of cubs in 33 days and on one occasion $2\frac{1}{2}$ brace were killed, all above ground—a fine performance for Hampshire with its really wild foxes. Sixty-five litters were paid for. On Boxing Day, 1929, a huge crowd turned out at Wokingham Market Place and saw three foxes accounted for, one in the middle of Wokingham. Anyone who sees the enthusiasm of Boxing Day meets can see how strong a hold foxhunting has on the ordinary people of the country. In the season 1929-30 58 brace of foxes were accounted for in 127 days, and 28 brace were also marked to ground.

The next season produced good sport with a pack used to killing their foxes, and 58 brace of foxes were again killed in 116 days. On the 12th January, 1931, an exceptionally good hunt took place from Poley Street. The first fox, from Paddock Wood, was marked to ground in Bigwood after a fast hunt. The next fox, from Millars Gorse, provided the hard-riding section of the field with a splendid gallop over grass, starting over a big ditch brim full, a stiff post and rails into Stanlake Park, and then over Mr. Barker's " oxer." Gates were ignored by the small number with hounds as the pace was too great to open them. Hounds ran past Camerons, below the old kennels by Honeys, through Billingbear Park, to the home covert, over the Fair Mile and Broad Common. Sharp turns here enabled the main body of the field to see the final burst over Haines Hill Park to ground by South Lodge. The only followers to stay with hounds during this hunt were Daniels, the huntsman, and the 1st whipper-in, Lord Dorchester, Major and Mrs. Wallington, the master of the Staff College Draghounds, Major Tanner of the Army Remount Depot and two ladies. The point made was small, but this accommodating fox gave a hunt on grass over big fences at a great pace, unusual in Hampshire, and just saved his brush.

To the general regret Colonel Barker decided to retire at the end of his three years, though his retirement has not prevented him being always ready to step into the breach and act as master whenever required. Colonel Barker was presented with his portrait by Mr. St. John H. Lander on 1st November, 1931, at the opening meet at Haines Hill. Mr. E. M. Sturgess, the President of the Garth Hunt Club, made the presentation ; about 1,500 people were present at the ceremony and 250 horsemen.

Q

Major Sir H. R. Cayzer and Mr. R. H. R. Palmer, 1931-36.

Sir Herbert Cayzer again became a joint master, taking Wednesdays and Fridays, and Mr. Reginald Howard Reed Palmer, M.C., of Hurst Grove, Twyford, took control on Mondays and Saturdays. Good sport continued and one fine point of 17½ miles deserves placing on record. On February 15th hounds found in Winnal's Wood. They ran through Coopers and Hartley Wood to Flood Farm. Thence, crossing the river, they ran into South Berks country below Tubbs Gully, past New Plantation, leaving the Four Horseshoes on their left, past Wingrove Farm and over the Devil's Highway to Spratleys. Crossing the Mortimer road to Woodcock Lane, hounds were finally beaten at the Brickfields at Spencer Wood.

Mr. Palmer had taken a great interest in hound breeding and his joint mastership was a happy one. Mr. Palmer, however, resigned in 1936 and Sir Herbert, now Lord Rotherwick carried on his third term of mastership with Miss Effie Barker, daughter of Colonel F. G. Barker of Stanlake Park, as joint master.

Col. The Lord Rotherwick and Miss Barker, 1936-39.

Miss Effie Lucile Barker had started as a child hunting two foxhound puppies, a fox terrier and a beagle with a horn out of a cracker, and mounted on a donkey. Afterwards she did a good deal of amateur whipping-in and now she attained her ambition. She had plenty to do as Lord Rotherwick was still a very busy man and had to be much away. At the Hunt meeting before this joint mastership commenced it was decided to hunt only three days a week and to lower the guarantee to £3,500.

In 1939 Lord Rotherwick's many duties forced him to resign the mastership and shortly afterwards he again became a part-time soldier commanding the Rotherwick Battalion of the Hampshire Home Guard during the 2nd World War. On December 30th Colonel Barker presented Lord Rotherwick with his mounted portrait; unfortunately frost prevented a suitable ending to the ceremony in a good hunt.

Miss Barker and The Earl of Northesk, 1939
(May to Sept.)

The 11th Earl of Northesk of Cedar House, Sherlock Row, Twyford, Berks, joined Miss Barker till September, when he was re-employed in military service as a Major in the Intelligence Corps.

A Committee, 1939 - present date.

Acting Masters, Colonel F. G. Barker and Miss Barker, 1939-45.

During the 2nd World War the hunt was carried on by a committee with Colonel Barker and Miss Barker as acting masters, hunting at first three days a week and then two days a week. Horses and hounds were drastically cut down.

Daniels remained as huntsman and Jack Vicars from the Blackmore Vale acted as whipper-in for the first war season. Mr. R. H. R. Palmer officiated as Hon. Secretary in place of Mr. Vivian Simonds who resigned. Vicars was called up in 1940 and Miss Barker acted as 1st whipper-in and a second horseman assisted. Three days were cut to two days. The Ministry of Food took the stables as a store. This was only one of the many difficulties successfully overcome by the committee.

In 1942 the old veteran Edward Taylor came back to help as whipper-in. No stopping was done and foxes were not too plentiful, but 20 couple of hounds were kept and the country was hunted.

Acting Masters, Mr. R. H. R. Palmer and Mr. V. P. Simonds, 1945-46.

Acting Masters, Mr. V. P. Simonds and Miss Barker, 1946 - present date.

Colonel Barker retired from his labours at the end of the war and Mr. Reginald Howard Reed Palmer and Mr. Vivian P. Simonds of Hall's Farm, Farley Hill, Reading, were appointed acting-masters for one year.

Wynham Daniels now retired after his long and successful career in good times and bad. He was presented with a cheque of £1,000 at the opening meet in 1946. H. F. Cooper from the South Berks succeeded Daniels as huntsman. After the huntsman was laid up by a broken ankle bone in 1947 Daniels volunteered to whip-in to the 1st whipper-in, J. Poile, a characteristic and most sporting action on his part. In 1949 the huntsman was unlucky again to break his arm and the whipper-in again hunted hounds.

The committee of the Hunt who have kept the hounds and the country going since the 2nd World War consists of the

following gentlemen in addition to the acting masters :—
R. H. R. Palmer, Esq. (Chairman), Colonel F. G. Barker, C.B.E.,
Brigadier H. V. S. Charrington, D.S.O., M.C., C. W. Booth, Esq.,
Major G. D. Edwards, F. W. Headington, Esq., C. C. Leversuch,
Esq., The Earl of Northesk, G. S. A. Scott, Esq., Major M. H.
Simonds (Hon. Treasurer) and Brigadier E. W. Chadwick, M.C.
(Hon. Secretary).

With so efficient a committee the affairs of the Hunt have
run very smoothly. Parts of the old Monday country, once
so fashionable, have been much built over. Arborfield Camp
has also destroyed a nice piece of hunting country where so many
point-to-point races have been held in the past. Windsor
Forest is now unhuntable. The Friday country is little changed
and the new owners of the Tylney Estate assist the Hunt. Wire
is, as in all countries, a considerable and growing menace. The
lack of good earth-stopping makes the killing of foxes much
more difficult. There is, however, hope of increasingly good
sport and the general support of landowners and farmers is
encouraging. Fields are very much smaller than formerly,
now some sixty on a Monday, and twenty on a Friday. This
must assist sport and take away a great burden of responsibility
from the masters.

ODE TO THE NORTH - EASTER.
By REV. CHARLES KINGSLEY.

Through the black fir forest,
Thunder harsh and dry,
Shattering down the snowflakes
Off the curdled sky.
Hark the brave north-easter,
Breast high lies the scent,
On by holt and headland,
Over heath and bent.
Chime, ye dappled darlings,
Through the sleet and snow,
Who can override you ?
Let the horses go !

Chime, ye dappled darlings,
Down the roaring blast
You shall see a fox die
Ere an hour be past.
Go ! and rest to-morrow,
Hunting in your dreams,
While our skates are singing
O'er the frozen streams.

CHAPTER IX.

THE TEDWORTH HUNT.

MASTERS OF THE TEDWORTH HUNT.

1826–58	Mr. T. A. Smith, Tedworth House, Hants.
1858–79	Marquis of Ailesbury and Committee.
1879–82	Sir R. H. Graham, Bart., Netheravon House.
1882–85	Hon. P. S. Wyndham, Clouds, East Knoyle, Wilts.
1885–88	Mr. F. Vaughan Williams.
1888–89	Mr. C. P. Shrubb, The Oaks, Andover.
1899–1906	Mr. W. J. Yorke Scarlett, Fyfield House, Weyhill.
1906–07	Mr. J. E. A. Willis Fleming.
1907–08	Mr. Henry Connop, Ramridge and Fyfield House.
1908–11	Capt. W. V. Faber.
1911–12	Capt. Malet, Wilbury Park.
1912–14	Mr. O. C. H. Riley, Huntsman's Cottage, Tedworth.
1914–15	Mr. H. W. Boileau, Huntsman's Cottage, Tedworth.
1915–18	A Committee.
1918–19	Capt. M. J. Kingscote.
1919–20	Mr. F. C. Giddens.
1920–21	Capt. Sir Alfred Hickman.
1921–24	Mrs. F. K. Simmons, Fyfield Grange.
1924–25	Sir Leonard Powell, Manningfold.
	Major Henry Connop.
1925–27	Mr. A. K. Kemble.
1927–28	Sir Peter W. Farquhar, Bart., Middlecot, Quarley, Hants.
1928–31	Sir Peter W. Farquhar, Bart., Middlecot, Quarley, Hants.
	Lord Melchett, Melchett Court, Romsey, Hants.
1931–34	Lord Melchett, Melchett Court, Romsey, Hants.
	Major A. E. Phillips, D.S.O.
1934–35	Lord Melchett, Melchett Court, Romsey, Hants.
1935–36	Lady Wright, Durley House, Burbage, Wilts.
1936–37	Lady Wright, Durley House, Burbage, Wilts.
	Sir H. Gordon Ley, Bart., Furze Down, King's Somborne, Hants.
1937–38	Sir H. Gordon Ley, Bart., Furze Down, King's Somborne, Hants.
	Mr. J. C. Porter (acting master).
1938–39	Capt. R. H. Palmer, Fittleton Manor.

1939–42   Mr. J. C. Porter (acting master), Sunnyhill House,
           Milton.
1942–46   Disbanded.
1946–49   Mr. J. C. Porter, Sunnyhill House, Milton, Wilts.
1949–   The Earl of Hardwicke, Rockley Manor House,
           Marlborough.
           Mr. P. Dunn.

TEDWORTH SECTION.

Mr. T. A. Smith, 1826-58.

The Tedworth Hounds owe their existence to the liberality,
energy and sporting genius of the famous Thomas Assheton
Smith.   Mr. Smith set up an establishment in 1826 at Penton
Lodge, Andover, to hunt that country during his father's lifetime ; this action was not at all with that gentleman's approval
who thought his son was wasting his time in such a country,
and preferred hearing of his son's great performances in the
Midlands.   It may be of interest to give some sketch of this
great sportsman's career.

Young " Tom Smith " was born on 2nd August, 1776.
His father had settled on a considerable estate at Tedworth,
but the family came from Ashley Hall in Cheshire where his
grandfather Thomas Assheton had lived.   The family were of
ancient Saxon lineage and originated at Assheton-under-Lynne
in the neighbouring county of Lancashire.   It was his grandfather who added the name of Smith on coming into his uncle
Captain William Smith's property.   " Young Tom " was sent
to Eton at the age of seven and remained there eleven years.
His most notable achievement at Eton was a great fight with
Jack Musters, a long and desperate battle, after which the two
future masters of hounds were very good friends.   He was
fond of boating and learnt to play cricket.   His skill at this
game was shown in 1806, among many other occasions, when
playing in the first match, Gentlemen *versus* Players, at Lords ;
in this match he made top score of 48 and his side won by an
innings and 13 runs.   Going up to Christ Church, Oxford, in
1794, he became a steady supporter of John Warde's hounds
and doubtless absorbed much hunting lore from that great
sportsman.   He proved a useful batsman, a good swimmer, and
he pulled a good oar ; his academic efforts are not known.
As a child he had had sport with rabbit beagles round Sidbury

Hill, and as a boy, with his father's harriers at Tedworth, and he had already attained a reputation as a promising horseman.

In 1806, without other experience, he succeeded Lord Foley as master of the Quorn, an ambitious start, but he soon made his establishment at Quorndon Hall an example of efficiency. The sport he showed has seldom been equalled. In 1816 he took the Burton country in Lincolnshire where he continued his success. His desperate riding stood him in good stead. His principle was to be with his hounds, and so he knew exactly what had happened at a check and no obstacle would daunt him in a cast ; if he thought that was the way of the fox he would jump a gate or tough bullfinch as soon as cast in the open field. He also kept his field in good discipline, not always appreciated, but he was so genuine in his desire to show sport and so successful in doing so, that he soon attained a reputation that was known throughout England. This was shown when he was presented at the French Court and was greeted by Napoleon as " le premier chasseur d'Angleterre."

In 1824 he gave up the Burton Hounds and after hunting a couple of years in the shires he came to live at Penton Lodge in 1826 in a country described by "Nimrod" as "nothing but a bed of flints with woodlands which were the worst country in the whole world." Nothing, however, was beyond Mr. Smith's judgment, patience and knowledge of hunting. He had only retained one couple of his old hounds and so he had to buy drafts from a dozen different packs to start his first year's hunting. He showed his skill by never " lifting " hounds and so they killed their foxes. Even with his scratch pack of hounds some notable hunts occurred in 1826. One from Collingbourne Woods, when, after a turn round the wood, the fox broke by Honey Bottom by Dean Farm to Scott Poors, then across the hills, leaving Fosbury Wood on the right, he ran on for Oxenwood and Botley Clump, down into the Vale, past the plantation on Shalbourne Hill and down this precipice the master raced, hat off, and screaming to his hounds. The fox ran on in the open, pointing for Stype, and was killed after forty-three minutes without a check of any kind. A sheep dog pitched into one of the hounds at the kill and the master kicked him head over heels. The shepherd, a burly man with a fighting face, resented this. The master prepared for action saying, " Take care what you do or I will serve you the same." The shepherd, after a good look at the irascible squire, decided on immediate retreat.

In another hunt of the first year from Lower Conholt Hanger by Mescombe Wood, through Wilster Wood to Netherton Hanger, down the steep pitch through the churchyard to Faccombe Wood, leaving the village on the left, to Privet and Charldown, on to Brick Hanger and into the Vale towards East Woodhay, up to a farm nearby, there was neither check nor turn; at the farm, however, hounds threw up but would not leave its neighbourhood. The master seized a countryman, whom he thought suspicious, by the collar and swore he would horsewhip him if he did not tell him what he had done with the fox. Hounds bayed at a stable door and there was the fox in a sack inside the corn bin. He was thrown out and soon accounted for. The taking of the fox was given away by the first yokel but the squire was mollified by his excuse[1] and gave him half-a-crown.

In 1828 a field of over 300 met his hounds at Weyhill which was a great tribute to his reputation. In the same year the purchase of Sir Richard Sutton's hounds helped him to found his own pack again which soon became famous. Sir Richard also gave him a hunter, " Rob Roy," which, he said, " perhaps he might ride, but no one down there could." That this was a fact he soon showed when out with Lord Kintore's hounds in the V.W.H. country. He led the field, beating his Lordship on his best two horses, for one of which he had recently given £400.

On 29th October, 1828, Mr. Smith married, when 51, Maria Webber of Binfield Lodge, Berkshire. His wife proved an ideal helpmate and hostess when he moved to Tedworth the following year. Till his father's death in 1828, Mr. Smith seldom gave more than £50 for a horse. His perfect seat and hands enabled him to ride horses that others could not attempt. After his father's death, Mr. Smith moved to Tedworth House, where the whole countryside was changed by his lavish expenditure and energy; and also, a very important point, by winning the support of the local landowners. He rebuilt the house on a much larger and more magnificent scale. Kennels and stables and gardens were completed on the same scale. Vast forests were partially felled and grubbed and provided with convenient rides. That he was able to accomplish so much was due to the income from his Welsh estates

---

[1] The yokel's answer was, " Please, sir, I zee'd a fox come into the yard, and thinking Parson Lance's hounds were worriting the poor crittur, I cotches him up, and was a-going to take him over to Squire Smith of Penton."

around Vaenol, which his energy and ability developed very greatly. He created the private port of Dinorwic and provided it with a private railway. Mr. Smith quadrupled the area of the slate quarries there and spent over £9,000 a month in wages and materials. The income of the Welsh estates of 47,000 acres at the time of his death was £40,000 a year. They were left to a grandson of Mrs. Astley, the Squire's sister. His mechanical skill was remarkable, too, in one so greatly absorbed in horses and hounds. At Tedworth, Vaenol, and at his London home Mr. Smith arranged a train system to bring all food from the kitchen to the dining room. As a member of the Royal Yacht Club he had five sailing yachts built for him, but he withdrew his name from the club when they refused to allow steam vessels the privileges of the club. In the years 1830–51 he had eight steam yachts built by Mr. Robert Napier of Glasgow, the tonnage of these yachts varying from 100 tons to 700 tons. He always wanted hollow lines and in 1838 insisted on the *Fire King* being built to his own plans with hollow lines and flat bottom. Against all expert opinion of the time, the ship proved most successful and the others were all built to his lines. Once, when the Duke of Wellington was staying at Tedworth, the Squire gave him his ideas about gun-boats. Next morning the Duke told him he had been thinking it over and thought there was a good deal in what he had said, and advised the Squire to write to the First Lord of the Admiralty. This was done, but no reply came from that august person. Meeting the First Lord afterwards in Regent Street, Mr. Smith asked him if he had received the letter. The First Lord replied that he had, but that the Admiralty could not pay attention to all the recommendations made to them. Mr. Smith raised his hat and, turning away, said, " What His Grace the Duke of Wellington has considered worthy of attention I think your Lordship might at least have condescended to notice."

Our ships at Kronstadt lay idle and useless off shore in consequence, but some ten years later Mr. Smith's ideas for gunboats were adopted, and these craft were of great use in China.

As a landowner, Mr. Smith's farms and cottages were made comfortable and efficient ; he built churches and schools also, and a fine hotel in Wales. His generosity was always free with deserving cases and Mrs. Smith ministered to all those in want of help. One day, returning from hunting, the Squire was caught in heavy rain at Chute, and was offered cover by an old labourer in a miserable hovel. The old man also brought a sack to put over his saddle. Next day a bricklayer and carpenter arrived to restore the whole cottage at the Squire's expense.

His strict field discipline was once the subject of amusement to all. At Chute Gorse everyone was correctly placed, when the Squire saw a white smock frock in a gap just where the fox should break. He halload and waved and, that failing, used most unparliamentary language. "Do ride up and make that scoundrel come back," he said to a friend. The friend reported that the man would not attend to anything he said. "Then, by Jove, if he does not walk off I will horsewhip him," said the irate master. He rode up, with whip ready, to discover a peaceful scarecrow to frighten away the rooks. All, including the master, then gave way to their mirth.

The Squire's first season only produced 4½ brace of foxes, but he averaged 50 brace during his thirty-two years' mastership and in one year killed 70 brace. These foxes were killed above ground. The Squire would never have a terrier in the kennel. His expenditure on hounds was lavish, as, besides buying Sir Richard Sutton's pack, he also bought Sir Thomas Boughey's hounds and the Duke of Grafton's pack of 60 couple in 1842. The number of hounds in kennel and at walk was very large; when George Carter arrived with the Grafton Hounds there were upwards of 200 couples, drafted down later to 104 couple.

The Squire hunted four days a week with a dog and a bitch pack both of 26 couple and George Carter hunted twice a week with about 50 couple of old hounds and young hounds. The Squire never took hounds to the meet himself or brought them home. He galloped out on a fast hack. He had, of course, many affairs to attend to and this gave him another hour or so of extra time.

In the picture of the hunt painted by Ferneley in 1829 at Penton, most of the Squire's favourite horses and hounds and his most efficient servants appear—Dick Burton, huntsman, who was with him 22 years, Tom Day, 1st whipper-in, and David Edwards,[2] 2nd whipper-in. Mistakes were not approved of; David Edwards once halload away a hare; when the Squire brought the hounds not a hound would speak: "I do not know, sir, whether you are ashamed of yourself, but my hounds, you see, are heartily ashamed of you." With Dick Burton and

---

[2] This was "Humpy David" from the New Forest Hunt.

Tom Day as whippers-in, the establishment was as near perfection as it could be, all perfectly mounted, all fine horsemen and masters of their work.

Little of the good sport shown has been recorded, but one wonderful hunt in December 1834 is outstanding. A fox was found in the ozier beds at Amesbury, but after a fast hunt this fox was lost. The second fox, found near the same spot, crossed the River Avon at Amesbury, and ran straight for the plain, past Stonehenge, through Barwick village to Wishford. The fox crossed the River Willy and ran up the hill to Gravelly Copse, where he was killed—a 16-mile point in one hour and fifteen minutes. Hounds required no help and travelled so fast as to out-distance even the Squire, though he was first in sight of the Plain.

Mr. Smith was one of the finest horsemen of his day and a great huntsman, too. He had cut off 1,500 brushes with a knife which he afterwards lost in the West Woods, all fairly hunted to their death above ground. If he had a fault as a horseman it was that he was a somewhat jealous rider. An amusing incident occurred once in the Shires when he and Mr. J. White were rivals. Coming one day to a large bullfinch with only one possible place to jump, Mr. White stuck fast in the fence. " Ram your spurs in and pray get out of my way," said Mr. Smith. " If you're in such a damned hurry, why don't you charge me," was the answer. No sooner said than done, and Mr. White was projected through the fence somehow and Mr. Smith went on as if nothing had happened. In the New Forest on one occasion he became jealous of Lord Cardigan, but in that very difficult country he actually was beaten with hounds. Old George Carter said the Squire " did not like caddling about after a fox, but preferred to leave a ringing fox and go and find another." With three horses out and 100 couple of first-rate hounds in kennel he could do what he liked and still keep up his tally. An old farmer described the hounds running into their fox as follows :—" They goes at 'un like my wether sheep into a tie of turnips—*all first*." Old George Carter was always patiently and quietly teaching the young hounds to hunt and by the time they reached the Squire's pack they knew their business. An ideal arrangement for a man of his very large means, but not one possible for the huntsman of to-day.

Mr. Smith received at various times tokens of the esteem in which he was generally held. In 1837, on March 22nd, a dinner was given to him at the Town Hall, Andover, at which eighty-two gentlemen sat down.   The Chair was taken by the Rt. Hon. H. Pierrepoint, supported by the Squire, and the Marquis of Douro, Lords Roderick and William Paulet, Sir Edmund Antrobus, Bart., Mr. R. Etwall, M.P., Messrs. E. R. Tunno, Henry Fellowes, Colonel Hicks Beach and John Poole, the Mayor of Andover, were among the company.

In 1840 he went on a visit to his friend and successor in Lincolnshire, Sir Richard Sutton.   Whilst staying with Sir Richard, he was asked by Mr. Green of Rolleston to bring his hounds once more to the Quorn country, and this he did. On March 20th some 2,000 horsemen met the Squire's hounds at Shankton Holt, coming from a very great radius.   The whole country was studded for miles with horsemen and foot people. Sport was unfortunately impossible, but the wonderful welcome overcame the great disappointment and the Squire kept quiet throughout the day.

Another interesting hunt in later years is recorded in Bell's *Life* on January 1st, 1852.   The Tedworth had a wonderful hunt from a meet at Ham Ashley.   They found at Riever's Hill, the fox first pointing for Stype, but, turning to Ham Church and threading Ham Sprays, went up the hill at Bull's Copse.   He then went away by Combe Wood and Vernham to Fosbury Wood and Oxenwood village, and back to Ham Ashley, down the hill with the pack in full cry and was rolled over at Bagshot Wood.   The fox was found in Wiltshire, run into Hampshire and killed in Berkshire.   The Squire rode like a boy, on a horse which he had never seen before.   At the end of the day he bought the horse, a handsome chestnut, from Mr. Samuel Reeves for 175 guineas and christened him " Ham Ashley " from the covert in which this good fox was found.

The Squire became alarmingly ill in Wales in 1856, and after that date he never recovered his health and strength.   At the great annual meet at Tedworth House on the 1st November, 1857, the Squire rode slowly to see his beloved hounds, but he did not wear his hunting clothes, fearing that hounds would not hunt if he had to leave them in his scarlet. A big field had come to greet the Squire ; among them were the Marquis and Marchioness of Winchester, the Marquis of Ailesbury, Lord Charles Wellesley, Sir Edmund Antrobus, Sir John Pollen, Sir Edward Poore, the Rt. Hon. Mr. Sydney Herbert and Lady Rose Lovell, Mr. and the Hon. Mrs. Pierrepoint, Messrs. John Bushe, Tyrwhitt Walker, Charles Pressley, Thomas Best, Chaffin Grove, Thomas Fowler, Wadham Knatchbull, M. Marsh, M.P.,

W. Tugwell, Mackrel Smith, T. Lamb, W. Everett, H. Sutton, Mr. and Mrs. W. Humphrey, Mr. and Mrs. J. H. Brewer, Mr. Edmund Antrobus, M.P., Mr. Robert Antrobus, R. Hetley, Major Eustace Heathcote, Colonel Montague, Colonel Newington, Messrs. John Pitt Ewart, Walter Flowers, J. B. Starkey and many others.[3] It is noteworthy that both houses of Parliament were well represented, as well as the well-known Dorset M.F.H., Mr. Chaffin Grove. After this meet his only riding was at a walk mounted on one of his favourite horses up and down the great corridor leading to the huge conservatory he had built for his wife ; it was 965 feet in length, glazed on one side and warmed by hot water pipes. The Squire died at Vaenol in August 1858, leaving everything to his wife who did not long survive him. He has been best described as " possessed of adamantine nerves, encased in a frame of iron, he would with dauntless courage ride at anything." Mr. Delmé Radcliffe, the author of *The Noble Science*, said of Mr. Smith : " He was an instance of the very rare union of coolness and consummate skill as a huntsman, combined with the impetuosity of so desperate a rider ; and not only was he the most determined of all riders, but equally remarkable as a horseman." His old friend the Duke of Wellington, in a letter to the Squire of 12th November, 1851, calls him the " Field Marshal of Foxhunters." A fitting epitaph to a mighty hunter.

A Committee, 1858-79.

Mrs. Smith handed over the hounds on the Squire's death to a committee of management over which the Marquis of Ailesbury presided. The other members were Sir John Pollen, Sir Edmund Antrobus of Amesbury, Mr. H. Fowle and Mr. W. Knatchbull. In one of the years 1858–60 the Tedworth had a special meet in honour of the great Dorset sportsman Mr. F. J. Farquharson of Langton House, M.F.H., 1806–58, after he had retired. He was staying with Mr. Best of Red Rice and thither the hounds were brought. Finding in Chalford Oakcuts, hounds ran very well over Danebury Hill, over the paddocks to Wallop where he was headed. Turning right-handed to Nuch Wood and Kents Barrow to Monkton Oakcuts, running down Red Rice Plantations, he was killed in the covert in which

[3] The Antrobus family representatives were Sir Edmund Antrobus of Amesbury Abbey, 2nd Baronet of Antrobus, Co. Chester, J.P., D.L., died 1870, and his two sons Edmund (afterwards Sir Edmund), M.P. for East Surrey, 1841–47, and Wilton 1855–77, and Robert Crawford Antrobus, J.P., Middlesex and London.

he had been found, after 62 minutes. Squire Farquharson followed keenly and the *Devizes Gazette* adds " Well may the sportsmen of Dorset be proud of such a man."

Mr. J. H. Brewer of Garlogs was Hon. Secretary and a subscription of £1,150 was raised to meet annual expenses. A good tale is told of this Mr. Brewer who was a master in Chancery of very large proportions and usually referred to as " the Master." One day the field had lost hounds ; then someone saw a large red object on the distant horizon. " There's old Brewer going over the hill ; hounds can't be far off," he said. All cheerfully galloped off to their mark and found a very large red-painted water-butt !

A very notable supporter of the Hunt at this period and for a good many years after was the Rev. John Henry Gale, nick-named " Rude Boreas." He was Vicar of Milton Lilbourne, near Marlborough, from 1846 to 1893 ; a great character as parson, foxhunter or magistrate. If the responses in church were not to his liking his clerk was audibly told " Holloa them on, John " ! It is also said that he regularly gave out the week's meets of the foxhounds in church.

Another parson in the 1840's attacked a farmer, by name John Elmore of Penton, for not coming to church. The attack took place when out hunting and went as follows :

Parson : " Everybody is compelled by statute to go to church."

Farmer : " You don't know, sir, what religion I am."

Parson : "Are you not a Protestant ? "

Farmer : " No sir, I am not."

Parson : "Are you a Roman Catholic ? "

Farmer : " No, sir, I am not."

Parson : "Are you a Wesleyan."

" No," said the farmer.

Finally the parson said in despair, " What are you then ? "

The answer came at once : " I am an infernal Quaker, sir, and I wish your reverence good morning."

The farmer then rode off in triumph, leaving a somewhat crestfallen parson.

The purchaser of the Tedworth property, Sir John Kelk, kindly gave the Hunt the use of two kennels at Tedworth House. George Carter, then 67, was kept on as huntsman until his retirement in 1865, and Jack Fricker and Will Brice whipped-in to him. A handsome sum was subscribed to help

Carter's well-earned rest and he had also a life pension left him by the Squire. The old man took a cottage in Milton in the Pewsey Vale and he was seen for a good many years in scarlet coat and velvet cap at the covert side, when hounds were in the neighbourhood. He died at the ripe age of 91, when his cap and scarlet coat, the insignia of his former office, were buried with him.

Jack Fricker succeeded to the horn. The Squire had first noticed how well he sat a carthorse when going to water. His father was a labourer on the estate and the Squire told the boy to go to his stables and get a job there. He worked his way to the top and was huntsman for twenty-three years, being very quick and with wonderful eyesight, always with hounds, but never interfering with them until necessary. He was a splendid huntsman, ending his career with a fine hunt of an hour and forty minutes from Carson Copse and killing his fox in a pig sty at East Tytherley—a 9-mile point and a fine hunting run.

Sir Edmund Antrobus, who had been master of the old Surrey from 1836–47, was often in control in the field, as he had been during the Squire's illness. In 1865 Mr. W. Knatchbull, who had arranged the meets and the draw, ceased these labours but continued to hunt for many years. The Marquis of Ailesbury then took a more active part in the management and became field master. He was followed by Mr. F. Raikes of Netheravon and then by the Duke of Somerset. The loaned New Forest country, Speery Well to Clarendon, was given up in 1865. In 1879 the 2nd Marquis of Ailesbury died and the committee's long management came to an end.

Sir R. H. Graham, Bart., 1879-82.

After the committee's long reign, the Hunt were lucky in attracting Sir Reginald Henry Graham, 8th Baronet of Norton Conyers, a well-known sportsman who had previously been master of the Cotswold Hunt, 1871–73 and the New Forest Hunt, 1874–78. Sir Reginald took a three-year lease of Netheravon House from Sir Michael Hicks-Beach. He retained Jack Fricker as huntsman but sometimes hunted hounds himself. John Bevan and Jack Thatcher were his whippers-in.

In his first season, 1879–80, though stopped by frost on 29 days, 41 brace were killed in 94 days' hunting. On November 24th, 1879, a good straight hunt took place from Fargo, killing at Wylye, an 8½-mile point. Another fox was killed at the same time by a whipper-in and a few couple. Two brace were killed in the day. On January 5th, 1880, a fox from Round Down, near Everley, was killed in the West Woods after a 9-mile point and also there was a fast 25 minutes from Pewsey gorse, killing at Upavon.

Jack Fricker had his hounds absolutely steady from riot and also they were so full of dash and determination that they would face any gorse, however thick.

The next season, 1880–81, hunting was greatly interfered with by frost and only 34½ brace were killed, but some very good sport was shown. On November 29th, 1880, from Wilbury, where the Hon. Percy Wyndham, M.P., then lived, a very busy day indeed was enjoyed. The first fox, from the Warren, gave a fast 30 minutes and was killed near the house. At Tower Hill three or four were on foot and one was quickly killed; another was viewed away by the South Western Railway and, after running a mile parallel with the line, went away from the open downs, leaving Old Lodge on the left, to ground near Roche Court, after a 25-minute gallop. Here the master harangued the field for overriding hounds. On the way back Lord Lawrence entertained the field at Old Court which doubtless restored their morale. Yet another fox jumped up at Folly Hill and was soon run to ground. Finally, the master again tried the Warren which held and a sharp gallop of 20 minutes resulted, the fox being killed under the windows of the house where the first fox of the morning had been eaten.

Tuesday, November 30th, produced a good hunt of an hour and fifty minutes from Rushall ozier bed. The fox swam the river and ran up to Wood Bridge; he crossed the highroad, pointing straight up the Pewsey Vale, which rode very deep indeed, past Manningford, over the fields to the railway, up the line and on to Wilcot, over the Canal Bridge, by Stowell to Wraycott, on towards Oare Hill, left-handed to Coker Wood, across the downs to the Wansdyke where hounds soon ran from scent to view and rolled over an old vixen as stiff as a poker. This made an eight-mile point, the dog pack hunting beautifully, and hounds were not over-ridden by even the most inveterate thrusters. During this season the master suffered much from sciatica. His last season was a very open one and on only two days did frost and fog prevent hunting. Thirty-nine brace were killed. This season, January 1882, produced a very unusual hunt. A fox was found in West Woods and forced out to Gore Coppice back to the great woodland and out again to Granham, past the house and on to White Horse Down,

Sir Reginald Graham, Bart.,
M.F.H. 1879-82, M.F.H. New Forest Hunt 1874-78

Mr. T. A. Smith, M.F.H. 1826-58, Founder of the Tedworth Hunt.

Lord Melchett, M.F.H.   Master and Joint Master, Tedworth Hunt, 1928-35.

running at racing pace, crossing the river into the college masters' garden at Marlborough, through the passage to the college court and into the racquet court, where he was killed. The mask was given to Mr. C. M. Bull. Another fox was found in the withy bed close to the college chapel, but was soon accounted for near Preshute House. In the spring of the year the Duke of Beaufort had a day by the invitation of the master. A very large field was attracted, but the sport is not recorded. It was a very windy day and a very bad scent, so presumably these famous hounds did not do very much. The chief supporters mentioned by Sir Reginald were as follows :—Sir John Kelk of Tedworth House ; the Hon. Percy Wyndham, M.P., of Wilbury House ; Lady Charles Wellesley of Conholt Park, with her two sons, Henry and Arthur, both to be Dukes of Wellington and great sportsmen ; Sir Edward Antrobus of Amesbury Abbey ; Sir John Astley of Everley (" The Mate," a great racing man) ; Lord Algernon St. Maur (afterwards 14th Duke of Somerset), a great sportsman and first-rate whip, who died driving a team ; Sir William Humphrey of Penton House ; Messrs. Stephen Butler of Stitcombe, William Hayward Fowler of Chute Lodge and Powell of Easton ; Sir Claude de Crespigny of Durrington, a former officer of the 60th Rifles, of iron nerve, who regarded locked railway gates and sheep hurdles with equal indifference ; the Rev. W. H. Awdrey of Ludgershall, and the redoubtable Rev. J. H. Gale who has been mentioned before.

Mr. Stephen Allen of Eastover and Mr. Thomas Lamb of Andover performed the duties of Hon. Secretaries during Sir Reginald's mastership. Sir Reginald was forced by circumstances to return to his Yorkshire home. He was master of the Hurworth from 1886–88, but found the 27 miles to kennels too much for him. He then soon got together a pack of 20-inch harriers which he hunted from home and hunted the fox with the Bedale and Lord Zetland. He died in 1920 at the age of 85. A great sportsman, but unfortunately his periods of mastership were always short.

Hon. P. S. Wyndham, 1882-85.

The Hon. Percy Scawen Wyndham, third son of the 1st Baron Leconfield, of Clouds, East Knoyle, Wiltshire, succeeded to the mastership. He showed very good sport and his resignation was much regretted. Mr. Wyndham was High Sheriff of Wilts in 1896, a J.P. and D.L. for the County and M.P. for West Cumberland for 1860–85, besides being a considerable

R

landowner. His other duties proved too great for him to continue his mastership. The same hunt staff continued in service.

Mr. F. V. Williams, 1885-88.

Mr. F. Vaughan Williams now became master. The reduction of hunting days to three a week in such a large country soon caused foxes to be difficult to find in some places as the country could not be properly hunted.

Mr. C. P. Shrubb, 1888-99.

Mr. C. P. Shrubb now took over and Fricker resigned soon afterwards. Mr. Shrubb had previous experience as master of the Burton Hounds, 1882–85 ; he hunted hounds himself on two days, his huntsman Denton officiating on the other two days a week. This arrangement did not last long and the master hunted the hounds himself with, firstly, Bevan as 1st whipper-in and J. Goater 2nd whipper-in ; then, F. Perrin, his kennel huntsman, turned hounds to him on Bevan's departure after three years. Mr. Shrubb was a very good and popular master and did everything well. He again took over the New Forest country formerly loaned but given up in 1865, and also Wherwell Wood. This vast covert had not been properly hunted since the Squire's day, when George Carter took his pack of 30 or 40 couple there every Wednesday, saying he had passed enough time in Wherwell Wood to entitle him to a living in the parish and he would rather go to Hades than visit it again. However, the Squire was quite right to have this great woodland fastness thoroughly and regularly disturbed. It was a home of foxes and if well hunted the foxes would lay out in small places and give good hunts. Mr Shrubb bore most of the expense himself and everything was going well. His sudden death in 1899 was a sad blow to the Hunt. He had previously hunted the Ripley and Knap Hill Harriers which gave him useful experience as an amateur huntsman.

Mr. W. J. Yorke Scarlett, 1899 - 1906.

Mr. William James Yorke Scarlett of Gigha, Argyllshire, took a house in Andover and then bought the Fyfield House Estate, Weyhill, and showed great keenness in promoting sport. Born in 1872, young and vigorous, a keen and very knowledgeable hound man, he kept an even pack of 50 couple of hounds. He spared no money or energy to keep the country going well.

The New Forest country was given up to the Hursley and Wherwell Wood was again relinquished. Fred Perrin and J. Goater continued to serve the master and proved excellent hunt servants with a thorough knowledge of the country. When Mr. Scarlett was living at Andover he used to walk to the kennels at Tedworth House and exercise the hounds and then walk the nine miles back. This was a good example of his keenness and also his hard condition.

The War Office were commencing their operations on the Plain but Mr. Assheton Smith's farms were not yet reduced to rubble. The downs were still downs and had not yet become birdcages of wire. Some wire did exist in the Pewsey Vale but it was still rideable, though not what it had been in earlier days. A good scent usually hung on the downs and in the vale and there was not a great deal of ploughed land. Among many enjoyable hunts one of the best was from Everley Ashes after a poor morning. The hounds found in the late afternoon in winter, with frost coming on ; they ran at top pace over Sidbury Hill, by Netheravon, crossed the River Avon and killed on Ell Barrow, without a check or being handled in any way. In exactly similar conditions Mr. Scarlett also had his best hunt with the Craven, making a 14-mile point. In the hunt mentioned horses could not keep with hounds and only two or three of the whole field were up, beside the master and his hunt servants. That good sportsman Mr. Tom Baily of Thruxton was one of the fortunate survivors.

During this mastership the Duke of Beaufort twice visited the country, meeting by permission at Savernake Forest, seat of the Marquis of Ailesbury who was chairman of the hunt. On the first occasion sport was bad and foxes in short supply, but on the second occasion the Duke had a very good hunt, finishing well in the Craven country.

A staunch supporter of the Hunt was Francis R. H. S. Sutton of Penton Lodge, a grandson of the famous Sir Richard Sutton, the old friend of Mr. Assheton Smith, for whom the favourite covert of Southgrove annually provided the right type of fox. The average number of foxes killed at this time was 40 brace, hunting four days a week, and in his best season Mr. Scarlett killed 45 brace.

Mr. Yorke Scarlett took over the mastership of the Craven Hounds from 1906–08 and continued with Mr. J. A. Fairhurst as joint master until 1919.

Mr. Yorke Scarlett then founded the Tedworth Woodland Pack of Welsh-cross hounds in 1923 which he continued to hunt, with the assistance of joint masters, until 1939, when the hounds were sold. (See Tedworth Woodland, pp. 250-51.)

Mr. J. E. A. Willis Fleming, 1906-07.

A series of short masterships now followed. Mr. John Edward Arthur Willis Fleming of Stoneham Park and Chilworth, undertook the mastership for one year only. He was subsequently master or joint master of the Isle of Wight Hounds from 1920-25.

Major H. Connop, 1907-08.

Major Henry Connop of Ramridge and Fyfield, succeeded for one year also. This gentleman was subsequently also master of the Wilton Hounds for one season, 1926-27. For a short time he lived at Ramridge House and then at Fyfield House for a period. Perrin acted as huntsman for Mr. Connop and for the two succeeding masters.

Lieut.-Colonel W. V. Faber, M.P., 1908-11.

Captain Walter Vavasour Faber was Member of Parliament for Andover from 1906-1918. Born in 1852, an ex-Captain, R.H.A., and afterwards Lieut.-Colonel Commanding Royal Wiltshire Imperial Yeomanry, he was fond of a hunt, of powerful physique and cheerful character. He was afterwards for one year only, 1918-19, master of the famous Pytchley.

Captain Malet, 1911-12.

Captain Malet of Wilbury Park reduced hunting to three days a week, always an unfortunate happening as much country does not get hunted.

Mr. O. C. H. Riley, 1912-14.

Mr. O. C. H. Riley lived in the huntsman's cottage at Tedworth House. A good sportsman who knew his work, he hunted hounds himself four days a week. Fifty couple of hounds were kept in kennel. Tom Astley came to the Hunt at this time and was of great value during the difficultwar years.

Mr. H. W. Boileau, 1914-15.

Mr. H. W. Boileau came for one season only, having previously been master of the South Berks Hounds, 1910-14.

A Committee, 1915-18.

A Committee took charge during the war years. Tom Astley hunted hounds and Mr. C. C. G. Hilton Green whipped-in to him. Major C. C. G. Hilton Green is now joint master and huntsman to the old Berkshire. Captain W. H. Alexander of Upavon, a sportsman of 6ft. 4in. nicknamed " Tiny," also whipped-in for Tom Astley. In addition, he assisted the late Mr. Arthur Hussey with his harriers which afterwards were taken over by the Royal Artillery. Full of good stories and well known to all racing and hunting folk over a large area. When too heavy to ride he founded the Pewsey Vale Beagles, a beautiful little pack of 14½-inch hounds, which he afterwards gave to Lord Melchett to amuse his boys and train them up in the way they should go.

Captain M. J. Kingscote, 1918-19.

Captain Maurice John Kingscote whose father lived at Latton, Wilts, hunted the pack for one season. He had served as a Captain in the Berkshire Yeomanry in the 1st World War. Subsequently he has become well known as an amateur huntsman. He has been master of the V.W.H., Cricklade, 1931–36, South Atherstone 1936–37, joint master of the Meynell 1937 to date, and from 1948 huntsman as well as joint master.

Short masterships continued after the 1st World War, giving no opportunity for any master to greatly influence either the country or the hounds.

Mr. F. C. Giddens, 1919-20.

Captain Sir A. E. Hickman, 1920-21.

Captain Sir Alfred Edward Hickman had served with the 4th/7th Dragoon Guards and afterwards as a Major in the Shropshire Yeomanry. Born in 1885, he served in the 1st World War and was wounded. He succeeded his grandfather in 1910.

Mrs. F. K. Simmons, 1921-24.

Mrs. F. K. Simmons of Fyfield Grange was the daughter of J. A. Fairhurst, Esq., of Arlington Manor, Newbury, joint master of the Craven Hunt 1908–19 and master 1919–21. She married Major-General Frank K. Simmons, C.B.E., M.V.O., M.C., in 1922.

Sir R. L. Powell and Major H. Connop, 1924-25.

Sir Robert Leonard Powell of Flowers Hill, Pangbourne, was a very well-known whip and a member of the Coaching Club. His neat team of roans often won in the show ring. Major Connop repeated his former single year of joint mastership. Sir Leonard lived at Manningford in the Pewsey Vale during his joint mastership.

Mr. A. K. E. Kemble, 1925-27.

Mr. Kenneth Kemble hunted hounds himself and proved himself an efficient huntsman. Percy Holland was his kennel huntsman.

Sir Peter W. Farquhar, Bart., 1927-28.

Sir Peter Walter Farquhar of Middlecot, Quarley, Hants, 6th Baronet, a Lieutenant in the Royal Scots Greys, 1926, and the 16th/5th Lancers, 1927–29, now hunted the country, carrying the horn himself with great success. He was assisted by some first-class amateur whippers-in. Mr. R. E. Field Marsham, M.F.H. and joint M.F.H. the Bicester 1936–42, and the brothers Fanshawe, R. M. and R.G., the former joint master of the South Oxfordshire 1938–46. Sir Peter has proved himself an authority on hound breeding and a fine amateur huntsman since leaving the Tedworth country, he has been M.F.H. the Meyvell 1931–34 and the Whaddon Chase 1934–38. He also proved his capacity as a soldier in the 2nd World War by good service in France, the Desert and Italy as Major, 9th Lancers, and Lieut.-Colonel Commanding 3rd Hussars. Since 1947 Lieut.-Colonel Sir Peter Farquhar has been joint master and huntsman of the Portman Hounds. Fred Funnel was his kennel huntsman.

Sir Peter W. Farquhar and Lord Melchett, 1928-31.

The 2nd Lord Melchett of Woodfalls, Melchett Court, Romsey, a very busy man with many large business and political interests, managed to find time to help the Hunt from 1928 to 1935 with the aid of joint masters. This was the longest period of mastership for some years. Unfortunately Lord Melchett found it necessary to sell the Melchett Court estate and after he moved to Bedfordshire became joint master of the Oakley Foxhounds from 1935–38.

Lord Melchett and Major A. E. Phillips, D.S.O., 1931-34.

Major Arthur Edward Phillips, D.S.O., of Elone House, Winterbourne, Daventry, Wilts, after a period of joint mastership with that fine sportsman Mr. Guy Hargreaves in the South

Berks country from 1928–31 now came to assist Lord Melchett. From 1931 to 1934 that distinguished soldier and sportsman Captain (now Brigadier) M. W. Selby Lowndes, D.S.O., acted as amateur huntsman. He had already had much experience of hunting hounds (see pages 91-93). Sport was consistently good and one hunt on March 9th, 1933, from Wooton Rivers, covering a great deal of the Marlborough Down country, gave an eight-mile point to ground above Allington. This hunt was one hour and forty minutes. Captain W. Howard Alexander, who has been mentioned before, had by this time increased in weight to nearly 20 stone. He was still heart and soul with all forms of hunting. The amateur huntsman and his amateur whipper-in went to call on him for supper at 7 p.m. : they talked fox hunting till 3 a.m. On another occasion this redoubtable giant returned from the Farmers' Ball at Marlborough at 6 a.m. The day after the ball had been very successful and Captain Selby Lowndes called in at Upavon to tell Captain Alexander all about the hunt which he much liked. He was still talking fox hunting with a friend who was staying with him, both still in their evening clothes of the night before, so presumably they had not stopped talking since breakfast time.

Another soldier whipper-in, a heavy dragoon of considerable weight, was a great man to go. A fair lady asked him if he was not frightened of falling at some of the obstacles which he took on. His reply was final : " My horses never fall. I think they are frightened I might roll on them."

During this joint mastership Fred Napper came from Lord Leconfield as kennel huntsman.

Major Phillips died in 1948.

Lord Melchett, 1934-35.

Mr. J. C. Porter of Sunnyhill House, Hon. Secretary since 1924, acted as deputy master for both Lord Melchett and Lady Wright.

Lord Melchett died in 1949, a great loss to all who knew him.

Lady Wright, 1935-36.

Lady Wright, wife of Sir Robert A. Wright, P.C. (Lord Wright) of Durley House, Burbage, Marlborough, now assumed control. Lady Wright was well known in every show ring in the country as a most successful show jumping rider with plenty of courage.

Lady Wright and Sir H. G. Ley, Bart., 1936-37.

Sir Henry Gordon Ley, 2nd Bart., born 1874, master of the Hursley Hounds 1932–36, joined Lady Wright, bringing with him Will James as huntsman. His brother, Charles James, was with the H.H. for some of the 2nd World War years and is now with the Tiverton.

Sir Gordon Ley, Bart., 1937-38.

Sir Gordon Ley continued for another season alone, Mr. J. C. Porter assisting.

Mr. R. H. Palmer, 1938-39.

Mr. Rodney H. Palmer (now Lieut.-Colonel R. H. Palmer, M.C., M.F.H., South Berks, 1947) took over the mastership until proceeding overseas with his regiment. He intended to hunt the country four days a week and wished to hunt Collingbourne Wood and Savernake Forest in conjunction with Mr. Yorke Scarlett of the Tedworth Woodland.

A Committee, 1939-42.
(Mr. J. C. Porter, Acting Master.)

Mr. Porter again acted as master during the commencement of the 2nd World War. After 1942, it became impossible to hunt the country as it became a military area almost entirely. Hounds were dispersed, most of them being given to the Wylye Valley Hunt and four couple were lent to the Craven, Will James going with them. The R.A. Harriers, Bulford, now R.A. Foxhounds, were allowed to hunt on and around Salisbury Plain.

Mr. J. C. Porter, 1946-49.

Mr. John C. Porter of Sunnyhill House, Milton, Marlborough, started again with practically a new pack of hounds. About 25 couple were in kennel and they hunted three days a week. Will James returned with the small nucleus of hounds from the Craven, then reduced to one and a half couple. Many difficulties have been overcome, some have to be endured. A new pack cannot be made in a year or two, but the young entry improves each year. The Forestry Commission create wire enclosures in Savernake Forest and Collingbourne Wood, and the military requirements do not improve foxhunting, but it is hoped that the new masters, the Earl of

Mr. J. C. Porter, M.F.H. 1946-49, Acting Master 1937-38 and 1939-42, on " Dawn "
at meet at Stowell Cross-roads 1948.

Tedworth Woodland Hunt.
E. Hope and Mr. Yorke Scarlett.

THE TEDWORTH WOODLAND HUNT.

From left to right.—Eleanor Lady Yarrow, M.F.H., Lord Wright, Lady Wright, M.F.H., Mr. W. J. Yorke Scarlett, M.F.H., founder of the Hunt, W. Swan, and E. Hope.

Hardwicke of Rockley Manor, Marlborough, and Mr. Philip Dunn, may stay long enough to get the Tedworth back to something like its original glories.

Some of the chief fox preservers, without whom no hunt can exist, have been during this period : firstly, the Marquis of Ailesbury ; the late Mr. Arthur Godding's covert Ram Alley never failed ; the late Mr. James Haines of East Wich and his successor Mr. Bob Haynes of the same farm ; Lady Ernest St. Maur of Wilcot Manor who always had a fox in Wilcot withy bed and hunted up to the age of 75 ; Mr. W. J. Yorke Scarlett always had numerous foxes in Collingbourne Wood ; the late Mr. George Young of Huish also kept a good supply and Mr. J. C. Porter always had several litters in Glass Wood which he rented for fourteen seasons, and his gorse by the new kennels also can be relied on for a litter. A grand sportsman was Mr. Bob House of Pewsey, nicknamed " Boadicea " because when too crippled with arthritis to ride, he followed in his two-wheeled milk float and never missed a day as long as he could get into his " chariot."

Up to the 2nd World War, about 25 brace of foxes were accounted for. During and after the war this number greatly decreased, as happened in many other hunts, who are now getting going again and gradually reaching their pre-war standard.

During the 20th century the country has changed greatly for the worse owing to the enormous amount of wire that has sprung up on the rolling downs.

The Hunt has had, however, some most useful and influential chairmen—Sir Edmund Antrobus, Mr. William Fowle of Chute Lodge, the Marquis of Ailesbury, Lord Cardigan, 1946, and now Mr. R. B. Butler of King's Hall, Milton.

After Mr. W. V. Faber gave up the duties of Hon. Secretary came Mr. Lamb of Andover, son of Mr. Lamb of Andover who held the post before for twenty-five years. Admiral Marx then took over the South side of the country and Mr. McNiven of Maningford took over the North side till 1929. Admiral Marx was a very keen sportsman and a fine sailor. On being told in 1914 there was no job for him in his rank, he said surely they could find a job for him as a Lieutenant. He was appointed to a mine sweeper and was promoted to be Commander to his great joy, just fifty years after he had reached that rank before. General H. R. Leader followed the Admiral till his death in a sailing accident in 1926. The sides were then amalgamated and Mr. J. C. Porter who already was looking after the North side, undertook the duties for the whole country until 1946, when Mr. G. A. Young of West Chisenbury was appointed. Mr. Young had managed the kennels and earth stopping during the 1st World War and had paid the poultry claims until 1924, when Mr. Porter undertook this important but thankless task.

The Earl of Hardwicke and Mr. P. Dunn, 1949-

The 9th Earl of Hardwicke, an old officer of the Life Guards, who served with the 1st Airborne Division in the 2nd World War, of Rockley Manor, Marlborough, and Mr. Philip Dunn of Stowell Park, Marlborough, have undertaken the mastership, with George Goodwin from the Woodland Pytchley, as huntsman; Mr. Roy Beddington of Esseborne Manor, Hurstbourne Tarrant, is now Hon. Secretary. Ben Butler and an amateur, Mr. J. Kunkler, act as whippers-in.

The pack has been brought up to about 30 couple and two days and a bye day are now hunted.

THE TEDWORTH WOODLAND.

In the season 1923-24 Mr. William James Yorke Scarlett of Fyfield House, Andover, provided the Tedworth Woodland Pack of 30 couple of Welch cross foxhounds to hunt, by permission of the Tedworth and Vine Hunts, the great woodlands in Hampshire and Wiltshire, including Savernake Forest, Collingbourne Wood, Doles Wood and Wherwell Wood. Mr. Scarlett knew the country well as master of the Tedworth 1899 to 1906, and he had the added experience of being master or joint master of the Craven Hounds from 1906 to 1919. By sound and knowledgeable breeding, he soon had a first-rate pack. Mr. Scarlett carried the horn himself and showed very good sport. E. Hope was his 1st whipper-in and kennel huntsman and W. Swan acted as 2nd whipper-in.

In 1924 Eleanor Lady Yarrow of Green Meadows, Clatford, joined Mr. Scarlett as joint master. She was the second wife and widow of Sir Alfred F. Yarrow, Bart., F.R.S., M.I.C.E.—a keen and very helpful partner.

In 1933 Captain R. P. L. Vigors, D.S.O., and Mrs. Vigors of East Kennett Manor, also became joint masters. No subscription was taken but followers were expected to subscribe to either the Tedworth or the Vine Hunts.

In 1937 Lady Wright of Durley House, near Marlborough, who had been master and joint master of the Tedworth Hunt, 1935–37, joined the joint masters, making five in all.

No great points were made in the woodland hunting and hounds were often disappointed of their prey by fresh foxes jumping up to save a beaten fox or by his reaching a friendly earth. Despite all difficulties Mr. Scarlett accounted for an average tally of twelve or thirteen brace during the fifteen years of the pack's existence.

In 1938 the Tedworth Hunt Committee wished to resume hunting their big woodlands in conjunction with the Woodland Pack. The Woodland masters decided not to continue hunting and the pack was dispersed. This was most unfortunate as both the Tedworth and the Vine Hunts had soon to give up hunting and a very large stretch of country remained unhunted until 1949.

Hounds were kennelled at Appleshaw and were hunted twice a week. Favourite meets were Biddesden Gate, Crawlboys Farm, Fox Inn, Tangley, Durley Gate, Leigh Hill, Postern Gate and Eight Walks.

CHAPTER X.

THE HURSLEY HUNT.

MASTERS OF THE HURSLEY HUNT.

1837–39	Rev. Sir J. B. Mill, Mottisfont Abbey.
1840–43	Mr. J. White, Ampfield, Romsey.
1843–50	Mr. R. D. Cockburn, The Kennels.
1850–52	Mr. G. A. E. Wall, Worthy Park, Winchester.
1852–57	Mr. S. Lowe, Lainston House, Winchester.
1857–62	Mr. J. Tregonwell, Lainston House, Winchester, and Cranbourne Lodge, Dorset.
1862–69	Mr. W. C. Standish, South Stoneham House, Southampton.
1869–88	Colonel S. J. E. Nicoll, Westbourne.
1888–92	Mr. A. Deane, Winchester.
1892–96	Sir C. E. Frederick, Bart., Shawford House. Mr. J. W. Baxendale, Hursley Park, Winchester.
1896–1902	Mr. J. W. Baxendale, Hursley Park, Winchester.
1902–03	Mr. W. Philpotts Williams.
1903–06	Mr. F. C. Swindell.
1906–08	Mr. W. V. Long.
1908–16	Sir G. A. Cooper, Bart., Hursley Park, Winchester.
1916–17	Mr. H. Johnson, Marsh Court, Stockbridge. Lieut.-Col. G. Philippi M.C., Crawley Court, Winchester.
1917–22	Mr. H. Johnson, Marsh Court, Stockbridge.
1922–24	Captain G. J. R. Cooper, Merdon Manor, Hursley.
1924–26	Major A. J. Wilkie, Wooley Green, Romsey.
1926–27	A Committee.
1927–30	Mr. H. Johnson, Marsh Court. Lieut.-Col. E. R. Kewley, D.S.O., M.C., Little Dean House, Stockbridge.
1930–31	Major L. A. Jackson, The Kennels, Braishfield.
1931–32	Major L. A. Jackson, The Kennels, Braishfield. Mr. E. S. Cattley, Sparsholt, Winchester.
1932–34	Major L. A. Jackson, The Kennels, Braishfield. Sir H. Gordon Ley, Bart., Furze Down, King's Somborne.
1834–36	Sir H. Gordon Ley, Bart., Furze Down.

1936–40   Mr. G. Singer, Norman Court.
1940–47   A Committee.
1947–49   Captain F. S. Faber, Ampfield House.
1949–50   Captain F. S. Faber, Ampfield House.
           Mr. J. Craig-Harvey, Lainston House.
1950   Captain F. S. Faber, Ampfield House.

Rev. Sir J. B. Mill, 1836-39.

The Reverend Sir John Barker Mill of Mottisfont Abbey was elected a member of the H.H. Club in 1836, and applied to the Club for permission to hunt the country west of the River Itchen. Permission was granted, but Norwood, Crab Wood, Worthy Groves, the Race Course and the Crawley Belts as far as Chilbolton were reserved exclusively by the H.H. and they also reserved the right of resuming the Hursley country at any future period. Sir John then bought the Sandbeck Hounds (afterwards the Grove) from North Nottinghamshire and engaged Sawyer as his huntsman who had served Mr. Villebois from 1814 till his death in 1837.

One authority describes the country as " a heart breaking one for a huntsman ; for a fox is no sooner out of one of these enormous woods than, after going a field or two, he is into another, and unless there is an extraordinary scent to drive him out, finishes the day there. . . . . It is divided into the upper and the lower country ; in the former a child may almost go where he likes on a donkey, and hounds are always overridden ; in the latter only a wild duck or moorhen can go straight over it, so hounds have it pretty much to themselves, and the field with few exceptions, ride about the roads." This authority was obviously no lover of hound work, and probably knew little of it. Before barbed wire, hounds could be seen well in much of the upper country and stout hearts got across the lower. When master of the H.H. Mr. Villebois had had a kennel at Hursley and his advent was eagerly awaited by many good sportsmen who lived there.

An amusing anecdote is told of a sturdy yeoman called Forder who lived at Mere Court Farm, Sparsholt, who himself kept a few couple of harriers. His wife, a woman of pronounced character, was no friend to fox hunting. One day Mr. Villebois was meeting at Crabwood. Mr. Forder said he would draw some hay for the sheep with a wagon and three horses, and took a strong lad to help him. His hunter, " Diamond," was the third horse and his saddle and bridle reposed safely in the bed of the wagon. When out of sight of the house Mr. Forder soon had the old horse stripped, saddled and bridled and, twisting his smock, tucked it into his breeches and trotted off to the hunt. He told Mr. Villebois, with whom he was a favourite, how he " had done his missus." A fox was found and they galloped on well through Bushes and Vauxhall and over the hill near the farmer's house, old " Diamond " well to the fore. A halloa brought Mrs. Forder out with her maid to see the fun. " Lor', Mary, who's that a-riding like a wild man in a round frock and without a hat ? " said the lady. " Don't 'e know, missus ? Why, that's our master on old ' Diamond.' " " Master, you fool, why he's gone to draw the hay, I see'd un start myself." A closer view, however, revealed her spouse for certain and Mr. Forder's good gallop had to be paid for on return. Old Diamond's son won the H.H. Cup later on, ridden by his nephew, Gilbert Biggs. The cup had to be filled so many times that it is said Farmer Forder took a week to return home. What his wife then said is not recorded.

Mr. Edward Godwin of Slackstead, a name till quite recently to the fore in Hampshire sport, was another favourite of Mr. Villebois in the Hursley country. He hunted a famous chestnut mare for twenty-four seasons.

The Mill family[1] had a tradition of hunting which they carried on from the Sandys family from whom they obtained Mottisfont by marriage. Certainly three Mills baronets used to hunt in the New Forest and their huntsmen were duly rewarded by the churchwardens for the fox masks brought to them as was the huntsman to Lord Sandys. The Mill baronetcy failed for the lack of a male heir on the death in 1835 of Sir Charles. However, his sister Mary had married John Barker of Wareham, Dorset, for her second husband, and their son the Reverend Sir John Barker Mill was created a Baronet in 1836. He was soon difficult to recognise as a clergyman ; the loudness of his check trousers and his cherry-coloured ties were quite renowned.

In addition to the country loaned by the H.H., Sir John hunted the Speery Well country, which Mr. T. A. Smith and Lord Radnor hunted afterwards.

[1] The 2nd Sir John Mill of Newton Berry married Margaret daughter of Colonel Henry 4th Lord Sandys of the Vyne. He died as the result of wounds received at Cheriton fight. His son William, 5th Lord Sandys, sold the Vyne to Mr. Chaloner Chute *c.* 1649. He retired to Mottisfont Abbey. Both his brothers died without heirs leaving Margaret heiress. Her son, the 3rd Sir John Mill, 1st of Mottisfont, kept hounds and was High Sheriff 1685. His two sons, Sir John and Sir Richard, High Sheriff 1722, both kept hounds. Sir Richard's son, another Sir Richard, was M.P. for Southampton and represented the county.

In 1838 a good run has been recorded from Parnholt, by West Wood, Westley, Philip's Heath, over the White Horse Downs to Barton Stacey Down ; thence down to Bullington water meadows which were very deep and boggy. Hounds crossed the river ,which is deep here, and with a big fence on the far side, and ran on to Freefolk Wood and to ground at Laverstoke. This hunt is about a 15-mile point and only four followers rode the hunt with hounds—Mr. William Sadler on a thoroughbred, Mr. Hopkins, Mr. R. Gessett and Mr. Walton.

On the 14th March of the same year Mr. Sam Day, the celebrated son of Mr. John Day of Danebury, sustained a very bad fall hunting with Sir John's hounds. The horse crushed his chest and he was taken to Mr. William Sadler's house near Stockbridge, his brother-in-law, where he died. Till then he was the youngest jockey to win the St. Leger. A very popular and skilful jockey, well liked and respected by all.

Sir John finished the 1839 season with a very good day from Rookley, but gave up the hounds on the plea of the wilful destruction of foxes in parts of the country. It is possible that his great predilection for racing had also something to do with his resignation. He always had some horses in training at Danebury, one of which, " Cymba," won the Oaks in 1848, though entered in the name of Mr. Hill. Only one personal story has survived about him; when a rather bumptious squarson was telling him how he had entertained a well-known trainer and his brother and given them some champagne as a treat. Sir John said, " Bless your soul, they have drunk more champagne out of tumblers than ever you saw in your life." On his retirement he was entertained to dinner at Hursley and presented with a gold snuff box. Mr. Thomas Chamberlayne of Cranbury Park, Mr. Waddilove, General Yates, Colonel Iremonger, Messrs. Waddington, J. H. Campbell, Charles Deane, W. Bulpett, both the latter well-known bankers and sportsmen of Winchester, J. Theobald and others were among those present at the dinner.

Mr. J. White, 1840-43.

1840 is the date of the birth of the Hursley Subscription Hounds with Mr. Joseph White of Ampfield as master. The H.H. now gave up for three years the country west of the River Itchen bounded by the Winchester—Andover turnpike road through Wherwell. George Sharp was his first huntsman, succeeded by Jack Bradley who had previously hunted Sir John

Halket's staghounds at Fareham. Drafts were obtained from the Duke of Beaufort, Mr. T. Assheton Smith, Mr. Codrington and Colonel Wyndham. Hounds were kennelled at Ampfield.

Mr. R. D. Cockburn, 1843-50.

On Mr. White's resignation Mr. Robert Drayton Cockburn, son of the Dean of York and nephew of Sir Robert Peel, Bart., succeeded to the mastership. He was a very good amateur huntsman, a good judge of hounds and knew how to manage his kennels. He also was a most popular master and showed good sport. He obtained from the H.H. permission to hunt the country for a further term of seven years on the same conditions as Mr. White. Mr. Cockburn attained the celebrity of a nickname, "Mahogany Bob," from his habit of wearing mahogany tops to his boots when fashion favoured white or pale pink.

The combined meet of the H.H., Hambledon and Hursley Hounds in 1846 and the combined hunt ball has been mentioned elsewhere (p. 69.)

In the same year a dinner was given to Mr. Cockburn at the King's Head, Hursley, by his friends in the country. Mr. John Fleming of Stoneham Park took the chair, being assisted by Mr. Walton of Merdon as vice-chairman. Both landlords and farmers showed their appreciation of the master and the master said he had never had a more successful season. The chairman, whose health was also drunk, said his coverts should swarm with foxes and that he would rather have his game destroyed by them than give encouragement to poachers.

Next year on January 15th, 1847, a good hunt is recorded from Chilworth Lodge over the Baddesley country. The hunt was a severe one of two hours and twenty minutes and unfortunately the fox was completely eaten except for the mask before any of the field arrived. Messrs. Gearing, Green, White junior and Burt, beside the master and his whipper-in Dick Teed, had all gone well. Up to that date the pack had hunted nineteen days and killed fourteen foxes, running five to ground. This record, a very good one for difficult country, was in the proper hunting season and did not include cub hunting.

On February 14th, 1848, Mr. Cockburn again had a fine hunt of one hour and forty-five minites from Rookley Pond. The covert belonged to Mr. W. Allee and during the season eleven foxes were found there and nine of them were killed, reflecting equal credit on covert owner and huntsman.

Rev. Sir John Barker Mill, M.F.H. 1837-39, and his hounds.
The first master of foxhounds in the separated Hursley country.

Colonel S J. E. Nicoll, M.F.H. 1869-88.

Mr. Cockburn showed what could be done in a difficult country by knowledge, activity and great keenness. His brother George assisted him and they lived together in a cottage near the kennels. He could not afford big prices for his horses, but the two brothers and Dick Teed managed to keep near hounds. A sort of parody of the tale told of Lord Craven (p. 30) is told of Mr. Cockburn. It shows, at any rate, that his reputation for killing foxes was considerable. A fox saw a woodman at work and stopped to have a chat with him. Suddenly hounds were heard at a distance. " Who is out to-day ? " asked Reynard. " Mahogany Bob," was the answer. " Then I must be off at once ; had it been —— I would have stayed and chatted an hour with you." Besides his outstanding qualities as a huntsman, he added the accomplishments of painting, poetry and music. He painted a picture of himself, his brother and Dick Teed with the hounds at Farley Mount. It is not known what has happened to this picture. He composed and sang with great effect his own hunting songs, but these have not been recorded.

Among many good hunts one is recorded from Toothill brick kilns to Stoneham where hounds killed after running some twenty miles without a check. In this hunt Mr. J. P. Fitt jumped a fence into a bog and was rolled on. When he emerged he was minus a boot. The master said to him, " Thank you, you have just saved me that."

Winchester was full of horses in his day, often brought by their owners from a considerable distance. After being out with the H.H. one day Mr. Cockburn met a very young officer in Winchester and, chatting with him, asked him if he intended to hunt the next day. He replied : " I think I shall go and have a look at Mahogany Bob," having no idea to whom he spoke. " Then I hope I shall show you good sport, sir," said the master, raising his cap.

During Mr. Cockburn's mastership two incidents happened of interest, both involuntary and both accomplished by Mr. Barton Wallop's[2] horses. On 2nd December, 1843, Mr. Wallop's groom was exercising two of his hunters. A dog jumped out of a fence and the horses bolted. After about a mile and a half they faced St. Cross turnpike gate and both

---

[2] The gentleman would appear to be William Barton Powlett Wallop William-Powlett, Captain, 60th Rifles, whose great-grandchildren Olivia Parry and Helen Vernon Wallop used to go very well with the H.H. in the 1930's as children, finding their way unaccompanied long distances from their home and taking excellent care of their ponies.

S

jumped it together successfully without the slightest damage.
The gate was 6 feet high. On March 15th, 1847, Mr. Barton
Wallop jumped a good fence 5 feet high, on the other side of
which was a chalk pit 10 feet deep. The horse landed on its
legs and no accident occurred. Others following were duly
warned, among them Prince Edward of Saxe Weimar and a
Grenadier officer. Lord Palmerston of Broadlands, the Prime
Minister, sometimes came out but was keener on racing than
hunting. One of his best horses was " Iliona " who won the
Cesarewitch in 1841. He once stayed with the Emperor
Napoleon III at Compiegne and joined the hunt in his Hampshire
hunting clothes. The other followers wore Louis XV coat and
waistcoat, cocked hat and long napoleon boots. The Emperor
urged him to put on a greatcoat as it was raining. " Oh no,
your Majesty," was the reply, " You know nothing ever gets
through our red coats." Mr. Thomas Chamberlayne of
Cranbury was a great supporter and was always well mounted.
Among other prominent supporters were Mr. W. T. Graeme,
Colonel William Gauntlett, Mr. J. White, the ex-master, and
his son Ben who went well, Mr. George Wall of Worthy Park,
the next master, Mr. Lowndes, Mr. Charles Deane, Major
Charles Lowth, Mr. John Tregonwell who afterwards was
master, the Hon. Arthur Arundell of Houghton Lodge, Mr.
William Colyer, and Mr. Edward Hopkins, Messrs. Edward,
George and Ben Bailey of Worthy and Stoke, a great family of
sportsmen, Mr. Allee of Rookley with his two sons William and
Charles, all first-rate sportsmen, Mr. William Pain of New Barn,
a hard man to hounds and with a name well known in Hampshire
sport, Messrs. Thomas and Henry Wheble of Marsh Court,
Mr. Nevill of Chilland, Mr. Benjamin Nevill of Slackstead and
his sons, and also Mr. Tom Nevill who was also a keen stag
hunter, and many others. Few ladies hunted in those days,
but the Misses Hill, daughters of Admiral Hill of Braishfield,
always stayed out till hounds went home and always walked
puppies. Parson John Lukin from the New Forest was well
to the fore with the Hursley, too. On one occasion when a
nasty blind ditch had engulfed a very smart gentleman the
parson shouted " Lie still, sir ; Lie still and let the old parson
ride over you," which he promptly did. Another well-known
supporter and excellent horseman was the Rev. G. B. Lee,
afterwards Warden of Winchester College (1861–1903). He
always rode thoroughbred horses and rode them well. His
daughter, Miss Lee, remained a keen supporter until her death
in 1947, though she had not been able to ride to hounds for

some ten years. In the author's days at Winchester College the dignified sight of the Warden in high hat and strapped overalls and Wellington boots issuing from Outer Gate was always a cheerful sight. The Warden was rightly proud of his ancestor Colonel John Bolles, son of Sir John Bolles of Louth Hall, Lincolnshire, who died fighting gallantly for his king on December 12th, 1643, in Alton Church. The brasses to his memory in Alton Church and Winchester Cathedral though doing him due honour are remarkable for inaccuracy in several respects. On one occasion he met the second master newly appointed (Mr. Montague Rendall)[3] in a cap and riding a penny-farthing bicycle. The Warden did not approve.

Mr. Cockburn's death in 1850 at his father's rectory at Kelston, near Bath, was a great loss to the country. He was greatly liked by all who knew him.

Mr. G. A. E. Wall, 1850-52.

Mr. George Alfred Ellis Wall of Worthy Park now sold his harriers to Mr. Robert Pearse of South Warnborough and bought Mr. Cockburn's hounds for £300. He hunted hounds himself with Henry Nason and William Fisher whipping-in. Everything was done well and he had a fine stud of weight-carrying horses. The H.H. gave him permission to draw Burntwood and the Race Course. A good gorse covert was fenced in there and provided good sport and he had a good hunt from Burntwood over the open by Norwood, Westley, Ashley, Parnholt to Ampfield. Another good hunt occurred on December 15th, 1851, from Sandy Down. After two or three turns round the covert and Phillip's Heath the fox broke over by Leckford and Newton, crossed Bransbury Common and was pulled down a field short of Wherwell Wood, Mr. Frederick Baily of Brown Candover being first up and taking the fox from the hounds. Mr. T. E. Edwards, J. Nevill and Mr. Barton Wallop on the " Sweep " were next up, followed closely by master and his staff and the chief constable. Despite showing good sport in 1852, Mr. Wall took the Hambledon Hounds and the Hursley had another short mastership.

Mr. S. Lowe, 1852-57.

Mr. Stanley Lowe bought the famous Rev. Jack Russell's hounds from North Devon. He lived first at Worthy then at

[3] Dr. M. J. Rendall, c.m.g., second Master 1899–1911, Headmaster of Winchester College 1911–24, of Butley Priory, Woodbridge, Suffolk, who died in 1950.

Sparsholt and finally made Lainston House habitable again. He tried hunting hounds himself with John Tubb, an Irishman, to turn hounds for him. This was not successful and he got W. Summers from the H.H. to hunt hounds. Summers did what he could, but was not well mounted and the Hursley sport lost the reputation gained under the two former masters.

Mr. J. Tregonwell, 1857-62.

Mr. John Tregonwell of Cranborne Lodge, Dorset, now took the hounds and lived at Lainston House. The kennels were at Crawley as in Mr. Cockburn's day. Summers carried the horn and James Roffey and George Summers turned hounds. James Roffey was succeeded by Edwin Summers. The Summers family were admirably brought up and useful in the choir at Crawley Church. When the hounds left Crawley, Archdeacon Jacob said he regretted the departure of the family but not of the smell of the soup kitchen ! The master knew the country well, rode well to hounds and had the knack of always keeping perfectly clean whatever the state of the country he rode over.

Sport much improved and one very fine open hunt was enjoyed from Norwood by the Rack and Manger, Spittlebushes to Leckford Hut and Titcombe Bridge. Turning right by Chilbolton, by Newton, away to Bullingdon, crossing the open at the back of Hunton, over the water at Stoke Charity, thence past Newdown and killed on the edge of Micheldever Wood. This hunt took them through thirteen parishes and lasted two hours and fifteen minutes, a fine performance both of hounds and huntsman.

The Hon. Arthur Arundell of Houghton Lodge, Captain and Mrs. Bidgood of Wallop House, Mr. F. Bowker of Winchester and his daughter, spoken of as a magnificent horse woman, the Hon. Ralph Dutton of Timsbury Mr. W. Gater, Mr. Fred Heysham and his nephew, Mr. W. N. Heysham and Mr. T. Cordery were among the master's staunch supporters.

Mr. W. C. Standish, 1862-68.

Mr. William Cecil Standish of South Stoneham House became master. He was the third son of Rowland Stephenson of Scaleby Castle who took the name and arms of Standish in 1832, his mother becoming heiress of Standish. Mr. Standish hunted hounds himself, W. Summers acting as kennel huntsman. Always well mounted and spending money liberally, Mr. Standish tried very hard to show good sport. He was well supported by the three large landowners, Lord Palmerston of Broadlands, Sir William Heathcote of Hursley and Mr. Chamberlayne of Cranbury Park. It is regretted that all landowners did not follow their excellent example.

In 1864 Mr. Standish moved the kennels from Crawley to some he had built himself on his own property at Hensting near Colden Common. Walter Bell and Edwin Summers were his whippers-in. In 1866 Mr. Standish had some reward for his trouble in a great hunt from the Decoy Pond at Stoneham, by West End, Botley, Durley, on to the Rookeries near Wickham, thence forced into the open he killed his fox by the Bold Forester, after a run of two hours and twenty minutes. This hunt gave a fourteen-mile point and about thirty miles as hounds ran. This hunt was over a deep country with high banks and wide ditches and so falls were numerous. A boy is said to have told Summers that he greatly enjoyed his day, for he had jumped a lot of fences, had three falls and eaten four oranges.

Another good hunt of an hour and a half occurred from the same meet. On this occasion the fox crossed the River Test into the New Forest country.

In 1867 he lost many hounds through " dumb madness," but made good his losses.

In the spring of 1869 Mr. Standish retired to take the mastership of the New Forest hounds. It is of interest to note that Mr. Standish had started the Pau hounds in the 40's when quite a young man, having been born in 1821.

Mr. William Everett of Abbots Wood was Hon. Secretary to Mr. Standish. Colonel Samuel Nicoll, a future master, was among the most keen supporters ; Messrs. George, Charles and Arthur Deane, another future master, are also mentioned. It is noteworthy that for the first time quite a number of ladies are mentioned. The Misses Chamberlayne of Cranbury, Mrs. Acheson Gray, Mrs. A. C. Bidwell, Miss Everett of Lainston House, Miss Jarrett, Miss Deane of Bishopstoke, the Misses Hitchcock of Weeke Manor, Mrs. Talbot, Mrs. Clara Wabey of Leckford. Lord Gardner of Wherwell Priory, Mr. Heathcote of Hursley, Doctor England of Winchester and Colonel Dowker of Winchester, very keen on hounds and a great puppy walker, were also among the later supporters.

Colonel S. J. E. Nicoll, 1869-88.

On Mr. Standish's retirement the affairs of the Hunt looked in poor case. The subscription was only £300 and it was owing to the energies of Colonel Samuel J. E. Nicoll of Westbourne, son of Mr. Sam Nicoll the well-known master of the New Forest Hunt for fourteen years, that a strong committee was formed to carry on. Colonel Nicoll had started his military career with the 60th Rifles. The Committee consisted of Mr .Chamberlayne of Cranbury, always a staunch supporter of sport, Colonel Nicoll, Colonel Dowker and Mr. James P. Fitt who acted as Hon. Secretary. On Colonel Dowker retiring from the Committee Mr. Tyrwhitt Walker of Bossington took his place. Richard Morris was first engaged as huntsman, followed the next year by Alfred Summers, and the New Forest Hounds were purchased. New kennels were built at Pitt owing to the generosity of Sir William Heathcote who allowed farm buildings there to be converted and provided most of the material. It is presumed that Colonel Nicoll always acted as master in the field. The subscription under his able management soon rose to £1,000 per annum. It is not now apparent when exactly Colonel Nicoll assumed the full role of master, but he was the moving spirit from the beginning. At the early age of 12 Colonel Nicoll had attracted the notice of the great " Nimrod " when visiting his father's hounds in the New Forest. " Nimrod " said that young Sam would rate and turn a hound with any man in England. His huntsman was Alfred Summers who had acted as kennel huntsman and 1st whipper-in to Mr. Deacon with the H.H. and so had a thoroughly good training by a first-rate huntsman. He had a very good voice and until his weight became too great he was a very useful woodland huntsman, and he showed very good sport. In 1873 in the spring a memorable hunt took place from Baddesley Common, by Slackstead, Parnholt, Ashley, North Park, on to Stockbridge. At Stockbridge he turned back to Ashley where this game fox fairly ran them out of scent, and as Summer's horse was completely done he stopped hounds. The fox had been headed by an over eager young follower at Ashley, time was lost and never regained. The Hursley country is one that seldom forgives mistakes, if a fox is to be killed.

Colonel Nicoll's twenty years of good management was one of the Hursley's best periods. Alfred Summers returned to the H.H. in 1885 and Mr. Arthur Deane acted as amateur huntsman for three years very successfully.

Mr. A. Deane, 1888-92.

Mr. Arthur Deane of Winchester then became master and carried the horn himself. In the season 1888–89 he killed 18½ brace of foxes, hunting two days a week. This is a very good record for a difficult country.

Three of his hunts in the early nineties are of considerable interest. The first took place after a lawn meet at Hursley Park, then owned by Mr. Joseph Baxendale. A stale line was picked up on the way to draw South Lynde plantation on the fringe of Grovelands Copse. Scent was catchy, but hounds took the line through the east end of Crab Wood, across Ham Green to Lainston and on through Northwood Park, where Mr. Van de Byl then lived. Hounds ran on by New Barn and Crawley Warren where they checked. A good cast hit off the line again, crossing the Winchester—Newbury road, through Lackwhistle Farm, whence they ran into the Race Course, now Worthy Down Aerodrome, and there Mr. Deane was beaten.

About a month later hounds met at Hursley Pound and, after a long morning's work in Ampfield where a fox was killed, Mr. Deane went to again try conclusions with the fox which had beaten him before. On reaching Merdon, a distant holloa was heard from the Grovelands Copse direction. A man ploughing told the master that a fox had stolen away from Pages Copse as soon as he heard the horn in the park (Page's is just south-east of Grovelands), and had made off towards Crab Wood. Mr. Deane realised he had to do with his old opponent. There was a cold miserable east wind and a poor scent, but hounds puzzled out the line and again reached the Race Course where they were completely beaten. Mr. Deane was determined not to be beaten and met again at Hursley Pound after a month's rest. This time he went straight to Pages Copse without using his horn. Lakin, his first whipper in, had been sent on by Grovelands and soon gave a " View halloa." Scent was good and hounds raced their fox to Westwood, by Sheddon Oak and Well Copse, on by Lainston to North Wood. From thence the fox took exactly the same line to the Race Course, hounds being close behind him. Again, however, he disappeared but this time it was obvious that he could not have vanished into thin air and a thorough search of the buildings was undertaken. The fox was discovered lying behind the slate in the gentlemen's lavatory. The most extraordinary feature of this " hide out " was that the door was a spring door and the mystery was, how did the fox get out on the other two occasions.   In this case the fine big fox was so stiff Mr. Deane thought he would never live if left, so he was broken up, though most reluctantly.   Mr. Deane felt him a worthy opponent who deserved his life for his ingenuity.

Unfortunately Mr. Deane's diaries cannot be found but Major Lionel Deane of Littleton, who kindly supplied me with this interesting episode, remembers another hunt from Braishfield when Mr. Deane killed in Netley churchyard.   He used up three horses during the hunt.   In those days wire was unknown in Hampshire.   Cattle fences were properly plashed or good stout rails were used.   There were also a great many wattle fences which made very good training jumps for young riders and their mounts.   In the last hunt mentioned there would now be almost a town of small houses, etc., to get through.

Sir C. E. Frederick, Bart., and Mr. J. W. Baxendale, 1892-96.

Sir Charles Edward Frederick, 7th Baronet, of Shawford House near Winchester, and Mr. Joseph William Baxendale who had purchased the Hursley Estate, became joint masters. Sir Frederick was J.P. and High Sheriff of Hants, 1889, and had served in both the 10th Hussars, 1861–73, and 21st Hussars, 1873–82.   Sir Charles retired in 1896, finding his other duties too great a burden.

In December, 1894, during this joint mastership, a remarkable feat of a little mare, 15 hands, is recorded.   She was the property of Major Warde.   Her owner put her at a quickset fence : " as he took off he saw a deep lane on the other side but the mare actually cleared both fences and landed over the fence on the other side of the lane in the field beyond.   Just failing to clear the second fence with her heels, she came down, but was quickly up again and finished the run."   The distance was carefully measured and found to be 34 feet 8 inches from the point of taking off to where the mare landed with her forefeet.   This feat is remarkable as, the lane being quite unexpected, the rider did not gallop at the fence as he would have done at a brook, and wide ditches are uncommon in the country.

Mr. J. W. Baxendale, 1896 - 1902.

Mr. Joseph William Baxendale continued as sole master. He served as High Sheriff, 1893, and was a J.P. and D.L.   He was an ideal master for the country, owning a large estate with many covers in the middle of the country, but unfortunately he found it necessary to retire after ten years of office. Both Sir Charles Frederick and Mr. Baxendale died in 1913.

Mr. W. Philpotts Williams, 1902-03.

Mr. W. Philpotts Williams' short reign had little effect on the country. The big woodlands probably frightened him away to East Cornwall where he served as joint master for nine seasons and sole master 1912–14.

Mr. F. C. Swindell, 1903-06.

Mr. F. C. Swindell's taking over boded well for the Hunt. He was very keen and had a thorough knowledge of hounds. From 1885–94 Mr. Swindell had hunted the Buntingford and Royston side of the Puckeridge country. Till 1890 Mr. Gosling had hunted the other half, a committee taking over on his retirement. Mr. Swindell not having been born in the country, he was apparently regarded as a "foreigner." Hunting became so unpleasant that he sold his fine pack for £1,200 to the Hon. L. J. Bathurst, who then sold it two years later to that great sportsman and well-known authority on hounds Mr. Edward Barclay, master for 52 years. Mr. Swindell was master of the old Berkshire, 1894–98, and the Taunton Vale from 1900–02. It was a great loss to the Hursley that he did not stay long enough to make his abilities more felt in improving hounds and the country. He, however, brought Ted Bailey with him as kennel huntsman who gave so many years of good service to the hunt, and after getting rid of the old pack he got together a very useful pack of hounds.

Mr. W. V. Long, 1906-08.

Mr. Walter Vansittart Long, formerly of Preshaw, who married the heiress of the Dunoon and Corhampton Estates and so became in 1909 W. V. Campbell-Wyndham Long. A thorough sportsman, son and grandson of Hambledon masters. He soon returned to the Hambledon and was for many years a staunch supporter of that pack and chairman of the Hunt Club for some years.

Sir George Cooper, Bart., 1908-16.

These very short masterships which are so bad for a hunt were brought to an end by Sir George Alexander Cooper, 1st Baronet, of Hursley Park. Sir George had recently purchased this fine estate and proved a kind and excellent landlord and very public spirited. The whole estate was kept up in model fashion in every way and a plentiful supply of foxes and pheasants was always available. He became the mainstay of the Hunt and remained so till his death in 1940. Without his generous assistance and plentiful supply of foxes the Hunt would have fallen on very evil days when enormous battues of tame pheasants became fashionable.

In 1911 Ted Bailey was promoted huntsman with Matt Townsend as 1st whipper-in and Will Maiden 2nd whipper-in. He had a good start at the kennel copse, killing two brace of cubs on September 22nd, 1911. In 1911–12 and 1912–13 there were four blank days in each season, 35½ brace and 15 brace being killed, including cub-hunting, three brace and five brace being marked to ground.

On February 13th, 1914, hounds had a good hunt from a root field by Winchester Racecourse, running over the Andover road in a ring to Fitts Copse, then over the Racecourse and both railways ; they killed their fox as stiff as a board after an hour's hard gallop by Micheldever Wood in the H.H. country.

The 1913–14 season produced the best sport during Ted Bailey's time. In 65 days 18 brace were killed and seven brace marked to ground. No blank days were experienced in the season proper, but one day's cub-hunting was blank.

On March 19th, 1915, the pack had a very busy day from Leckford Hut. The first fox was killed after a fifteen minutes' gallop to Common Down. The next was bolted from a tree below Marsh Court and he soon was rolled over. A good forty minutes' hunt followed, but both huntsman and 1st whipper-in got a bad start, their horses being the other side of the railway. This fox was lost at Hoplands. Going back to Leckford, another fox provided a fast fifteen minutes and was killed. Most unusually, scent was very good, the air cold and frosty.

During the last two years of Sir George's mastership the tallies fell to 12 and 10 brace, though no blank day was noted in 1914–15.

The Honorary Secretary, the Hon. George Hewitt, was a great help to Sir George and started the Point-to-Point Races at Hursley in 1910.

Among staunch supporters for many years were Generals Crosbie and Vibart, Colonels Little and Toogood and Major Warde, the Chief Constable, Captain Crawford, R.N.; Mesdames Mottram Hewett, Bather, and Clowes; Misses Clayton Mitchell,

THE HURSLEY HUNT AT HURSLEY PARK, 1921.

Mr. Herbert Johnson, M.F.H.,
Master or Joint Master, 1916-22 and 1927-30.

Toogood and Warde, a strong Winchester contingent. South-ampton was represented by Mr. Graham Day and his two brothers. Sir George relied entirely on the Duke of Beaufort's pack for drafts.

Mr. H. Johnson and Lieut-Col. G. Philippi, M.C., 1916-17.

On Sir George's retirement Mr. Herbert Johnson of Marsh Court and Lieut.-Col. George Philippi, M.C., of Crawley Court became joint masters. Mr. Johnson, well known to a very large circle of friends as "Johnnie," had built Marsh Court entirely with hard chalk, from Sir Edwin Lutyen's plans. He was well known in almost every sport. A good fisherman, both on the River Test and with salmon, a keen stalker, a big game shot and his high pheasants were renowned. He also proved a good helmsman, racing his six- and eight-metre yachts on the Solent. Above all, a most kind, generous and hospitable host, well aided by his charming wife, the widow of Captain Bertram Meeking of the 10th Royal Hussars. His active interest in the Hunt lasted till 1930, when increasing blindness and deafness prevented any active hunting or shooting. Mr. Johnson also had to sell Marsh Court, but his pluck and cheerfulness remained to the end when he died in Winchester aged 93 in 1949.

Bailey remained as huntsman until called up for service in 1917, when Charles Isaac, the old Cottesmore huntsman, carried on till his return in 1919.

Lieut.-Col. George Philippi owned the fine estate of Crawley Court and the beautiful village, all of which, except the house and park, has now been broken up. He did not long continue his interest in the Hunt, but Mr. Johnson carried on alone till 1922.

Mr. H. Johnson, 1917-22.

Sport was fairly good and in 1919–20 sixty days' hunting were enjoyed without a blank day. Probably during the war years stopping was not properly carried out as the tally fell to 6 brace killed and 6½ brace marked to ground in that year. The 1920–21 season was somewhat better, but in 1921-22 there were many disappointing days and a scarcity of foxes.

Captain Lionel Edwards of Buckholt, West Tytherley, the great sporting artist and keen supporter of the Hursley, has given the author some recollections of hunts during these years.

In 1919 the field were confronted by a brook on Cross Oaks Farm. It was not a large brook but had boggy banks ; only three followers are reported as jumping it—a veterinary surgeon and two Remount officers from Romsey. Charles Isaac, Fernie's old huntsman, carried the horn in the absence of Ted Bailey who had been called up. In 1922, January 30th, a very fast hunt over good country was enjoyed from Hound Wood, by Farley, Knightwood, through Clarendon, back to Aldeberry, where hounds lost on the railway.

Bailey resumed his duties in the 1920–21 season when 11 brace were killed and 7 brace marked to ground, but three blank days again were noted.

On March 21st, 1921, a fox was found at Northpark and gave a good hour and thirty-five minutes' hunt through Winterdown, Up Somborne, Ashley, Forest Farm, to Crab Wood, nearly to the Leigh road, then left-handed by Ashley to the King's Somborne road where he jinked back to Ashley and was killed. In 1921–22 season the scent was generally poor and only 5½ brace were killed and 8 brace run to ground.

In 1921 young Sam Newman, son of Tom Newman,[1] the Beaufort huntsman, came as 2nd whipper-in. Tom Newman had himself learnt his work in the Hursley woodlands under Summers.

Captain G. J. R. Cooper, 1922-24.

Captain George James Robertson Cooper of Merdon Manor, the eldest son of Sir George A. Cooper of Hursley Park, who had served as a Captain in the Royal Scots Greys, now took over the mastership with Ted Bailey as huntsman. Captain Cooper did not long keep the hounds, but as hon. secretary, joint hon. secretary, master, and, after the death of Sir George in 1940, chairman of the Hunt, he has kept his interest and, as in his father's time, his many coverts hold foxes.

Major A. H. Wilkie, 1924-26.

Captain Cooper now handed over control to his brother-in-law, Major Archibald Hanning Wilkie of Woolley Green, Romsey, late of the 60th Rifles. Major Wilkie had acted as hon. secretary to Mr. H. Johnson and also as field master.

1 " Tom " Newman's real name was Ernest, he was the son of Walter Newman, huntsman to the Hambledon Hunt, see p. 191.

On December 16th, 1924, a 12-mile hunt took place from Blackmore. After two turns round Bentley Great Wood, the fox returned to Blackmore, but ran on to Hound Wood, Pitton and Clarendon Park, where he was lost.

A good fox was found after a meet at the ex-master's home at Merdon, which ran straight nearly to Barton Stacey, a point of about eight miles. Unfortunately again the fox was not accounted for.

A Committee, 1926-27.

A committee including Captain J. A. F. Dalgety of Lockerley Hall, Captain G. J. R. Cooper of Merdon, Lieut.-Commander W. F. G. North, R.N., and Captain Lionel Edwards took over. Fred Gosden hunted hounds and Commander North, the Hon. Secretary, has helped the Hunt through many crises.

The Hunt went through one of its many crises which was terminated by Mr. H. Johnson again coming forward with Lieut.-Colonel Edward Rigby Kewley, D.S.O., M.C., late Rifle Brigade, of Little Dean House, Stockbridge to help him.

Mr. H. Johnson and Lieut.-Colonel E. R. Kewley, D.S.O., M.C., 1927-30.

Some useful hunts took place during this mastership, including a six-mile point from Dean Copse, by Bentley to Clarendon Park on March 9th, 1928, and an eight-mile point on December 3rd. No details, however, are available.

On January 6th, 1930, Hound Wood provided a good fox who ran via Farley Copse, Pitton, Folliot's Plantation to Thorny Down (Gas School), on to Old Lodge, Golden City, Roche Court, back to Old Lodge and to ground in the Tedworth country—a hunt of about 14 miles with a point of five miles.

On Tuesday, April 17th, a considerable thrill was given to the whole hunting community by the Duke of Beaufort bringing his hounds to Ashley village at the invitation of the joint masters. Naturally a big gathering attended the meet. Six masters of other packs were out, including Mr. George Evans (H.H.) and Lieut.-Colonel C. M. Borwick (Middleton). Three ex-masters were also present on foot. Great expectations were roused in some and some scepticism in others. The Duke soon proved, however, that his hounds could hunt and kill a Hampshire fox. Their first draw was Ashley, unfortunately blank, but Parnholt as usual provided a brace. Hounds forced one away to Forest of Bere Farm where he was unfortinately headed. He came back *via* Farley Mount to Parnholt, where he was well hustled up and down until forced again to quit. He was pulled down in Berrydown Plantations after fifty-five minutes—an old fox who had probably defeated hounds on many occasions. Crabwood was then drawn and a fox was soon on foot. He was driven to West Wood and on to Farley Mount where the field pressed on hounds too closely. The Duke put hounds right after a short check, and they ran on through Parnholt and Berry Down towards the Point-to-Point Course, but turned into the Warren, through Ten Acres, back to Crabwood. The scent was poor and the ground much foiled, but hounds patiently pushed their fox through, despite all difficulties, to Nomansland and would certainly have accounted for this fox, too, had the Duke not been forced to stop them after an hour and twenty minutes in order to catch his train back to Badminton and he was six miles from the station.

The author is indebted to the courtesy of the editor of the *Hampshire Chronicle* for the particulars of this interesting day, which proved that the famous Beaufort pack could hunt well in most difficult, poor-scenting woodland country.

The Duke of Beaufort again visited the Hursley country on April 14th, 1930. The meet was at Stockbridge. Despite a poor scent, hounds ran well through Upper Somborne Wood to Shedden Oak. Here the fox was viewed but hounds did not kill as scent failed. The Duke carried the horn and hounds hunted with great drive though unsuccessful.

Major L. A. Jackson, 1930-31.

Major L. A. Jackson was an experienced amateur huntsman who had already a knowledge of Hampshire hunting with the Garth Hunt for three seasons, 1919 to 1922. He had also been master of the Cotswold for two seasons, 1922 to 1924.

Major L. A. Jackson and Mr. E. S. Cattley, 1931-32.

Mr. Eric S. Cattley of Sparsholt Manor joined Major Jackson for one season.

Major L. A. Jackson and Sir H. G. Ley, 1932-34.

Sir Henry Gordon Ley, 2nd Baronet, of Furze Down, King's Somborne, and Lagonly Hall, Cumberland, joined Major Jackson. A curious incident happened in 1932 after a meet at Farley Church. Captain Lionel Edwards saw the hunted fox, found at Hound Wood, and running near Farley village, kill three fowls in front of hounds. It was a very bad scenting day and it would seem to be an act of bravado. Foxes certainly know what sort of scent there is. The case of a pheasant being snatched up by a hunted fox was reported to Mr. Tom Smith who had never heard of a case himself. This appears in his *Reminiscences* written by a friend.

Sir H. G. Ley, 1934-36.

Sir Henry Gordon Ley took the sole control in 1934 and engaged Will James as huntsman. The great change that took place in the country during these years between the two wars, apart from the general increase of wire, was the disappearance of the old type of yeoman farmer, formerly so typical of the country.

Mr. Aylward of Lockerley Water, who had been a good man to hounds and a great sportsman, still came out after the 1st World War, but few others. Mr. Lamb who farmed near the Duke's Head Inn was also a firm supporter. He rode a brown cob, wore a brown bowler, brown coat, brown breeches and box cloth gaiters. Hearing, on one occasion, the M.F.H. complaining of the expenses, he produced a wad of notes and handed them to the M.F.H. Mr. Gavin of Whitenap, Romsey, and Mr. Frampton of Ranville's Farm, Romsey, were also two of the exceptions.

H. Goddard, the present huntsman of the Bramham Moor, served his apprenticeship with the Hursley, also the Summers family, and the famous Tom Newman of the Beaufort Hounds.

Mr. Grant Singer, 1936-40.

Mr. Grant Singer of Norman Court now took over the mastership. He introduced youth and great keenness, and Norman Court was a large estate. Charles James was his huntsman (who went afterwards to the H.H.) and J. Beck his 1st whipper-in. Mr. Singer worked hard on the wire. Had this good sportsman survived the war undoubtedly he would have made an excellent master of hounds, but he was killed in the 2nd World War whilst serving in the 10th Royal Hussars. When Mr. Singer joined the Army, a Committee carried on with Fred Gosden as huntsman.

A Committee, 1940-47.

In 1943, on February 16th, from a meet at Dean Station, hounds found in Dean Copse at once and ran very fast the whole length of Bentley Great Wood, through Norman Court, Buckholt, over the Salisbury—Stockbridge road to Lobscombe Corner Aerodrome, then on to the Salisbury—Andover road where the fox was headed. He then ran to Middle Wallop and was lost at Garlogs. The whipper-in's horse dropped dead and the huntsman got hounds back alone in the dark, arriving at the kennels at 11 p.m. A comment of the times in a 1940 cub hunt was that A.A. fire and sirens made more noise than the hounds.

Captain F. S. Faber, 1947-49.
Captain F. S. Faber and Captain J. Craig Harvey, 1949-50.
Captain F. S. Faber, 1950-

Captain Frank Stanley Faber of Ampfield House, late Captain in the 3rd County of London Yeomanry, came to the rescue of the Hunt in another crisis and took over the mastership, being joined in 1949 by Captain John Craig Harvey of Lainston House, but only for one year. Fred Gosden retired from his position of huntsman, receiving a handsome testimonial from his many friends in the country.

Jack Baily now carries the horn, and Jack Peacock turns hounds for him.

The best hunt of 1949–50 season was on December 16th from the Swamp by Lockerley Mill. Hounds ran by the western end of Holbury, through Morgan's Piece, driving right through 1000 acres of Bentley Wood into Houndwood. The fox circled this covert and ran on through Pitton and was lost near a farm N.W. of Pitton. This made a 6½-mile point and hounds were unlucky not to kill.

HURSLEY HOUNDS AT LAINSTON HOUSE, 1946-47.
J. Taylor, whipper-in ; F. Gosden, huntsman ; Captain F. S. Faber, M.F.H.

The "old hero" of the poem.

The "old Hero."

The illustration opposite shows an earthstopper to the Hursley Hunt, who, on attaining his jubilee in 1853, wrote the following lines :—

" For fifty long years this old hero can say
He stopt all his earths by the break of the day,
And one thing more to add to his lot
When the fox ran to Humbers[5] he found the earth stopt.
There's Foster[6] and Sawyer[7] can both justly say
When they came to Humbers by night or by day
They were pleased and surprised to have the good luck
To find the old Hero had all the earths stopt.
For six separate masters[8] he also can say
He has stopt all his earths by the break of the day,
When the fox came to Humbers how sad was his lot
To find the old Hero had all the earths stopt.
And now for his Jubilee to carry the sway
By all the brave sportsmen that's riding that way,
Let the hounds run to Humbers be it ever so hot,
They will find the old Hero has all the earths stopt."

Though no poet, the old earthstopper has obviously played his part nobly by doing an arduous and somewhat thankless task. Few realise his work in awful weather except the master and huntsman.

The doggerel was in Mr. George Alfred Ellis Wall's diary and the picture was in his possession and is reproduced by the courtesy of Mrs. Butchart of Worthy Park, his grand-daughter. Unfortunately the name of the " old Hero " is now lost.

---

[5] Humbers, a covert 1½ miles south of King's Somborne, no longer a noted fox-covert.

[6] Richard Foster came to Mr. J. T. Villebois, master of the H.H. (of which country the Hursley formed a part) in 1813. He had served Lord Foley in Worcestershire before. He had started under Mr. Smith of Lowlebrooke Lodge, Northamptonshire, as pad groom. He then went to Lord Southampton for ten years and then to Lord Foley as 1st whipper-in. Foster stayed with Mr. Villebois till the latter's death in 1837 and then was huntsman to Major Barrett till 1840. He died at Andover in 1855 and was buried near his old master Mr. Villebois in Old Alresford churchyard. One of the best huntsmen Hampshire has known.

[7] Sawyer. First served Lord Clanricarde 1807–08. He then was with Mr. Powlett-Powlett, M.F.H., and one year with Mr. T. Delme. He served Mr. Villebois, M.F.H., from 1814 to 1837, when he went to Sir John Barker-Mill, M.F.H., and Mr. White of Ampfield, M.F.H. He was a first-rate whipper-in. Still living in Mr. Wall's time, 1850, who occasionally mounted him.

[8] The six masters were presumably Mr. W. Powlett-Powlett to 1802, Mr. J. T. Villebois to 1837, masters of the H.H., and Sir J. Barker-Mill to 1839, Mr. White to 1843, Mr. R. Cockburn to 1850 and Mr. G. A. E. Wall 1850–52, masters of the Hursley.

T

CHAPTER XI.

THE NEW FOREST BUCKHOUNDS.

MASTERS OF THE NEW FOREST BUCKHOUNDS.

1858–83 (unofficial)	Mr. F. F. Lovell, Hinchelsea.
1883	The date of official recognition of the New Forest Buckhounds by the Crown authorities.
1883–93	Mr. F. F. Lovell, Hinchelsea.
1893–94	Mr. E. St. L. Walker.
1894–95	Mr. E. St. L. Walker.
	Mr. E. Festus Kelly, Northerwood Park.
1895–1901	Mr. E. Festus Kelly, Northerwood Park.
1901–08	Mr. O. T. Price, New Park, Brockenhurst.
1908–10	Mr. G. J. Thursby, Fountain Court, Lyndhurst.
	Captain H. T. Timson, Tatchbury Mount.
1910–36	Sir George J. Thursby, Bart., Fountain Court, Lyndhurst.
1936–38	Sir John Buchanan Jardine, Bart.
	Mr. A. W. H. Dalgety.
1938–40	Mr. H. J. Colebrook.
	Miss Colebrook.
1940–41	A Committee.
1941–42	Mr. H. J. Colebrook.
	Mrs. Collins (*née* Miss Colebrook).
1942–44	No hunting.
1944–47	Mr. A. W. H. Dalgety.
	Lady Daresbury.
1947–49	Mr. H. J. Colebrook.
1949–50	A Committee.
1950	Lieut.-Colonel Sir D. B. Forwood, Bart., C.M.G.

NEW FOREST BUCKHOUNDS.

The New Forest Buckhounds, though hunting the stag or buck, in a forest devoted to their chase for some 900 years, are the youngest of Hampshire packs. They owe their existence to the effects of the Deer Removal Act of 1851. The Royal Staghounds had taken all the stock they wanted by 1852. After that time the deer were persecuted and destroyed in every possible way. The deer soon were reduced to very small

274

numbers and it occurred to various people, after the lust for killing had expended itself, that good sport could be enjoyed by hunting them. No Lord Warden had succeeded the Duke of Cambridge, who died in 1850, the Commissioneer of Woods and Forests was Sir Henry Loch. The previous Commissioner, Mr. J. K. Howard, was a kindly official who did not want to be bothered with the quarrels of rival packs of hounds of a somewhat "bobbery" nature. The Hon. Gerald Lascelles was appointed Deputy Surveyor in 1880 and for two years watched the squabbling and then induced the Commissioneer to act in the same way as the Lord Warden had acted in 1784. A conference was held in 1883 ; the Master of the Foxhounds was first asked what days he wished to hunt. He adhered to the original permission given them for Tuesday, Thursday and Saturday. Mr. Francis Frederick Lovell of Hinchelsea had the best regulated pack at the time and this was constituted the official pack of buckhounds. He handed over his hounds and the use of his kennels at Hinchelsea to the managing committee appointed. This pack was duly allotted Monday and Friday as hunting days.

Mr. F. F. Lovell, 1883-93 (unofficial 1858-83.)

Mr. Henry Buckworth Powell of Wilverley Park had hunted a small pack in 1854–58 and Mr. Francis Frederick Lovell of Hinchelsea had continued to hunt in the spring only with a stable boy and his two daughters to assist him from 1858 till the day of formation of the official pack in 1883. Mr. Lovell was the fourth son of P. H. Lovell, Esq., of Cole Park, Wiltshire, an old Life Guards Officer and a fine horseman. Though he had lost an arm in a shooting accident, he hunted hounds himself.

Mr. Lovell was a great sportsman and his ideals are well shown by Mr. Horace Hutchinson in his book *The New Forest Beautiful*. He is there quoted as saying " I have tried to put somewhat on the ancient footing, in the New Forest, the oldest sport of all English sports, and to show, as the French ' limier ' has so often shown, how much is to be gained by patience, in making good a scent after the lapse, not of six or seven minutes, but at least of as many hours." Here Mr. Lovell is referring to the difficult art of " tufting." The stag must be well harboured, not by any means an easy matter in itself. It must be a warrantable stag or buck and the one the master wishes to hunt. The harbourer may be sure from slot or fewmets,[1] that a warrantable stag has entered some covert. It is not so easy to know that he has not left it, also there may be other deer in the same covert, and it is often a very difficult and arduous task to separate the stag which is to be hunted from the others, before the pack can be laid on to advantage. In the old days the harbourer would come to the master with the fewmets in his horn to prove his work, and, of course, he would have measured the slot exactly. Though Mr. Lovell did not have the mediaeval grandeur of the chase in his modest establishment, he had all the real sportsmanship and knowledge of true venery. He was born in 1821 and by 1883 was very glad of some knowledgeable assistant. This help Mr. Lascelles gave him.

In 1885 Mr. Lovell could not hunt, owing to the death of his wife, Lady Rose Lovell, a daughter of Henry, 7th Duke of Beaufort. Mr. Lascelles carried the horn for this season and killed eight deer in the fourteen days of the spring hunting—a good performance for an amateur, often on strange horses kindly lent by Lord Londesborough.

On April 27th hounds ran well and killed a buck after forty-five minutes in the morning, and in the afternoon they ran a buck from Rhinefield into the Avon Valley beyond High Wood, and then turning into the Forest, bayed him at 7 p.m. in the stream by Burley Manor, after a very varied hunt of some three hours. The first hound to bay the stag was badly punished, being caught against the high bank whilst swimming. Though able to come home with the pack, blood poisoning set in, and he lost every hair on his body before recovery. This showed the partial truth, at any rate, of George Turberville's[2] line in the *Noble Arts of Venerie* in 1575 : " If thou be hurt with horne of Harte, 't will bring thee to thy bier."

In 1886 Mr. Lovell was laid up with illness, so it was arranged that W. Perkins, who had been engaged as professional whipper-in, should hunt the hounds and that Mr. Lascelles should act as field master, another whipper-in being also engaged to help Perkins. The spring hunting again produced eight deer. April 12th produced a good point of nine miles and a two-hour hunt from Buskett's Wood right across the Forest to Linford. A week later two stags were hunted from Busketts, without

---

[1] Fewmet = excrement (French fumée), sometimes fumes of hart, croteys of buck or roe.

[2] Member of the well known Dorset family of Bere Regis and Wool Manor House. Scholar of Winchester College and Fellow of New College 1561. Author of other scholarly works. The first writer to use blank verse.

the long delay in separating them, one hour's tufting proving of no good. The stags raced together to Roe Wood, about eight miles away, and there the stags separated. Hounds brought back the warrantable stag right across the Forest, and they killed at Canterton—about seventeen miles in three hours.

The next season the services of a really good huntsman of long experience with foxhounds and harriers were obtained by engaging Robert Allen. Born and bred in the Bramham Moor country, Allen had been in various services, the most important being huntsman to Mr. Nicholas Parry with the Puckeridge and also to Sir George Brooke's Harriers in Co. Dublin. A splendid type of hunt servant and a first-rate hound man.

Mr. George Lane Fox of the Bramham Moor Hunt sent yearly a nice draft of dog hounds. Lord Portman and Lord Yarborough also often sent some useful young unentered dogs not quite big enough for their standard. A pack of 23 inches only was aimed at, but of the best blood. It was considered that size was the least objectionable reason for drafting.

Mr. Lovell found in 1893 that the strain of the long days' hunting in all weathers was too much for him, and he retired. Mr. Lovell died in 1906. His huntsman, Robert Allen, carried on with his successor, having become a great character in the Forest, noted for his invariable courtesy and dry humour. Two stories of him are worth recording. Hounds had met at Bushy Bratley and a deer had been harboured in Lord Normanton's coverts some four or five miles to the westward. When the pack was laid on, the deer had laid down in some thick furze and so they fresh found him and raced away for twenty-five minutes, straight back to Bushy Bratley. Colonel W. Martin Powell of Brooklands had just arrived and viewed the deer. Off went his hat and hounds turned short from him and ran into their buck about half-a-mile further on, never having checked for a second. Riding up to old Allen, the Colonel said, " Well, Allen, I killed that deer for you." Though this was rather a startling remark, Allen received it with grave courtesy. " Thank you, Colonel, but," looking down at his hounds, " *they'll* never believe that." On another occasion hounds were running well late in April and the field were making for a gap which seemed the best exit. Allen was in front and held up his hand as if for danger. On being questioned afterwards as to what was the trouble, the huntsman replied : " There's an 'ard turkey hen sitting on her eggs i' that gap, and I didn't want them to disturb her, ye see." An unusual hunting obstacle, but doubtless the owner of the turkey blessed the considerate huntsman.

Mr. E. St. L. Walker, 1893-94.

In 1893 Mr. Edward H. St. Ledger Walker came from the Croome country where he had been master since 1889. He remained sole master for only one season.

Mr. E. St. L. Walker and Mr. E. F. Kelly, 1894-95.

In 1894 Mr. Edward Festus Kelly joined Mr. Walker. Mr. Kelly bought Northerwood Park, Lyndhurst, from Mr. Keppel Pulteney, where very ample stabling existed. Lord Londesborough used to rent this fine place for the spring hunting, always bringing some thirty horses with him for coaching and hunting.

Mr. E. F. Kelly, 1895 - 1901.

In 1895 Mr. Walker retired, and Mr. Kelly carried on alone. Mr. Kelly experimented by importing some French deerhounds of ancient lineage and also some half-bred foxhounds and blue mottled Gascon hounds. A few were still in the pack in the next master's time but they do not seem to have been a great success. They would hardly mix well ; the French hound is very true to the line but has not the dash of an English fox-hound. He is not interfered with by the huntsman, and he prefers to hunt the line out even if the stag is in view.

Up to 1897 Robert Allen, despite often suffering a good deal of pain, had carried on and shown good sport. The time came when he could not continue hunting hounds and he retired, regretted by all. He did not long survive his retirement and was buried in Lyndhurst churchyard, his memorial stone being put up by Mrs. Cheape, a very staunch friend of the old huntsman.

Harry White, who had served Mr. Charles Wright when master of the FitzWilliam and also had experience with the Vere and Dumfries-shire packs, succeeded Allen and proved also an excellent houndman. Despite miserable accommodation, being at one time reduced to a range of pig sties, a small cow byre and one horse box, hounds always were in first-rate condition. This was due to the fact that he was always out with them at exercise in the Forest in all weathers and for most of the day.

Mr. O. T. Price, 1901-08.

Mr. Owen T. Price now became master and took up his residence at New Park in 1904. There he created much improved quarters for both men and hounds. His hunt servants were Will Roberts, huntsman, and Jim Wateridge as whipper-in, both smart and efficient at their work.

In 1905 Mr. Price killed 71 deer in 68 hunting days. Hounds ran in collars, the " leaders " releasing the swivels to allow the pack to join the tufters who ran on with the pack. No hound was ever hung up by his collar, despite the thick brambles and high undergrowth they had to push through.

Mr. Price ran bitches with his pack, which was rather an innovation.

No man living knows more of the Forest and the ways of its animals than Mr. Price. A pillar still of the foxhounds, he also founded, during his mastership of the Buckhounds, a pack of beagles which became very popular, and when he left another pack was carried on by the Lyndhurst residents with Mr. Day as master. Mr. Price hunted stag or buck in August and September ; in November, December, January and February doe or pricket were hunted and in March and April stag or buck.

Mr. G. J. Thursby and Captain H. T. Timson, 1908-10.

In 1908 Mr. George James Thursby of Fountain Court, Lyndhurst, and Captain H. T. Timson of Tatchbury, became joint masters. Mr. Thursby had previous experience of hunting hounds, having carried the horn when his father, Sir John J. Thursby, was master of the New Forest Foxhounds (Western Portion) 1891–95. He had also been master of the Ledbury Hunt from 1895–97. Mr. Thursby was, without doubt, the greatest licensed amateur jockey of his day, riding " John of Gaunt " into second place in the Derby of 1904, and in the 1906 Derby riding " Picton " again into second place. Captain Timson, a descendent of the Rev. E. Timson, M.F.H. the New Forest Foxhounds in 1854–60, undertook the tufting arrangements and turned hounds during the hunt. Mr. Thursby hunted the pack. After two seasons Captain Timson resigned and Mr. Thursby carried on alone till 1936.

Mr. (afterwards Sir) George J. Thursby, Bart., 1910-36.

This mastership was the greatest period in the history of the Buckhounds. The master, born in 1869, was a splendid horseman, a great huntsman and a good judge of hounds. Owing to the Rugby Hound Sales, it was not now possible to rely on an annual draft from a good pack. These sales, too, had made hounds more expensive. Mr. Thursby decided to buy 26in. doghounds who were really good hounds but too big for most foxhound packs. The Devon and Somerset Hunt was his only competitor for hounds of this size. Mr. Thursby had no lumberers, and no hounds covered the Forest faster. Under his control they were as smart and quick as any smaller hounds could have been. They had complete trust in their huntsman and with reason. Some very fine hunts took place during Sir George's long period of office but few have been recorded.

In one hunt from Franchise Wood on the North Edge of the Forest in Wiltshire a young stag raced across the whole Forest passing its southern boundary, to be bayed and killed near Milton, one mile short of the sea, for which he was doubtless making. For the first seven miles the master, Mr. Compton and Mr. Lascelles were well with hounds but were misled by a false halloa. Mr. Thursby, on a race horse, got up to hounds again by Brockenhurst. In Milton he changed on to a hotel fly horse and got to his hounds on this animal as hounds pulled down their stag in a ditch after a fourteen-mile point at a great pace.

In April, 1913, a fallow buck from Loosehanger, outside the Forest in the north, ran straight over the Ashley Hills, by Broomy Lodge and then due south. Running through fresh deer at Roe Wood, the pack ran on to Ridley Wood where for the first time a check occurred. The master soon put the hounds right and they went on across the open over the Forest boundary on to Mr. Mills' property at Bisterne where they killed him about a mile from Mr. Mills' house. The point was eleven miles in an hour and a half. Lord and Lady Leconfield and several other masters of hounds saw this great hunt.

After the 1st World War hounds were difficult to obtain and so Mr. Thursby lowered his standard to 25-inch to get a greater number of hounds to pick from. Experiments were made but Mr. Thursby found that the pure-bred English fox-hound was the best hound for the work. During his mastership he stuck to the fallow buck rather than the stag or roe. The three Fry brothers in corduroy keeper's coats, breeches and gaiters and hats were " leaders " for many years. They added considerably to the picturesqueness of the meets as their

SIR GEORGE THURSBY, Bart, Master New Forest Buckhounds 1908-36, and
FRANK MAIER, 1st whipper-in and kennel hand.

THE FRY BROTHERS.

SIR GEORGE THURSBY AND HUNT STAFF.

portrait opposite shows. They were succeeded by the three Witcher brothers. Mr. Thursby succeeded his half-brother Sir John O. S. Thursby as 3rd Baronet in 1920. Frank Maier was 1st whip and Kestrell kennel huntsman for some thirty years. Sir George Thursby died in 1941 leaving no heir.

Sir J. W. Buchanan Jardine, Bart., and Mr. A. W. H. Dalgety, 1936-38.

The Buckhounds were now taken over by two experienced masters of foxhounds—Sir John William Buchanan Jardine, Bart., of Castle Milk, Lockerbie, master of the Dumfries-shire Hunt since 1921, and Mr. Arthur William Hugh Dalgety (late 9th Lancers) of Ringmer, Sussex, who had been master or joint master of the Vine Hunt, 1923–29, and the Southdown Hunt from 1929. Both remained master of their foxhound packs and still are in control. Mr. Dalgety also had some experience of hunting the deer from his period with the Vine when he kept a few couple of hounds for the purpose.

Jack Slightham, a keen sportsman who knew the Forest from boyhood and had been a Forest keeper, came as 1st whipper-in and kennel huntsman. He also was in charge of tufting operations. He has been the mainstay of the pack since that time. The Witcher brothers had become rather old and retired from their job as pack holders. The hound van was used to kennel the pack until laid on. Generally the fallow buck was hunted, the red stag was also hunted when one was harboured ; does and hinds were not hunted.

In 1936 a good nine-mile point was enjoyed with a buck from Hollyhatch to Tanting Wood, and in 1937 a magnificent stag was roused on the Ashley Hills and hunted beyond Trafalgar where he was killed in the River Avon. This stag was a seventeen-pointer and probably the biggest stag killed by hounds for many years. Its head adorns Mr. Dalgety's home in Sussex.

Sport was good but it was a considerable disadvantage that both masters lived far from the Forest.

Mr. H. J. Colebrook and Miss Colebrook, 1938-40.

Mr. H. John Colebrook of Fulmer Hall, Bucks, and his daughter now became joint masters. Both were well known for the fine teams of hackneys which Miss Colebrook usually drove in the show ring and drove very well, winning many prizes.   The Compton Arms, owned by Mr. Colebrook, provided a useful headquarters in the Forest.

A Committee, 1940-41.

A Committee took over for one year before the pack was again taken by Mr. Colebrook and his daughter who had now married.

Mr. H. J. Colebrook and Mrs. Collins, 1941-42.
No hunting, 1942-44.
Mr. A. W. H. Dalgety and Lady Daresbury, 1944-47.

To start the hunting again with no pack was by no means easy, but Mr. Dalgety brought seven or eight couple of fox-hounds from Sussex, which though not very staunch to, fox were equally not very staunch to deer and were apt to change from deer to fox and from the hunted deer to another.

Lord Daresbury was joint master of the Belvoir from 1934–47 and Lady Daresbury's father, Brig.-General Sir Joseph Laycock, K.C.M.G., D.S.O., T.D. (late 2nd Life Guards) was also a good sportsman.

Though sport was naturally not up to the standard of a properly broken pack of buckhounds some good hunts were enjoyed.   One buck roused in the Avon Valley in the extreme northern boundary of the Forest was hunted by Bramshot Telegraph and Rufus Stone past Canterton Manor and beyond.

Mr. H. J. Colebrook, 1947-49.

Mr. Colebrook again came to the rescue and took much trouble in collecting a small pack of useful hounds.   Black and tan were found to be very good in their work and the pack of 13½ couple are still his—loaned now to the committee of management.   Two couple of bitches run with the dogs.   The pack are now about 24 inches.

In his last season good sport was shown and two hunts deserve recording.   A buck roused on Broom Hill ran through Salisbury Trench, King's Garm Gutter, past the Rufus Stone to Shave Green and Brockis Hill ; then, crossing Bartley Water to Foxhills, he ran on to Matley Heath.   Thence by Matley Wood leaving Ashurst Lodge on the left, and across Matley Bog to Little Holmhill Enclosure, on by Denny Wood to Stubby Copse Enclosure where hounds ran in to him.   This good hunt of an hour and a half was run very fast and gave a point of about eight miles and more as hounds ran. Again on Easter Monday, April 18th, hounds met on Lyndhurst Racecourse and were laid on under London Minstead. They ran into Shave Green, back to London Minstead, on to Brockis Hill, over Bartley Water to Foxhills, thence by Longwater to Ashurst Lodge, right-handed to Matley Wood. They crossed the road to Denny, Parkhill, and on through Ramnor and Balmer Lawn, left-handed over Whitley Ridge to Ivy Gutter, across the river to Brockenhurst Park, left-handed by Boldre Church and on to Pilly where they killed. This season's tally was twenty buck.

During the difficult years since 1940 Mrs. G. Witherby of Spy Holms acted as Hon. Secretary and did all she could to keep the pack going.

A Committee, 1949-50.

No master coming forward, a Committee under the chairmanship of Lieut.-Colonel Sir Dudley B. Forwood, c.m.g., took over the management. The Committee consisted of Mrs. George Jonas of Hall Close, Fordingbridge, who is also Honorary Secretary, Mrs. Mackworth-Praed of Castle Top, Burley, the Hon. Robert Manners, Tyrrell's Ford, Avon, Mr. G. Moore, Hightown Close, Ringwood, Major N. H. C. Russell, D.S.O., Bearground, Brockenhurst, the Lady Rachel Stuart, Harthill House, Redlynch, Mrs. G. Witherby, Spy Holms, Burley (Hon. Secretary, 1940–49), Mr. J. Talford Wood, Paddock House, Burley.

In addition to these the chief supporters at the present time are Colonel Cash, Miss C. Chamberlain, Mr. Dudley Forwood, Mr. J. Gee, Brigadier Howes, D.S.O., M.C., Dr. G. G. Meade, M.C., Captain Timothy Moore, Mis Newby-Vincent, Miss S. Rowe, Mr. and Mrs. Taylor and Miss Anne Wood.

Lt.-Col. Sir D. B. Forwood, Bart., C.M.G., 1950-

The pack, after a series of crises, has at last got a local master in Lieut.-Colonel Sir Dudley Baines Forwood, Bart, c.m.g., of Stoney Cross Lodge. Much trouble has been taken to arouse interest and support and it is to be hoped that the pack may again rise to its former fame. Sir John Buchanan Jardine has kindly presented four couple of Black and Tan hounds and other drafts have been acquired. The pack is again held during tufting operations and the tufters run on with the pack. Both dogs and bitches are now hunted. Slightham remains as huntsman and continues to show good sport.

CHAPTER XII.

STAGHOUNDS IN HAMPSHIRE.

H.R.H. The Prince of Wales, 1791-93.

The description of this pack is given in Chapter III.

Mr. C. Shard, 1825-26.

Mr. Charles Shard of Somborne House bought from Mr. Lucas the North Devon Staghounds. These big lemon pied hounds were real staghounds and the last pack of real staghounds in England. They probably descended from the pack kept by Hugh Pollard, the Ranger of Exmoor Forest, in Queen Elizabeth's time. Sharp was his huntsman who had served with the Hon. Lumley Savile, and his son assisted him. Two of his friends, Mr. Smith of Somborne and Mr. Lovell of Rookley, acted as yeomen prickers. As the *Sporting Magazine* said, " Whatever Mr. Shard does, he does with spirit." He turned out beautifully mounted, and wearing the correct handsome belt which carried his bugle. Fifteen deer were kept in his paddocks but he was short of hounds, some of the North Devon pack having to be put down. Some replacements from the Royal Staghounds were acquired. When taken, the stag was blooded in the tail; this did not prevent a stag after a gallop from Flowerdown to Crawley Warren and about three miles beyond, severely injuring the huntsman that evening in the paddock. On November 11th, 1825, about 200 horsemen turned out to a meet at Ball Down. The stag was uncarted and ran to Crawley and then in view for some six miles until taken at Titcomb Bridge. At the end of the season of 1826 the pack were sold, part going to Germany and some to Epping Forest.

Hon. G. A. Craven, 1835-36.

The Hon. George Augustus Craven, son of the 1st Earl of Craven. Mr. Craven married in 1833 Georgiana Smythe of Brambridge Park where the hounds were kept. On November 23rd, 1835, after Mr. Chamberlayne of Cranbury Park had entertained the field a stag was uncarted at Oliver's Battery. He went over Winchester Racecourse, through Worthy and

284

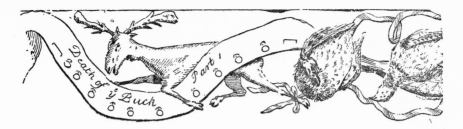

Easton and was taken at Avington Park. On November 30th a stag was uncarted at Farley Mount and ran by Pitt to Yew Hill, Bishopstoke, Durley, Bishop's Waltham and Botley. Here he took soil but was driven out and ran to Bursledon and escaped. Mr. Craven died on July 26th, 1836 at the early, age of 26. His son William George, a Life Guards officer, was a keen foxhunter in the shires but the staghounds were dispersed.

Commander Sir John Halkett, R.N., 1839-40.

Commander Sir John Halkett, 7th Baronet, kept a pack of staghounds at Fareham. He was a member of the Hambledon Hunt and a hard rider. Mr. Alfred Dyson hunted hounds for him the first season and then Mr. Jack Bradley, the son of a farmer at Tanworth, hunted them in 1840. A good hunt took place on January 29th, 1840, from Barton Stacey. The stag ran by Tidbury Ring, Ashe Park, St. John's Wood and was taken at Manydown, a distance of eighteen miles. Only ten followers were up and Sir John hunted hounds himself for the latter part of the hunt, Bradley's horse being dead beat. The hounds were sold to the Marquis of Waterford, and Bradley accompanied them to Lincolnshire. Then after a time with Mr. Yeatman of Stock House, Dorset, Bradley came to hunt the Hursley for Mr. White.

Mr. T. Nevill, c. 1840 - c. 62.

Mr. Thomas Nevill of Chilland kept a pack of bloodhounds at Worthy. These hounds he originally acquired from the New Forest and they were black St. Hubert hounds of ancient lineage. Mr. Nevill kept about twenty couple and the pack earned considerable renown. His huntsman George Gaiger and whipper-in Thomas Lock had been with the hounds from childhood and so well understood their temperament. Mr. Nevill himself had a wonderful power over animals and was able at the end of a run to call his stag to him and he would trot home

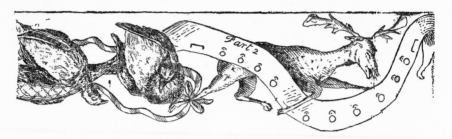

with Mr. Nevill, keeping close by his stirrup. One stag called
" Monarch " always followed him home even after a hard run.
One day he ran from the Racecourse to Wonston, by Hill Farm
to Norwood, through Littleton, and he took soil in a pond at
Winchester. When called he left the water with a bound and
went home with Mr. Nevill. His mate, " Princess," roamed
away from her meadow and was absent for six months when
she was reported at Burntwood. With 2½ couple of hounds,
his father and hunt servants, Mr. Nevill went to take her. She
ran by Shrowner to the Grange Park past the Candovers, by
Wield, College Wood, Chawton Park, Newton Common to Inna
Down, where she was left at dusk ; all horses were beat after a
hunt of some thirty miles. Three weeks later she was reported in
Bushey Leaze. She again ran hard for an hour and joined some
cows. Gaiger halload to a man to open the yard gate and she
entered with the cows. Mr. Nevill dismounted and entered
the yard and called the deer who instantly came to him and he
had some difficulty in keeping her from treading on his feet.
These hounds would hunt rats, water fowl, swans, badgers,
foxes or apparently anything which their master wished them
to hunt.

In 1852 Mr. Tunno gave him a jackal. He was turned out
on the Racecourse, gave a good run and was taken uninjured.

In August, 1839, Mr. Nevill alone with one bitch brought
home an outlying fallow deer after a severe hunt. He himself
was a fine horseman and once rode his famous horse " Dartmoor"
from Chilland to the New Forest, had a fine hunt with the
Queen's Hounds and returned to Chilland the same evening.
" Dartmoor " was buried at Chilland, aged 30, with some
hounds and a deer for company and an oak tree was planted
over him.

In 1850 a fallow deer became so tame that Mr. Nevill took
her for exercise with the hounds, he then would turn her before
the hounds and she would run straight home and join the cows in

the meadow. She used to push through the hounds when feeding and eat their meal with them until it was all gone. These fine hounds were also occasionally used to recover stolen property from a thief.

In 1860 the Duke of Beaufort presented Mr. Nevill with some red deer and doubtless they soon were happy members of this unusual family party, all members of which appeared to thoroughly enjoy themselves.

Captain H. B. Powell, 1854-58.

Mr. Henry Buckworth Powell, D.L., of Wilverley Park, near Lyndhurst, kept a small pack to hunt the New Forest deer after they had been nearly exterminated in 1851. An old officer of the Grenadier Guards and a good sportsman, he revived the most ancient sport in the New Forest, hunting only in April and August. In 1871 he added the name of Montgomery to that of Powell which is so well known in New Forest sport. Mr. Powell-Montgomery died in 1898.

CHAPTER XIII.

HARRIER PACKS IN HAMPSHIRE.

This list cannot claim to be complete, but gives the names of the gentlemen who hunted their packs as far as the author can ascertain.

Mr. J. Anderson, c. 1862.

Mr. Joseph Anderson of Longstock House, Stockbridge, kept harriers there and hunted deer also at the end of the season. He bought the pack formerly belonging to Mr. Longman of Farnborough.

The Andover Harriers, c. 1818.

Messrs. Footner and Todd were the chief supporters.

Mr. H. Barnard, 1854-56 ?

Mr. Henry Barnard of Park Farm, East Meon, had a pack of black and white harriers. In November 1861 he had a run of one hour and fifteen minutes without a check at Meonstoke. A great supporter of the Hambledon Hunt, he once had eight foxes in a small covert, all of which gave good runs.

Major Barton, c. 1819.

Major Barton of Ropley had about fifteen couple, and hunted round Ropley, Medstead and Bighton. George Hall, huntsman.

Mr. R. Bailey, c. 1833-43.

Mr. Richard Bailey of King's Worthy, a hospitable old sportsman, and a member of a great fox-hunting family.

Mr. Bennet, c. 1835.

Mr. Bennet, joint master of Lymington Harriers with Mr. St. Barbe.

Mr. T. Blake, c. 1803-16.

Mr. Thomas Blake of Winchester hunted harriers for many years, but chiefly in Wiltshire. He continued to hunt with

288

his nephew Mr. John Blake till his death at Stratford, near Old Sarum, in 1851.

Mr. T. Bonham, c. 1782 - 1820.

Mr. Thomas Bonham of Buriton, a member of the old H.H. Club. He bought Sir John Dashwood's pack which had some renown. Mr. Mullins obtained some of this blood from him, *q.v.*

Mr. T. Butler, 1823-34.

Mr. Thomas Butler of Bury Lodge, Hambledon, the first master of the Hambledon Hunt, acquired Mr. Hale's pack of harriers at his death in 1823.

Mr. T. Chamberlayne, c. 1829.

Mr. Thomas Chamberlayne of Cranbury Park, member of the Hambledon Hunt, hunted harriers for two seasons and then gave the pack to Mr. John King, M.F.H. A great supporter of hunting and of cricket.

Mr. H. Chaplin and Mr. E. Chaplin, 1850-59.

Mr. Horace Chaplin and Mr. Ernest Chaplin of Ewhurst hunted the country between Basingstoke and Whitchurch for one season and then Mr. Ernest hunted there till 1859 when Mr. Horace Chaplin died. (See Mr. P. Kelly.)

Mr. W. J. Chute, c. 1790 -95 or 96.

Mr. W. J. Chute of the Vyne hunted harriers around his home till changing to foxhounds in 1796 and founding the Vine Hunt. He may have acquired his original harriers from a Mr. Erle, a picture of whom with two servants exists at the Vyne.

Captain L. Curtis (afterwards Rear Admiral Sir L. Curtis, Bart., C.B.), c. 1822.

Captain Lucius Curtis of Ramsbridge Cottage, Weyhill, hunted around Andover and Chilbolton. Offered by Mr. T. A. Smith " the best hunter that money can buy " to give up his hounds. Mr. Smith had started foxhounds at Penton Lodge, 1826.

Mr. J. Day, c. 1858-61.

Mr. John Day of Danebury, the famous trainer of race horses, hunted harriers assisted by his son and Judd a jockey. His country was around Stockbridge.

Major-General T. de Burgh (afterwards Lord Clanricarde), c. 1806-08.

Major-General Thomas de Burgh of Belmont (Warnford Park), had, before proceeding on service abroad in 1800, a pack of foxhounds which he gave to the Prince of Wales. On return he purchased a pack of harriers. Phil Gosling was his huntsman, Sawyer was whipper-in 1807–08. Lord Clanricarde died in 1808.

Mr. J. Dear, c. 1853.

Mr. James Dear of Winchester, with Thomas Wilding, an ex-bombardier of the R.A. who served in the Crimean War, as kennelman and assistant. Showed very good sport and was well supported. Presented by the ladies with a silver horn, 1862.

Captain Evans, c. 1852.

Captain Evans of Broxmore Park, near Romsey, hunted a level pack of 15-inch harriers which he brought from Oxford-shire, where he was known as the " Flying Captain." In

Oxfordshire he used a retriever " Sam " as a whipper-in to turn hounds and this intelligent dog also would lead a horse home with the bridle in his mouth. In the house Sam acted as valet and would bring any article of dress required to his master.

Mr. R. Eyles, c. 1810.

Mr. Richard Eyles of Berely House kept a pack of harriers

Mr. T. Frere, 1841-50, 1851-

Mr. Tobias Frere of Odiham hunted Dr. Leech's old country, *q.v.*, and had also assisted Dr. Leech latterly. On moving to Whitchurch he continued to hunt harriers in that country with great success. One very remarkable run deserves record. A hare found at Hunton ran over Winchester Racecourse and then by Waller's Ash. He crossed the turnpike road by the Coach and Horses Inn at King's Worthy and took to the water meadows. He swam the River Itchen and was pulled down at Easton. An eight-mile point in fifty minutes. Such a hunt in a country well stocked with hares must be nearly unique.

Mr. N. Fuller, c. 1839-

Mr. Neston Fuller hunted around Winchfield. Several runs reported in Bell's *Life*.

Hon. T. W. Gage, 1822-

Hon. T. William Gage of Westbury, brother of Lord Gage, member of the H.H. 1818, and of the Hambledon Hunt, 1827, and one of the best horsemen in the county. Cannons, his keeper, whipped-in to him. These hounds came from Mr. Twynam, *q.v.*

Mr. E. Hale, 1797 - 1823.

Mr. E. Hale of Hambledon hunted harriers for thirty years and at his death Mr. T. Butler took them over, *q.v.*

Mr. Harwood, c. 1790.

Mr. Harwood of Dean House, Basingstoke, kept a pack of harriers. His finances were ruined by association with the Prince of Wales.

Messrs. W. and G. Higgens, 1834-44.

Messrs. William and Godfrey Higgens took over the pack formerly hunted around Hambledon by Mr. E. Hale and Mr. T. Butler, *q.v.*

Mr. G. P. Jervoise, M.P., c. 1805-

Mr. George Purefoy Jervoise, M.P., of Herriard Park, kept a pack of harriers. A notable though very irregular feat of $3\frac{1}{2}$ couple of these hounds is worthy of record. In December, 1808 or 1809, $3\frac{1}{2}$ couple of these hounds, with Mr. Stephen Terry of Dummer then living at Tunworth, ran a fox from Hen Wood over the Alton road near Winslade, by Ellisfield Down and Moundsmere Farm, leaving Preston Oakhills on the north side, *via* Medstead, south of Windmill Hill, to a point some two miles from Petersfield. The country beyond Windmill Hill was unknown to Mr. Terry. The hunt occupied about three hours and Mr. Terry killed the fox, a deed which would not have been so popular later on. Mr. Terry relates that these hounds always showed him special attachment afterwards. The distance must have been about twenty miles with a point of some thirteen miles. Mr. Terry reached the kennel at Herriard between 10 and 11 p.m., having refreshed himself, his horse and his small pack at Alresford.

Mr. P. Kelly, 1859-

Mr. Peter Kelly took over Mr. Chaplin's hounds and hunted the Basingstoke—Whitchurch country for some years. He subsequently hunted the Calpé Hounds at Gibraltar.

Colonel the Hon. G. T. Keppel (afterwards General and 6th Earl of Albemarle), c. 1841.

Colonel the Hon. George Thomas Keppel of Lymington hunted the country formerly hunted by Messrs. St. Barbe and Bennet in the 1830's. Colonel Keppel was M.P. for Lymington 1847–50 and had served at Waterloo in the 14th Regiment.

Mr. Lechmere, 1824.

Mr. Lechmere of Wilbury in Wiltshire hunted in Hampshire the Quarley—Cholderton country.

Dr. Leech, 1782 - 1838.

Dr. Leech of Odiham hunted his renowned harriers for fifty-six years. Mr. Frere joined him for the latter part of his long mastership. He always wore a blue coat with brass buttons and not harrier green. He was a patron also of cock-fighting. A coloured print of this old sportsman was published in 1838 by J. H. Brown of Odiham. It was inscribed to Mr. Tobias Frere. A good hunt from North Warnborough of two hours and twenty-five minutes is recorded in the *Sporting Magazine*, p. 446. In 1838 he was 79 and is called the oldest sportsman in England. This is a proud boast, but he was possibly the oldest master of hounds at the time.

Mr. L. Lywood, 1862-63.

Mr. L. Lywood hunted for one season the country round Upham, Owslebury, Fair Oak, finishing the season hunting deer in the New Forest.

Lt.-Col. J. May, c. 1885.

Lieut.-Colonel John May of Basingstoke kept a pack for four years kennelled in the farm opposite the Brewery in Brook Street. A keen supporter of foxhunting, he commanded his local volunteer battalion and was a great supporter of cricket.

Mr. J. Mills, c. 1875-85.

Mr. John Mills of Bisterne, Ringwood, had a first-class pack of harriers at his place which he kept till becoming M.F.H., Western Portion, New Forest Hunt. George Sears was his huntsman to both harriers and foxhounds.

Mr. J. S. Moody, c. 1817.

Mr. John Sadleir Moody of Southampton kept a pack of harriers and sometimes hunted stag. He became Hon. Secretary of the Hambledon Hunt in 1839 and remained in that position many years. A fine horseman and good sportsman.

Mr. Mullins, 1809-26.

Mr. Mullins kept his hounds at Skippet's Inn, near Basing-stoke, and had a very staunch level pack absolutely proof to riot. He showed this with great success to some ill-mannered people who asked him to hunt and turned a bagged fox out which they halload. Not a hound spoke and they would not touch the line. He hunted his hounds very well though 18 stone. Mr. John Portal bought the pack at his death.

Mr. R. Norris, c. 1821.

Mr. Richard Norris of Basing Park, member of the H.H. Club, 1811. A good sportsman and, with the Hon. T. W. Gage, another harrier master, rode Tom Smith's great hunt January 18th, 1825.

Mr. C. Owton, 1854-62.

Mr. Caleb Owton of Owslebury hunted the country round Owslebury, Upham and Fair Oak. Renowned for a wonderful mule he rode. Mr. Lywood took over in 1862, *q.v.*

Mr. R. C. T. Pearse, 1850-52.

Mr. Robert C. T. Pearse of South Warnborough Lodge, who had bought Mr. Wall's harriers, hunted the country between Odiham and Alton. His brother William assisted him. Mr. Pearse was elected a member of the H.H. Club in 1849 and became master of the H.H. in 1852 and showed as good sport with fox as with hare.

Sir P. Pole, c. 1790.

Sir Peter Pole of Wolverton Park kept harriers managed by his son, the Rev. Henry Pole.

Mr. J. Portal, 1826-

Mr. John Portal of Freefolk House, having bought Mr. Mullins' pack, hunted the Laverstoke—Overton country for some years. A prominent supporter of the Vine and a good horseman.

The Portsea Harriers, c. 1803.

These hounds were kept by Mr. Pittis and hunted regularly twice a week.

Mr. C. Rumbold, c. 1830.

Mr. Charles Rumbold of Preston House, near Basingstoke, member of the H.H. Club, 1834, hunted around Preston Candover. His groom whipped-in to him.

Mr. J. St. John, c. 1850.

Mr. John St. John of Banisters, son of Rev. Ellis St. John of West Court, Finchampstead, master of harriers 1790–1810 and of foxhounds 1810–16. Came to hunt round Winchester for several seasons, hunting alternate days with Mr. Dear. A good horseman, huntsman and cricketer.

Mr. T. Scotland, 1815-c. 1850.

Mr. Thomas Scotland first started keeping small harriers in 1815 at Charlton and then he removed to Penton and then to Bishop's Sutton, in each place becoming very well known as a first-class houndman and sportsman. A very keen supporter of Mr. Villebois, from whose drafts he started his last pack. In 1823 on April 27th Mr. Scotland was lowered down a well at Bighton 35 feet deep and seized a fox which had fallen in, by the poll and extracted him. He and Sawyer were first up in the pantry hunt with the H.H. on January 11th, 1825. This was from Black House to Townhill, three miles from Southampton, and again distinguished himself on November 2nd, 1841, in the good run with the H.H. from Cheriton Wood to the mill in the Grange Lake. Mr. Fred Yates, another master of harriers, son in law to Mr. Scotland, also distinguished himself. Mr. Scotland had a great knowledge of hounds and hares. After Christmas he used to hunt deer, but his hounds remained steady. " Gelert " said of him in 1849 that he had " an acquaintance with all the packs of foxhounds in Hampshire, but literally, it may be said, with each individual hound composing those packs."

Mr. T. Smith, c. 1790 - 1828.

Mr. Thomas Smith of Tedworth kept for many years a beautiful pack of harriers with which he occasionally hunted fox. The famous Thomas Assheton Smith, his son, learnt much from hunting with them as a boy.

Mr. Smither, c. 1770.

Mr. Smither of Hale, presumably a forebear of Mr. Stephen Smither, hunted on the borders of Hampshire and Surrey. George Bradley was his huntsman who is rescued from oblivion by his encounter with William Cobbett at the age of eight. The hounds ran into their hare on Seal Common near Waverley Abbey. Young Cobbett jumped in amongst them, took the hare away and secured the scut. He received a cut from the huntsman's whip for his effrontery. The boy meditated a cunning revenge. When hounds again came to Seal Common, not far from his home in Farnham, he laid in wait with a red herring. After a hare was viewed away to the south, he got the pack on to his drag to the west, up a very steep hill, over all the toughest country he could find into Moor Park where he made a most complicated drag and went finally down a precipitous hanger into a swamp. The herring was then consigned to a swift stream and Cobbett awaited the hunt. At dusk a bedraggled party arrived in the drizzling rain, some of them half covered with mud and all in bad tempers. The huntsman tried on, but of course failed, and there was nothing for him to do but to go home in the rain. Mr. Cobbett brings this tale of the red herring into a letter to the Hon. John Stuart Wortley on equitable adjustment (Register v. 81, p. 514).

Mr. S. Smither, late 1850's and 60's.

Mr. Stephen Smither of Down Farm, Odiham, hunted Dr. Leach's old country regularly on Mondays and Thursdays, and showed very good sport. In 1858 the hunted hare went over the edge of Odiham chalk pit, hounds following. Many were killed or damaged beyond recovery. Followers wished to subscribe for their replacement, but Mr. Smither did not care to accept this gift, so they gave him a mounted portrait with his hounds, by Mr. Garland of Winchester, instead.

Mr. St. Barbe, c. 1835.

Mr. St. Barbe was joint master of the Lymington Harriers with Mr. Bennet.

Mr. T. Terry, c. 1790.

Mr. Thomas Terry of Dummer hunted a small country round that village.

The Steep, 1824-25.

These hounds were advertised in the *Hampshire Chronicle* for that season.

Mr. C. Taylor, M.P. (afterwards Sir Charles Taylor,) c. 1824.

Mr. C. Taylor, M.P., of Hollycombe, hunted the Stockbridge country. His huntsman bore the appropriate name of Jelly. " Nimrod " visited his hounds and reports them as full 20 inches but running well together. Mr. Taylor found Hollycombe country very bad for hounds and so had a cottage near Stockbridge where he kept his hounds. He was M.P. for Wells.

DR. LEACH, Master of Odiham Harriers, 1782 - 1838.

MR. STEPHEN SMITHER, Master of Odiham Harriers,
c. 1860.

Mr. G. A. E. WALL, M.H. 1848-59, M.F.H. Hursley Hunt 1850-52, Hambledon Hunt 1852-56.

The Tytherley Harriers, 1843.

General Yates kept a pack of 12 to 14 couple of harriers at Tytherley and had some good hunts reported in the *Hampshire Chronicle*.

Mr. J. Twynam, 1812-18.

Mr. J. Twynam of Whitchurch, with Mr. T. James' assistance, hunted that neighbourhood with hounds obtained from Mr. Portal. In 1818 most of the pack went back to Mr. Portal.

Mr. G. Twynam, 1819-31.

Mr. George Twynam kept some of these hounds and continued to hunt the district with the help of Mr. W. B. Allen, but with quite a small pack. Mr. Twynam died in 1846. The Hennessys assisted, father and son, "Old Pop" and "George Pop." "Pop" Hennessy was 2nd whipper-in to Mr. Villebois with the H.H. and huntsman to the East Sussex in 1832.

Mr. G. A. E. Wall, 1848-59.

Mr. George Alfred Ellis Wall of Worthy Park had bought the Isle of Wight Harriers from Mr. Harvey of Newport in 1846. He took these first to Hallow Park, Worcestershire, and then came and hunted round Winchester from Worthy Park which estate his father had bought in 1825. George Davis was his whipper-in. He hunted three days a week. Mr. Wall became a member of the H.H. Club in 1850 and soon aspired to be a master of foxhounds and was master of the Hursley 1850-52 and the Hambledon 1852–56. He had a good hunt with a hare from the plantation by Hunton ozier beds over Hunton Farm to Weston and Stoke Charity, over the railway to Stratton Lodge and he whipped-off in Micheldever Wood, a nice 12-mile hunt. Mr. Robert Pearse (*q.v.*) bought his hounds. He also established the Worthy Park Cricket Club.

Mr. J. Wickham, 1830-32.

Mr. James Wickham of Sutton Scotney kept twelve couple of hounds and hunted round Micheldever, Wonston, Chilbolton and Littleton. They were of Mr. Mullins' breed. In 1832 he gave the pack to Mr. Chamberlayne of Cranbury, *q.v.*

Mr. J. T. Villebois, c. 1796-1802.

Mr. John Trueman Villebois, tenant of Preston House, member of the H.H. Club 1796, hunted the country around Preston

Candover till becoming chief manager of the H.H. in 1802 and master in 1803.　His harriers once brought a fox from Preston Copse and killed by Amory Wood (see Chapter IV, p. 60).

Mr. F. Yates, 1861- c. 80.

Mr. Frederick Yates of Bishop's Sutton hunted round the Wield, Medstead, Bighton, Bishop's Sutton country with great success.　Many of his runs are described in Bell's *Life*.　His son, Mr. Arthur Yates, the well-known amateur steeplechase jockey, also hunted the hounds.　It was a first-rate pack, well hunted and doubtless owed much to Mr. Thomas Scotland's advice.

CHAPTER XIV.

BEAGLES.

Formerly some beagles were kept by most squires and farmers to amuse them on their own ground. This was so common as seldom to be mentioned and they were not often regular packs. In a deed of 1613 wherein John Wither of Manydown Park makes over everything to his eldest son William, he reserves certain amenities to himself, among others that his son should keep for him " two servants, a horse, three couple of beagles and one greyhound for his pleasure."

H.R.H. The Prince of Wales at Kempshott Park, 1791-95

It is recorded in William Poyntz's diary that a pack of beagles was kept by H.R.H. The Prince of Wales and they are the first " pack " noticed in the county though Anne of Denmark, wife of James I, had a pack very early in the seventeenth century. It is unlikely, however, that these hounds hunted in Hampshire.

The Stockbridge Union Beagles, c. 1840.

The Stockbridge Union Beagles' chief supporters were Mr. William Sadler and Mr. John Day, the famous trainer. " Cecil " says in the *Sporting Magazine* " They are Lilliputian foxhounds, and show more dash and courage than I ever witnessed before in such little creatures."

The Aldershot Beagles, 1882 to date
(except for the period 1939 to 1945 when dormant).

This sporting pack was founded by Captain Stopford, 18th Royal Irish Regiment. It was revived by Captain D. Treffry, R.A., in 1946 and now has about 14 couples. The country hunted for the most part is by permission of the H.H. on both sides of the main Aldershot—Farnham—Alton roads. The kennels are at Iveley Farm, Farnborough, and hounds hunt Wednesdays and Saturdays. It does much to keep sport alive in the Army in these horseless days.

Mrs. O. T. Price, 1903-08.

Mrs. O. T. Price hunted a private pack of beagles from New Park, Brocklehurst, whilst Mr. O. T. Price, M.H., had the New Forest Buckhounds. They hunted part of the New Forest.

Mr. O. T. Price, 1909-10.

Mr. O. T. Price took over the pack and hunted the New Forest one day a week.

The New Forest Beagles, 1910-17.

Mr. Frederick Day bought some of Mr. Price's hounds and started a subscription pack. In 1917 both Mr. Frederick and Mr. Ernest Day went on active service overseas. Mr. Philip Gurney bought the pack and hunted them at Caversham. They became the Cranwell Beagles in 1920.

Roke Manor Beagles, 1920-23.

Captain Keith Gladstone bought the Leigh Park Beagles for £500 and hunted them in the New Forest once a week on Wednesdays by permission. They were a private pack.

The Ringwood Beagles, 1921.

Captain Gladstone changed their name to the Ringwood Beagles which became a subscription pack in 1922. Mr. Ernest Day acted as Hon. Secretary and Treasurer.

New Forest Beagles,
1923-29.

The name was again changed in 1923 to the New Forest Beagles. In 1929 Captain Gladstone sold the pack to the country and Mr. Ernest Day became Master, Hon. Secretary and Treasurer. Kennels were built at Bartley.

Mr. E. Day, 1929-46.

Mr. Ernest Day continued his arduous task of bearing all the work single-handed and hunting the hounds. This he did very successfully. In his best year, 1936–37, in 57 days with two blank days, 51 hares were accounted for. In the Forest in 37 days with two blanks, 39 hares were killed. Hares are scarce in the Forest itself; the Manors maintain a supply. The rough heath holds a wonderful scent in wet weather and even in dry weather hounds can run owing to the side scent.

Mr. E. Day, and Mr. B. Day, 1946-50.

Mr. Bryan Day joined Mr. Ernest Day as joint master. The masters are busy rebuilding the pack to what it was before the war. During the war no hounds were bred owing to food shortage. Both the joint masters retired at the end of the 1949-50 season, Mr. Ernest Day completing 20 years as master and 27 years as Honorary Secretary. He was presented with his portrait with the pack, painted by Captain Lionel Edwards, at the opening meet on 30th September, 1950.

Mr. C. R. Swayne.

Mr. C. R. Swayne of Hill Top, North Baddesley, then took over the mastership with A. Bennett as huntsman.

Pewsey Vale Beagles, c. 1920-23.

These beagles were founded by that great sportsman Captain Howard Alexander of Upavon when he could no longer ride to hounds. In 1931 he presented them to the 2nd Lord Melchett, M.F.H. the Tedworth Hunt, who kept them till he left the country in 1934. Major A. E. Philipps, D.S.O., M.F.H., was joint master, Lowsley Williams, Esq., amateur huntsman, and Messrs. Young and H. W. Cole amateur whippers-in.

Farley Hill Beagles

Mr. G. P. Simonds and Mr. V. P. Simonds, 1919-39.

Mr. G. P. Simonds, and Mr. V. P. Simonds, were joint masters of a private pack kennelled at Farley Hill. The country hunted was chiefly in Hampshire, but parts of Berkshire were also hunted.

Mr. G. P. Simonds, 1339-45.

In 1939 Mr. V. P. Simonds became a master of the Garth and Mr. G. P. Simonds remained sole master until 1945.

Mr. G. P. Simonds and Mr. H. M. Hermon Worsley, m.c., 1945 to date.

Mr. G. P. Simonds, Upper Mosses, Farley Hill, Reading, was joined by Mr. H. M. Hermon-Worsley, M.C., of Bensgrove Farm, Goring Heath, Oxfordshire, where the hounds are now kennelled and Mr. Hermon-Worsley hunts the hounds. Parts of South Oxfordshire are now hunted. S. Hale is kennel huntsman.

A subscription is now taken, but the pack is the property of the joint masters. This pack hunts Wednesdays and Saturdays.

The Dummer Beagles, 1939 to date.

The Dummer Beagles were established by R. N. Rycroft, Esq., son of Sir Nelson E. D. Rycroft, Bart., then living at Dummer House, near Basingstoke. They hunted in the Vine, Craven and parts of the H.H. country. About eight couples were kept. Owing to the war service of the master the hounds suffered various changes. Disbanded in 1943, except for a few breeding bitches, in 1946 they again hunted at Dummer and in 1947 they were temporarily joined with the Wye College Beagles, Mr. R. N. Rycroft and Mr. J. G. R. Stevens being masters of the amalgamated pack for the season 1947–48. In 1948–49 they were again hunted at Dummer and then followed Mr. Rycroft to Gloucestershire where he now lives.

Beagles (Meon Valley), 1949-

Joint Masters, Mrs. Vivian, Mrs. Arnold and Mrs. C. A. James. Fourteen couples are kennelled at West End House.

APPENDIX A

AN ACCOUNT OF AN 18TH CENTURY HUNT.

This detailed account of a hunt in the 18th century was preserved among the papers of Admiral Sir Edward Codrington, G.C.B., K.S.L., K.S.G., to whom the letter is written. His great-grandson, Colonel G. R. Codrington, C.B., C.B.E., D.S.O., T.D., gave the letter to Colonel J. B. Scott of Rotherfield Park. The letter is now published by the courtesy of both these gentlemen :—

' MY DEAR SIR,

With much pleasure I send you herewith a memorandum of our famous Farmers chace, writing it over has brought it all again fresh to my memory, and the perusal of which I hope will afford you some amusement.

Every place put down may be distinctly seen upon the map of Hampshire—where I have said in my statement turned to the right or left—I suppose you going from Preston Oakhills to Littleton, which as you look at the map will be quite the reverse.

I believe if the ground could be measured it would not vary a mile—the only two points that there was the least difficulty of ascertaining—were from the top of Preston Oakhills to the point in the common field going towards Wield, where the fox was headed for Preston Candover—and the circuit the fox made round Worthy down and the common field adjoining.

It was a wonderful chace to think on. I do not think the annals of foxhunting can produce anything equal to it for distance in so short a time for a body of hounds, the hounds must have been stout and in good condition to have done it.

Mr. Meynel was of opinion I have been told that no hounds ever ran twelve miles an hour for two hours together—he must allude I conceive to a body of hounds—as the speed of a foxhound is much beyond that pace—Mr. Barry's Bluecap and Wanton having run four miles over Newmarket a train scent in eight minutes—and Col. Thornton's (Merlin ?) ran four miles in seven minutes and half a second.

Our chace certainly exceeded in speed anything Mr. Meynel had an idea of—and the distance we went never could have been done within the time if the chapter of accidents had not been decidedly in our favor—I will endeavour to bring that chapter to your recollection.

In the first burst from Preston Oakhills, just as we came up with the hounds as they were going towards Wield Wood—there was a halloa in the bottom towards Preston village, in going over to that Hallo the fox was viewed at a great distance going over the hill behind[1] Mr. Hall's house for Preston Copse—there we got the first nick at the fox—that head back for Preston Copse brought up the rear—at that time much behind—from Preston Copse round Chilton Wood over a wattle fence on to Becketsdown to the turnip field hedge close to Thorneydown we went as fast as we could ride the moment you had dismounted near Thorneydown I heard a Hallo to our right which hallo carried us to Woodmancot Holt—and the moment we were thro' Woodmancot a third Hallo carried us to Popham

---

[1] Mr. Thomas Hall (junior), born 1728, built North Hall, Preston Candover, probably in 1769, certainly before 1790. His daughter, Elizabeth, married G. P. Jervoise of Herriard in 1798. Mr. Hall died 1812.

Wood—to this point it was more like racing than hunting—here we got another good nick on the fox who could never afterwards get away from the hounds—the next check or pause was at a gate going on to Worthydown (where a Gentleman observed to me that his horse was fresher than he was in the morning—not being able he said for the last halfhour to get him thro' a gateway without running against the posts)—such symptoms of freshness are generally succeeded by the tail of the horse standing erect and his nose close to the ground.

I conceive those three Halloos to have been the occasion of our great speed for the whole of our chace and that it would have been nearly impossible if the hounds had hunted every inch of ground to have got so near their fox in so short a time.

Drummer	Damon	
Ransom	Griper	
Vocal	Lucifer	these seven and a half couple of hounds were out that day and were the speediest body of chace hounds I ever saw together in one pack.
Whisper	Lasher	
Damper	Bluecap	
Guider	Dowager	
Lawyer	Daphne	
	Dancer	

Bluecap and Dowager you perhaps may recollect—the former was nearly loosing me a good run by Greene Copse near Henwood by Skirting and the other was leading in great style over the heath for Bagshot park when Prospero fell with you—

The best appology I can make to you for writing so much upon a favorite subject is to wish you may see half a dozen as good runs before the end of the season.

I am
Dear Sir,
Yours sincerely
Jos. Russell.

Hoddington House,
  Near Odiham.
18 *March* 1808.

MEMORANDUM OF A CHACE WITH THE ODIHAM HOUNDS
ON THE 21ST DECEMBER, 1798.

Blossom
Bashful
Banker
Drummer
Duster
Damsel
Guilty
Labourer
Madam
Ranter
Ransom
Venery
Vocal
Wilful
Whisper
Honesty
Captious
Music
Vicious
The above 9½ *couple bred by Lord Egremont.*

Damper
Guider
Bowler
Tickler
Vexer
2½ couple bred by Lord Stawell.

Lawyer
Pillager
Crowner
Vanish
2 couple bred by the Duke of Richmond.

Dealer
Damon
Juno
Laundress
Plunder
Griper
Vulcan
Gameboy
The above four couple bought of the Marquis of Donegal, and mostly bred by Ld. Fitzwilliam.

Lucifer
Lasher
Hamlet
Pirate
Bluecap
Stinger
Vaunter
Daphne

After drawing a great deal of Country without finding—we found a fox in Preston Oakhills about one o'clock in that part of the Oakhills next Bradley Lane—the fox went down the Oakhills towards Ilsfield (Ellisfield) down, kept along the bottom of the Oakhills by the side of the down to Moundsmere Copse and turned short back up the Copse to the furze common at the top of the Oakhills next to Preston Candover - - 1½ ms.

from the furze common over some large fields part of Preston down towards Wield Wood - 2½
turned short back to the right to Mr. Hall's house in Preston Village - - - - 1½
—through Preston Copse to Chilton wood - 1
turned to the right in Chilton Wood and made nearly a circle of the wood and broke cover at the lower end of Chilton Wood for the furzes on Becketsdown - - - - - 1½
—to the skirts of Thorneydown - - 1½
—headed by a shepherd, and turn'd—went thro' a part of Woodmancot Holt—Popham Wood, and crossed the Winton turnpike road about two miles from Popham Lane to Waltham Trimleys - 3
—thro' a part of Waltham Trimleys keeping on the north side of the western turnpike road to Blackwood where he was headed and turned back and recrossed the above road nearly where Sir F. Baring's new Lodge now stands - - 2½
—round Stratton Park to East Stratton keeping the park on ye. right hand - - - 2
—crossed the Winton road at East Stratton near the Blacksmith's shop to the village of Weston - 2
—was headed back through Micheldever Village and recrossed the Winton road to Micheldever Wood - - - - - - 1½
—went up the long ride in Micheldever Wood to the road that leads from Northington to the Winton road - - - - - 1½
—turned short to the right and recrossed the Winton road at the five mile stone from Winton 1
—bore away for the Windmill between Micheldever village and Stoke Charity - - 1½
—turned for Ash Farm - - - 2
to Wallers Ash - - - - 1
—to Worthy Down - - - - 1
round the down to the Andover road, crossed the 2
Andover road and along ye. top of the common ½
field almost back again to the Andover road and round the common field - - - 1

X

Dowager	headed back and went round Littleton village and
Dancer	was kill'd in a Hogstye - - - I
Dainty	
Desperate	
The above six	33 ms.
couple bred by Jos.	after a chace of Two hours and a quarter one couple of
Russell.	hounds only missing out of Twenty-four couple—

24 couples.

the ground went well for the horses, very few leaps,
earths all open—
—the Whipper-in's horse tired early in the day—
The field that started on the other side—
Dramatis Personae as per Margin.

[2]Wm. Harrison mounted on Old Hock ; Mat Archer mounted on Young Highflyer ; [3]J. Russell mounted on Honeysuckle ; Sr. Robt. Sloper mounted on Count ; [4]Capt. Codrington mounted on Jago ; Dickinson mounted on Volunteer ; Sparrow mounted on Magog ; [5]Mrs. Russell on Johnny Gilpin, the first time of riding him; Beaufoy on a bay gelding; [6]Parson Jervoise on a grey gelding; Mrs. Parker on a bay mare with a white face ; Farmer Murrel on a bay gelding afterwards sold to Lord Stawell ; Mrs. Russell's servant on Capricomb ; Sr. Ro. Sloper's servt. on Pagan.

N.B.—Not any person joined in the chace which was singular considering the length of ground we went over.

[2] William Harrison, huntsman. Portrait see page 33. Mat Archer probably whipper-in.

[3] Joseph Russell, M.F.H., see p. 36-7, writer of the letter.

[4] Admiral Sir Edward Codrington, G.C.B., K.S.L., K.S.G., grandson of Sir William Codrington of Doddington, receipient of the letter. Commanded H.M.S. *Orien* at Trafalgar and the allied fleets at Navarnio, 1827. M.P., Devonport, 1832-39. Died 1851. Great-grandfather of Colonel G. R. Codrington, C.B., C.B.E., D.S.O., T.D., who gave the letter to Colonel J. B. Scott.

[5] Lady Betty Russell, wife of the master, see page 36.

[6] Rev. George Huddleston Jervoise of Britford and Shalstone, succeeded to Herriard Estate on the death of his elder brother, Tristram H. Jervoise, in 1794. Died 1805. Father of George Purefoy Jervoise, see p. 292.

APPENDIX B

AN ACCOUNT OF A REMARKABLE RIDE OF A HAMPSHIRE MAN.

Stow records a feat of riding performed on 17th July, 1621, by Bernard Calvert of Andover. He left Shoreditch, London, 3 a.m., he rode to Dover, visited Calais in a barge, returned to Dover and thence back to St. George's Church in Shoreditch, arriving at 8 p.m. in the evening of the same day. The riding part of the journey was 142 miles.

BIBLIOGRAPHY

Acton, C. R. *Sport and Sportsmen in the New Forest.* 1936.

Apperley, C. J. ("Nimrod"). *The Chace, the Turf and the Road.* 1837.

Apperley, C. J. ("Nimrod"). *Hunting Reminiscenses.* 1826.

Baillie-Grohman, William A. and F. *The Master of Game,* by Edward de Langley, 2nd Duke of York, 1909 (written 1406-13).

Barrow, A. G. ("Sabretache"). *Monarchy and the Chase.* 1948.

Beaufort, His Grace the Duke of, K.G., and Mr. Mowbray-Morris, *Hunting.* The Badminton Library. 1885.

Beckford, Peter. *Thoughts upon Hare and Fox Hunting.* 1796.

Bell, Isaac. *A Huntsman's Log Book.* 1947.

Burrows, M. *The Family of Brocas.* 1886.

Capes, W. W. *Scenes of Rural Life in Hampshire.* 1901.

Chalmers, Patrick. *The History of Hunting* (Lonsdale Library, Vol. XXIII). 1901.

Chute, C. W. *A History of the Vyne in Hampshire.* 1888.

Cobbett, William. *Rural Rides.* 1853.

Cook, Colonel J. *Observations on Hunting* (written 1826). 1922.

Creston, Dormer. *The Regent and his daughter.* 1943.

Cuming, E. D. *Squire Osbaldeston : His Autobiography.* 1926.

Curtis, William. *History of Alton.* 1896.

De Trafford, Sir Humphrey F., Bart. *Foxhounds of Great Britain and Ireland.* 1906.

Dixon, W. Scarth. *Hunting in the Olden Days.* 1912.

Eggar, J. A. *Remembrances of Life and Customs in Gilbert White's, Cobbett's and Charles Kingsley's Country.*

Eversley, The Lord. *Commons, Forests and Footpaths.* 1910.

FitzGerald, Brian Vesey. *Hampshire and the Isle of Wight.* 1949.

Graham, Sir Reginald, Bart. *Fox Hunting Recollections.* 1908.

Hampshire, Victoria History of. 1908.

Heysham, W. N. ("Aesop"). *Sporting Reminiscences of Hampshire, 1745-1862.* 1864.

Higginson, A. Henry. *Try Back.* 1932.

Higginson, A. Henry. *The Meynell of the West.* 1936.

Hore, J. *History of the Royal Buckhounds.* 1893.

Howard, S. Jackson, and Hughes, H. S. *Part II Arundell Genealogical Collection* (printed for private circulation).

Jeans, G. E. *Memories of Old Hampshire.* 1906.

Kenchington, F. E. *The Commoners' New Forest.*

Lascelles, Hon. Gerald C. B. *Thirty-five Years in the New Forest.* 1915.

Leach, A. F., *A History of Winchester College.* 1899.

308

Leigh, Rev. J. E. Austen- ("Sexagenarian"). *Recollections of the Early Days of the Vine Hunt.* 1865.

Leigh, W. Austen-, and Knight, Montagu George. *Chawton Manor and its Owners.* 1911.

Lewis, Peter. *A Foxhunter's Anthology.* 1934.

Milner, Rt. Rev. John, D.D., F.S.A. *The History and Survey of the Antiquities of Winchester.* 1798.

Nisbet, John. *Our Woods and Forests.* Haddon Hall Library. 1900.

Paget, J. Otho. *Hunting.* Haddon Hall Library. 1900.

Radcliffe, F. P. Delmé. *The Noble Science* (written 1839). 1892.

Read, D. H. Moutray. *The Highways and Byways in Hampshire.* 1928.

Ribblesdale, The Lord. *The Queen's Hounds.*

Simpson, C. Charles, R.I. *Trencher and Kennel.* 1927.

Simpson, John. *Church, Manor and Plough.* Vol. 1. 1946.

Smith, T. *Sporting Incidents in the Life of another Tom Smith* by a friend. 1867.

Smith, T. *Extracts from the Diary of a Huntsman* (written 1838). 1921.

Smith, T. *The Life of a Fox* (written 1843). 1920.

Stirling, A. M. W. *The Diaries of Dummer.* 1934.

Strickland, Agnes. *The Lives of the Queens of England.* 1864.

White, Gilbert. *The Natural History of and the Antiquities of Selborne* (written 1788). 1900.

Wilmot, Sir John Eardley, Bart. *Reminiscences of the late Thomas Assheton Smith.* 1862.

Wise, J. R. *The New Forest.* 1867.

Wither, Rev. R. F. Bigg-. *Materials for a History of the Wither Family.* 1907.